Financial Structure and
Economic Growth

Financial Structure and Economic Growth

A Cross-Country Comparison of Banks, Markets, and Development

Edited by
Aslı Demirgüç-Kunt and
Ross Levine

The MIT Press
Cambridge, Massachusetts
London, England

This book was set in Palatino by Asco Typesetters, Hong Kong, on 3B2.
Printed and bound in the United States of America.

Library of Congress Cataloging-in-Publication Data

Financial structure and economic growth : a cross-country comparison of banks, markets, and development / edited by Aslı Demirgüç-Kunt and Ross Levine.
    p. cm.
  Includes bibliographical references and index.
  ISBN 0-262-04198-7 (hc. : alk. paper)
        anking—Case studies. 2. Financial institutions—Case studies.
      anges—Case studies. 4. Economic development—Case studies.
     Kunt, Aslı, 1961– II. Levine, Ross.
         2001

                                                        2001044154

Contents

Acknowledgments

Many people made this book possible. We are especially grateful to Gerard Caprio for his intellectual leadership and support. We would like to thank Joe Stiglitz and Paul Collier for their guidance at key stages of the research.

Over the course of two years, Thorsten Beck went from constructing the data sets and commenting on our papers to being a valued coauthor. Many colleagues helped by discussing and by providing comments: Franklin Allen, John Boyd, Chun Chang, Stijn Claessens, Augusto De la Torre, Cevdet Denizer, Bulent Gultekin, James Hanson, Patrick Honohan, Enrico Perotti, Guillermo Perry, Raghu Rajan, Lemma Senbet, Andrew Sheng, Mary Shirley, Dimitri Vittas, and John Williamson. Participants at the World Bank Conference on Financial Structures and Economic Development, February 10–11, 2000, provided valuable input. Many thanks are due to the authors for their contributions to this volume.

Bo Wang and Anqing Shi provided valuable research assistance. Paramjit K. Gill read many versions of the manuscript. We are also grateful to Polly Means and Kari Labrie who went out of their way to help produce the manuscript.

We would also like to thank our families, who lovingly let us substitute research for leisure during this project.

I   Introduction

1 Financial Structure and Economic Growth: Perspectives and Lessons

Aslı Demirgüç-Kunt and
Ross Levine

1.1 Motivation and Scope

In *Financial Structure and Development*, Raymond W. Goldsmith
(1969) sought to accomplish three goals. His first goal was to document how financial structure—the mixture of financial instruments,
markets, and intermediaries operating in an economy—changes as
economies grow. Thus, he sought to trace the evolution of the
structure of national financial systems as economies develop. Second, Goldsmith wanted to assess the impact of overall financial development—the overall quantity and quality of financial instruments,
markets, and intermediaries—on economic growth. He sought to
answer the question: Does finance exert a causal influence on economic growth? Finally, Goldsmith sought to evaluate whether financial structure influences the pace of economic growth. Does the
mixture of markets and intermediaries functioning in an economy
influence economic development? Indeed, Goldsmith (1969) summarized his motivation for studying the last two questions as follows: "One of the most important problems in the field of finance, if
not the single most important one, almost everyone would agree, is
the effect that financial structure and development have on economic
growth" (390).

Goldsmith (1969) met with varying degrees of success in achieving
each of these three goals. Goldsmith was largely successful in documenting the evolution of national financial systems, particularly
the evolution of financial intermediaries. Specifically, he showed that
banks tend to become larger relative to national output as countries
develop. He also presented evidence suggesting that nonbank financial intermediaries and stock markets frequently—though certainly
not always—grow relative to banks in size and importance as countries expand economically.

Goldsmith met with more limited success in assessing the links between the level of financial development and economic growth. He clearly documented a positive correlation between financial development and the level of economic activity in thirty-five countries, using data prior to 1964. He just as clearly indicated that he was unwilling to draw causal interpretations from his graphical presentations. Thus, Goldsmith was unwilling to assert that financial development exerts a causal influence on economic growth.

On the third question, the relationship between economic development and the mixture of financial markets and intermediaries operating in an economy, Goldsmith was unable to provide much cross-country evidence due to data limitations. Instead, Goldsmith—like many researchers before and after him—relied on careful comparisons of Germany and the United Kingdom. Detailed studies comparing financial structure in Germany and the United Kingdom, and later the United States and Japan, produced illuminating insights on the operation of *these* financial systems. Nevertheless, it is not clear that researchers can extend the conclusions garnered from these countries to very different countries. Indeed, Goldsmith expressed hope that others would follow his lead and produce broad cross-country evidence on the relationship between financial structure and economic growth.

Recent research has made substantial progress in expanding the analysis of Goldsmith's (1969) second goal: the connection between financial development and economic growth. In particular, researchers have provided additional findings on the finance-growth nexus and have offered a much bolder appraisal of the causal relationship: firm-level, industry-level, and cross-country studies all suggest that the level of financial development exerts a large, positive impact on economic growth.[1] Furthermore, building on La Porta, Lopez-de-Silanes, Shleifer, and Vishny (1998), a growing body of work suggests that cross-country differences in legal systems influence the level of financial development with important implications for economic growth.[2] This line of research is substantively improving our understanding of the relationship between financial development and economic growth.

Recent research, however, has not substantially updated and extended Goldsmith's documentation of the evolution of financial structures by using data from the last forty years, nor has recent research completed Goldsmith's third goal of assessing the relationship between financial structure and economic growth in a broad cross-section of countries. It is true that researchers have developed rigorous theories of the evolution of the financial structures and how the mixture of markets and banks influences economic development. Allen and Gale (2000) provide a comprehensive study of the theory of comparative financial systems. It is also true that researchers have conducted detailed country studies of the connections between financial structure and growth, especially in Germany, Japan, the United Kingdom, and the United States. Again, Allen and Gale (2000) integrate these country studies into their analytic comparisons of different financial systems. The research presented in this book, however, is different in that it dissects the relationship between financial structure—the degree to which a country has a bank-based or market-based financial system—and long-run economic growth using a broad cross-section of countries.

This book sheds additional empirical evidence on each of Goldsmith's three questions. Part II updates Goldsmith's documentation of the evolution of financial structure during the process of economic growth. The work represents the fruits of a two-year data gathering process that produced a unique dataset on financial systems around the world. This database is available on the CD that accompanies this book. Part III uses this cross-country dataset to assess Goldsmith's next two questions: the relationship between economic growth and both the level of overall financial development and the structure of financial systems. Part IV includes a collection of detailed country studies of developing countries that examine the relationship between economic development and financial structure.

1.2   The Measurement and Evolution of Financial Systems

The absence of cross-country data on the structure of financial systems has hampered research on the determinants and implications of different financial structures. While Goldsmith (1969) documented how the structure of financial systems changes as countries develop, he examined only thirty-five countries and his data stopped in 1963. Difficulties in assembling comparable data on banks, insurance companies, private pension funds, mutual funds, and securities markets across a broad cross-section of countries have dissuaded researchers from extending Goldsmith's efforts and either confirming or refuting his findings.

Chapter 2 presents the fruits of a two-year data gathering effort. Specifically, in "The Financial Structure Database," Thorsten Beck, Aslı Demirgüç-Kunt, and Ross Levine discuss a comprehensive cross-country database that has information on the size, efficiency, and activity of banks, insurance companies, pension funds, mutual funds, finance companies, stock markets, and bond markets in up to 150 countries. Thus, the chapter computes measures of overall financial development as well as measures of the degree to which each country is more bank-based or market-based. The dataset also contains a wealth of information on each country's political, economic, and social environment. The authors make all of this information available on the World Wide Web.

In assembling, publishing, and making this database easily available, Beck, Demirgüç-Kunt, and Levine hope to augment the marginal product of future research on financial structure and economic development. The data are neither perfect nor complete, as the chapter makes clear. Nevertheless, chapter 2 potentially lowers the entry barriers to cross-country research on financial systems.

Chapter 3, "Bank-Based and Market-Based Financial Systems: Cross-Country Comparisons," takes this new database and documents how financial structure differs across countries and changes as economies develop. Specifically, Demirgüç-Kunt and Levine find that banks, nonbanks, stock markets, and bond markets are larger, more active, and more efficient in richer countries. Thus, the data show—unsurprisingly—that financial systems, on average, are more developed in richer countries. Moreover, the data show that in higher-income countries, stock markets tend to become more active and efficient relative to banks. This finding does not suggest that there is a unique path along which financial systems evolve. The data do, however, illustrate a general tendency for national financial systems to become more market-oriented as they become richer.

Besides documenting the evolution of financial structure, chapter 3 assesses the relationship between financial systems and key legal, regulatory, and political characteristics. Specifically, the chapter finds that countries with a common law tradition (as distinct from a civil law tradition), strong protection of minority shareholder rights, good accounting systems, low levels of corruption, and no explicit deposit insurance tend to have more market-oriented financial systems. This is consistent with theories emphasizing that higher information costs and weaker legal codes regarding individual investor rights will tend to favor banks over atomistic markets. Besides examining financial structure, Demirgüç-Kunt and Levine also examine the overall level of financial development. They find that underdeveloped financial systems have a greater tendency to have a French civil law tradition, poor protection of minority shareholder rights and creditor rights, poor contract enforcement in general, higher levels of corruption, poor accounting standards, commercial banking regulations that heavily restrict the activities of banks, and high inflation rates. Chapter 3 simply documents some broad proclivities in the data and does not evaluate specific theoretical predictions. The relationships, however, are consistent with many theories discussed in Allen and Gale (2000) and in René Stulz's review of the theoretical literature (chapter 4).

1.3   Financial Development, Structure, and Growth

Part III focuses on the relationship between financial structure and growth but also provides additional evidence on the connection between overall financial development and economic growth. In chapter 4, "Does Financial Structure Matter for Economic Growth? A Corporate Finance Perspective," René Stulz reviews the literature on financial structure and economic growth by emphasizing the connections between financial arrangements and corporate finance. He emphasizes that, by lowering information and transaction costs, overall financial development can facilitate the efficient flow of capital and thereby influence economic growth. Stulz also notes that legal, regulatory, and policy factors influence the effectiveness with which the overall financial system channels capital to productive ends.

This chapter also investigates the comparative merits of bank-based and market-based financial systems. A variety of theories specify the conditions under which bank-based systems will do a better job of funneling capital to its most productive ends than more market-based systems. In particular, banks may be particularly effective in underdeveloped countries with poorly functioning legal and accounting systems (Gerschenkron 1962). Powerful banks can more effectively induce firms to reveal information and pay debts than atomistic markets that rely on efficient legal and accounting systems. Furthermore, banks may be more effective in providing external resources to new firms that require staged financing because banks can more credibly commit to making additional funding available as the project develops, while markets have a more difficult time making credible, long-term commitments.

Alternatively, some theories highlight the conditions under which market-based systems are effective at allocating society's savings. Powerful banks frequently stymie innovation and competition. Banks may extract information rents from firms and thereby reduce the incentives of firms to undertake profitable projects (Rajan 1992). By encouraging competition, market-based systems create greater incentives for R&D and growth. Furthermore, powerful bankers may collude with managers against other outside investors and thereby thwart competition, efficient resource allocation, and growth (Wenger and Kaserer 1998; Weinstein and Yafeh 1998; Morck and Nakamura 1999). Thus, some theories stress the advantages of market-based systems, especially in the promotion of innovative, more R&D–based industries (Allen 1993). In reviewing the literature, Stulz sets the analytical stage for the empirical work that follows.

Chapter 5, "Financial Structure and Economic Development: Firm, Industry, and Country Evidence" by Thorsten Beck, Aslı Demirgüç-Kunt, Ross Levine, and Vojislav Maksimovic, conducts a comprehensive assessment of the relationship between economic performance and financial structure. To measure financial structure, the authors use the data assembled by Beck, Demirgüç-Kunt, and Levine for this book. They then combine this data with firm-level, industry-level, and pure cross-country datasets. Specifically, the chapter relies on (1) pure cross-country comparisons, (2) cross-industry, cross-country methods, and (3) firm-level data across many countries, to examine the connections between financial structure and economic growth.

Using very different data and econometric methodologies, the authors of chapter 5 find astonishingly consistent results. First, no evidence exists that distinguishing countries by financial structure helps explain differences in economic performance. More precisely, countries do not grow faster, financially dependent industries do not expand at higher rates, new firms are not created more easily, firms' access to external finance is not easier, and firms do not grow faster in either market-based or bank-based financial systems. Second, chapter 5 finds that distinguishing countries by overall financial development does help explain cross-country differences in economic performance. Measures of bank development and market development are strongly linked to economic growth. More specifically, the data indicate that economies grow faster, industries depending heavily on external finance expand at faster rates, new firms form more easily, firms' access to external financing is easier, and firms grow more rapidly in economies with higher levels of overall financial-sector development. Finally, chapter 5 emphasizes the role of the legal system in producing growth-enhancing financial systems. Specifically, the component of overall financial development explained by the legal rights of outside investors and the efficiency of the legal system in enforcing contracts is strongly and positively linked to firm, industry, and national economic success.

In chapter 6, "Financial Structure and Bank Profitability," Aslı Demirgüç-Kunt and Harry Huizinga focus on the performance of the banking sector itself across different financial structures. Their research shows that banks have higher profits and larger interest-rate margins in underdeveloped financial systems. After controlling for the overall level of financial development, the relative development of banks versus markets does not have an independent effect on bank profitability or interest margins. Thus, it is the level of bank and stock market development that translates into differences in banking sector efficiency, not financial structure per se.

In Chapter 7, "International Evidence on Aggregate Corporate Financing Decisions," Ian Domowitz, Jack Glen, and Ananth Madhavan assemble a new cross-country dataset on bond and stock issues and investigate how the role played by these markets varies with financial structure. This is a first-time effort to systematically document the magnitude of primary market financing, both across countries and over time. The authors examine the determinants of primary market activity, focusing on the role of various institutional and macroeconomic factors. They show that macroeconomic stability is highly correlated with the choice of external financing and that the institutional framework plays an equally crucial role in financing decisions. Key institutional factors include liquidity in the stock market, concentration in the banking system, and the relative size of the banking sector and the stock market. Finally, the authors observe that market-based systems are more dependent on foreign securities, which turns out to be mostly driven by a reliance on foreign bonds.

1.4   Financial Structure and Performance: Country Studies

The country studies echo the cross-country, industry-level, and firm-level findings: Overall financial development is very important for economic success, but financial structure as such is not a distinguishing characteristic of success. While studying financial structure, each of the country studies naturally focuses on the particular issues facing the country under consideration.

In chapter 8, "Financial Structure in Chile," Francisco Gallego and Norman Loayza investigate the development of Chile's financial system over the last two decades. They use firm-level data and panel-econometric techniques to assess a number of hypotheses. They show that Chilean firms have become less cash constrained in their investment decisions with the substantial improvement in Chile's financial system. Thus, overall financial development in Chile has eased cash-flow constraints and thereby facilitated a more efficient allocation of capital. Furthermore, they show that the rapid development of the banking system induced an increased reliance on debt. This occurred even while capital market development lowered the cost of firms raising capital by issuing equity. Thus, bank and capital market development improved firm access to capital, and on net, an increase in firm leverage ratios occurred. Finally, Gallego and Loayza emphasize the internationalization of Chile's financial system. Access to international capital markets positively influenced firm debt-equity ratios. Specifically, the ability of Chilean firms to issue American Depository Receipts sent a positive signal of future performance that eased borrowing constraints. Thus, Chile is a country that has developed better markets and strong banks and has gained greater access to international equity and debt markets. The improvement in overall financial development has enhanced capital allocation. While debt ratios have risen, no evidence exists that changes in financial structure per se have significantly influenced firm performance in Chile.

In chapter 9, "Firms' Financing Choices in Bank-Based and Market-Based Economies," Sergio Schmukler and Esteban Vesperoni investigate the impact of internationalization on firm financing decisions and whether this impact depends on financial structure. Specifically, the chapter examines whether international liberalization alters financing choices of firms, and whether the level of domestic financial development and structure influences the impact of international liberalization on firm financing decisions. The authors use firm-level data from Asia and Latin America. They show that international liberalization has less of an impact on firm financing choices in countries with well-developed financial systems. Schmukler and

Vesperoni also show that financial structure—the degree to which countries are bank-based or market-based—does not influence the impact of liberalization on firm financing choices. Again, the evidence suggests that it is overall financial development that influences decisions and not financial structure as such.

In chapter 10, "Corporate Groups, Financial Liberalization, and Growth: The Case of Indonesia," Andy Chui, Sheridan Titman, and K. C. John Wei examine the case of Indonesia. They study whether firms connected to corporate groups responded differently to financial liberalization than did independent firms. Corporate groups control a significant portion of their economies' assets in many developing countries and are controlled by politically powerful families. These groups may have greater power than independent firms in terms of (1) access to capital and (2) the ability to influence and circumvent government regulations. Under these conditions, these groups may impede financial market liberalization because liberalization may tend to reduce their power. In particular, powerful groups may favor a concentrated, bank-based system rather than atomistic, difficult-to-control markets. To explore these possibilities, Chui, Titman, and Wei empirically examine the effects of financial liberalization on corporate groups and independent firms in Indonesia. They do not detect a difference: Corporate groups do not respond differently than independent firms do. This result holds over a period during which stock market development increased dramatically in Indonesia.

1.5   Lessons

This book tackles three broad questions.

1. What happens to national financial systems as countries develop?

2. Does overall financial development influence economic growth and firm performance?

3. Does the structure of the financial system—bank-based or market-based—influence economic growth and firm performance?

Through a diverse set of analyses, the answers are surprisingly clear. First, we find that national financial systems tend to become more developed overall and more market-oriented as they become richer. Second, we find that overall financial development tends to accelerate economic growth, facilitate new firm formation, ease firm access to external financing, and boost firm growth. Moreover, the evidence strongly suggests the following: Legal systems that effectively protect the rights of outside investors and that enforce contracts efficiently improve the operation of financial markets and intermediaries with positive ramifications on long-run growth. Third, financial structure is not an analytically very useful way to distinguish among national financial systems. Countries do not grow faster, new firms are not created more easily, firms' access to external finance is not easier, and firms do not grow faster in either market- or bank-based financial systems.

At the risk of oversimplifying, we can summarize the findings of this book as follows: Overall financial development matters for economic success, but financial structure per se does not seem to matter much. Thus, policymakers may achieve greater returns by focusing less on the extent to which their country is bank-based or market-based and more on legal, regulatory, and policy reforms that boost the functioning of markets *and* banks.

Before concluding this introduction, we stress an important qualification: Because no universally accepted definition of financial structure exists, our measures may be prone to error. The research presented here uses a variety of different measures that, combined with different analytical procedures, all point to the same conclusion. Nevertheless, one can reject all of the measures of financial structure and thereby reject this book's conclusions. We fully accept this possibility. We hope that our efforts improve the marginal product of those who will further investigate financial structure and economic development. Perhaps, Goldsmith (1969, x) put this best in discussing his own efforts: "I cannot expect to have escaped statistical errors and oversights.... All I can do is to take comfort in the proverb, nothing ventured, nothing gained, and to put my faith in those who will plow the field over again and may produce a richer harvest, in particular obtaining a higher yield per hour for their labor."

Notes

1. Specifically, firm-level studies (Demirgüç-Kunt and Maksimovic 1998), industry-level studies (Rajan and Zingales 1998; Wurgler 2000), cross-country studies (King and Levine 1993a, b; Levine and Zervos 1998), and pooled cross-country, time-series studies (Beck, Levine, and Loayza 2000) find that financial development is positively related to growth, and this relationship is not due only to simultaneity bias.

2. See Demirgüç-Kunt and Maksimovic 1999; Levine 1998, 1999, forthcoming; and Levine, Loayza, and Beck 2000.

References

Allen, Franklin. 1993. Stock markets and resource allocation. In *Capital markets and financial intermediation*, ed. C. Mayer and X. Vives, 148–151. Cambridge: Cambridge University Press.

Allen, Franklin, and Douglas Gale. 2000. *Comparing financial systems*. Cambridge, MA: MIT Press.

Beck, Thorsten, Ross Levine, and Norman Loayza. 2000. Finance and the sources of growth. *Journal of Financial Economics* 58(1):261–300.

Demirgüç-Kunt, Aslı, and Maksimovic Vojislav. 1998. Law, finance, and firm growth. *Journal of Finance* 53(6):2107–2137 (December).

Demirgüç-Kunt, Aslı, and Vojislav Maksimovic. 1999. Institutions, financial markets, and firm debt maturity. *Journal of Financial Economics* 54:295–336.

Gerschenkron, Alexander. 1962. *Economic backwardness in historical perspective, a book of essays*. Cambridge, MA: Harvard University Press.

Goldsmith, Raymond W. 1969. *Financial structure and development*. New Haven, CT: Yale University Press.

King, Robert G., and Ross Levine. 1993a. Finance and growth: Schumpeter might be right. *Quarterly Journal of Economics* 108:717–738.

King, Robert G., and Ross Levine. 1993b. Finance, entrepreneurship, and growth: Theory and evidence. *Journal of Monetary Economics* 32:513–542.

La Porta, Rafael, Florencio Lopez-de-Silanes, Andrei Shleifer, and Robert W. Vishny. 1998. Law and finance. *Journal of Political Economy* 106(6):1113–1155.

Levine, Ross. 1998. The legal environment, banks, and long-run economic growth. *Journal of Money, Credit, and Banking* 30(3, Pt. 2):596–620 (August).

Levine, Ross. 1999. Law, finance, and economic growth. *Journal of Financial Intermediation* 8(1/2):36–67.

Levine, Ross. Forthcoming. Napoleon, Bourses, and growth: With a focus on Latin America. In *Market augmenting government*, ed. Omar Azfar and Charles Cadwell. Ann Arbor: University of Michigan Press.

Levine, Ross, and Sara Zervos. 1998. Stock markets, banks, and economic growth. *American Economic Review* 88(3):537–558 (June).

Levine, Ross, Norman Loayza, and Thorsten Beck. 2000. Financial intermediation and growth: Causality and causes. *Journal of Monetary Economics* 46(1):31–77 (August).

Morck, Randall, and Masao Nakamura. 1999. Banks and corporate control in Japan. *Journal of Finance* 54:319–340.

Rajan, Raghuram G. 1992. Insiders and outsiders: The choice between informed and arms length debt. *Journal of Finance* 47(4):1367–1400 (September).

Rajan, Raghuram G., and Luigi Zingales. 1998. Financial dependence and growth. *American Economic Review* 88(3):559–586 (June).

Weinstein, David E., and Yishay Yafeh. 1998. On the costs of a bank-centered financial system: Evidence from the changing main bank relations in Japan. *Journal of Finance* 53(2):635–672.

Wenger, Ekkehard, and Christoph Kaserer. 1998. The German system of corporate governance: A model which should not be imitated in competition and convergence. In *Financial markets: The German and Anglo-American Models*, ed. Stanley W. Black and Mathias Moersch, 41–78. New York: North-Holland Press.

Wurgler, Jeffrey. 2000. Financial markets and the allocation of capital. *Journal of Financial Economics* 58(1):187–214.

II

Measurement and Determinants of Financial Structure

2   The Financial Structure Database

Thorsten Beck, Aslı
Demirgüç-Kunt, and Ross
Levine

2.1 Introduction

A recent and expanding literature establishes the importance of financial development for economic growth.[1] Measures of the size of the banking sector and the size and liquidity of the stock market are highly correlated with subsequent gross domestic product (GDP) per capita growth. Moreover, emerging evidence suggests that both the level of banking-sector development and stock market development exert a causal impact on economic growth.[2] Recent financial crises in South East Asia and Latin America further underscore the importance of a well-functioning financial sector for the whole economy.

This chapter introduces a new database that for the first time provides financial analysts and researchers with a comprehensive assessment of the development, structure, and performance of the financial sector. This database, which is available with the book, includes statistics on the size, activity, and efficiency of various financial intermediaries and markets across a broad spectrum of countries and over time. The database will thus enable financial analysts and researchers to compare the level of financial development and the structure of the financial sector of a specific country with that of other countries in the region or countries with a similar GDP per capita level. It allows comparisons of financial systems for a given year and over time.

Previously, financial analysts and researchers have relied on a few indicators of the banking sector and the stock market, using data from the International Monetary Fund's (IMF's) International Financial Statistics (IFS) and the International Finance Corporation's (IFC's) Emerging Market Database. This new database draws on a wider array of sources and constructs indicators of the size, activity, and efficiency of a much broader set of financial institutions and markets. Specifically, this database uses bank-specific data to construct indicators of the market structure and efficiency of commercial banks. Furthermore, this is the first systematic compilation of data on the split of public versus private ownership in the banking sector. This database is the first attempt to define and construct indicators of the size and activity of nonbank financial intermediaries, such as insurance companies, pension funds, and nondeposit money banks. Finally, this database is the first to include indicators of the size of primary equity markets and primary and secondary bond markets. This results in a unique set of indicators that capture the development and structure of the financial sector across countries and over time along many different dimensions.

The remainder of this chapter is organized as follows. Section 2.2 discusses indicators of the size and activity of financial intermediaries. Section 2.3 introduces indicators of the efficiency and market structure of commercial banks. In section 2.4 we define indicators of the size and activity of other financial institutions. Stock and bond market indicators are introduced in section 2.5. Each section presents the indicators, the sources and the sample, and the variance of the indicators across income groups of countries. Section 2.6 offers concluding remarks. Table 2.1 provides an overview of all indicators with cross-country and time-series coverage. The appendix presents the sources and construction of the measures.

2.2 The Size and Activity of Financial Intermediaries

A first set of measures compares the size and activity of central banks, deposit money banks, and other financial institutions relative to each other and relative to GDP. We use data from the IMF's International Financial Statistics to construct these indicators. The data cover the period from 1960 to 1997 and 175 countries.

2.2.1 Groups of Financial Institutions

The indicators in this section distinguish among three groups of financial institutions: central banks, deposit money banks, and other financial institutions.[3] The three groups are defined as in the IFS. The first group comprises the central bank and other institutions that perform functions of the monetary authorities.[4] The second group,

Table 2.1
Coverage of the Variables

	Time span	Number of countries	Number of observations
Central bank assets to total financial assets	1960–1997	79	2,177
Deposit money banks assets to total financial assets	1960–1997	79	2,177
Other financial institutions assets to total financial assets	1960–1997	79	2,177
Deposit money versus central bank assets	1960–1997	169	4,651
Liquid liabilities to GDP	1960–1997	159	3,873
Central bank assets to GDP	1960–1997	153	3,671
Deposit money bank assets to GDP	1960–1997	160	3,912
Other financial institution assets to GDP	1960–1997	80	2,008
Private credit by deposit money banks to GDP	1960–1997	160	3,901
Private credit by deposit money banks and other financial institutions to GDP	1960–1997	161	3,923
Net interest margin	1990–1997	129	721
Overhead costs	1990–1997	129	719
Concentration	1990–1997	137	822
Foreign bank share (assets)	1990–1997	111	673
Foreign bank share (number)	1990–1997	111	673
Public share	1980–1997	41	213
Total assets of other banklike institutions to GDP	1980–1997	54	766
Total assets of life insurance companies to GDP	1980–1997	24	333
Total assets of insurance companies to GDP	1980–1997	40	547
Total assets of private pension and provident funds to GDP	1980–1997	16	185
Total assets of pooled investment schemes to GDP	1980–1997	27	295
Total assets of development banks to GDP	1980–1997	46	634
Private credit by other banklike institutions to GDP	1980–1997	43	652
Private credit by life insurance companies to GDP	1980–1997	17	258
Private credit by insurance companies to GDP	1980–1997	19	275

Table 2.1
(continued)

	Time span	Number of countries	Number of observations
Private credit by private pension and provident funds to GDP	1980–1997	11	126
Private credit by pooled investment schemes to GDP	1980–1997	10	106
Private credit by development banks to GDP	1980–1997	38	555
Life insurance penetration	1987–1996	85	682
Life insurance density	1987–1996	85	682
Stock market capitalization to GDP	1976–1997	93	1,171
Stock market total value traded to GDP	1975–1997	93	1,264
Stock market turnover to GDP	1976–1997	93	1,154
Private bond market capitalization to GDP	1990–1997	37	287
Public bond market capitalization to GDP	1990–1997	37	287
Equity issues to GDP	1980–1995	42	586
Long-term private debt issues to GDP	1980–1995	40	508

deposit money banks, consists of all financial institutions that have liabilities in the form of deposits transferable by check or otherwise usable in making payments (IMF 1984, 29). The third group—other financial institutions—is made up of other banklike institutions and nonbank financial institutions. These are institutions that serve as financial intermediaries, while not incurring liabilities usable as means of payment. Other banklike institutions include (1) institutions that accept deposits, but do not provide transferable deposit facilities, (2) intermediaries that finance themselves mainly through issuance of negotiable bonds, (3) development banks, and (4) offshore units. Nonbank financial institutions include insurance companies, provident and pension funds, trust and custody accounts, real investment schemes, other pooled investment schemes, and compulsory savings schemes. Whereas data on other banklike institutions are usually current and complete, only fragmentary data are available for nonbank financial institutions.

We distinguish between two different balance-sheet items: total claims on domestic nonfinancial sectors (lines a through d) and claims on the private sector (line d).[5] In what follows, we denote the first with assets and the second with private credit. Whereas assets refers to total domestic financial intermediation that the respective intermediary performs, private credit captures the financial inter-mediation with the private nonfinancial sector. For both measures, we exclude claims on central banks, deposit money banks, and other financial institutions (lines e through g) and therefore any cross-claims of one financial sector on another.

2.2.2 *Measures of Size of Financial Intermediaries*

We present two groups of size indicators. The relative size indicators measure the importance of the three financial sectors relative to each other; the absolute size indicators measure their size relative to GDP.

Relative Size Measures
The first three indicators are only presented if data are available on all three financial sectors. These indicators are:

• Central Bank Assets to Total Financial Assets
• Deposit Money Banks Assets to Total Financial Assets
• Other Financial Institutions Assets to Total Financial Assets

where Total Financial Assets are the sum of central bank, deposit money banks, and other financial institutions assets.

Since these measures are calculated only if data are available for all three categories, we construct an alternative indicator that measures the relative importance of deposit money banks relative to central banks: Deposit Money versus Central Bank Assets. This measure has been used as a measure of financial development by, among others, King and Levine (1993a, b) and Levine, Loayza, and Beck (2000) and equals the ratio of deposit money bank assets and the sum of deposit money and central bank assets.

Absolute Size Measures
The following three indicators measure the size of the three financial sectors relative to GDP:

• Central Bank Assets to GDP
• Deposit Money Banks Assets to GDP
• Other Financial Institutions Assets to GDP

These measures give evidence of the importance of the financial services performed by the three financial sectors relative to the size of the economy. The assets include claims on the whole nonfinancial real sector, including government, public enterprises, and the private sector.

Since many researchers have focused on the liability side of the balance sheet, we include a measure of absolute size based on liabilities. Liquid Liabilities to GDP equals currency plus demand and interest-bearing liabilities of banks and other financial intermediaries divided by GDP. This is the broadest available indicator of financial intermediation, since it includes all three financial sectors. For the numerator we use either line 55l or, where not available, line 35l. Whereas line 35l includes monetary authorities and deposit money banks, line 55l also includes other banking institutions, as defined by the IMF. Line 35l is often also referred to as M2. Liquid Liabilities is a typical measure of financial depth and thus of the overall size of the financial sector, without distinguishing among the financial sectors or among the use of liabilities.

2.2.3 *Measures of Activity of Financial Intermediaries*

While the size measures do not distinguish whether the claims of financial intermediaries are on the public or the private sector, the following two indicators concentrate on claims on the private sector:

- Private Credit by Deposit Money Banks to GDP
- Private Credit by Deposit Money Banks and Other Financial Institutions to GDP

Whereas the first equals claims on the private sector by deposit money banks divided by GDP, the second includes claims by both deposit money banks and other financial institutions. Both measures isolate credit issued to the private sector as opposed to credit issued to governments and public enterprises. Furthermore, they concentrate on credit issued by intermediaries other than the central bank. They are the measures of the activity of financial intermediaries in one of its main functions: channeling savings to investors. Both indicators have been used by researchers, the first by Levine and Zervos (1998), and the second by Levine, Loayza, and Beck (1999) and Beck, Levine, and Loayza (1999).

2.2.4   A Note on Deflating

We can distinguish between two groups of measures depending on the denominator. The first group consists of ratios of two stock variables, whereas the measures in the second group are ratios of a stock variable and a flow variable, specifically GDP. Whereas stock variables are measured at the end of a period, flow variables are defined relative to a period. This presents problems in the second group of indicators, both in terms of correct timing and in terms of deflating correctly. To address these problems, we deflate the end-of-year financial balance-sheet items (FD) by end-of-year consumer price indices (CPI) and deflate the GDP series by the annual CPI.[6] Then, we compute the average of the real financial balance sheet item in year t and $t-1$ and divide this average by real GDP measured in year t. The end-of-year CPI is either the value for December or, where not available, the value for the last quarter. The formula is the following:

$$\frac{0.5 * \left(\dfrac{FD_t}{CPI_{e,t}} + \dfrac{FD_{t-1}}{CPI_{e,t-1}} \right)}{\dfrac{GDP_t}{CPI_{a,t}}}, \tag{2.1}$$

where e indicates end of period and a average for the period.

2.2.5   Financial Intermediary Development across Income Groups and over Time

As exhibited by figures 2.1–2.3, our indicators of financial intermediary development show considerable variation across countries and over time.[7] Figure 2.1 shows that central banks lose relative importance as we move from low- to high-income countries, whereas other financial institutions gain relative importance. Deposit money banks gain importance versus Central Banks with a higher income level.[8] As can be seen in figure 2.2, financial depth, as measured by Liquid Liabilities to GDP, increases with the income level. Deposit money banks and other financial institutions are bigger and more active in richer countries, whereas central banks are smaller. Figure 2.3 shows that Liquid Liabilities to GDP and Private Credit by Deposit Money Banks to GDP have increased constantly since the

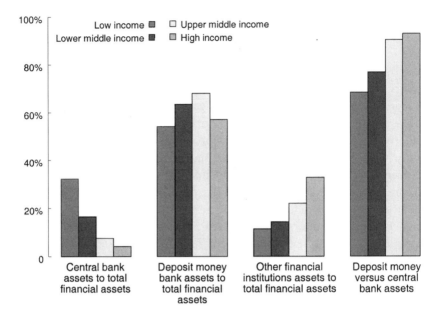

Figure 2.1
Financial intermediary development across income groups.

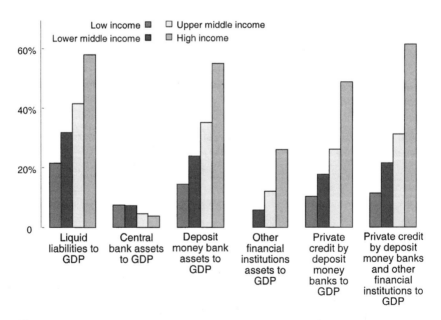

Figure 2.2
Financial intermediary development across income groups.

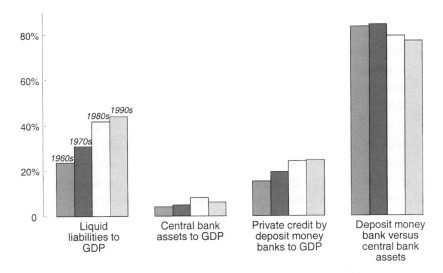

Figure 2.3
Financial intermediary development over time.

1960s. Central Bank Assets to GDP first increased from the 1960s to
the 1980s and then decreased again in the 1990s. Deposit Money
Banks versus Central Bank Assets first increased and then decreased
over time, a pattern mainly driven by low-income countries.

2.3 Efficiency and Market Structure of Commercial Banks

This section provides indicators of the efficiency and market structure of commercial banks.[9] The data were collected from individual
banks' balance sheets provided by IBCA's Bankscope database and
from individual country sources such as central bank and supervisory body publications.[10]

2.3.1 Measures of Efficiency

One of the main functions of financial intermediaries is to channel
funds from savers to investors. We construct two potential measures
of the efficiency with which commercial banks perform this function.
The net interest margin equals the accounting value of a bank's net
interest revenue as a share of its total assets.[11] Overhead cost equals

the accounting value of a bank's overhead costs as share of its total assets.

Unlike in the previous section, we do not deflate numerator and denominator of these two measures, although they are ratios of a flow and a stock variable and therefore measured at different points of time, for several reasons. First, unlike for macroeconomic variables, there is no obvious deflator for individual banks' assets and income flows. Second, unlike macroeconomic variables and financial-sector assets, bank-individual flows and stocks are directly related. Third, financial assets and flows do not equal quantity times price, as does the GDP. Finally, we would lose around 25 percent of the observations.[12]

2.3.2   Measures of Market Structure

Here we collect and present data on the concentration of commercial banks, foreign bank penetration, and public versus private ownership of commercial banks.

We use a concentration measure that is defined as the ratio of the three largest banks' assets to total banking-sector assets. A highly concentrated commercial banking sector might result in lack of competitive pressure to attract savings and channel them efficiently to investors. A highly fragmented market might be evidence of under-capitalized banks.

We present two measures of foreign bank penetration: the foreign bank share (number), which equals the number of foreign banks in total banks, and the foreign bank share (assets), which equals the share of foreign bank assets in total banking-sector assets.[13] Claessens, Demirgüç-Kunt, and Huizinga (1997) show that an increase in foreign bank penetration leads to lower profitability and overhead expenses for banks. Demirgüç-Kunt, Levine, and Min (1998) show that higher foreign bank penetration enhances economic growth by boosting domestic banking efficiency. A bank is defined as "foreign" if at least 50 percent of the equity is owned by foreigners.

Public versus private ownership has become an increasingly important issue not only for researchers and policymakers in the banking sector, but also for the whole economy.[14] This database includes the first compilation of panel data on the public ownership of commercial banks. Public Share equals the share of publicly owned commercial bank assets in total commercial bank assets. A bank is defined as

"public" if at least 50 percent of the equity is held by the government
or a public institution.

2.3.3 Sources and Coverage

Data on the net interest margin, overhead costs, concentration, and
foreign bank penetration use income statements and balance sheet
data of commercial banks from the Bank Scope Database provided
by IBCA. Data are available for 137 countries and for the years
since 1990. To ensure a reasonable coverage, only countries with at
least three banks in a given year are included. Although on average
around 90 percent of the banking sector assets in a given country and
year are covered in IBCA, sampling error and bias are possible. Net
interest margin and overhead costs are calculated as averages for a
country in a given year. Whereas for the two efficiency measures we
use only unconsolidated balance sheets, we use both unconsolidated
and consolidated balance sheets for the concentration index and the
foreign bank penetration measures.[15]

Data on public versus private ownership are from Bankscope,
Gardener and Molyneux (1990), and individual country sources,
such as central bank or supervisory body publications.[16] Data are
available for forty-one developed and developing countries and for
selected years in the 1980s and 1990s. Numbers from Bankscope
were double-checked with estimates from other sources.

2.3.4 The Efficiency and Market Structure of Commercial Banks across Income Groups

As can be seen in figure 2.4, commercial banks are more efficient in
high- and upper-middle-income countries. A negative correlation
exists between the income level and the concentration of the commercial banking sector. There is a higher degree of foreign bank
penetration in low- and lower-middle-income countries, both in
terms of number and assets of foreign banks.

The most striking variance can be observed for public versus private ownership of commercial banks. Whereas public bank assets
constitute over 70 percent of commercial bank assets in low-income
countries, their share is around 40 percent in middle-income and 0
percent in high-income countries.[17]

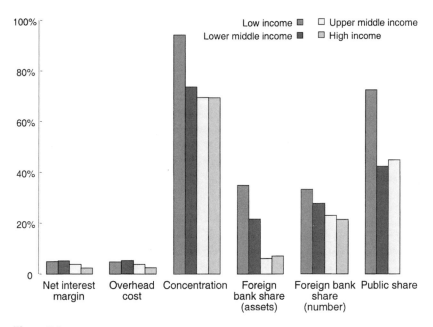

Figure 2.4
Efficiency and market structure of commercial banks across income groups.

2.4   Other Financial Institutions

This section of the database presents the first systematic effort to collect data on financial intermediaries other than central and deposit money banks.

2.4.1   Categories of Other Financial Institutions

In section 2.2 we included all financial intermediaries other than central and deposit money banks in one group, called "other financial institutions." In this section we try to get a better picture by breaking this sector into five subgroups.

   1. Banklike Institutions: This category comprises two groups of institutions: (a) intermediaries that accept deposits without providing transferable deposit facilities, and (b) intermediaries that raise funds on the financial market mainly in the form of negotiable bonds. Examples of the first group are savings banks, cooperative banks, mortgage banks, and building societies. Examples of the

second group include finance companies. Often these institutions have specialized in specific activities, for historic, legal, or tax reasons.[18]

2. Insurance Companies: Within the category of insurance companies, we can distinguish between life insurance companies and other insurance companies. We do not include insurance funds that are part of a government social security system.

3. Private Pension and Provident Funds: Like life insurance companies, pension and provident funds serve the purpose of risk pooling and wealth accumulation. We do not include pension funds that are part of a government social security system.

4. Pooled Investment Schemes: These financial institutions invest on behalf of their shareholders in a certain type of asset, such as real estate investment schemes or mutual funds.

5. Development Banks: These financial institutions derive their funds mainly from the government, other financial institutions, and supranational organizations. On the asset side, they are often concentrated on specific groups of borrowers. Most of these institutions were set up after World War II or after independence in an effort to foster economic development.

2.4.2 Measures of the Size and Activity of Other Financial Institutions

Here we present size and activity indicators similar to the ones in section 2.2, plus some additional measures of insurance development.

For all five other financial institution groups, we construct measures of their size relative to GDP by calculating the ratio of total assets to GDP. Unlike in section 2.2, total assets refer to total assets from balance sheet.[19] We also construct activity indicators by measuring the claims on the private sector relative to GDP.

For the insurance sector, we include an additional size and two additional activity measures: We present assets and private credit of the life insurance sector where disaggregated data are available. We also present life insurance penetration, measured by premiums/GDP and life insurance density, measured by premiums/population. The first indicator provides evidence on the importance of the life insurance sector relative to the total economy, and the second evidence on the expenditure per capita on life insurance provision.[20]

2.4.3 Sources

Data on the size and activity of other financial institutions were collected mostly from the IFS and individual country sources, such as central banks, bank and insurance supervisory bodies, and statistical yearbooks.[21] These data are available for sixty-five countries and for the years since 1980.

Data on life insurance penetration and life insurance density come from SIGMA, a monthly publication by Swiss Re. Their data are based on direct premium volume of commercially active insurers, regardless of whether they are in state or private ownership (SIGMA 1998, 4:4). Only domestic insurance business, regardless whether conducted by domestic or foreign insurers, is included. Data are available for eighty-eight developing and developed countries, and for years since 1987.[22]

2.4.4 Development of Other Financial Institutions across Income Groups

Figure 2.5 shows that the private credit by all five categories of other financial institutions increases as we move from low- to high-income countries.[23] Figure 2.6 shows that the private credit by life insurance companies, the life insurance penetration, and the life insurance density increase with GDP per capita. Interestingly, for the first two measures, the lower-middle-income group exhibits the lowest medians. Also note that the high-income countries exhibit a life insurance penetration ten times as high as lower-middle-income countries and a life insurance density nearly one hundred times higher than that of low-income countries.

2.5 Stock and Bond Market Development

This part of the database defines measures of the size, the activity, and the efficiency of primary and secondary stock and bond markets. By including bond markets and primary equity markets, this database improves significantly on previous work. Sources and coverage are presented, as well as the variance of these indicators over time and across income groups.

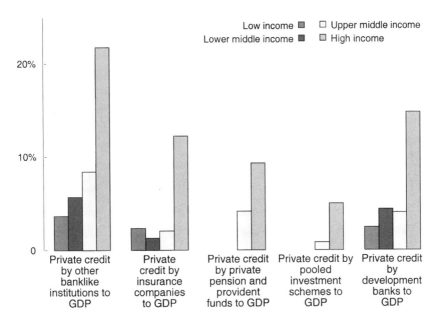

Figure 2.5
Private credit by other financial institutions across income groups.

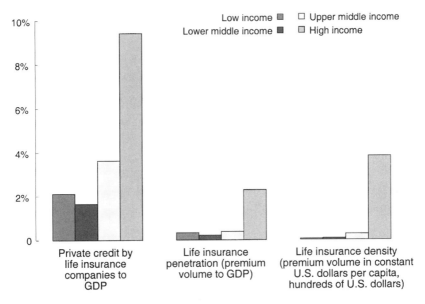

Figure 2.6
Life insurance development across income groups.

2.5.1   Indicators of Stock Market Size, Activity, and Efficiency

As an indicator of the size of the stock market, we use the stock market capitalization to GDP ratio, which equals the value of listed shares divided by GDP. Both numerator and denominator are deflated appropriately, with the numerator equaling the average of the end-of-year value for year t and year $t-1$, both deflated by the respective end-of-year CPI, and the GDP deflated by the annual value of the CPI.

To measure the activity or liquidity of the stock markets, we use stock market total value traded to GDP, which is defined as total shares traded on the stock market exchange divided by GDP. Since both numerator and denominator are flow variables measured over the same time period, deflating is not necessary in this case.

We use the stock market turnover ratio as efficiency indicator of stock markets. It is defined as the ratio of the value of total shares traded to market capitalization. It measures the activity or liquidity of a stock market relative to its size. A small but active stock market will have a high turnover ratio whereas a large, less liquid stock market will have a low turnover ratio. Since this indicator is the ratio of a stock to a flow variable, we apply a deflating procedure similar to that of the market capitalization indicator.

2.5.2   Indicators of Bond Market Size

As indicators of the size of the domestic bond market, we use the private and public bond market capitalization to GDP, which equals the total amount of outstanding domestic debt securities issued by private or public domestic entities divided by GDP. Both numerator and denominator are deflated appropriately, with the numerator equaling the average of the end-of-year value for year t and year $t-1$, both deflated by the end-of-year CPI, and the GDP deflated by the annual value of the CPI.

2.5.3   Indicators of Primary Stock and Bond Market Size

As an indicator of the size of primary equity and debt markets, we use Equity Issues to GDP (Long-term Private Debt Issues to GDP), which equals equity issues (long-term private debt issues) divided by GDP. Both numerator and denominator are in nominal terms, since both are flow variables.

2.5.4   Sources

Most of the secondary stock market data come from the IFC's Emerging Market Database. Additional data come from Goldman Sachs' International Investment Research (1986). Some of the data are in local currency, some in U.S. dollars. To deflate in a consistent way, we use the local CPI and the U.S. CPI respectively.[24] Data on the secondary bond market come from the Bank for International Settlement (BIS) *Quarterly Review on International Banking and Financial Market Development* and are in U.S. dollars. Data on the primary equity and debt market come from country-specific sources and were collected by Aylward and Glen (1999) and from the OECD Financial Statistics Monthly.[25] They are partly in local currency, partly in U.S. dollars. GDP numbers in local currency and the CPI numbers are from the International Financial Statistics, while GDP numbers in U.S. dollars are from the World Bank.

Secondary stock market data are available for ninety-three countries starting in 1975. Secondary bond market data are available for thirty-seven countries, mostly industrialized, and for the years since 1990. Primary market data are available for forty-two countries, both industrialized and developing, for the years 1980–1995.

2.5.5   Stock and Bond Market Development across Income Groups

There is a significant variation in size, activity, and efficiency of stock markets across income groups, as evident in figure 2.7. Countries with a higher level of GDP per capita have bigger, more active, more efficient stock markets. Richer countries also have larger bond markets and issue more equity—in particular, private bonds.[26] Stock markets have increased in size, activity, and efficiency over the last three decades, as can be seen in figure 2.8.

2.6   Concluding Remarks

This chapter introduced a new and unique compilation of indicators of the size, activity, and efficiency of financial intermediaries and markets across countries and over time. It enables financial analysts

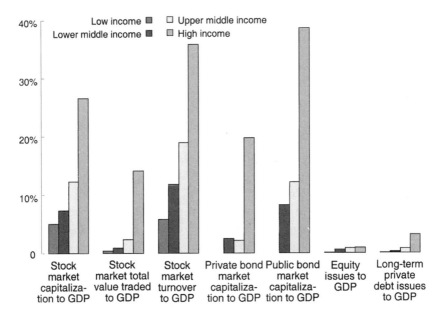

Figure 2.7
Stock and bond market development across income groups.

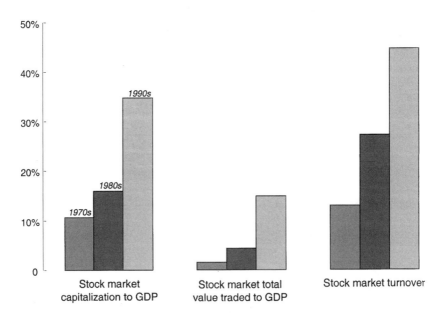

Figure 2.8
Stock market development over time.

to make a comprehensive assessment of the development and structure of the financial sector of countries compared to other countries and over time. It allows researchers to address a rich set of questions and issues in financial economics.

The database is part of a broader research project that tries to understand the determinants of financial structure and its importance for economic development. Specifically, the compiled data permit the construction of financial structure indicators that measure the relative size, activity, and efficiency of banks compared to stock markets. These indicators can then be used to investigate the empirical link between the legal, regulatory, and policy environment and the financial structure indicators (chapter 3) as well as the implications of financial structure for economic growth.

Appendix 2.1:   Sources

Section 2.2

All raw data are from the electronic version of the IMF's International Financial Statistics.

The following lines are included in Central Bank Assets, if available:

12AN.ZF	Claims on government (net)
12A.ZF	MONAUTH: claims on central government (local currency)
12BX.ZF	MONAUTH: claims on off entities (local currency)
12B.ZF	MONAUTH: claims on state and local governments (local currency)
12CD.ZF	Claims on nonfinancial enterprises
12C.ZF	MONAUTH: claims on nonfinancial public enterprises (local currency)
12D.ZF	MONAUTH: claims on private sector (local currency)

The following lines are included in Deposit Money Bank Assets, if available:

22ANHZF	Claims on central government (net)
22A.HZF	Claims on central government
22A.MZF	Claims on central government
22A.TZF	Claims on central government
22A.GZF	Claims on government
22AN.ZF	Claims on government (net)
22AE.ZF	Claims on national property fund
22A.ZF	DEPMONBKS: claims on central government (local currency)

22B.MZF	Claims on local government
22B.GZF	Claims on official entities
22B.TZF	Claims on state and local governments
22BX.ZF	DEPMONBKS: claims on official entities (local currency)
22B.ZF	DEPMONBKS: claims on state and local governments (local currency)
22CB.ZF	Claims on cooperatives
22C.HZF	Claims on nonfinancial public enterprises
22CA.ZF	Claims on public corporations
22C.ZF	DEPMONBKS: claims on nonfinancial public enterprises (local currency)
22D.GZF	Claims on private sector
22D.HZF	Claims on private sector
22D.MZF	Claims on private sector
22D.TZF	Claims on private sector
22DA.ZF	Claims on socialist sector
22D..ZF	DEPMONBKS: claims on private sector (local currency)
22D.IZF	Treasury: claims on private sector

The following lines are included in Other Financial Institutions Assets, if available:

42BXLZF	Local and semi-government securities
42BXKZF	Claims on official entities
42B.SZF	Claims on local governments
42B.GZF	Claims on local governments
42B.BZF	Claims on official entities
42B.FZF	Claims on official entities
42B.KZF	Claims on official entities
42B.NZF	Claims on state and local governments
42B.LZF	Claims on state and local governments
42BX.ZF	OTHFININST: claims on official entities (local currency)
42B.ZF	OTHFININST: claims on state and local governments (local currency)
42A.LZF	Claims on central government
42A.NZF	Claims on central government
42A.PZF	Claims on central government
42A.BZF	Claims on government
42A.FZF	Claims on government
42A.GZF	Claims on government

42A.HZF	Claims on government
42A.IZF	Claims on government
42A.KZF	Claims on government
42A.MZF	Claims on government
42A.SZF	Claims on government
42AN.ZF	Claims on government (net)
42A..ZF	OTHFININST: claims on central government (local currency)
42C.SZF	Claims on nonfinancial public enterprise
42C.NZF	Claims on nonfinancial public enterprise
42C.LZF	Claims on nonfinancial public enterprise
42C.MZF	Claims on nonfinancial public enterprise
42C.GZF	Claims on public enterprises
42C.FZF	Claims on public enterprises
42C.ZF	OTHFININST: claims on nonfinancial public enterprises (local currency)
42D.BZF	Claims on private sector
42D.FZF	Claims on private sector
42D.GZF	Claims on private sector
42D.HZF	Claims on private sector
42D.IZF	Claims on private sector
42D.KZF	Claims on private sector
42D.LZF	Claims on private sector
42D.MZF	Claims on private sector
42D.NZF	Claims on private sector
42D.PZF	Claims on private sector
42D.SZF	Claims on private sector
42D.ZF	OTHFININST: claims on private sector (local currency)
42H.SZF	Fixed asset/real estate
42H.LZF	Real estate

The following line is included in Liquid Liabilities:

55L.ZF	FINSURVEY: liquid liabilities (local currency)

if not available: 35L.ZF—MONSURVEY: money plus quasi-money (M2) (local currency)

The following lines are included in Private Credit by Deposit Money Banks, if available:

22D.GZF	Claims on private sector
22D.HZF	Claims on private sector

22D.MZF	Claims on private sector
22D.TZF	Claims on private sector
22DA.ZF	Claims on private sector
22D.ZF	DEPMONBKS: claims on private sector (local currency)
22D.IZF	TREAS: claims on private sector

The following lines are included in Private Credit by Deposit Money Banks and Other Financial Institutions, if available:

22D.GZF	Claims on private sector
22D.HZF	Claims on private sector
22D.MZF	Claims on private sector
22D.TZF	Claims on private sector
22DA.ZF	Claims on socialist sector
22D.ZF	DEPMONBKS: claims on private sector (local currency)
22D.IZF	TREAS: claims on private sector
42D.BZF	Claims on private sector
42D.FZF	Claims on private sector
42D.GZF	Claims on private sector
42D.HZF	Claims on private sector
42D.IZF	Claims on private sector
42D.KZF	Claims on private sector
42D.LZF	Claims on private sector
42D.MZF	Claims on private sector
42D.NZF	Claims on private sector
42D.PZF	Claims on private sector
42D.SZF	Claims on private sector
42D.ZF	OTHFININST: claims on private sector (local currency)

For GDP in local currency, the following line is used 99B.ZF—NA: gross domestic product (local currency) if not available: 99B.CZF—Gross domestic product. For the annual deflator the Consumer Price index, line 64.ZF is used. For the end-of-period deflator the December value of the Consumer Price index, line 64M.ZF or, if not available, the fourth quarter value of line 64Q.ZF is used.

Section 2.3

Data on all variables, except Public Share are from IBCA's Bankscope database. The data for Public Share were collected from the following sources. If the public banks are not clearly marked in the publication, the classification is also added.

Argentina

Source: Banco Central de la Republica Argentina, Informacion de Entidades Financieras

Dates available: 1995–1997

Austria

Source: Gardener and Molyneux

Dates available: 1983, 1988

Bangladesh

Source: Bangladesh Bank, Bangladesh Bank Bulletin

Dates available: 1980–1997

Belgium

Source: Gardener and Molyneux

Dates available: 1982, 1988

Bolivia

Source: Banco Central de Bolivia, Boletin Estadistico

Dates available: 1980–1997

Brazil

Source: Banco Central do Brazil, Boletim Mensal

Dates available: 1980–1997

Canada

Source: Bankscope

Dates available: 1997

Colombia

Source: Banco de la Republica, Informe Annual del Gerente a la Junta Directiva

Dates available: 1986–1991

Costa Rica

Source: Bankscope

Dates available: 1992–1997

Denmark

Source: Gardener and Molyneux

Dates available: 1983, 1988

Ecuador

Source: Bankscope

Dates available: 1997

Egypt
Source: Bankscope
Dates available: 1990–1997

Finland
Source: Statistical Yearbook of Finland (share of Postpankki assets in total commercial bank assets)
Dates available: 1980–1988

France
Source: Gardener and Molyneux
Dates available: 1983, 1988

Germany
Source: Gardener and Molyneux
Dates available: 1983, 1988

Ghana
Source: Internal World Bank information
Dates available: 1988

Greece
Source: Gardener and Molyneux (credit instead of assets)
Dates available: 1988

Guatemala
Source: Superintendencia de Bancos, Boletin Annual de Estadisticas del Sistema Financiero
Dates available: 1980–1997

India
Source: Reserve Bank of India, Statistical Tables Relating to Banks in India
Dates available: 1980–1996

Indonesia
Source: Bank Indonesia, Indonesia Financial Statistics (commercial banks other than private exchange and foreign and joint exchange banks)
Dates available: 1986–1997

Ireland
Source: Gardener and Molyneux
Dates available: 1983, 1988

Italy
Source: Gardener and Molyneux
Dates available: 1983, 1988

Japan
Source: Bankscope
Dates available: 1997

Mexico
Source: Bankscope
Dates available: 1993–1994

Netherlands
Source: Gardener and Molyneux
Dates available: 1983, 1988

New Zealand
Source: Bankscope
Dates available: 1997

Norway
Source: Gardener and Molyneux
Dates available: 1983, 1988

Pakistan
Source: Bankscope
Dates available: 1990–1996

Philippines
Source: The World Bank, Philippine Financial Sector Study, 7177-
                       PH.
Dates available: 1980, 1986

Portugal
Source: Banco de Portugal, Annual Report 1997 (credit instead of
                       assets)
Dates available: 1984, 1989, 1997

Spain
Source: Gardener and Molyneux
Dates available: 1983, 1988

Sri Lanka
Source: Bankscope
Dates available: 1992–1996

Sweden
Source: Gardener and Molyneux
Dates available: 1983, 1988

Switzerland
Source: Banque Nationale Suisse, Les Banques Suisses en 19 (share
                   of cantonal bank assets in total commercial bank assets)
Dates available: 1980–1997

Thailand
Source: The World Bank's report: FSS, 8043-TH
Dates available: 1980, 1985–1988

Tunisia
Source: Information from the country economist
Dates available: 1987, 1992

Turkey
Source: Banks Association of Turkey, Banks in Turkey
Dates available: 1985, 1990, 1992

United Kingdom
Source: Gardener and Molyneux
Dates available: 1988

United States
Source: Bankscope
Dates available: 1997

Uruguay
Source: Bankscope
Dates available: 1990–1996

Zambia
Source: The World Bank's Financial Sector Report No. 12387-ZA
Dates available: 1992

Section 2.4

The following information lists the sources, the time span, and the definition
of the categories for each country. All numbers are total assets or total financial assets, unless otherwise stated. The raw numbers are for December,
unless otherwise noted. If the raw numbers are for other months, the deflating process is adjusted correspondingly. An asterisk denotes series for which
data points had to be extrapolated. The sources for life penetration and

density are listed at the end. Data on GDP in local currency and CPI are from the electronic version of the IFS, as described in the appendix for section 2.2.

Argentina

Sources: (a) Banco Central de la Republica Argentina, *Boletin Esta-distico*
                      (b) IFS

Dates available: 1980–1987, 1992–1997

Assets (Source a)

Banklike Institutions: Finance companies
                                    Credit companies
                                    Building societies

Private credit (Source b)

Banklike Institutions: Investment finance companies
                                    Credit cooperatives
                                    Savings and loan associations

Australia

Source: Reserve Bank of Australia, *Bulletin*

Dates available: 1980–1996

All raw numbers are for June.

Assets

Banklike Institutions: Permanent building societies
                                    Credit cooperatives
                                    Money market corporations
                                    Pastoral financial companies
                                    Finance companies
                                    General financiers
                                    Intragroup financiers
                                    Other financial corporations
                                    Cooperative housing societies
                                    Securization vehicles

Insurance Companies: Life insurance offices
                                    General insurance offices
                                    Friendly societies

Private Pension Funds: Superannuation funds

Pooled Investment Schemes: Other managed funds (cash management
                                    trusts, common funds)
                                    Public unit trusts

Development Banks: Other banks (Australian Resource Develop-
                                    ment Bank, Commonwealth Development
                                    Bank, and, prior to reclassification in 1988 to

trading banks, the Primary Industry Bank of Australia)

Private credit
Lines included total loans excluding loans to related companies, unless otherwise noted.

Banklike Institutions:	Permanent building societies
	Credit cooperatives
	Money market corporations
	Pastoral financial companies
	Finance companies
	General financiers
	Securization vehicles (all assets except other assets)
Insurance Companies:	Life insurance offices (debentures and notes, shares, other investments, and loans)
Private Pension Funds:	Superannuation funds (bills of exchange, debentures and notes, domestic shares, and loans)
Pooled Investment Schemes:	Cash management trusts (bills of exchange and other promissory notes)
	Public unit trusts (bills of exchange, debentures and notes, domestic shares and loans)
Development Banks:	Other banks (Australian Resource Development Bank, Commonwealth Development Bank, and, prior to reclassification in 1988 to trading banks, the Primary Industry Bank of Australia)

Austria

Source:	Oesterreichische Nationalbank, *Mitteilungen*
Dates available:	1980–1997

Assets

Banklike Institutions:	Building societies
Insurance Companies:	All insurance companies
Private Pension Funds:	Pension funds
Pooled Investment Schemes:	Investment funds

Private credit
Lines included other domestic bonds, other domestic obligations, shares, other domestic loans.

Banklike Institutions:	Building societies
Insurance Companies:	All insurance companies
Private Pension Funds:	Pension funds
Pooled Investment Schemes:	Investment funds

Bahamas

Sources:	(a) Central Bank of the Bahamas, *Statistical Digest*
	(b) IFS
Dates available:	1980–1997

Assets (Source a)

Banklike Institutions:	Other local financial institutions
	P.O. Savings Bank
Development Banks:	Bahamas Development Bank

Private credit

Banklike Institutions (Source b):	Licensed banks and trust companies other than commercial banks corresponds to other local financial institutions)
Development Banks (Source a):	Bahamas Development Bank (total loans)

Barbados

Sources:	(a) through 1995: Central Bank of Barbados, *Annual Statistical Digest*, and after 1995: Central Bank of Barbados, *Economic and Financial Statistics*
	(b) IFS
Dates available:	1980–1997

Assets (Source a)

Banklike Institutions:	Mortgage and finance companies
	Finance companies and merchant banks
Insurance Companies	National Insurance Fund
Development Banks:	Barbados Development Bank

Private credit (Source b)

Banklike Institutions:	Trust companies

Belgium

Sources:	(a) *Bulletin of Banque Nationale de Belgique*
	(b) *Annuaire Statistique de la Belgique*
	(c) *OECD Methodological Supplement*
Dates available:	1980–1993, incomplete data

Assets

Banklike Institutions:	Savings banks (Source a)
	Caisse generale d'epargne et de retraite (Source a)
	Mortgage companies and capital redemption companies (Source c)
Insurance Companies:	Insurance companies (includes life insurance, Source b)
	Life insurance companies (Source a)

Private Pension Funds: Pension funds (Source c)
Pooled Investment Schemes: Institutions pour placement collectif
                              (Source b)
Development Banks: Public financial credit intermediaries
                              (Source c)

Belize

Sources: (a) Central Bank of Belize, *Quarterly Review*
                  (b) IFS
Dates available: 1980–1997

Assets (Source a)
Development Banks: Development Finance Corporation

Private credit (Source b)
Development Banks: Development Finance Corporation

Bolivia

Sources: (a) Banco Central de Bolivia, *Boletin estadistico*
                  (b) IFS
Dates available: 1980–1997

Assets (Source a)
Development Banks: Specialized banks

Private credit (Source b)
Development Banks: Specialized banks (Mining Bank, Agricultural
                             Bank, Industrial Bank, Industrial Financing
                             Bank)

Brazil

Source: Banco do Brazil, *Boletim Mensal*
Dates available: 1980–1997

Assets
Banklike Institutions: Investment banks
                             Housing credit companies
                             S&L associations
                             Leasing companies
Insurance Companies: Insurance companies
Private Pension Funds: Private pension funds
Pooled Investment Schemes: Mutual Funds
                             Investment institutions and investment funds
Development Banks: National Bank of Economic and Social
                             Development
                             State development banks
                             Credit Society of Finance and Investment

                              National Housing Bank
                              National Bank of Cooperative Credit
                              Special Industrial Financing Agency

Private credit
Line included total credit to private nonfinancial sector.
Banklike Institutions: Investment banks
                              Housing credit companies
                              Leasing companies
Development Banks: National Bank of Economic and Social
                              Development
                              State development banks
                              Credit Society of Finance and Investment
                              National Bank of Cooperative Credit

Canada
Sources: (a) National Balance Sheet Accounts, *Statistics Canada*
                  (b) IFS
Dates available: 1980–1997

Assets (Source a)
Banklike Institutions: Quebec Savings Bank, since 1987 classified as
                              deposit money bank
                              Credit unions and caisses populaires
                              Sales finance and consumer loan companies
                              Other financial institutions (venture capital
                              companies, finance leasing companies, and
                              investment and holding companies)
                              Trust companies and mortgage loan
                              companies
Private Pension Funds: Trusteed pension plans
Insurance Companies: Life insurance business and segregated funds
                              of life insurance companies
                              Property and casualty insurance companies
                              and accident and sickness branches of life
                              insurance companies
Pooled Investment Schemes: Mutual funds
Development Banks: Public financial institutions

Private credit
The following lines are included in data collected from Source a: trade
receivables, consumer credit, other loans, mortgages, other bonds, and
shares.
Banklike Institutions   Quebec Savings Bank, since 1987 classified
(Source b):   as deposit money bank
                               Credit unions and caisses populaires

	Sales finance and consumer loan companies
	Trust companies and mortgage loan companies
Private Pension Funds:	Trusteed pension plans (Source a)
Insurance Companies (Source a):	Life insurance business and segregated funds of life insurance companies
	Property and casualty insurance companies and accident and sickness branches of life insurance companies
Pooled Investment Schemes:	Mutual funds (Source a)
Development Banks (Source a):	Public financial institutions

Chile

Sources:	(a) Banco Central de Chile, *Boletin Mensual*
	(b) Chile finanzas, Web page
	(c) IFS
Dates available:	1980–1997

Assets

Banklike Institutions:	Financial companies (Source a)
Insurance Companies:	Life and nonlife insurance companies (Source b)
Private Pension Funds:	Private pension funds (Source b)
Pooled Investment Schemes:	Foreign capital investment funds (Source b)
	Investment funds (Source b)
	Mutual funds (Source b)

Private credit

Lines included in data collected from Source b: stocks, mortgage backed securities, corporate bonds.

Banklike Institutions:	Financial companies (Source c)
Insurance Companies:	Life and nonlife insurance companies (Source b)
Private Pension Funds:	Private pension funds (Source b)
Pooled Investment Schemes:	Foreign capital investment funds (Source b)
	Investment funds (Source b)
	Mutual funds (Source b)

Colombia

Source:	Banco de la Republica, *Revista del Banco de la Republica*
Dates available:	1980–1996

Assets

Banklike Institutions:	Savings and housing corporations
	Private finance companies
	Trade finance companies

	Financial coporations
	Banco Central Hipotecario
	Caja Social de Ahorros
Development Banks:	Caja de Credito Agrario, Industrial y Minero
	Financiera Energetica Nacional
	Instituto de Fomento Industrial

Private credit
Line included credito al sector privado.

Banklike Institutions:	Savings and housing corporations
	Private finance companies
	Trade finance companies
	Financial coporations
	Banco Central Hipotecario
	Caja Social de Ahorros
Development Banks:	Caja de Credito Agrario, Industrial y Minero
	Financiera Energetica Nacional
	Instituto de Fomento Industrial

Denmark

Sources:	(a) *Statistical Yearbook of Denmark*
	(b) Reports and Accounts for the Year…, Danmarks Nationalbank
Dates available:	1980–1995

Assets

Banklike Institutions:	Mortgage credit associations and local governments' credit associations (Source a)
	Financing companies (Source b)
	Denmarks Skibskreditfond (Source a)
	Manufacturing and Manual Industries' Finance Corporation (Source a)
Banklike Institutions:	Private nonfinancial intermediaries (development banks, mortgage banks, and S&L associations)
Development Banks:	Public nonfinancial intermediaries

Dominican Republic

Source:	Banco Central de la Republica Dominicana, *Boletin Mensual*
Dates available:	1980–1997

Assets

Banklike Institutions:	Private nonfinancial intermediaries (development banks, mortgage banks, and S&L associations)

Development Banks: Public nonfinancial intermediaries

Private credit
Line included credito interno al sector privado.
Development Banks: National Development Bank
                                National Housing Bank
                                National Financial Corporation

Ecuador

Sources: (a) Banco Central de Ecuador, *Boletin anuario*
                    (b) Banco Central de Ecuador, *Memoria anual*
Dates available: 1980–1994

Assets
Banklike Institutions: S&L associations
                                Private finance companies
Insurance Companies: Insurance companies
                                Reinsurance companies
                                Life insurance companies
Development Banks: National Development Bank
                                National Housing Bank
                                National Financial Corporation

Private credit (Source b)
Line included credito al sector privado.
Banklike Institutions: S&L associations
                                Private finance companies
                                The Mortgage Bank of the Kingdom of
                                Denmark (Source a)
                                The Fisheries Bank of the Kingdom of
                                Denmark (Source a)
Insurance Companies   Life insurance companies
(Source a):   Non–life insurance companies
Private Pension Funds: Private pension funds (Source a)
Pooled Investment Schemes: Investment associations (Source b)

Private credit (Source b)
Banklike Institutions: Financing companies (leasing assets and
                                loans)
                                Mortgage credit associations (total lending)

Egypt

Sources: (a) Central Bank of Egypt, *Economic Review*
                    (b) Central Bank of Egypt, *Annual Report*
                    (c) IFS
Dates available: 1980–1997

All raw numbers except the ones from Source c are for June.

Assets

Development Banks:	Specialized banks (Source a)
Insurance Companies:	Investment by insurance companies (Source b)

Private credit

Development Banks:	Specialized banks (Source c)
Insurance Companies:	Insurance companies (Source b, *included lines*: securities and loans, other than of/to government)

El Salvador

Sources: (a) Banco Central de Reserva de El Salvador, Boletin tri-
                mestral

                (b) Superintendencia del Sistema Financiero, Estados e
                indicadores financieros

                (c) Superintendencia de Bancos y Otras Instituciones,
                Estadisticas: Seguros, Fianzas, Bancos

                (d) IFS

Dates available: 1980–1997

Assets

Banklike Institutions:	Finance companies (Source a), earlier called S&L associations
	General warehouses (Source b)
Insurance Companies:	Insurance companies (Source c)
Development Banks:	Official credit institutions (Source b)

Private credit (Source d)

Banklike Institutions:	Finance companies

Fiji

Sources: (a) Bureau of Statistics, *Current Economic Statistics*
                (b) IFS

Dates available: 1980–1997

Assets (Source a)

Insurance Companies:	Non–life insurance companies
	Life insurance companies

Private credit (Source b)

Insurance Companies:	Life insurance companies

Finland

Sources: (a) Statistical yearbook of Finland
                (b) OECD Methodological Supplement

Dates available: 1980–1994

Assets

Banklike Institutions:	Mortgage banks (Source b)
	Finance companies (Source b)
	Others (development and investment companies, banking houses, holding companies, and pawnshops) (Source b)
Insurance Companies:	Insurance companies and associations (Source b)
Pooled Investment Schemes:	Mutual funds (Source a)
	Unit trusts (Source a)
Development Banks:	Development credit institutions (Source b)

France

Source: Banque de France, Statistiques monetaires et financieres annuelles

Dates available: 1980–1996

Assets

Banklike Institutions:	Finance companies and security houses
Pooled Investment Funds:	Fonds comuns de creances
	OPCVM (organismes de placement collectif en valeurs mobilieres)
Development Banks:	Specialized financial institutions

Private credit

Line included creance sur l'economie.

Banklike Institutions:	Finance companies and security houses
Pooled Investment Schemes:	Fonds comuns de creances
	OPCVM (organismes de placement collectif en valeurs mobilieres)
Development Banks:	Specialized financial institutions

Germany

Sources: (a) Bundesbank, *Monthly Bulletin*
                  (b) Bundesbank, *Capital Market Statistics*
                  (c) IFS

Dates available: 1980–1997

Assets

Banklike Institutions:	Building societies (Source a)
Pooled Investment Schemes:	Investment and securities-based investment funds (Source b)

Private credit (Source c)

Banklike Institutions:	Building societies

Greece

Sources: (a) Bank of Greece, *Monthly Statistical Bulletin*
                  (b) Bank of Greece, *Annual Report*
                  (c) IFS

Dates available: 1980–1997

Assets

Pooled Investment Schemes: Mutual funds (Source b)

Development Banks: Specialized credit institutions including
                             Agricultural Bank, National Mortgage Bank,
                             Investment Bank, National Investment Bank
                             for Industrial Development, Hellenic Indus-
                             trial Development Bank, National Housing
                             Bank, Deposits and Loan Fund and Postal
                             Savings Banks (Source a)

Private credit (Source c)

Development Banks: Specialized credit institutions

Guatemala

Source: Superintendencia de Bancos, *Boletin annual de estadisticas
                 del sistema financiero*

Dates available: 1980–1997

Assets

Banklike Institutions: Private finance companies
                             General warehouses
                             Trust accounts

Insurance Companies: Insurance companies

Development Banks: National Financial Corporation

Guyana

Source: Bank of Guyana, *Statistical Bulletin*

Dates available: 1980–1992

Assets

Banklike Institutions: New Building Society
                             Trust companies
                             Guyana Co-operative Mortgage Finance Bank

Insurance Companies: Life insurance companies
                             Non–life insurance companies

Private Pension Funds: Pension schemes

Private credit

Line included private sector.

Banklike Institutions: New Building Society
                             Trust companies
                             Guyana Co-operative Mortgage Finance Bank

Insurance Companies: Life insurance companies
                            Non–life insurance companies
Private Pension Funds: Pension schemes

Honduras
Sources: (a) Banco Central de Honduras, *Boletin de estadisticas de*
                  seguros
                  (b) Banco Central de Honduras, *Boletin estadistico*
Dates available: 1980–1997

Assets
Banklike Institutions   Specialized finance companies
(Source b):
Insurance Companies: Insurance companies (Source a)
Development Banks   Development banks
(Source b):

Private credit (Source b)
Line included credito e inversiones, sector privado.
Banklike Institutions   Specialized finance companies
(Source b):
Development Banks   Development banks
(Source b):

India
Sources: (a) Reseve Bank of India, *Report on Currency and Finance*
                  (b) Life Insurance Corporation of India, *Annual Report*
                  (c) IFS
Dates available: 1980–1995, missing data
The raw numbers from sources b and c are for March or June.

Assets
Insurance Companies: Life Insurance Corporation of India (Source b)
Pooled Investment Schemes   Private mutual funds
(Source a):   Unit trust
Development Banks   State Financial Corporation
(Source a):   Industrial Financial Corporation of India
                            Industrial Development Bank of India
                            Industrial Credit and Investment Corporation
                            of India Limited
                            Export-Import Bank of India
                            National Housing Bank
                            Small Industries Development Bank of India
                            Industrial Investment Bank of India
                            Discount and Finance House
                            National Bank for Agricultural and Rural
                            Development

Private credit (Source c)
Development Banks: Development banks

Indonesia
Source: Bank Indonesia, *Indonesia Financial Statistics*
Dates available: 1980–1994

Assets
Banklike Institutions: State and private savings banks (since 1989
                            included in deposit money banks)
                            Financial companies
Development Banks: Development banks

Private credit
Line included claims on private enterprises and individuals.
Development Banks: Development banks

Ireland
Sources: (a) Central Bank of Ireland, *Annual Report*
                   (b) IFS
Dates available: 1980–1996

Assets (Source a)
Banklike Institutions: Nonassociated banks
                            Other credit institutions; TSB Bank, ACC
                            Bank, ICC Bank, and ICC Investment Bank
                            Building societies
                            Hire-purchase finance companies
Pooled Investment Schemes: Collective investment schemes, authorized by
                            the CB—total net asset values

Private credit (Source b)
Banklike Institutions: Definition varies over time

Israel
Sources: (a) Central Bureau of Statistics, *Statistical Abstract of Israel*
                   (b) Central Bureau of Statistics, *Monthly Bulletin of
                   Statistics*
Dates available: 1980–1995

Assets
Banklike Institutions   Industrial investment finance banks
(Source a):   Mortgage banks
Insurance Companies: Insurance companies (Source a)
Pooled Investment Schemes: Mutual funds (Source b)

Private credit
Lines included loans, shares, nontradeable bonds, private bonds, credit to
the public.

Banklike Institutions   Industrial investment finance banks
(Source a):   Mortgage banks
Pooled Investment Schemes: Mutual funds (Source b)

Italy
Sources: (a) Annuario Statistico
                  (b) Banca d'Italia, *Economic Bulletin*
Dates available: 1980–1996

Assets
Banklike Institutions: Specialized credit institutions (Source a)
Insurance Companies   Life insurance companies
(Source a):   Other insurance companies
Pooled Investment Schemes: Investment funds and securities investment
                             funds (Source b)

Jamaica
Sources: (a) Bank of Jamaica, Statistical Digest
                  (b) Bank of Jamaica, Annual Report
                  (c) IFS
Dates available: 1980–1996

Assets
Banklike Institutions   Finance houses and trust companies
(Source a):   Merchant banks
                             Building societies
                             Credit unions
                             Trust companies
Development Banks   National Development Bank
(Source b):   Agricultural Credit Bank
                             Trafalgar Development Bank

Private credit (Source c)
Banklike Institutions: Merchant banks, finance houses, and trust
                             companies

Japan
Sources: (a) Research and Statistics Department, Bank of Japan,
                      Economic Statistics Annual
                  (b) Research and Statistics Department, Bank of Japan,
                      Economic Statistics Monthly
Dates available: 1980–1997
For most categories total assets, for some categories sum of principal assets.

Assets
Banklike Institutions   Zenshinren banks
(Source a):   Credit cooperatives

	Shinkumi Federation Bank/National Federation of Credit Cooperatives Labor credit associations
	National Federation of Labor Credit Associations Agricultural cooperatives
	Credit Federation of Agricultural Cooperatives
	Fishery cooperatives
	Credit Federation of Fishery Cooperatives
	Postal Savings Bank—total deposits
	Foreign banks
	Securities finance companies
	Securities investment trusts
	Trust accounts of deposit money banks (includes city, regional, and trust banks)
	Postal Life Insurance and Postal Annuity
Insurance Companies (Source b):	Life insurance companies
	Non–life insurance companies
	Mutual insurance federations of agricultural cooperatives
Development Banks (Source b):	Government financial institutions: Japan Development Bank, Export-Import Bank, Hokkaido and Tohoku Development Corp., People's Finance Corp., Housing Loan Corp., Agriculture, Forestry and Fisheries Finance Corp., Small Business Corp., Japan Finance Corp. for Municipal Enterprises, Small Business Credit Insurance Corp., Environmental Sanitation Business Finance Corp., Okinawa Development Finance and Medical Care Facilities Finance Corp.
	Trust Fund Bureau

Private credit

Lines included loans, corporate bonds, stocks.

Banklike Institutions (Source a):	Zenshinren banks
	Credit cooperatives
	Shinkumi Federation Bank/National Federation of Credit Cooperatives Labor credit associations
	National Federation of Labor Credit Associations
	Agricultural cooperatives
	Credit Federation of Agricultural Cooperatives

	Fishery cooperatives
	Credit Federation of Fishery Cooperatives
	Foreign banks
	Securities finance companies
	Securities investment trusts
	Trust accounts of deposit money banks (includes city, regional, and trust banks)
Insurance Companies (Source b):	Life insurance companies
	Non–life insurance companies
	Mutual insurance federations of agricultural cooperatives
Development Banks (Source b):	Government financial institutions

Jordan

Sources: (a) *Monthly Statistical Bulletin*
                   (b) Central Bank of Jordan, *Annual Report*
                   (c) IFS

Dates available: 1980–1996 with missing data

Assets

Banklike Institutions (Source a):	Other financial corporations including finance companies, investment companies, securities companies. However, institutions included may change from time to time.
Insurance Companies:	Insurance companies (Source b)
Development Banks:	Specialized credit institutions including Cities and Village Development Bank, Industrial Development Banks, Housing and Development Corporation, Agricultural Credit Corporations and Jordan Co-operative Organization

Private credit

Banklike Institutions (Source a):	Other financial corporations (loans and corporate bonds/shares
Insurance Companies (Source b):	Insurance companies (investment in shares)
Development Banks (Source c):	Specialized credit institutions (included institutions vary over time)

Kenya

Sources: (a) Central Bank of Kenya, *Quarterly Economic Review*
                   (b) Central Bank of Kenya, *Statistical Bulletin*
                   (c) IFS

Dates available: 1980–1997

Assets

Banklike Institutions: Kenya Post Office Savings Bank (data since 1984 from Source b, before 1984 from Source a)

Nonbank financial institutions (Source b)

Private credit (Source c)

Banklike Institutions: Banklike financial institutions

Korea

Sources: (a) Bank of Korea, *Monthly Statistical Bulletin*
(b) IFS

Dates available: 1980–1997

Assets (Source a)

Banklike Institutions: Mutual savings and finance companies
Credit unions
Community credit cooperatives
Postal Savings and Postal Life Insurance
Mutual credits
Investment institutions
Investment and finance institutions, since 1993 included in merchant banks
Merchant banking companies
Investment trust companies
Korea securities and finance companies
Trust accounts of banks

Insurance Companies: Non–life insurance companies
Life insurance companies

Development Banks: Korea Development Bank
Export-Import Bank of Korea
Korea Long-Term Credit Bank

Private credit

Lines included in data collected from Source a: loans, stocks, debentures.

Banklike Institutions: Mutual savings and finance companies (Source a)
Credit unions (Source a)
Community credit cooperatives (Source a)
Mutual credits (Source a)
Trust accounts of banks (Source b)

Insurance Companies: Life insurance companies (Source b)

Development Banks: Development banks (Source b)

Malawi

Source: Reserve Bank of Malawi, *Financial and Economic Review*
Dates available: 1981–1997

Assets

Banklike institutions: New Building Society
                             P.O. Savings Bank
                             National Finance Company
                             Leasing and Finance Company
Insurance Companies: Insurance companies and assurance
                             companies
Development Banks: Investment and Development Bank

Private credit

Lines included private sector.

Banklike institutions: New Building Society
                             National Finance Company
Insurance Companies: Insurance companies and assurance
                             companies
Development Banks: Investment and Development Bank

Malaysia

Sources: (a) Bank Negara Malaysia, *Quarterly Bulletin*
                     (b) Bank Negara Malaysia, *Money and Banking in Malaysia*
                     (c) Annual Report of the Director General of Insurance
                     Companies
Dates available: 1980–1997

Assets

Banklike Institutions: National Savings Bank (Source b)
                             Cooperative societies (Source b)
                             Merchant banks (Source a)
                             Discount houses (Source b)
                             Finance companies (Source a)
                             Building societies, Pilgrims Management
                             and Fund Board, Cagamas Berhard, Credit
                             Guarantee Corporation, leasing, factoring,
                             and venture capital companies (Source b)
Insurance Companies   Life insurance funds
(Source c):   General insurance funds
Pooled Investment Schemes: Unit trust (Source b)
Development Banks: Development institutions (Malaysia Indus-
                             trial Development Finance, Agricultural
                             Bank, Borneo, Development Corporation,
                             Sabah Credit Corporation, Development

                                    Bank of Malaysia, Industrial Bank of Malaysia,
                                    Sabah Development Bank) (Source b)

Private credit
Lines included loans and corporate bonds/stocks.
Banklike Institutions: National Savings Bank (Source b)
                                    Cooperative societies (Source b)
                                    Merchant banks (Source a)
                                    Discount houses (Source b)
                                    Finance companies (Source a)
                                    Building societies, Pilgrims Management
                                    and Fund Board, Cagamas Berhad, Credit
                                    Guarantee Corporation, leasing, factoring,
                                    and venture capital companies (Source b)
Insurance Companies   Life insurance funds
(Source c):   General insurance funds
Development Banks: Development institutions (Malaysia Indus-
                                    trial Development Finance, Agricultural
                                    Bank, Borneo, Development Corporation,
                                    Sabah Credit Corporation, Development
                                    Bank of Malaysia, Industrial Bank of Malay-
                                    sia, Sabah Development Bank) (Source b)

Malta
Source: IFS
Dates available: 1980–1997

Private credit
Banklike Institutions: Banks that grant long-term loans and do not
                                    offer deposits

Mexico
Sources: (a) Banco de Mexico, *Indicadores Economicos*
                    (b) IFS
Dates available: 1980–1997
All numbers are recursos totales.

Assets (Source a)
Banklike Institutions: Factoring companies
                                    Leasing companies
                                    Warehouse companies
Insurance Companies: Insurance companies
Development Banks: Development banks
                                    Development funds

Private credit
Banklike Institutions   Factoring companies (cartera de factoraje con
(Source a):   recursos y deudores diversos)

	Leasing companies (cartera vigente)
	Warehouse companies (otras inversiones,
	creditos, deudores diversos)
Insurance Companies	Insurance companies (inversiones, pre-
(Source a):	stamos/creditos al sector privado, deudores)
Development Banks	Development banks
(Source b):	Development funds

Morocco

Source: IFS
Dates available: 1980–1996

Private credit
Development Banks: National Development Bank, National Agri-
                          culture Bank, Credit Immobilier et Hotelier
                          Caisse de Depots et de Gestion, Caisse des
                          Marches

Netherlands

Sources: (a) Nederlandse Bank, *Annual Bulletin*
                   There are varying definitions of the different groups and in
                   different sources.
                   (b) OECD, *Methodological Supplement*
                   The *Statistical Yearbook* presents significantly different
                   numbers
Dates available: 1980–1996

Assets
Banklike Institutions: Mortgage banks and building societies
                          (Source b)
                          Private-sector financial institutions (lombard
                          banks/finance companies, special institu-
                          tions for financing export and industry, bill
                          brokers, municipal credit banks) (Source b)
                          Savings banks until 1982 (classification
                          according to OECD) (Source b)
Insurance Companies: Life and non–life insurance companies
                          (Source a)
Private Pension Funds: Private pension funds (Source a)
Pooled Investment Schemes: Open-end investment companies (Source b)
                          until 1990
                          Investment institutions (Source a) since 1991
Development Banks: Local government banks (Source b)

Private credit (Source a)
Lines included: are short-term claims on persons/businesses, domestic
securities by private sector, loans to the private-sector shares, mortgage
loans.

Insurance Companies: Life and nonlife insurance companies
Private Pension Funds: Private pension funds

New Zealand
Sources: (a) Reserve Bank of New Zealand, *Bulletin*
                  (b) IFS
Dates available: 1980–1996

Assets (Source a)
Insurance Companies: Life insurance companies

Private credit
Insurance Companies: Life insurance companies

Nigeria
Source: Central Bank of Nigeria, *Annual Report*
Dates available: 1980–1995 with missing data

Assets
Banklike Institutions: Community banks, privately owned micro-
                              finance institutions
                              Discount houses
                              Primary mortgage institutions
                              Finance companies
Insurance Companies: Insurance companies
Development Banks: Nigerian Bank for Commerce and Industry
                              People's Bank of Nigeria
                              Nigerian Agricultural and Co-operative Bank
                              Federal Mortgage Bank of Nigeria
                              Nigerian Industrial Development Bank

Private credit
Lines included: loans and private securities.
Banklike Institutions: Community banks, privately owned micro-
                              finance institutions
                              Primary mortgage institutions
                              Finance companies
Insurance Companies: Insurance companies
Development Banks: Nigerian Bank for Commerce and Industry
                              People's Bank of Nigeria

Norway
Sources: (a) Central Bureau of Statistics of Norway, *Statistical
                  Yearbook*
                  (b) Bank of Norway, *Economic Bulletin*
                  (c) IFS

Dates available: 1980–1995

Assets (Source a)

Banklike Institutions:	Private credit enterprises/mortgage institutions
	Private financial companies
Insurance Companies:	Life insurance companies
	Non–life insurance companies
Private Pension Funds:	Private and municipal pension schemes
Pooled Investment Schemes:	Unit trust funds
Development Banks:	State lending institutions

Private credit

Lines included in data collected from Source b: other bonds, other certificates, loans to the public/nonfinancial enterprises and municipalities, shares. Definitions vary over time and across categories.

Banklike Institutions (Source b):	Private credit enterprises/mortgage institutions
	Private financial companies
Insurance Companies (Source b):	Life insurance companies
	Non–life insurance companies
Private Pension Funds (Source b):	Private and municipal pension schemes
Pooled Investment Schemes:	Unit trust funds
Development Banks (Source c):	State lending institutions

Pakistan

Sources:	(a) State Bank of Pakistan, *Banking Statistics*
	(b) *The Pakistan Insurance Yearbook*

Dates available: 1980–1995

The raw numbers for Development Banks are for either June or December.

Assets

Insurance Companies (Source b):	State Life Insurance Corporation
	Non–life insurance companies
Development Banks (Source a):	Agricultural Development Bank of Pakistan
	Industrial Development Bank of Pakistan
	Pakistan Industrial Credit and Investment Corporation
	National Development Finance Corporation
	House Building Finance Corporations
	Pakistan-Kuwait Investment Company Ltd.
	Pak-Libya Holding Company Ltd.
	Saudi-Pak Industrial and Agricultural Investment Company Ltd.
	Bankers Equity Ltd.

Paraguay

Source: Banco Central de Paraguay, *Boletin Estadistico*

Assets

Banklike Institutions: S&L associations for housing
                                 Finance companies
Development Banks: National Development Bank
                                 Cattle Fund

Peru

Source: IFS
Dates available: 1980–1997

Private credit

Development Banks: Five development banks

Philippines

Source: National Census and Statistics Office, *Philippine Yearbook*
Dates available: 1980–1990
All numbers are total resources.

Assets

Banklike Institutions: Thriftbanks (Savings banks, private develop-
                                 ment banks, stock S&L associations)
                                 Rural nondeposit banks
                                 Financing companies
                                 Venture capital corporations
                                 Pawnshops
                                 Lending investors
                                 Nonstock savings and loan associations
                                 Mutual building and loan associations
Insurance Companies: Life insurance companies
                                 Non–life insurance companies
Private Pension Funds: Funds manager
Pooled Investment Schemes: Investment companies
Development Banks: Specialized government banks (Development
                                 Bank of the Philippines, Land Bank of the
                                 Philippines, Philippine Amanah Bank)

Portugal

Source: Instituto Nacional de Estatistica, *Estatisticas monetarias e
                 financeiras*
Dates available: 1980–1988, 1991–1996

Assets

Banklike Institutions: Agricultural credit cooperatives
                                 Central agricultural credit cooperative

	Finance and credit companies
	Other intermediaries
Insurance Companies:	Life insurance companies
	Non–life insurance companies
Private Pension Funds:	Private pension funds
Pooled Investment Schemes:	Investment funds
Development Banks:	National Development Bank

Rwanda
Source: IFS
Dates available: 1980–1996

Private credit
Development Banks: Development Bank

Saudi Arabia
Source: IFS
Dates available: 1980–1996

Private credit
Development Banks: Saudi Agricultural Bank, Saudi Industrial
                             Development Fund, Public Investment Fund,
                             Real Estate Development Fund, Saudi Credit
                             Bank

Singapore
Sources: (a) Monetary Authority of Singapore, *Monthly Statistical
                     Bulletin*
                 (b) Monetary Authority of Singapore, *Annual Report*
                 (c) Development Bank of Singapore, *Annual Report*
                 (d) IFS
Dates available: 1980–1996

Assets
Banklike Institutions: Finance companies (Source a)
                             Merchant banks (Source a)
                             Total amount lent by pawnbrokers (Source a)
Insurance Companies: Insurance companies (Source b)
Development Bank: Development Bank of Singapore (Source c)

Private credit
Banklike Institutions: Finance companies (Source d)
Insurance Companies: Life insurance offices (Source d)
Development Bank: Development Bank of Singapore (Source c,
                             lines included: loans, investments, equity and
                             corporate bonds)

Solomon Islands
Source: Central Bank of Solomon Islands, *Annual Report*
Dates available: 1985–1993

Assets
Banklike institutions: Other local financial institutions
Development Banks: Development Bank of Solomon Islands

South Africa
Source: South African Reserve Bank, *Quarterly Bulletin*
Dates available: 1980–1997

Assets
Banklike Institutions: Participation mortgage bond schemes
excluding hire-purchase finance companies,
factoring and other similar finance companies
not registered as financial institutions—total
funds received and invested
Finance companies
Insurance Companies: Long-term insurers (life)
Short-term insurers (nonlife)
Pooled Investment Schemes: Unit trusts
Private Pension Funds: Private self-administered pension and provi-
dent funds
Development Bank: National Finance Corporation of South Africa
Land and Agricultural Bank of South Africa

Private credit
Lines included are loans other than to public sector and other securities.
Insurance Companies: Long-term insurers (life)
Short-term insurers (nonlife)
Private Pension Funds: Private self-administered pension and provi-
dent funds

Spain
Sources: (a) Banco de Espana, *Boletin Estadistico*
(b) Banco de Espana, *Cuentas financieras de la economia espanola*
(c) IFS
Dates available: 1980–1997

Assets
Banklike Institutions
(Source a): Specialized credit institutions (money market
intermediary companies, mortgage loan
companies, financial leasing companies,
finance and factoring companies, and other
specialized credit institutions

Insurance Companies (Source b):	Insurance companies (financial assets)
Pooled Investment Schemes (Source a)	Portfolio investment institutions
Development Banks (Source a):	Official credit institutions (official credit institute and until 1993 official credit banks)

Private credit

| Banklike Institutions (Source c): | Specialized credit institutions (money market intermediary companies, mortgage loan companies, financial leasing companies, finance and factoring companies, and other specialized credit institutions |
| Insurance Companies (Source b): | Insurance companies (short-term securities, bonds, shares, and loans, all of these to nonfinancial enterprises and households) |

Sri Lanka

Sources: (a) Central Bank of Sri Lanka, *Bulletin*
                  (b) *Annual Report of National Savings Bank*
                  (c) *Annual Report of National Development Bank*
                  (d) *Annual Report of Development Finance Corporation*

Dates available: 1980–1996

The raw numbers for the Development Finance Corporation are for March.

Assets

Banklike Institutions:	National Savings Bank (Source b)
Development Banks:	Development Finance Corporation, total loans and equities outstanding (Source d)
	State Mortgage and Investment Bank, total loans outstanding (Source a)
	National Development Bank (Source c)

Private credit
Included line: total loans.

Banklike Institutions:	National Savings Bank (Source b)
Development Banks:	Development Finance Corporation (Source d)
	National Development Bank (Source c)

Sweden

Sources: (a) Sveriges Riksbank, *Statistical Yearbook*
                  (b) IFS

Dates available: 1980–1997

Assets (Source a)

| Banklike Institutions: | Finance companies |
| | Mortgage companies (local government |

                                  credit institutions and business credit
                                  institutions)
                                  Housing credit institutions
Insurance Companies: Life insurance companies
                                  Non–life insurance companies
Pooled Investment Schemes: Mutual funds

Private credit (Source b)
Banklike Institutions: Finance companies
                                  Mortgage companies (local government credit
                                  institutions and business credit
                                  institutions)
                                  Housing credit institutions
Insurance Companies: Life insurance companies
                                  Non–life insurance companies

Switzerland
Source: (a) Banque Nationale Suisse, *Les banques suisses en ...*
                   (b) Swiss National Bank, *Monthly Bulletin*
                   (c) IFS
Dates available: 1980–1997

Assets
Banklike Institutions   Private banks (trust accounts, security
(Source a):   companies)
                                  Mortgage banks
                                  Clearing banks (three banks, one owned by
                                  agricultural cooperatives, one by regional
                                  banks, and the third an international clearing
                                  bank)
Pooled Investment Schemes: Investment funds (Source b)

Private credit
Insurance Companies: Life insurance offices

Taiwan
Source: Central Bank of China, *Financial Statistics Monthly*
Dates available: 1980–1997

Assets
Banklike Institutions: Credit cooperative associations
                                  Credit departments of farmers'
                                  and fishermen's associations
                                  Postal Savings System
                                  Bills finance companies
                                  Fuh-Hua securities finance companies
                                  Investment and trust companies

Insurance Companies: Life insurance companies
                              Property and casualty insurance companies

Private credit
Lines included: loans, securities private sector, corporate bonds, and commercial papers.
Banklike Institutions: Credit cooperative associations
                              Credit departments of farmers' and fishermen's associations
                              Postal Savings System
                              Bills finance companies
                              Fuh-Hua securities finance companies
                              Investment and trust companies
Insurance Companies: Life insurance companies
                              Property and casualty insurance companies

Thailand
Sources: (a) Bank of Thailand, *Quarterly Bulletin*
                  (b) IFS
Dates available: 1980–1997

Assets (Source a)
Banklike Institutions: Government Savings Bank
                              Finance and securities companies
Development Banks: Bank for Agriculture and Agricultural Cooperatives
                              Government Housing Bank
                              Industrial Finance Corporation of Thailand
                              Export-Import Bank

Private credit (Source b)
Banklike Institutions: Government Savings Bank
                              Finance and securities companies
Development Banks: Bank for Agriculture and Agricultural Cooperatives
                              Government Housing Bank
                              Industrial Finance Corporation of Thailand
                              Export-Import Bank

Tonga
Source: IFS
Dates available: 1980–1997

Private credit
Development Banks: Tonga Development Bank

Trinidad and Tobago

Sources: (a) Central Bank of Trinidad and Tobago, *Quarterly Statistical Digest*
                  (b) IFS

Dates available: 1980–1996

Assets (Source a)

Banklike Institutions: Finance companies and merchant banks
                                Trust and mortgage finance companies
                                Thrift institutions
Insurance Companies: Life insurance companies
Development Banks: Development banks

Private credit

Banklike Institutions: Finance companies and merchant banks
                                Trust and mortgage finance companies
                                Thrift institutions
Insurance Companies: Life insurance companies
Development Banks: Development banks

Tunisia

Source: Banque centrale de Tunisie, *Statistiques financieres*
Dates available: 1990–1997

Assets

Banklike Institutions: Leasing companies
                                Off-shore banks
Development Banks: Development banks

Private credit
Line included creance/credit a l'economie.

Banklike Institutions: Leasing companies
                                Offshore banks
Development Banks: Development banks

Turkey

Sources: (a) Central Bank of Republic of Turkey, *Quarterly Bulletin of Statistics*
                  (b) IFS

Dates available: 1987–1997

Assets (Source a)

Banklike Institutions: Special finance houses
Development Banks: Investment and development banks

Private credit (Source b)

Development Banks: Investment and development banks

United Kingdom

Sources: (a) Central Statistical Office, *Annual Abstract of Statistics*
                 (b) Office for National Statistics, *Financial Statistics*

Dates available: 1980–1997

Assets (Source a)

Banklike Institutions:	Discount houses
	Finance houses and other specialized credit-granting institutions (data after 1989 from Source b)
	Investment trusts
Insurance Companies:	Insurance companies—long-term
	Friendly societies (included with life insurance)
	Insurance companies—other than long-term
Private Pension Funds:	Self-administered pension funds
	Industrial and provident societies
Pooled Investment Schemes:	Unit trusts

Private credit (Source a)

Included lines are company securities, loans, and mortgages.

Banklike Institutions:	Finance houses and other specialized credit-granting institutions (data after 1989 from Source b)
	Investment trusts
Insurance Companies:	Insurance companies—long-term
	Insurance companies—other than long-term
Private Pension Funds:	Self-administered pension funds
Pooled Investment Schemes:	Unit trusts

United States

Source: Federal Reserve System, *Flow of Funds Accounts*

Dates available: 1980–1997

All asset numbers are total financial assets.

Assets

Banklike Institutions:	Issuers of asset-backed securities
	Finance companies
	Mortgage companies
	Funding corporations (funding subsidiaries, nonbank financial holding companies, and custodial accounts for reinvested collateral of securities lending operations)
	Bank personal trusts and estates
Insurance Companies:	Life insurance companies
	Other insurance companies

Private Pension Funds:	Private pension funds (includes Federal Employees' Retirement System Thrift Savings Plan)
Pooled Investment Schemes:	Mutual funds and closed-end funds Real estate investment trusts
Development Banks:	Government-sponsored enterprises (Federal Home Loan Banks, National Mortgage Association, Federal Home Loan Mortgage Corp., Farm Credit System, the Financing Corp., the Resolution Funding Corp., and the Student Loan Marketing Association), federally related mortgage pools (GNMA, FNMA, FHLMC), and Farmers Home Administration pools

Private credit

Lines included are corporate and foreign bonds, corporate equities, other loan and advances, consumer credit, and mortgages.

Banklike Institutions:	Issuers of asset-backed securities Finance companies Mortgage companies Funding corporations (funding subsidiaries, nonbank financial holding companies, and custodial accounts for reinvested collateral of securities lending operations) Bank personal trusts and estates
Insurance Companies:	Life insurance companies Other insurance companies
Private Pension Funds:	Private pension funds (includes Federal Employees' Retirement System Thrift Savings Plan)
Pooled Investment Schemes:	Mutual funds and closed-end funds Real Estate Investment Trusts
Development Banks:	Government-sponsored enterprises (Federal Home Loan Banks, National Mortgage Association, Federal Home Loan Mortgage Corp., Farm Credit System, the Financing Corp., the Resolution Funding Corp., and the Student Loan Marketing Association), federally related mortgage pools (GNMA, FNMA, FHLMC) and Farmers Home Administration pools

Uruguay

Source:		Banco Central del Uruguay, *Boletin Estadistico*
Dates available:	1980–1996

Private credit
Line included credito al sector privado.
Banklike Institutions: Banco Hipotecario
                                    S&L associations

Venezuela
Sources: (a) Banco Central de Venezuela, *Boletin Mensual*
                (b) Oficina Central de Estadistica e Informatica, *Anuario Estadistico de Venezuela*
Dates available: 1980–1992, 1994–1995

Assets
Banklike Institutions   Mortgage banks
(Source a):   Venezuela Workers Bank
                                National S&L System
                                Finance companies
                                Investment banks
                                Leasing companies
Insurance Companies: Insurance companies (Source b)
Pooled Investment Schemes Mutual funds
(Source a):   Money market funds
Development Banks   Agricultural Development Bank
(Source a):

Private credit (Source a)
Lines included sector privado en conceptos monetarios.
Banklike Institutions: Mortgage banks
                                  Venezuela Workers Bank
                                National S&L System
                                Finance companies (prestamos e inversiones al sector privado)
                                  Investment banks
Pooled Investment Schemes: Mutual funds
Development Banks: Agricultural Development Bank

Zimbabwe
Sources: (a) Reserve Bank of Zimbabwe, *Quarterly Economic and Statistical Review*
                (b) Central Statistical Office, *Monthly Digest of Statistics*
                (c) Annual Report of Zimbabwe Development Bank
                (d) Report of the Registrar of Insurance
                (e) Reports of the Registrar of Pension and Provident Funds
                (f) IFS
Dates available: 1980–1996
The raw numbers for building societies and the Zimbabwe Development Bank are for June.

Assets

Banklike Institutions (Source a):	Building societies P.O. Savings Bank Finance houses
Insurance Companies (Source d):	Life insurance companies Nonlife insurance companies
Private Pension Funds:	Pension and provident funds (Source e)
Development Banks:	Agricultural Finance Corporation (Source b) Zimbabwe Development Bank (Source c)

Private credit

Except for data from Source f, lines included loans, debentures, and stocks/shares.

Banklike Institutions (Source f):	Building societies P.O. Savings Bank Finance houses
Insurance Companies (Source d):	Life insurance companies Non–life insurance companies
Development Banks:	Agricultural Finance Corporation (Source b) Zimbabwe Development Bank (Source c)

Life Insurance Penetration and Density

Data on life insurance premium volume are from various issues of *Sigma*.

Data on total population and the purchasing power parity conversion factor (local currency unit per international dollar) are from the electronic version of the World Development Indicators.

Data on GDP in local currency are from the electronic version of the IFS, either line 99B.ZF or, if not available, line 99B.CZF.

The deflators in U.S. dollars are from the IFS, as described in the appendix for section 2.2.

Section 2.5

Stock Market Data

Data on market capitalization and total value traded are mostly from the IFC's Emerging Market Database, with additional data from Goldman Sachs (1986).

Data on GDP in U.S. dollars are from the electronic version of the World Development Indicators.

Data on GDP in local currency are from the electronic version of the IFS, either line 99B. .ZF or, if not available, line 99B.CZF.

The deflators in local currency and in U.S. dollars are from the IFS, as described in the appendix for section 2.2.

Bond Market Data

Data on private and public market capitalization are from the Bank for International Settlement Quarterly Review on International Banking and Financial Market Development. They were downloaded from the BIS Web page and are from Table 15: Domestic Debt Securities, by sector and country of issuer.

Data on GDP in U.S. dollars are from the electronic version of the World Development Indicators.

The deflators in U.S. dollars are from the IFS, as described in the appendix for section 2.2.

Primary Market Data

Data for the following countries were obtained from Aylward and Glen (1998).

They were obtained from national sources. Contributing organizations are:

Argentina	Bolsa de Comercio de Buenos Aires
Brazil	Comissão de Valores Mobiliários, Bolsa de Valores do Rio de Janeiro
Chile	Banco Central de Chile, Superintendencia de Valores y Seguros
China, P.R.	China Securities Regulatory Commission
Columbia	Superintendencia de Valores, Banco de la República
Hong Kong	Hong Kong Monetary Authority
Hungary	Hungarian State Treasury, Government Debt Management Agency
India	Reserve Bank of India
Malaysia	Kuala Lumpur Stock Exchange, Bank Negara Malaysia
Indonesia	Capital Market Supervisory Agency
Jamaica	The Jamaica Stock Exchange
Jordan	Amman Financial Market
Kenya	Capital Markets Authority
Korea	The Bank of Korea
Mauritius	Bank of Mauritius, Stock Exchange Commision
Mexico	Bolsa Mexicana de Valores, Comisión Nacional Bancaria y de Valores, Banco de México
Morocco	Bank Al-Maghrib, Moroccan Securities Commission
Pakistan	Corporate Law Authority, Karachi Stock Exchange (Guarantee) Ltd.
Peru	Comisión Nacional Supervisora de Empresas y Valores

Philippines	Bangko Sentral Pilipinas
Portugal	Comissão do Mercado de Valores Mobiliároios
Singapore	Monetary Authority of Singapore
Sri Lanka	Colombo Stock Exchange, Securites and Exchange Commission of Sri Lanka
Taiwan, R.C.	Central Bank of China
Thailand	Bank of Thailand, Securities and Exchange Commission, The Stock Exchange of Thailand
Tunisia	Conseil du Marché Financier
Turkey	Capital Market Board of Turkey
Venezuela	Comisión Nacional de Valores
Germany	OECD Financial Statistics Monthly
Japan	OECD Financial Statistics Monthly
United States	OECD Financial Statistics Monthly
Great Britain	OECD Financial Statistics Monthly

The following country data were taken from OECD Financial Statistics Monthly. Listed will be the country and line numbers for equity and debt issues.

Austria	Shares: A.1	Bonds: B.1.1 + B.1.2 c + d + e
Canada	Shares: A.1	Bonds: B.1.1 + B.1.2 d + e + f + g
Denmark	Shares: A.1	Bonds: B.1.1 c + d + e
Finland	Shares: N/A	Bonds: B.1.1 c + d + e + B.1.2 c + d + e
France	Shares: A.1 a + b + c	Bonds: B.1.1 c + d + e
Greece	Shares: A.1 b + c	Bonds: B.1.1 c + d + e
Italy	Shares: A.1	Bonds: B.1.1 c + d + e
Luxembourg	Shares: A.1	Bonds: B.1.1 c + d + e B.1.2 e
Netherlands	Shares: A.1 b + c	Bonds: B.1.1 c + d + e1 + e2 + B.1.2 e
Norway	Shares: N/A	Bonds: B.1.1 + B.1.2 c + d + e
Portugal	Shares: A.1	Bonds: B.1.1 + B.1.2 c + d + e
Spain	Shares: A.1	Bonds: B.1.1 c + d + e
Sweden	Shares: A.1 a + b + c	Bonds: B.1.1 c + d + e
Switzerland	Shares: A.1.1 a + b + c	Bonds: B.1.1 c + d + e + B.1.2 c + d + e

Data on GDP in U.S. dollars are from the electronic version of the World Development Indicators.

Data on GDP in local currency are from the electronic version of the IFS, either line 99B. .ZF or, if not available, line 99B.CZF.

The deflators in local currency and in U.S. dollars are from the IFS, as described in the appendix for section 2.2.

Notes

1. For an overview of this literature, see Levine 1997.

2. See King and Levine 1993a, b and Levine and Zervos 1998 for correlation. See Levine, Loayza, and Beck 2000; Beck, Levine, and Loayza 2000; Neusser and Kugler 1998; and Rousseau and Wachtel 1998 for evidence on causality. In addition, Demirgüç-Kunt and Maksimovic (1998) show that firms in countries with an active stock market and large banking sector grow faster than predicted by individual firm characteristics. Rajan and Zingales (1998) show that industries that rely more heavily on external finance grow faster in countries with better-developed financial systems.

3. For a detailed description of the three financial sectors, see IMF 1984. The three groups correspond to lines 12, 22, and 42 of the IFS.

4. Exchange stabilization funds are the most typical case of monetary authority functions that are performed separately from the central bank's balance sheets. Furthermore, the central bank might perform commercial banking tasks. Where possible, these are excluded from the central bank balance sheets when reported in the IFS.

5. In the case of other financial institutions, we also include line 42h, claims on real estate in total claims on domestic nonfinancial sectors and in private credit.

6. For the CPI numbers, we use line 64 and for GDP line 99b from the IFS.

7. To assess the size and activity of financial intermediaries across countries, we use the World Bank classification of countries according to their income levels (World Bank 1997). We can distinguish between four country groups: high-income countries with a GNP per capita in 1997 higher than $9,656, upper-middle-income countries with a GNP per capita between $3,126 and $9,655, lower-middle-income countries with a GNP per capita between $786 and $3,125, and low-income countries with a GNP per capita of less than $786.

8. We use medians for the four income groups to avoid the impact of outliers.

9. The classification's commercial and deposit money banks are close, but not exactly the same. Whereas IFS defines deposit money banks consistently across countries, Bankscope uses country-specific definitions of commercial banks.

10. Unfortunately, the coverage of Bankscope is less than 100 percent of most countries' banking sector. This poses relatively few problems in the case of the efficiency measures, but more so in the case of the measures of market structure.

11. Ex post spreads are preferable to ex ante spreads, since the latter reflect the perceived loan risk, so that different levels of risk faced by bankers distort these spreads. Ex post spreads also pose some problems though. So might interest income and loan loss reserving associated with a particular loan that incur in different periods. See Demirgüç-Kunt and Huizinga (1998).

12. We also calculated numbers deflated by the CPI. The correlation between the deflated numbers and the nominal numbers is 91 percent in the panel and 96 percent in the cross-section.

13. Both foreign bank indicator and the concentration measure might be biased upward for developing countries, if foreign and large banks are more likely to report than are domestic and smaller banks. There is an additional caveat concerning the two for-

eign penetration measures: Since a bank is defined as foreign if it was foreign in 1998, takeovers of domestic banks by foreign banks are not taken into account.

14. See Demirgüç-Kunt and Levine 1996.

15. We use unconsolidated balance sheets for the efficiency measures to insure consistency. In the case of the concentration index and the measures of foreign bank penetration, we want to maximize the number of banks.

16. See appendix 2.1 for the listing of sources.

17. Note that these numbers, like in all graphs, are medians. The means for the income groups are 64 percent for low-income groups, 38 and 39 percent for lower- and upper-middle-income groups and 23 percent for high-income countries.

18. Note that this definition is more restrictive than the IFS's definition of other banklike institutions.

19. Using balance sheets' total assets is problematic since they might include cross-claims within a category of other financial institutions and claims on other groups of financial intermediaries. A size measure that includes only claims on the nonfinancial sector, such as that described in section 2.2, is therefore preferable but not available for most countries.

20. Life insurance density is constructed as premiums in local currency divided by the purchasing power parity conversion factor, obtained from the World Development Indicators, and the population. To obtain the real density, we adjust these numbers by the annual CPI of the United States.

21. A complete list of sources is available in appendix 2.1.

22. We are grateful to Ian Webb for technical assistance in obtaining these data.

23. Using total assets instead of private credit yields a very similar picture. The graph might give a distorted picture, especially in the case of development banks, since values of zeros are treated as nonavailable.

24. Using this method assumes a flexible exchange rate with respect to the U.S. dollar, so that inflation differentials are reflected by changes in the exchange rates. Although this method is far from perfect, it is relatively accurate.

25. We are grateful to Joe Attia for collecting the data from the OECD *Financial Statistics Monthly*.

26. We combine the low- and lower-middle-income groups for the bond measures, since India is the only low-income country for which data are available.

References

Aylward, Anthony, and Jack Glen. 1999. Primary securities markets: Cross-country findings. Discussion Paper 39, Emerging Primary Markets. Washington, DC: International Finance Corporation.

Bank for International Settlement. Various dates. *Quarterly Review on International Banking and Financial Market Development*.

Beck, Thorsten, Ross Levine, and Norman Loayza. 2000. Finance and the sources of growth. *Journal of Financial Economics* 58(1):261–300.

Claessens, Stijn, Aslı Demirgüç-Kunt, and Harry Huizinga. 1997. How does foreign entry affect the domestic banking market? Mimeo, Policy Research Department, World Bank (June).

Demirgüç-Kunt, Aslı, and Harry Huizinga. 1998. Determinants of commercial bank interest margins and profitability. Policy Research Working Paper 1900, World Bank (March).

Demirgüç-Kunt, Aslı, and Ross Levine. 1996. The financial system and public enterprise reform: Concepts and cases. In *Financial development and economic growth*, ed. Neil Hermes and Robert Lensink, 247–286. London: Routledge.

Demirgüç-Kunt, Aslı, and Vojislav Maksimovic. 1998. Law, finance, and firm growth. *Journal of Finance* 53:2107–2137.

Demirgüç-Kunt, Aslı, Ross Levine, and Hong G. Min. 1998. Opening to foreign banks: Issues of stability, efficiency, and growth. Mimeo, Policy Research Department, World Bank (July).

Gardener, Edward P. M., and Philip Molyneux. 1990. *Changes in Western European banking*. London: Unwin Hyman.

Goldman Sachs. 1986. Anatomy of the world's equity markets. *International Investment Research* (September).

IMF (International Monetary Fund). 1984. A guide to money and banking statistics, *International Financial Statistics* (December).

King, Robert G., and Ross Levine. 1993a. Finance and growth: Schumpeter might be right. *Quarterly Journal of Economics* 108(3):717–738 (August).

King, Robert G., and Ross Levine. 1993b. Finance, entrepreneurship, and growth: Theory and evidence. *Journal of Monetary Economics* 32(3):513–542 (December).

Levine, Ross. 1997. Financial development and economic growth: Views and agenda. *Journal of Economic Literature* 35(2):688–726 (June).

Levine, Ross, and Sara Zervos. 1998. Stock markets, banks, and economic growth. *American Economic Review* 88:537–558 (June).

Levine, Ross, Norman Loayza, and Thorsten Beck. 2000. Financial intermediation and growth: Causality and causes. *Journal of Monetary Economics* 46(1):31–77.

Neusser, Klaus, and Maurice Kugler. 1998. Manufacturing growth and financial development: Evidence from OECD countries. *Review of Economics and Statistics* 80:636–646 (November).

OECD. Various dates. *Financial Statistics Monthly*.

Rajan, Raghuram G., and Luigi Zingales. 1998. Financial dependence and growth. *American Economic Review* 88:559–586 (June).

Rousseau, Peter L., and Paul Wachtel. 1998. Financial intermediation and economic performance: Historical evidence from five industrial countries. *Journal of Money, Credit, and Banking* 30:657–678.

SIGMA (monthly). 1998. Zurich, Switzerland: Swiss Re.

World Bank. 1997. *World Development Indicators 1997*.

3

Bank-Based and Market-Based Financial Systems: Cross-Country Comparisons

Aslı Demirgüç-Kunt and Ross Levine

3.1 Introduction

Economists have long debated the advantages and disadvantages of bank-based financial systems vis-à-vis market-based systems.[1] This debate has primarily focused on four countries. In bank-based financial systems such as Germany and Japan, banks play a leading role in mobilizing savings, allocating capital, overseeing the investment decisions of corporate managers, and providing risk management vehicles. In market-based financial systems such as England and the United States, securities markets share center stage with banks in terms of getting society's savings to firms, exerting corporate control, and easing risk management. Some analysts suggest that markets are more effective at providing financial services. Others tout the advantages of intermediaries. The debate is unresolved and hampers the formation of sound policy advice.

There is a major shortcoming with existing comparisons of market-based versus bank-based financial systems; they focus on a narrow set of countries with similar levels of GDP per capita, so that the countries have very similar long-run growth rates. Thus, if one accepts that Germany and Japan are bank-based and that England and the United States are market-based, and if one recognizes that these countries all have very similar long-run growth rates, then this implies that financial structure did not matter much.[2] To provide greater information on both the economic importance and determinants of financial structure, economists need to broaden the debate to include a wider array of national experiences.

To expand the debate to a broader cross-section of countries, we need new data. Based on a newly constructed data set, this chapter examines financial structure for a cross-section of up to 150 countries. We use simple graphs, correlations, and regressions to illustrate the relationships between financial structure and economic development. Furthermore, we provide empirical evidence on the potential legal, regulatory, and policy determinants of financial structure. This is the first systematic examination of financial structure and economic development for a large cross-section of countries since Goldsmith's (1969) influential book. It should be noted, however, that this chapter does not examine whether financial structure—whether the country is bank-based or market-based—exerts a causal influence on economic growth and firm performance. Chapter 5 conducts these analyses. This chapter, however, presents stylized facts concerning the relationship between financial structure and economic development and the links between financial structure and legal, regulatory, and policy determinants for a broad cross-section of countries.

More specifically, we provide international comparisons regarding three issues:

• economic development and bank, nonbank, and stock market development

• economic development and bank-based versus market-based systems

• the legal, regulatory, tax, and macroeconomic determinants of financial structure

To analyze financial structure, we must classify countries as either market-based or bank-based. We construct a conglomerate index of financial structure based on measures of size, activity and efficiency. Specifically, we study ratios of banking sector development (measured in terms of size, activity, and efficiency) relative to stock market development (also measured in terms of size, activity, and efficiency). Countries with larger ratios are classified as bank-based. Countries where the conglomerate ratio of banking sector development to stock market development is below the mean are classified as market-based. Thus, this grouping system produces two categories of countries: bank-based and market-based.

While a useful starting point, this bivariate classification system presents a number of complications. Uncomfortably, this method identifies countries as bank-based even though their banking systems are poorly developed by international comparisons. This occurs because their stock markets are very underdeveloped by international standards. Similarly, this method identifies countries as market-based even though their markets are underdeveloped by international comparisons because their banks are extremely underdeveloped. Consequently, we develop another grouping system where we first identify countries with highly underdeveloped financial systems. A country's financial system is considered underdeveloped if it has below median values of *both* bank and market development. This produces three categories of financial structure: underdeveloped, bank-based, and market-based. While this classification system also has problems, it helps in comparing financial structures across a broad cross-section of countries because very underdeveloped financial systems have more in common with each other than with better-developed financial systems that fall into either the bank-based or market-based group. Although we obtain similar results when only considering bank-based versus market-based financial systems, we observe much clearer patterns when we consider three categories of financial structure: underdeveloped, bank-based, and market-based.

We find the following:

• Banks, nonbanks, and stock markets are larger, more active, and more efficient in richer countries. Financial systems, on average, are more developed in richer countries.

• In higher-income countries, stock markets become more active and efficient relative to banks. There is some tendency for national financial systems to become more market oriented, as they become richer.

• Countries with a Common Law tradition, strong protection of shareholder rights, good accounting regulations, low levels of corruption, and no explicit deposit insurance tend to be more market-based.

• Countries with a French Civil Law tradition, poor protection of shareholder and creditor rights, poor contract enforcement, high levels of corruption, poor accounting standards, restrictive banking regulations, and high inflation tend to have underdeveloped financial systems.

The rest of the chapter is organized as follows. Section 3.2 presents evidence on how financial systems differ across income per capita

groups. Section 3.3 defines financial structure empirically and provides cross-country comparisons. In section 3.4, we examine the
legal, regulatory, tax, and policy determinants of financial structure.
We summarize the findings in section 3.5.

3.2   Financial Systems Differ across Income per Capita Groups

There are large differences in financial systems across countries. This
section uses newly collected data on a cross-section of up to 150
countries to illustrate how financial systems differ as one compares
poorer with richer countries (measured in terms of GDP per capita).
While not all measures of financial sector development vary in a
systematic way across income groups, some notable patterns
emerge. Namely, financial sector development—as measured by the
size, activity, and efficiency of banks, nonbank financial intermediaries, and equity markets—tends to be greater in richer countries. The analysis focuses on data collected in the 1990s.[3] We obtain
very similar results when we conduct the analysis over the 1980s,
1970s, or 1960s (data permitting). The appendix shows how financial
systems differ over time. Chapter 2 provides detailed information on
data sources.

3.2.1   Intermediaries

In higher income countries, banks and other financial intermediaries
tend to be larger, more active, and more efficient.
    Consider four measures. First, *Liquid liabilities/GDP* equals the ratio
of liquid liabilities of bank and nonbank financial intermediaries to
GDP. By aggregating the liquid liabilities of a broad range of banks
and nonbanks, *Liquid liabilities/GDP* is a general indicator of the size
of financial intermediaries relative to the size of the economy. *Liquid
liabilities/GDP* is frequently used as an overall measure of financial
sector development (King and Levine 1993a, b). Second, *Bank assets/
GDP* equals the ratio of the total domestic assets of deposit money
banks divided by GDP. *Bank assets/GDP* provides a measure of the
overall size of the banking sector. Third, *Claims of deposit money banks
on private sector/GDP* equals deposit money bank credits to (and
other claims on) the private sector as a share of GDP. This measure
excludes credits to the public sector (central and local governments
and public enterprises). By aggregating bank claims on the private
sector, *Claims of deposit money banks on private sector/GDP* is a general

indicator of bank activity in the private sector. Fourth, *Claims of other financial institutions on private sector/GDP* focuses on insurance companies, finance companies, pooled investment schemes (mutual funds), savings banks, private pension funds, and development banks. *Claims of other financial institutions on private sector/GDP* equals nonbank credits to (and other claims on) the private sector as a share of GDP measures the assets side as a share of GDP. Thus, *Claims of other financial institutions on private sector/GDP* provides a broad measure of nonbank activity in the private sector.

After computing these measures of financial intermediary size and activity, we group countries into low, lower-middle, upper-middle, and high-income countries as defined in 1997 World Development Indicators.[4] Based on this ranking of income, we end up with roughly the same number of countries in each quartile. Then, for each quartile we compute the average value of the financial intermediary development indicators. Table 3.1 gives the data for each country. Figure 3.1 shows that *Liquid liabilities/GDP*, *Bank assets/GDP*, *Claims of deposit money banks on private sector/GDP*, and *Claims of other financial institutions on private sector/GDP* all rise when comparing richer with poorer groups of countries. These patterns are statistically significant. The correlations between GDP per capita and *Liquid liabilities/GDP*, *Bank assets/GDP*, *Claims of deposit money banks on private sector/GDP*, and *Claims of other financial institutions on private sector/GDP* are all significant at the 0.05 level as shown in table 3.2. In terms of specific countries, Austria, France, Germany, Great Britain, Hong Kong, Japan, the Netherlands, and Switzerland have comparatively large, active banking systems (table 3.1). On the other hand, Argentina, Colombia, Costa Rica, Ghana, Nepal, Nigeria, Peru, Turkey, and Zimbabwe have particularly small, inactive banking systems. In terms of nonbanks, Japan, Korea, the Netherlands, South Africa, Sweden, and the United States have very large financial intermediaries (table 3.1). Indeed, in the United States, Sweden, and Korea, other financial intermediaries issue more credit to the private sector than the deposit money banks issue. Also, note that in richer countries, the direct role of the central bank in credit allocation is smaller (figure 3.1 and table 3.2).

Now, consider two measures of banking-sector efficiency. *Overhead costs* equals the ratio of bank overhead costs to the total assets of the banks. While not unambiguous, we interpret lower overhead costs as a sign of greater efficiency. Excessive overhead expenditures may reflect waste and a lack of competition. It should also be recognized,

Table 3.1
Financial Intermediary and Equity Market Development across Countries

Country name	GDP per capita 1990–1995	Liquid liabilities/ GDP	Bank assets/ GDP	Claims of deposit money banks on private sector/ GDP	Claims of other inter-medi-aries/ GDP	Central bank assets/ GDP
Argentina	4039.12	0.15	0.21	0.15	0.00	0.04
Australia	14313.95	0.61	0.77	0.70	0.27	0.03
Austria	13177.30	0.89	1.26	0.93		0.00
Bangladesh	194.31	0.34	0.31	0.22		0.02
Barbados	4777.04	0.64	0.52	0.35	0.11	0.05
Belgium	14481.78	0.69	1.18	0.56		0.01
Bolivia	754.98	0.35	0.37	0.36	0.02	0.22
Brazil	2346.36	0.23	0.32	0.23	0.05	0.14
Canada	17284.79	0.76	0.66	0.57	0.24	0.04
Chile	2725.16	0.38	0.46	0.45	0.12	0.20
Colombia	1432.39	0.30	0.18	0.16	0.15	0.02
Costa Rica	1866.60	0.37	0.17	0.15	0.01	0.10
Cyprus	6588.45	1.24	0.81	0.69	0.39	0.11
Denmark	17022.55	0.58	0.48	0.38		0.02
Ecuador	1322.40	0.24	0.17	0.17	0.04	0.09
Egypt	1042.35	0.81	0.63	0.26	0.04	0.34
Finland	15892.44	0.58	0.80	0.77		0.01
France	15232.41	0.64	1.02	0.89		0.01
Germany	16573.02	0.66	1.21	0.94	0.05	0.01
Ghana	553.23	0.16	0.06	0.05		0.16
Great Britain	11794.31	0.96	1.16	1.14		0.03
Greece	6551.64	0.60	0.41	0.18	0.14	0.19
Honduras	751.32	0.29	0.25	0.21	0.04	0.07
Hong Kong	10537.98	1.63	1.49	1.42		
Iceland	18939.92	0.37	0.49	0.45		0.03
India	385.43	0.44	0.34	0.24		0.13
Indonesia	609.76	0.42	0.49	0.46		0.02
Iran	2397.40	0.44		0.22	0.20	0.06
Ireland	9014.40	0.52	0.36	0.29	0.37	0.01
Israel	9259.58	0.69	0.92	0.60		0.06
Italy	11504.72	0.65	0.74	0.52		0.10
Jamaica	1711.34	0.43	0.28	0.21	0.07	0.06
Japan	15705.68	1.91	1.31	1.17	0.85	0.05

Over-head costs	Bank net interest margin/ GDP	Bank concen-tration index	Foreign bank assets in total bank	Public share in com-mercial bank assets	Market capital-ization/ GDP	Total value traded/ GDP	Turn-over ratio
0.01	0.07	0.50	0.16	0.34	0.11	0.04	0.34
0.03	0.02	0.65	0.01		0.71	0.33	0.43
0.03	0.02	0.72	0.03	0.98	0.12	0.08	0.64
0.02	0.01	0.64	0.20	0.72	0.04	0.01	0.09
0.05	0.03	1.00			0.21	0.00	0.02
0.03	0.02	0.65	0.03	0.00	0.36	0.05	0.15
0.05	0.04	0.48	0.29	0.13	0.02	0.00	0.01
0.11	0.11	0.60	0.05	0.56	0.19	0.12	0.56
0.02	0.02	0.58	0.07	0.00	0.59	0.29	0.47
0.03	0.04	0.47	0.04		0.84	0.09	0.10
0.08	0.06	0.44	0.15	0.58	0.13	0.01	0.10
0.06	0.05	0.80	0.05	0.33	0.07	0.00	0.03
0.04	0.06	0.88	0.48		0.22	0.02	0.11
0.04	0.05	0.74	0.00	0.00	0.34	0.16	0.45
0.08	0.07	0.40	0.06	0.00	0.10	0.01	0.14
0.02	0.01	0.65			0.10	0.02	0.14
0.02	0.02	0.88		0.18	0.29	0.12	0.34
0.04	0.03	0.41	0.06	0.74	0.33	0.17	0.50
0.03	0.02	0.45	0.04	0.00	0.24	0.28	1.13
0.06	0.08	0.89		0.79	0.15	0.00	0.03
0.03	0.02	0.56			1.13	0.55	0.48
0.04	0.03	0.77	0.02	0.77	0.15	0.06	0.36
0.04	0.07	0.44	0.19		0.05	0.02	0.67
0.02	0.02	0.72			1.96	1.08	0.52
	1.00			0.11	0.01	0.08	
	0.03	0.47	0.06	0.88	0.28	0.08	0.35
0.03	0.04	0.42	0.23	0.57	0.18	0.08	0.45
0.03					0.04	0.01	0.21
0.26	0.01	0.74	0.31	0.00	0.26	0.14	0.62
0.01	0.03	0.84	0.03		0.33	0.19	0.70
0.04	0.03	0.36	0.00	0.65	0.17	0.08	0.42
0.08	0.10	0.82			0.42	0.05	0.10
0.01	0.02	0.22	0.00	0.00	0.79	0.28	0.36

Table 3.1
(continued)

Country name	GDP per capita 1990–1995	Liquid liabil- ities/ GDP	Bank assets/ GDP	Claims of deposit money banks on private sector/ GDP	Claims of other inter- medi- aries/ GDP	Central bank assets/ GDP
Jordan	1288.78	1.11	0.71	0.62	0.07	0.21
Kenya	440.62	0.46	0.29	0.21	0.10	0.11
Korea	3908.74	0.65	0.55	0.53	0.59	0.01
Malaysia	2629.22	0.97	0.82	0.75	0.28	0.01
Mauritius	2124.69	0.68	0.54	0.39		0.02
Mexico	2951.55	0.25	0.24	0.22	0.03	0.01
Nepal	199.61	0.33	0.22	0.16		0.11
Netherlands	13954.71	0.83	1.12	0.90	0.55	0.01
New Zealand	9492.46	0.73	0.85	0.78	0.04	0.03
Nigeria	550.95	0.20	0.11	0.08	0.03	0.20
Norway	20134.81	0.57	0.69	0.57	0.34	0.02
Pakistan	435.90	0.41	0.36	0.23		0.14
Panama	1950.45	0.53	0.58	0.56		0.21
Peru	1292.36	0.15	0.12	0.09	0.01	0.00
Philippines	734.06	0.45	0.37	0.28	0.05	0.09
Portugal	4822.10	0.71	0.79	0.54		0.04
Singapore	11152.47	1.12	0.95	0.83	0.17	
South Africa	2379.26	0.44	0.66	0.61	0.51	0.03
Spain	7286.25	0.76	0.96	0.69	0.06	0.04
Sri Lanka	537.67	0.37	0.27	0.21		0.10
Sweden	18981.50	0.47	0.54	0.46	0.73	0.06
Switzerland	19529.79	1.44	1.77	1.65	0.39	0.01
Thailand	1502.88	0.77	0.82	0.78	0.30	0.02
Trinidad and Tobago	3684.84	0.52	0.37	0.30	0.17	0.08
Tunisia	1534.16	0.47	0.55	0.51	0.13	0.01
Turkey	2258.77	0.22	0.19	0.13	0.01	0.06
United States	19413.52	0.60	0.73	0.64	0.91	0.05
Uruguay	2514.33	0.39	0.28	0.24		0.15
Venezuela	3166.58	0.29	0.15	0.12	0.05	0.06
Zimbabwe	803.59	0.35	0.21	0.16	0.08	0.10
MEAN	6546.68	0.59	0.58	0.48	0.21	0.08

Over-head costs	Bank net interest margin/ GDP	Bank concen-tration index	Foreign bank assets in total bank	Public share in com-mercial bank assets	Market capital-ization/ GDP	Total value traded/ GDP	Turn-over ratio
0.03	0.02	0.91			0.65	0.12	0.20
0.04	0.74	0.03			0.16	0.00	0.03
0.02	0.02	0.31			0.37	0.44	1.22
0.02	0.03	0.49	0.06		2.01	1.14	0.50
0.02	0.03	0.94	0.03		0.27	0.01	0.05
0.05	0.05	0.58	0.01	0.00	0.32	0.13	0.41
0.02	0.04	0.90	0.96		0.05	0.00	0.04
0.01	0.01	0.74	0.10	0.00	0.69	0.43	0.56
0.03	0.02	0.69		0.00	0.49	0.14	0.27
0.08	0.05	0.81	0.08		0.06	0.00	0.01
0.02	0.03	0.84	0.01	0.00	0.26	0.14	0.53
0.03	0.03	0.74	0.20	0.52	0.16	0.06	0.34
0.02	0.02	0.42	0.42		0.09	0.00	0.04
0.10	0.08	0.69	0.42		0.11	0.04	0.30
0.05	0.04	0.47	0.30	0.19	0.52	0.15	0.26
0.02	0.03	0.46	0.06	0.68	0.13	0.05	0.38
0.01	0.02	0.71	0.33		1.37	0.70	0.50
0.04	0.04	0.77	0.01		1.66	0.15	0.08
0.03	0.04	0.47	0.10	0.07	0.30	0.23	0.63
0.05	0.05	0.82		0.56	0.16	0.02	0.12
0.03	0.03	0.88	0.03	0.26	0.62	0.33	0.47
0.05	0.02	0.76	0.08	0.19	0.98	0.76	0.74
0.02	0.03	0.53	0.05	0.17	0.57	0.40	0.77
0.04	0.04	0.76		0.12	0.01	0.10	
0.02	0.02	0.59	0.24	0.73	0.10	0.01	0.09
0.06	0.10	0.44	0.01	0.51	0.14	0.16	1.04
0.04	0.04	0.19	0.04	0.00	0.80	0.62	0.73
0.06	0.06	0.87	0.17	0.68	0.01	0.00	0.03
0.07	0.09	0.52	0.24		0.12	0.03	0.26
0.05	0.05	0.82	0.62		0.23	0.01	0.07
0.04	0.04	0.65	0.15	0.35	0.39	0.17	0.35

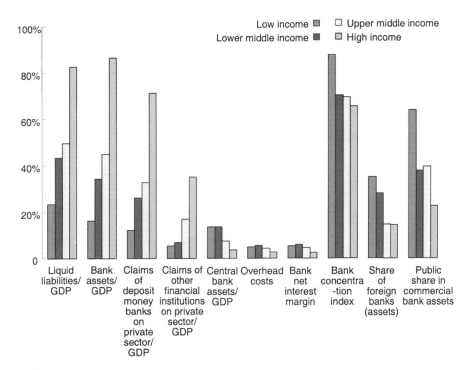

Figure 3.1
Financial intermediary development in the 1990s.

however, that competitive banks may undertake substantial investments to provide high-quality financial services. These productivity-
enhancing investments may boost overhead costs. Low overhead
costs, therefore, may reflect insufficient competition and insufficient
investment in providing superior banking services. Thus, *Overhead
costs* is not an unambiguously clear measure of efficiency.

A second measure of bank efficiency, *Bank net interest margin*,
equals the bank interest income minus interest expense over total
assets. While many factors influence interest margins, tighter interest
margins are frequently viewed as representing greater competition
and efficiency. We obtain *Overhead costs and Bank net interest margin*
from bank-level data across eighty countries. For each country, we
then compute the average across the individual banks. Figure 3.1
illustrates that higher income countries tend to have lower average
Overhead costs and lower average *Bank net interest margin*. The correlations (and p-values) between GDP per capita and *Overhead costs*

Table 3.2
Correlations of Financial Intermediary and Equity Market Development with GDP per Capita

	Correlation	p-value
Liquid liabilities/GDP	0.465	(0.001)
Bank assets/GDP	0.663	(0.001)
Claims of deposit money banks on private sector/GDP	0.639	(0.001)
Claims of other financial institutions on private sector/GDP	0.636	(0.001)
Central bank assets/GDP	−0.442	(0.001)
Overhead costs	−0.353	(0.005)
Bank net interest margin	−0.443	(0.001)
Bank concentration index	0.017	(0.898)
Foreign bank assets in total bank assets	−0.371	(0.009)
Public share in total bank assets	−0.462	(0.004)
Market capitalization/GDP	0.282	(0.025)
Total value traded/GDP	0.409	(0.001)
Turnover ratio	0.424	(0.001)

and *Bank net interest margin* further demonstrate the significant, negative relationship between GDP per capita and bank efficiency (table 3.2).

A statistically significant link does not exist between bank concentration and GDP per capita. We measure banking-sector concentration as share of the assets of the three largest banks in total banking sector assets and call this measure the *Bank concentration index*. Figure 3.1 shows that as we move from lower to higher income countries, bank concentration tends to fall. This drop in banking-sector concentration, however, is not statistically significant as shown in table 3.2.

In table 3.1 we also report *Foreign bank share* and *Public bank share* in total assets. Both of these measures decrease as we move to high-income countries (figure 3.1). These relationships are also statistically significant as we can see from table 3.2.

3.2.2 Equity Markets across Countries

In higher income countries, stock markets tend to be larger, more active, and more efficient.

To measure market size, we use *Market capitalization as a share of GDP*, which equals the ratio of the value of domestic equities (that are traded on domestic exchanges) to GDP. To measure market activity, we use *Total value traded as a share of GDP*, which equals the value of the trades of domestic equities on domestic exchanges divided by GDP. *Total value traded as a share of GDP* measures the value of stock transactions relative to the size of the economy. *Total value traded as a share of GDP* is frequently used to gauge market liquidity because it measures trading relative to economic activity (Levine and Zervos 1998). Finally, to measure the efficiency of the market, we use the *Turnover ratio*, which equals the value of the trades of domestic equities on domestic exchanges as a share of the value of domestic equities (that are traded on domestic exchanges). The *Turnover ratio* is not a direct measure of efficiency. It does not measure trading costs. Rather, the *Turnover ratio* measures the value of stock transactions relative to the size of the market, and it is frequently used as a measure of market liquidity (Demirgüç-Kunt and Levine 1996).

As shown in figure 3.2, *Market capitalization as a share of GDP, Total value traded as a share of GDP*, and *Turnover ratio* rise when we move from the poorest quartile of countries across to the highest quartile of countries. The correlations between GDP per capita and both *Total value traded as a share of GDP* and the *Turnover ratio* are about 0.4 and significant at the 0.01 level. The correlation between GDP per capita and *Market capitalization* is almost 0.3 and is significant at the 0.05 level. Stock markets are more developed in richer countries. In terms of individual countries, rankings can depend importantly on the particular measure of stock market development. Some countries show up as well-developed by all measures (Australia, Great Britain, Hong Kong, Malaysia, the Netherlands, Singapore, Sweden, Switzerland, Thailand, and the United States as shown in table 3.1). Some countries are large and illiquid, such as Chile and South Africa (table 3.1). Other countries have active but small stock markets; especially noteworthy are Korea and Germany.

3.2.3 Nonbank Financial Intermediaries across Countries

Insurance companies, pension funds, mutual funds, and other non-bank financial intermediaries are larger as a share of GDP in richer countries.

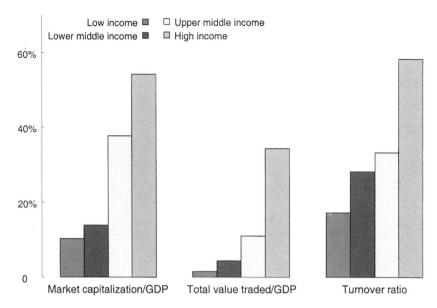

Figure 3.2
Equity market development in the 1990s.

Specifically, we measure credits to the private sector issued by insurance companies, pension funds, pooled investment schemes (mutual funds), development banks, and other nonbank financial institutions. These measures are computed as a share of GDP. Figure 3.3A shows that each of these measures of nonbank financial intermediary size is larger in richer countries. But as countries get richer, the role of insurance companies, pension funds, and mutual funds rises relative to the role of development banks and other nonbanks (figure 3.3B).

For the life insurance sector we include an additional size and two additional activity measures (figure 3.3C). The size of the life insurance sector, defined as the private credit by life insurance companies as a percentage of GDP, increases with income. The activity measures, life insurance penetration, measured by premiums to GDP, and life insurance density, measured by premiums to population also follow a similar pattern. The high-income countries exhibit a life insurance penetration ten times as high as lower-middle-income countries and a life insurance density nearly one hundred times higher than low-income countries.

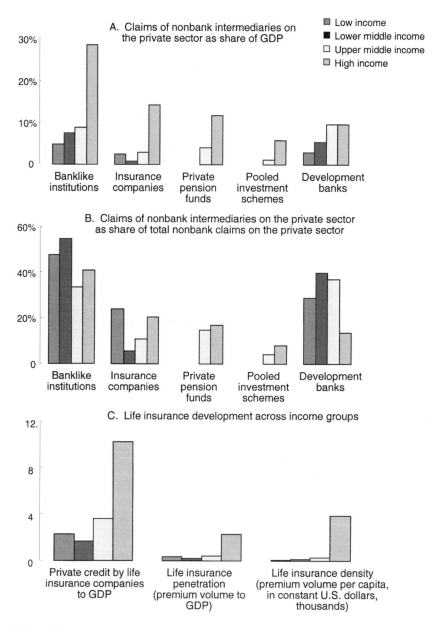

Figure 3.3
Nonbank intermediary development over the 1990s.

3.2.4   Overall Efficiency

In higher income countries, the overall financial system becomes larger, more active, and more efficient.

Until now, we have focused on either intermediaries or stock markets. Here, we analyze measures of the *overall* financial system (table 3.3). We consider five measures of overall financial sector development. First, we measure the overall size of the financial system. To do this, we sum the domestic assets of deposit money banks with stock market capitalization and divide by GDP. Rajan and Zingales (1998) use a similar indicator to measure the overall level of financial sector development. As shown in figure 3.4, the overall size of the financial sector rises sharply with GDP per capita, and the correlation is significant at the 0.01 level (table 3.4).

Next, we consider four measures of overall financial sector development, where we mix-and-match different measures of stock market and banking development. We use both *Turnover* and *Total value traded/GDP* to measure stock market liquidity, such that we interpret higher levels as indicating more efficiently operating equity markets. For gauging stock market development on an economy-wide basis, we prefer the *Total value traded/GDP* measure to the *Turnover* ratio. *Total value traded/GDP* measures trading relative to the size of the economy, where as *Turnover* measures trading relative to the size of the market. Thus, a small active market may have high *Turnover* and low *Total value traded/GDP*. Since we are seeking to measure the ease of trading ownership of a country's firms, *Total value traded/GDP* measures this more directly. Nonetheless, we provide the results using both. Similarly, we use both *Overhead costs* and *Bank net interest margin* to measure banking sector *inefficiency*. Here, we interpret higher levels as indicating *less* efficiently operating banks. Thus, we construct four measures of overall financial sector development by dividing each of the stock market indictors by each of the banking sector inefficiency measures.

The results using measures of the overall efficiency of the financial sector are plotted in figure 3.4, where the countries are broken-up into income quartiles. As shown, richer countries tend to have more efficient financial systems and the positive relationship is economically significant at the 0.05 significance level for all of the measures (table 3.4). Some countries stand out in terms of overall financial sector efficiency. In particular, Malaysia, Hong Kong, Singapore,

Table 3.3
Overall Size and Efficiency of the Financial Sector across Countries

Country name	GDP per capita 1990–1995	Overall size [(domestic assets of deposit money banks + stock market capitalization)/GDP]	Overall efficiency (total value traded/net interest margin)	Overall efficiency (total value traded/ overhead costs)	Overall efficiency (turnover/ net interest margin)	Overall efficiency (turnover/ overhead costs)
Argentina	4039.12	0.32	0.50	0.36	4.70	3.38
Australia	14313.95	1.48	16.30	12.87	21.10	16.67
Austria	13177.30	1.38	4.22	2.90	34.37	23.65
Bangladesh	194.31	0.35	0.70	0.26	11.30	4.20
Barbados	4777.04	0.74	0.11	0.08	0.47	0.34
Belgium	14481.78	1.53	2.37	1.87	7.03	5.56
Bolivia	754.98	0.38				
Brazil	2346.36	0.50	1.09	1.10	5.17	5.20
Canada	17284.79	1.24	16.80	12.86	26.76	20.49
Chile	2725.16	1.30	1.96	2.78	2.20	3.13
Colombia	1432.39	0.31	0.21	0.16	1.51	1.18
Costa Rica	1866.60	0.24	0.03	0.02	0.52	0.43
Cyprus	6588.45	1.03	0.39	0.57	1.77	2.57
Denmark	17022.55	0.82	3.31	4.43	9.53	12.74
Ecuador	1322.40	0.28	0.19	0.18	2.07	1.91
Egypt	1042.35	0.73	1.44	1.13	10.23	7.98
Finland	15892.44	1.09	7.42	7.03	21.22	20.12
France	15232.41	1.35	4.91	3.87	14.47	11.41

Germany	16573.02	1.45	11.18	10.01	45.39	40.64
Ghana	553.23	0.21	0.05	0.07	0.38	0.53
Great Britain	11794.31	2.29	26.97	20.65	23.54	18.02
Greece	6551.64	0.56	1.73	1.48	10.55	9.01
Honduras	751.32	0.30	0.29	0.48	9.57	16.09
Hong Kong	10537.98	3.45	45.54	44.90	22.10	21.79
Iceland	18939.92	0.60				
India	385.43	0.62	2.58	2.86	11.72	13.02
Indonesia	609.76	0.68	1.85	2.70	10.76	15.68
Iran	2397.40	0.26				
Ireland	9014.40	0.63	9.95	19.95	43.49	87.18
Israel	9259.58	1.25	5.86	5.16	22.13	19.51
Italy	11504.72	0.91	2.18	2.15	12.26	12.07
Jamaica	1711.34	0.70	0.55	0.63	1.09	1.25
Japan	15705.68	2.10	15.84	20.17	19.80	25.22
Jordan	1288.78	1.36	5.35	4.82	8.54	7.69
Kenya	440.62	0.45	0.08	0.13	0.44	0.75
Korea	3908.74	0.92	19.77	17.86	54.93	49.60
Malaysia	2629.22	2.83	44.24	74.91	19.45	32.93
Mauritius	2124.69	0.81	0.45	0.75	1.63	2.74
Mexico	2951.55	0.56	2.54	2.44	8.21	7.88
Nepal	199.61	0.27	0.06	0.10	0.95	1.56
Netherlands	13954.71	1.80	28.83	38.70	37.45	50.27
New Zealand	9492.46	1.34	6.06	5.66	11.35	10.60
Nigeria	550.95	0.17				
Norway	20134.81	0.95	4.82	5.94	17.88	22.03
Pakistan	435.90	0.52	2.17	2.05	12.14	11.46

Table 3.3
(continued)

Country name	GDP per capita 1990–1995	Overall size [(domestic assets of deposit money banks + stock market capitalization)/ GDP]	Overall efficiency (total value traded/net interest margin)	Overall efficiency (total value traded/ overhead costs)	Overall efficiency (turnover/ net interest margin)	Overall efficiency (turnover/ overhead costs)
Panama	1950.45	0.66	0.12	0.15	1.76	2.13
Peru	1292.36	0.23	0.51	0.39	3.91	3.05
Philippines	734.06	0.88	3.88	3.15	6.73	5.46
Portugal	4822.10	0.92	1.55	1.93	12.55	15.64
Singapore	11152.47	2.32	32.20	54.62	23.04	39.08
South Africa	2379.26	2.32	3.46	4.07	1.98	2.33
Spain	7286.25	1.27	6.30	6.65	17.17	18.11
Sri Lanka	537.67	0.43	0.43	0.45	2.44	2.57
Sweden	18981.50	1.16	12.91	12.24	18.43	17.48
Switzerland	19529.79	2.75	47.04	15.76	45.92	15.38
Thailand	1502.88	1.39	13.70	19.72	26.35	37.93
Trinidad and Tobago	3684.84	0.49	0.38	0.32	2.54	2.13
Tunisia	1534.16	0.65	0.52	0.59	3.99	4.60
Turkey	2258.77	0.33	1.61	2.57	10.72	17.06
United States	19413.52	1.53	15.76	16.95	18.64	20.05
Uruguay	2514.33	0.30				
Venezuela	3166.58	0.27	0.38	0.49	3.03	3.84
Zimbabwe	803.59	0.44	0.30	0.30	1.48	1.50

Table 3.4
Correlations of Overall Size and Efficiency of the Financial Sector with GDP per Capita

	Correlation	p-value
Overall size [(domestic assets of deposit money banks + stock market capitalization)/GDP]	0.519	(0.001)
Overall efficiency (total value traded/bank net interest margin)	0.470	(0.001)
Overall efficiency (total value traded/overhead costs)	0.304	(0.020)
Overall efficiency (turnover ratio/bank net interest margin)	0.574	(0.001)
Overall efficiency (turnover ratio/overhead costs)	0.400	(0.002)

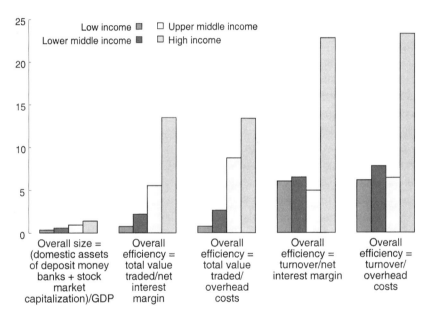

Figure 3.4
Overall size and efficiency of the financial system.

the Netherlands, Japan, Thailand, Korea, Great Britain, the United States, Switzerland, and Australia are ranked very high by our two preferred measures of overall financial sector efficiency (those based on the stock market indicator, *Total value traded/GDP*, and the two bank efficiency measures *Overhead costs* and *Bank net interest margin*).

3.3 Financial Structure: Comparisons and Definitions

We now turn to financial structure, having shown that intermediaries and stock markets tend to be larger, more active, and more efficient in countries with higher levels of GDP per capita. This section focuses on banks *relative* to stock markets. Furthermore, we also distinguish among economies with underdeveloped and developed financial systems. This provides additional information about financial structure, that is, if a particular bank-based (market-based) system has banks (markets) that can be considered developed by international standards. For example, both Germany and Pakistan are classified as bank-based systems, but in Pakistan banks cannot perform the functions expected of a bank-based system because they are not as well developed as German banks. Similarly, the United States and the Philippines are both market-based systems, but the markets in the Philippines are not as effective at providing financial services. Indeed, when we look at determinants of financial structure we see countries like Pakistan and the Philippines have more in common with each other than their respective bank-based and market-based counterparts.

3.3.1 Size

In higher income countries, banks do not become larger or smaller relative to the size of domestic stock markets.

Consider measures of financial structure based on size. Specifically, *Bank vs. capitalization* equals the domestic assets of deposit money banks relative to domestic stock market capitalization (i.e., *Bank vs. capitalization* equals *Bank assets* divided by *Market capitalization*). As in earlier figures, figure 3.5 graphs *Bank vs. capitalization* by income quartile. The first bar in the figure lists the average level of *Bank vs. capitalization* for the low-income countries. As shown, there is not a strong relationship between income level and the size of domestic bank assets relative to the size of the domestic stock market.

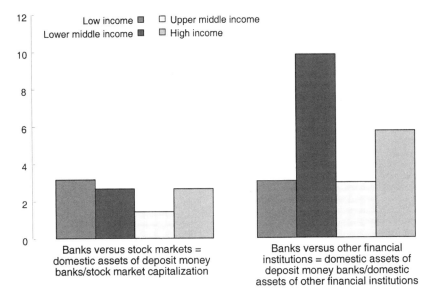

Figure 3.5
Relative size of bank, stock markets, and other financial institutions.

Now consider how *Bank vs. capitalization* classifies particular countries as having bank-based versus market-based financial structures. This relative size measure is given in table 3.5, which ranks countries from lowest to highest based on *Bank vs. capitalization*. There is a large range, from 0.40 (South Africa) to 10.24 (Austria). Consider the ten countries that have the largest markets relative to the size of the banks. These include the United States, Sweden, Hong Kong, Singapore, and Malaysia, which many observers classify as market-based. However, the *Bank vs. capitalization* measure classifies Jamaica, Mexico, and the Philippines as market-based. It does this primarily because banks are very small and underdeveloped in these countries, not because their stock markets are particularly well developed. Indeed, Mexico's stock market capitalization ratio is below the sample mean. Similarly, the *Bank vs. capitalization* measure identifies Chile and South Africa as market-based even though not much trading is done on their stock markets as noted below.

At the other end of the bank- versus market-based range, we find the same issues. Consider the ten countries that have the largest banks relative to the size of domestic stock markets. The relative size measure of financial structure identifies Austria, Panama, Portugal,

Table 3.5
Banks versus Capitalization

Country name	GDP per capita	Domestic assets of deposit money banks/ GDP	Market capital- ization/ GDP	Domestic assets of deposit money banks/market capitalization
South Africa	2379.26	0.66	1.66	0.40
Malaysia	2629.22	0.82	2.01	0.41
Chile	2725.16	0.46	0.84	0.55
Jamaica	1711.34	0.28	0.42	0.67
Singapore	11152.47	0.95	1.37	0.70
Philippines	734.06	0.37	0.52	0.71
Mexico	2951.55	0.24	0.32	0.76
Hong Kong	10537.98	1.49	1.96	0.76
Sweden	18981.50	0.54	0.62	0.86
United States	19413.52	0.73	0.80	0.91
Zimbabwe	803.59	0.21	0.23	0.95
Peru	1292.36	0.12	0.11	1.01
Great Britain	11794.31	1.16	1.13	1.03
Australia	14313.95	0.77	0.71	1.08
Jordan	1288.78	0.71	0.65	1.10
Canada	17284.79	0.66	0.59	1.12
Venezuela	3166.58	0.15	0.12	1.21
India	385.43	0.34	0.28	1.24
Colombia	1432.39	0.18	0.13	1.34
Turkey	2258.77	0.19	0.14	1.35
Ireland	9014.40	0.36	0.26	1.36
Denmark	17022.55	0.48	0.34	1.40
Thailand	1502.88	0.82	0.57	1.44
Korea	3908.74	0.55	0.37	1.48
Netherlands	13954.71	1.12	0.69	1.63
Japan	15705.68	1.31	0.79	1.66
Ecuador	1322.40	0.17	0.10	1.68
Sri Lanka	537.67	0.27	0.16	1.69
Brazil	2346.36	0.32	0.19	1.70
New Zealand	9492.46	0.85	0.49	1.73
Kenya	440.62	0.29	0.16	1.80
Switzerland	19529.79	1.77	0.98	1.80
Nigeria	550.95	0.11	0.06	1.88
Argentina	4039.12	0.21	0.11	1.90
Mauritius	2124.69	0.54	0.27	2.04
Pakistan	435.90	0.36	0.16	2.17

Table 3.5
(continued)

Country name	GDP per capita	Domestic assets of deposit money banks/ GDP	Market capital- ization/ GDP	Domestic assets of deposit money banks/market capitalization
Barbados	4777.04	0.52	0.21	2.44
Costa Rica	1866.60	0.17	0.07	2.51
Indonesia	609.76	0.49	0.18	2.67
Norway	20134.81	0.69	0.26	2.69
Finland	15892.44	0.80	0.29	2.71
Israel	9259.58	0.92	0.33	2.76
Greece	6551.64	0.41	0.15	2.78
Trinidad and Tobago	3684.84	0.37	0.12	2.95
France	15232.41	1.02	0.33	3.11
Spain	7286.25	0.96	0.30	3.20
Belgium	14481.78	1.18	0.36	3.31
Cyprus	6588.45	0.81	0.22	3.73
Nepal	199.61	0.22	0.05	4.30
Italy	11504.72	0.74	0.17	4.45
Iceland	18939.92	0.49	0.11	4.50
Germany	16573.02	1.21	0.24	5.01
Honduras	751.32	0.25	0.05	5.22
Iran	2397.40	0.22	0.04	5.24
Tunisia	1534.16	0.55	0.10	5.79
Portugal	4822.10	0.79	0.13	5.84
Egypt	1042.35	0.63	0.10	6.10
Panama	1950.45	0.58	0.09	6.74
Bangladesh	194.31	0.31	0.04	7.76
Austria	13177.30	1.26	0.12	10.24

Tunisia, and Germany as bank-based. However, the *Bank vs. capitalization* measure also classifies Bangladesh, Egypt, and Iran as bank-based. Again, these are classified as bank-based primarily because their stock markets are small and underdeveloped, not because their banks are particularly well developed. Specifically, Bangladesh, Egypt, and Iran have banks that are smaller as a share of GDP than the sample mean. Thus, while the relative size measure provides useful information about the relative size of banks versus stock markets, it has obvious limitations. Notably, if a country has a large value of the *Bank vs. capitalization* measure, this does not necessarily indicate that it has a well-developed banking system relative to the banking systems of other countries. Similarly, if a country has a very low value of the *Bank vs. capitalization* measure, this does not necessarily indicate that it has a well-developed equity market relative to the equity markets of other countries.

We also examined banks relative to nonbank financial intermediaries. Specifically, we constructed a measure of the size of banks relative to the size of nonbanks called *Bank vs. other financial institutions*, which equals the domestic assets of deposit money banks divided by domestic assets of other financial intermediaries. We can see from figure 3.5 and table 3.6 that there is not a strong tendency for banks to grow or shrink relative to nonbanks when moving across income quartiles.

3.3.2 Activity

In higher income countries, domestic stock markets tend to become more active relative to domestic banks.

To measure financial structure based on activity, consider the ratio of private credit by deposit money banks relative to the total value of stock transactions on domestic exchanges, and call this ratio *Bank credit vs. trading*. The *Bank credit vs. trading* measure of financial structure will be larger in countries where banks are actively engaged in funneling credit to the private sector relative to the value of trading on domestic stock markets. Figure 3.6 shows that richer groups of countries tend to have lower values of the ratio *Bank credit vs. trading* measure of financial structure; countries tend to become more market-based as they grow richer. Similarly, stock markets also tend to become more active relative to nonbank financial intermediaries as indicated in the same figure.

Now, let's consider individual country rankings using the relative activity measure of banks versus markets. The relative activity measure of financial structure (*Bank credit vs. trading*) yields a somewhat different classification of countries than the relative size measure (*Bank vs. capitalization*). Table 3.7 ranks countries from lowest to highest based on the *Bank credit vs. trading* measure of financial structure. Values range from 0.7 to 196, though the extremely high values correspond to countries where there is virtually no trading on their stock exchanges. Consider the ten countries that have the least active banks relative their markets. These include the United States,

Table 3.6
Banks versus other Financial Institutions

Country name	GDP per capita	Domestic assets of deposit money banks/ GDP	Domestic assets of other financial institutions/ GDP	Domestic assets of deposit money banks/ domestic assets of other financial institutions
Sweden	18981.50	0.54	0.82	0.66
United States	19413.52	0.73	1.11	0.66
Ireland	9014.40	0.36	0.45	0.81
South Africa	2379.26	0.66	0.77	0.86
Korea	3908.74	0.55	0.60	0.92
Japan	15705.68	1.31	1.41	0.93
Colombia	1432.39	0.18	0.19	0.95
Netherlands	13954.71	1.12	0.96	1.16
Zimbabwe	803.59	0.21	0.15	1.41
Norway	20134.81	0.69	0.46	1.51
Greece	6551.64	0.41	0.27	1.54
Trinidad and Tobago	3684.84	0.37	0.20	1.87
Cyprus	6588.45	0.81	0.39	2.06
Kenya	440.62	0.29	0.13	2.15
Thailand	1502.88	0.82	0.34	2.42
Mexico	2951.55	0.24	0.10	2.46
Canada	17284.79	0.66	0.26	2.56
Malaysia	2629.22	0.82	0.31	2.60
Venezuela	3166.58	0.15	0.06	2.64
Australia	14313.95	0.77	0.27	2.81
Iran	2397.40	0.22	0.06	3.35
Chile	2725.16	0.46	0.13	3.56
Jamaica	1711.34	0.28	0.08	3.68
Nigeria	550.95	0.11	0.03	3.73
Switzerland	19529.79	1.77	0.44	3.98
Tunisia	1534.16	0.55	0.13	4.20
Ecuador	1322.40	0.17	0.04	4.24
Barbados	4777.04	0.52	0.11	4.67
Honduras	751.32	0.25	0.05	4.90
Brazil	2346.36	0.32	0.06	5.06
Singapore	11152.47	0.95	0.18	5.25
Philippines	734.06	0.37	0.06	6.65
New Zealand	9492.46	0.85	0.09	9.94
Jordan	1288.78	0.71	0.07	10.27

Table 3.6
(continued)

Country name	GDP per capita	Domestic assets of deposit money banks/ GDP	Domestic assets of other financial institu-tions/ GDP	Domestic assets of deposit money banks/ domestic assets of other financial institutions
Egypt	1042.35	0.63	0.06	11.42
Peru	1292.36	0.12	0.01	11.48
Turkey	2258.77	0.19	0.01	15.26
Spain	7286.25	0.96	0.06	16.47
Germany	16573.02	1.21	0.05	22.68
Austria	13177.30	1.26	0.05	23.35
Bolivia	754.98	0.37	0.02	24.31
Costa Rica	1866.60	0.17	0.01	29.54

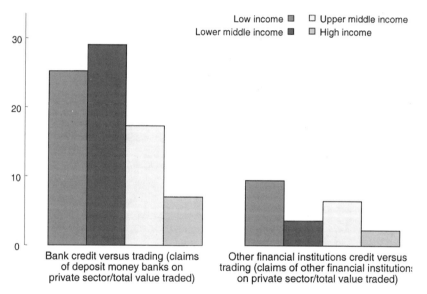

Figure 3.6
Activity of banks, stock markets and other financial institutions.

Table 3.7
Bank Credit versus Trading

Country name	GDP per capita	Claims of deposit money banks on private sector/ GDP	Total value traded/ GDP	Claims of deposit money banks on private sector/total value traded
Malaysia	2629.22	0.75	1.14	0.66
Turkey	2258.77	0.13	0.16	0.85
United States	19413.52	0.64	0.62	1.05
Singapore	11152.47	0.83	0.70	1.18
Korea	3908.74	0.53	0.44	1.21
Hong Kong	10537.98	1.42	1.08	1.32
Sweden	18981.50	0.46	0.33	1.38
Mexico	2951.55	0.22	0.13	1.71
Philippines	734.06	0.28	0.15	1.87
Brazil	2346.36	0.23	0.12	1.92
Canada	17284.79	0.57	0.29	1.93
Thailand	1502.88	0.78	0.40	1.96
Great Britain	11794.31	1.14	0.55	2.06
Ireland	9014.40	0.29	0.14	2.07
Australia	14313.95	0.70	0.33	2.10
Netherlands	13954.71	0.90	0.43	2.11
Switzerland	19529.79	1.65	0.76	2.18
Denmark	17022.55	0.38	0.16	2.40
Peru	1292.36	0.09	0.04	2.44
Spain	7286.25	0.69	0.23	2.98
Greece	6551.64	0.18	0.06	3.13
India	385.43	0.24	0.08	3.17
Israel	9259.58	0.60	0.19	3.20
Germany	16573.02	0.94	0.28	3.40
Venezuela	3166.58	0.12	0.03	3.52
Pakistan	435.90	0.23	0.06	3.78
Jamaica	1711.34	0.21	0.05	3.92
Norway	20134.81	0.57	0.14	4.01
Japan	15705.68	1.17	0.28	4.11
South Africa	2379.26	0.61	0.15	4.14
Argentina	4039.12	0.15	0.04	4.17
Jordan	1288.78	0.62	0.12	4.98
France	15232.41	0.89	0.17	5.21
Chile	2725.16	0.45	0.09	5.28
New Zealand	9492.46	0.78	0.14	5.44

Table 3.7
(continued)

Country name	GDP per capita	Claims of deposit money banks on private sector/ GDP	Total value traded/ GDP	Claims of deposit money banks on private sector/total value traded
Indonesia	609.76	0.46	0.08	5.99
Finland	15892.44	0.77	0.12	6.55
Italy	11504.72	0.52	0.08	6.90
Sri Lanka	537.67	0.21	0.02	9.80
Honduras	751.32	0.21	0.02	10.39
Belgium	14481.78	0.56	0.05	10.81
Zimbabwe	803.59	0.16	0.01	11.15
Portugal	4822.10	0.54	0.05	11.35
Colombia	1432.39	0.16	0.01	11.64
Austria	13177.30	0.93	0.08	11.91
Ecuador	1322.40	0.17	0.01	12.78
Egypt	1042.35	0.26	0.02	13.58
Trinidad and Tobago	3684.84	0.30	0.01	21.03
Iran	2397.40	0.20	0.01	27.07
Mauritius	2124.69	0.39	0.01	27.14
Cyprus	6588.45	0.69	0.02	28.39
Bangladesh	194.31	0.22	0.01	38.61
Kenya	440.62	0.21	0.00	42.55
Tunisia	1534.16	0.51	0.01	43.98
Iceland	18939.92	0.45	0.01	61.65
Nepal	199.61	0.16	0.00	67.27
Costa Rica	1866.60	0.15	0.00	98.50
Barbados	4777.04	0.35	0.00	103.40
Panama	1950.45	0.56	0.00	196.18

Sweden, Hong Kong, Singapore, and Malaysia, which were also classified as market-based by the size measure of financial structure (*Bank vs. capitalization*). The relative activity measure also classifies Korea as market-based. Korea has an active, though not very large, stock market and over the last fifteen years nonbanks have played an increasingly large role, so that deposit money bank credit to the private sector is not a large share of GDP. The relative activity measure, *Bank credit vs. trading*, also classifies Turkey, Mexico, and Brazil as market-based. This occurs because banks are very inactive and underdeveloped in these countries, not because they have active stock markets. Indeed, *Trading* in these countries is less than the sample average. Also, note that Chile and South Africa no longer enter as market-based. These two countries have large but relatively inactive stock exchanges.

The *Bank credit vs. trading* measure of financial structure faces even greater problems in identifying bank-based financial systems because a large number of countries have very inactive stock markets, which boosts the *Bank credit vs. trading* measure as shown in table 3.7.[5] To mitigate this problem, consider only countries where bank credit to the private sector relative to GDP is greater than the sample mean. Then, the relative activity measure of financial structure identifies Panama, Tunisia, Cyprus, Austria, Portugal, Cyprus, Belgium, Italy, and Finland as bank-based, which is consistent with our expectations. Thus, while the relative activity measure provides useful information about the relative activity of banks versus stock markets, it also has specific limitations. As with the relative size measure, if a country has a large value of the *Bank credit vs. trading* measure, this does not necessarily indicate that it has a very active banking system relative to the banking systems of other countries.

We also compared stock markets with nonbank financial intermediaries. Specifically, we constructed a measure of the activity of stock markets relative to nonbank financial intermediaries. The activity of nonbanks relative to the activity of the stock market is called *Other financial institutions vs. trading*, which equals private credit of nonbanks divided by the value of stock transactions. We see from figure 3.6 and table 3.8 that nonbanks tend to shrink relative to stock market activity when moving to higher income quartiles.

3.3.3 Efficiency

In higher-income countries, domestic stock markets tend to become more efficient relative to domestic banks.

To measure financial structure based on efficiency, we focus on two measures of market- versus bank-based financial structures. For markets, we concentrate on the value of stock market transaction relative to the size of the economy (*Total value as share of GDP*). We do not use the *Turnover* ratio to avoid classifying countries with active, but small, markets as market-based. To classify a country as market-based, we want them to have a large and an active stock

Table 3.8
Other Financial Institutions versus Trading

Country name	GDP per capita	Claims of other financial institutions on private sector/ GDP	Total value traded/ GDP	Claims of other financial institutions on private sector/total value traded
Turkey	2258.77	0.01	0.16	0.06
Germany	16573.02	0.05	0.28	0.18
Peru	1292.36	0.01	0.04	0.23
Singapore	11152.47	0.17	0.70	0.24
Malaysia	2629.22	0.28	1.14	0.25
Spain	7286.25	0.06	0.23	0.25
Mexico	2951.55	0.03	0.13	0.26
New Zealand	9492.46	0.04	0.14	0.29
Philippines	734.06	0.05	0.15	0.33
Brazil	2346.36	0.05	0.12	0.39
Switzerland	19529.79	0.39	0.76	0.51
Jordan	1288.78	0.07	0.12	0.56
Thailand	1502.88	0.30	0.40	0.75
Australia	14313.95	0.27	0.33	0.81
Canada	17284.79	0.24	0.29	0.83
Jamaica	1711.34	0.07	0.05	1.26
Netherlands	13954.71	0.55	0.43	1.28
Korea	3908.74	0.59	0.44	1.33
Chile	2725.16	0.12	0.09	1.46
United States	19413.52	0.91	0.62	1.49
Venezuela	3166.58	0.05	0.03	1.50
Sweden	18981.50	0.73	0.33	2.18
Honduras	751.32	0.04	0.02	2.20
Egypt	1042.35	0.04	0.02	2.22
Greece	6551.64	0.14	0.06	2.35
Norway	20134.81	0.34	0.14	2.40
Ireland	9014.40	0.37	0.14	2.63
Japan	15705.68	0.85	0.28	2.98
Ecuador	1322.40	0.04	0.01	3.09
South Africa	2379.26	0.51	0.15	3.42
Costa Rica	1866.60	0.01	0.00	3.62
Zimbabwe	803.59	0.08	0.01	5.80
Iran	2397.40	0.06	0.01	8.69
Tunisia	1534.16	0.13	0.01	11.27

Table 3.8
(continued)

Country name	GDP per capita	Claims of other financial institutions on private sector/ GDP	Total value traded/ GDP	Claims of other financial institutions on private sector/total value traded
Colombia	1432.39	0.15	0.01	11.38
Trinidad and Tobago	3684.84	0.17	0.01	12.00
Cyprus	6588.45	0.39	0.02	16.22
Kenya	440.62	0.10	0.00	20.35
Barbados	4777.04	0.11	0.00	32.44

market relative to their banking system. For banks, we use two measures: *Overhead costs* and *Bank net interest margin*. Thus, we focus on two measures of financial structure based on efficiency: (1) *Trading vs. overhead costs*, which equals *Total value traded/GDP* multiplied by *Overhead costs*; and (2) *Trading vs. interest margin*, which equals *Total value traded/GDP* multiplied by *Bank net interest margin*.

Figure 3.7 shows that richer countries tend to have higher levels *Trading vs. overhead costs* and *Trading vs. interest margin*. According to these relative efficiency measures of financial structure, countries tend to become more market-based as they grow richer.

Turning to specific countries, the *Trading vs. interest margin* and the *Trading vs. overhead costs* measures of financial structure identify nine countries that (1) have very high values, which signifies market-based economies and (2) have *Total value traded/GDP* values greater than the sample mean (tables 3.9 and 3.10). Thus, Malaysia, Hong Kong, the United States, Singapore, Great Britain, Switzerland, Sweden, Thailand, and Korea have active stock markets relative to their banks and relative to world markets. While the *Trading vs. interest margin* and the *Trading vs. overhead cost* measures of financial structure also classify Brazil and Turkey market-based, these markets are not very active. Specifically, *Total value traded/GDP* in Brazil and Turkey are below the sample mean.

In terms of classifying countries as bank-based, we again run into the problem that many countries have very inactive markets. Thus, the *Trading vs. interest margin* and the *Trading vs. overhead cost* measures of financial structure classify these countries as bank-based

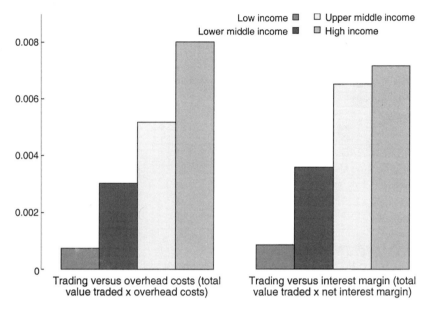

Figure 3.7
Efficiency of stock markets versus banks.

even when their banking system are not well developed. Thus, to identify bank-based countries we again use two-step criteria. If (1) both *Trading vs. interest margin* and the *Trading vs. overhead cost* measures of financial structure have low values, which signifies bank-based economies and (2) the country has a *Private credit of deposit money banks/GDP* value of grater than the sample mean, we consider the country bank-based. These criteria identify Panama, Tunisia, Cyprus, Portugal, Belgium, Austria, Italy, Jordan, Norway, and Japan as bank-based financial systems.

3.3.4 Conglomerate Indexes of Financial Structure

In higher income countries, financial systems tend to be more market-based.

This subsection constructs a conglomerate index of financial structure based on measures of size, activity, and efficiency. Since (1) measures of relative size, activity, and efficiency place countries into slightly different places along market-based versus bank-based spectrum and (2) there is little reason to favor one particular measure of

Table 3.9
Trading versus Overhead Costs

Country name	GDP per capita	Total value traded	Over-head costs	Total value traded × overhead costs
Panama	1950.45	0.00	0.02	0.00
Nepal	199.61	0.00	0.02	0.00
Costa Rica	1866.60	0.00	0.06	0.00
Bangladesh	194.31	0.01	0.02	0.00
Barbados	4777.04	0.00	0.05	0.00
Kenya	440.62	0.00	0.04	0.00
Tunisia	1534.16	0.01	0.02	0.00
Ghana	553.23	0.00	0.06	0.00
Mauritius	2124.69	0.01	0.02	0.00
Egypt	1042.35	0.02	0.02	0.00
Trinidad and Tobago	3684.84	0.01	0.04	0.00
Zimbabwe	803.59	0.01	0.05	0.00
Honduras	751.32	0.02	0.04	0.00
Ireland	9014.40	0.14	0.01	0.00
Ecuador	1322.40	0.01	0.08	0.00
Sri Lanka	537.67	0.02	0.05	0.00
Cyprus	6588.45	0.02	0.04	0.00
Colombia	1432.39	0.01	0.08	0.00
Portugal	4822.10	0.05	0.02	0.00
Belgium	14481.78	0.05	0.03	0.00
Pakistan	435.90	0.06	0.03	0.00
Finland	15892.44	0.12	0.02	0.00
India	385.43	0.08	0.03	0.00
Austria	13177.30	0.08	0.03	0.00
Indonesia	609.76	0.08	0.03	0.00
Venezuela	3166.58	0.03	0.07	0.00
Greece	6551.64	0.06	0.04	0.00
Chile	2725.16	0.09	0.03	0.00
Italy	11504.72	0.08	0.04	0.00
Jordan	1288.78	0.12	0.03	0.00
Norway	20134.81	0.14	0.02	0.00
New Zealand	9492.46	0.14	0.03	0.00
Argentina	4039.12	0.04	0.10	0.00
Peru	1292.36	0.04	0.10	0.00
Japan	15705.68	0.28	0.01	0.00
Jamaica	1711.34	0.05	0.08	0.00

Table 3.9
(continued)

Country name	GDP per capita	Total value traded	Over-head costs	Total value traded × overhead costs
Netherlands	13954.71	0.43	0.01	0.00
South Africa	2379.26	0.15	0.04	0.01
Denmark	17022.55	0.16	0.04	0.01
Mexico	2951.55	0.13	0.05	0.01
Canada	17284.79	0.29	0.02	0.01
Israel	9259.58	0.19	0.04	0.01
Philippines	734.06	0.15	0.05	0.01
France	15232.41	0.17	0.04	0.01
Germany	16573.02	0.28	0.03	0.01
Spain	7286.25	0.23	0.03	0.01
Thailand	1502.88	0.40	0.02	0.01
Australia	14313.95	0.33	0.03	0.01
Sweden	18981.50	0.33	0.03	0.01
Singapore	11152.47	0.70	0.01	0.01
Turkey	2258.77	0.16	0.06	0.01
Korea	3908.74	0.44	0.02	0.01
Brazil	2346.36	0.12	0.11	0.01
Great Britain	11794.31	0.55	0.03	0.01
Malaysia	2629.22	1.14	0.02	0.02
United States	19413.52	0.62	0.04	0.02
Hong Kong	10537.98	1.08	0.02	0.03
Switzerland	19529.79	0.76	0.05	0.04

financial structure over another, this subsection merges three different measures to produce a conglomerate index of financial structure.

Specifically, after removing the means of each series, we take the average of *Capitalization vs. bank*, *Trading vs. bank credit*, and *Trading vs. overhead cost* and call the result *Structure*. Higher values of *Structure* signify a higher degree of stock market development relative to the development of the banking system. We also conducted the analysis using the means-removed average of *Capitalization vs. bank*, *Trading vs. bank credit*, and *Turnover vs. overhead cost* and obtained virtually identical rankings and results.

Figure 3.8 shows that richer countries tend to have higher levels of stock market development relative to the development of their

Table 3.10
Trading versus Interest Margin

Country name	GDP per capita	Total value traded	Net interest margin	Total value traded × net interest margin
Bangladesh	194.31	0.01	0.01	0.00
Panama	1950.45	0.00	0.02	0.00
Costa Rica	1866.60	0.00	0.05	0.00
Nepal	199.61	0.00	0.04	0.00
Barbados	4777.04	0.00	0.03	0.00
Tunisia	1534.16	0.01	0.02	0.00
Egypt	1042.35	0.02	0.01	0.00
Ghana	553.23	0.00	0.08	0.00
Kenya	440.62	0.00	0.07	0.00
Mauritius	2124.69	0.01	0.03	0.00
Trinidad and Tobago	3684.84	0.01	0.04	0.00
Zimbabwe	803.59	0.01	0.05	0.00
Colombia	1432.39	0.01	0.06	0.00
Ecuador	1322.40	0.01	0.07	0.00
Sri Lanka	537.67	0.02	0.05	0.00
Belgium	14481.78	0.05	0.02	0.00
Honduras	751.32	0.02	0.07	0.00
Portugal	4822.10	0.05	0.03	0.00
Austria	13177.30	0.08	0.02	0.00
Cyprus	6588.45	0.02	0.06	0.00
Pakistan	435.90	0.06	0.03	0.00
Finland	15892.44	0.12	0.02	0.00
Greece	6551.64	0.06	0.03	0.00
Ireland	9014.40	0.14	0.01	0.00
India	385.43	0.08	0.03	0.00
Italy	11504.72	0.08	0.03	0.00
Argentina	4039.12	0.04	0.07	0.00
Jordan	1288.78	0.12	0.02	0.00
Venezuela	3166.58	0.03	0.09	0.00
Peru	1292.36	0.04	0.08	0.00
Indonesia	609.76	0.08	0.04	0.00
New Zealand	9492.46	0.14	0.02	0.00
Chile	2725.16	0.09	0.04	0.00
Norway	20134.81	0.14	0.03	0.00
Canada	17284.79	0.29	0.02	0.01
Japan	15705.68	0.28	0.02	0.01
Jamaica	1711.34	0.05	0.10	0.01

Table 3.10
(continued)

Country name	GDP per capita	Total value traded	Net interest margin	Total value traded × net interest margin
Philippines	734.06	0.15	0.04	0.01
France	15232.41	0.17	0.03	0.01
Israel	9259.58	0.19	0.03	0.01
Mexico	2951.55	0.13	0.05	0.01
South Africa	2379.26	0.15	0.04	0.01
Netherlands	13954.71	0.43	0.01	0.01
Australia	14313.95	0.33	0.02	0.01
Germany	16573.02	0.28	0.02	0.01
Denmark	17022.55	0.16	0.05	0.01
Spain	7286.25	0.23	0.04	0.01
Sweden	18981.50	0.33	0.03	0.01
Korea	3908.74	0.44	0.02	0.01
Great Britain	11794.31	0.55	0.02	0.01
Thailand	1502.88	0.40	0.03	0.01
Switzerland	19529.79	0.76	0.02	0.01
Brazil	2346.36	0.12	0.11	0.01
Turkey	2258.77	0.16	0.10	0.02
Singapore	11152.47	0.70	0.02	0.02
United States	19413.52	0.62	0.04	0.02
Hong Kong	10537.98	1.08	0.02	0.03
Malaysia	2629.22	1.14	0.03	0.03

banking systems. The correlation between *Structure* and real per capita GDP is .29 and is significant at the 0.05 level.

Even with this conglomerate index, however, we observe some problems with classifying countries as market-based or bank-based (table 3.11). For example, *Structure* classifies Turkey as market-based since the value of *Structure* for Turkey is in the top ten countries. Yet, Turkey has below-average measure of stock market development, as measured by the *Total valued traded/GDP* ratio. As we saw above, some countries are classified as market-based because they have poorly developed banks. The same is true at the other end of the spectrum. *Structure* classifies Bangladesh, Nepal, Costa Rica, and Honduras as bank-based because the value of *Structure* for these countries is in the bottom ten of the sample. Yet, each of these

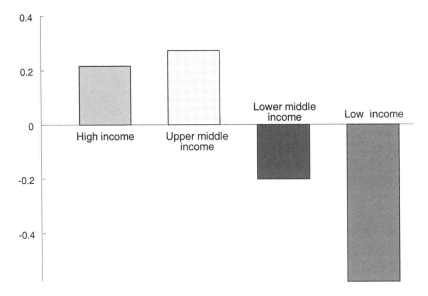

Figure 3.8
Financial structure index.

countries has below average values of most of the banking sector development indicators. There may be potential advantages to considering a country as bank-based only if it has well-developed banks relative to other countries *and* if its banks are well developed relative to its markets.

3.3.5 *Financial Structure in Developed versus Underdeveloped Financial Systems*

Measures of financial structure produce intuitively plausible classifications of countries as either bank-based or market-based for both financially developed and underdeveloped economies.

Here we create four categories of countries based on the structure and level of development of their financial systems: (1) underdeveloped and bank-based, (2) underdeveloped and market-based, (3) developed and bank-based, and (4) developed and market-based. We do not use a simple bank-based, market-based classification since we want to avoid classifying two countries in the same bank-based category if one has poorly developed banks by international standards. Similarly, we want to avoid classifying countries in a single market-based category when some have poorly developed markets

Table 3.11
Financial Structure across Countries

Country name	GDP per capita	Structure index	Market capital- ization/ assets of deposit money banks	Trading versus banks	Trading versus overhead costs
Panama	1950.45	−0.92	0.15	0.01	0.00
Bangladesh	194.31	−0.90	0.13	0.03	0.00
Tunisia	1534.16	−0.88	0.17	0.02	0.00
Nepal	199.61	−0.87	0.23	0.01	0.00
Egypt	1042.35	−0.82	0.16	0.07	0.00
Costa Rica	1866.60	−0.79	0.40	0.01	0.00
Barbados	4777.04	−0.78	0.41	0.01	0.00
Cyprus	6588.45	−0.77	0.27	0.04	0.00
Honduras	751.32	−0.75	0.19	0.10	0.00
Portugal	4822.10	−0.75	0.17	0.09	0.00
Trinidad and Tobago	3684.84	−0.74	0.34	0.05	0.00
Austria	13177.30	−0.73	0.10	0.08	0.00
Mauritius	2124.69	−0.70	0.49	0.04	0.00
Kenya	440.62	−0.69	0.56	0.02	0.00
Belgium	14481.78	−0.66	0.30	0.09	0.00
Italy	11504.72	−0.57	0.22	0.15	0.00
Ecuador	1322.40	−0.56	0.60	0.08	0.00
Sri Lanka	537.67	−0.54	0.59	0.10	0.00
Finland	15892.44	−0.53	0.37	0.15	0.00
Indonesia	609.76	−0.50	0.37	0.17	0.00
Colombia	1432.39	−0.47	0.75	0.09	0.00
Pakistan	435.90	−0.38	0.46	0.26	0.00
Zimbabwe	803.59	−0.34	1.06	0.09	0.00
Greece	6551.64	−0.34	0.36	0.32	0.00
Norway	20134.81	−0.33	0.37	0.25	0.00
New Zealand	9492.46	−0.29	0.58	0.18	0.00
Argentina	4039.12	−0.25	0.53	0.24	0.00
Japan	15705.68	−0.19	0.60	0.24	0.00
France	15232.41	−0.17	0.32	0.19	0.01
Venezuela	3166.58	−0.15	0.83	0.28	0.00
India	385.43	−0.14	0.81	0.32	0.00
Jordan	1288.78	−0.14	0.91	0.20	0.00
Germany	16573.02	−0.10	0.20	0.29	0.01
Israel	9259.58	−0.06	0.36	0.31	0.01
Ireland	9014.40	−0.06	0.73	0.48	0.00

Table 3.11
(continued)

Country name	GDP per capita	Structure index	Market capital-ization/ assets of deposit money banks	Trading versus banks	Trading versus overhead costs
Spain	7286.25	0.02	0.31	0.34	0.01
Netherlands	13954.71	0.11	0.61	0.47	0.00
Denmark	17022.55	0.15	0.72	0.42	0.01
Peru	1292.36	0.16	0.99	0.41	0.00
Chile	2725.16	0.25	1.80	0.19	0.00
Jamaica	1711.34	0.28	1.49	0.26	0.00
Thailand	1502.88	0.39	0.69	0.51	0.01
Canada	17284.79	0.41	0.90	0.52	0.01
Australia	14313.95	0.50	0.93	0.48	0.01
Brazil	2346.36	0.65	0.59	0.52	0.01
Mexico	2951.55	0.68	1.32	0.58	0.01
Philippines	734.06	0.71	1.40	0.54	0.01
South Africa	2379.26	0.83	2.50	0.24	0.01
Korea	3908.74	0.89	0.68	0.82	0.01
Sweden	18981.50	0.91	1.16	0.72	0.01
Great Britain	11794.31	0.92	0.97	0.48	0.01
Singapore	11152.47	1.18	1.43	0.85	0.01
Turkey	2258.77	1.23	0.74	1.18	0.01
United States	19413.52	1.96	1.09	0.96	0.02
Switzerland	19529.79	2.03	0.55	0.46	0.04
Hong Kong	10537.98	2.10	1.32	0.76	0.03
Malaysia	2629.22	2.93	2.47	1.52	0.02

by international standards. Therefore, we distinguish countries that have underdeveloped financial systems from those that have developed systems. We define a country as having an underdeveloped financial system if both of the following hold: (1) *Claims of deposit money banks on the private sector/GDP* is less than the sample mean, and (2) *Total value traded as a share of GDP* is less than the sample mean, as reported at the foot of table 3.1. Thus, we only classify a country's financial system as underdeveloped if it has poorly developed banks and markets.

Market-based versus bank-based split is determined by the *Structure* index. Using the *Structure* measure of financial structure, table

3.11 ranks countries along the spectrum from bank-based to market-based, where higher values of *Structure* indicate higher levels of stock market development relative to banking-sector development. Countries that have above the mean values of *Structure* are then classified as market-based. Countries that have below the mean values of *Structure* are classified as bank-based.

Table 3.12 lists the four categories of countries. As shown, this simple classification system produces intuitively appealing results. For instance, developed economies such as Austria, Belgium, France, Germany, Italy, Japan, Portugal, and Spain are classified as bank-based. Three developing countries are also classified as financially developed and bank-based: Panama, Tunisia, and Jordan. This classification system also identifies economies with large, active stock markets. For example, Great Britain, Hong Kong, Malaysia, Singapore, United States, and Switzerland are each identified as having market-based financial systems. Interestingly, Korea, which many authors consider to be dominated by large banks (Park 1993), is also identified as having a market-based financial system. Korea is classified as market-based because it has a very active, efficient equity market, as reflected in high *Turnover* and *Total valued traded/GDP* ratios (table 3.1). Moreover, nonbanks play a substantial role in Korea. Indeed, nonbanks issue more credit to the private sector than banks in Korea. Thus, while intermediaries play a relatively large role in Korea, nonbanks share center stage with banks (table 3.1).

Looking at financially underdeveloped economies, we see that they are disproportionately bank-based as expected, since financial structures become more market-based as countries develop. The classification of countries like Chile, Mexico, Turkey, and the Philippines as market-based reflects the significant development of their stock markets since the second half of the 1980s. Other countries like Bangladesh, Nepal, Kenya, and Costa Rica remain bank-based since their stock markets are not yet developed. Yet other countries like India, Indonesia, and Pakistan have seen some development of their stock markets, but are classified as bank-based because their banks still play a more important role in their financial systems.[6]

3.4   The Legal, Regulatory, Tax, and Macroeconomic Determinants of Financial Structure

A rich literature examines how features of the legal, regulatory, tax, and macroeconomic environment influence financial contracting and

Table 3.12
Country Classification of Financial Structure

Financially underdeveloped economies		Financially developed economies	
Country name	Structure index	Country name	Structure index
Bank-based economies		*Bank-based economies*	
Bangladesh	−0.90	Panama	−0.92
Nepal	−0.87	Tunisia	−0.88
Egypt	−0.82	Cyprus	−0.77
Costa Rica	−0.79	Portugal	−0.75
Barbados	−0.78	Austria	−0.73
Honduras	−0.75	Belgium	−0.66
Trinidad and Tobago	−0.74	Italy	−0.57
Mauritius	−0.70	Finland	−0.53
Kenya	−0.69	Norway	−0.33
Ecuador	−0.56	New Zealand	−0.29
Sri Lanka	−0.54	Japan	−0.19
Indonesia	−0.50	France	−0.17
Colombia	−0.47	Jordan	−0.14
Pakistan	−0.38	Germany	−0.10
Zimbabwe	−0.34	Israel	−0.06
Greece	−0.34	Spain	0.02
Argentina	−0.25	Group-mean	−0.44
Venezuela	−0.15	*Market-based economies*	
India	−0.14	Netherlands	0.11
Ireland	−0.06	Thailand	0.39
Group-mean	−0.54	Canada	0.41
Market-based economies		Australia	0.50
Denmark	0.15	South Africa	0.83
Peru	0.16	Korea	0.89
Chile	0.25	Sweden	0.91
Jamaica	0.28	Great Britain	0.92
Brazil	0.65	Singapore	1.18
Mexico	0.68	United States	1.96
Philippines	0.71	Switzerland	2.03
Turkey	1.23	Hong Kong	2.10
Group-mean	0.52	Malaysia	2.93
Financially underdeveloped		Group-mean	1.17
countries	−0.24	*Financially developed*	
Overall mean	0.03	*countries*	0.28

the functioning of intermediaries and markets. This chapter collects cross-country information on many of the legal, regulatory, tax, and macroeconomic determinants of financial development proposed by the literature. We then examine whether countries with different financial structures have different legal, regulatory, tax, and macroeconomic characteristics. We find the most significant differences in means exist between underdeveloped (regardless of bank-based or market-based), developed bank-based, and developed market-based financial systems. For brevity, we name these categories underdeveloped, bank-based, and market-based, respectively. We also examine the correlations between these potential determinants and the three categories and the financial structure index. Finally, we use simple regressions that control for the level of real per capita GDP to assess the relationship between the legal, regulatory, tax, and macroeconomic variables, and measures of financial structure. Caution, however, should be exercised in interpreting the results. We use the word *determinant* because theory and past work suggests that these variables exert a causal influence on the functioning of the financial system. We do not, however, provide any statistical evidence on causation. We simply present summary statistics.

3.4.1   The Legal Environment

La Porta et al. (1998) explain how countries with different legal origins develop distinct laws governing debt and equity contracts. Specifically, legal scholars have identified four major legal families: English Common Law, French Civil Law, German Civil Law, and Scandinavian Civil Law. Legal systems spread primarily through conquest and colonization. These legal families treat equity and debt contracting differently. The consequent differences in the contracting environment have had profound implications on the evolution of intermediaries and securities markets as demonstrated by La Porta et al. (1997, 1998), Levine (1998, 1999, forthcoming), Levine, Loayza, and Beck (2000), and Demirgüç-Kunt and Maksimovic (1998, 1999). Here, we use La Porta et al. measures of the legal environment.

Legal Origin
Common Law countries are more likely to have market-based financial systems than countries with other legal origins. Underdeveloped financial systems are more likely to have French Civil Law legal systems than other legal origins.

In terms of legal origin, La Porta et al. focus on the difference between countries that have common law origins and countries with a French Civil Law tradition. La Porta et al. show that Common Law countries tend to stress the rights of minority shareholders with beneficial implications for securities market development (La Porta et al. 1997). In contrast, countries with a French legal tradition do not emphasize the rights of minority shareholders with adverse effects on the functioning of equity markets (Levine forthcoming). In terms of debt contracts, legal systems that stress creditor rights tend to generate beneficial repercussions for financial intermediary development (Levine 1998, 1999; Levine, Loayza, and Beck 2000). The few countries with German legal foundations tend to stress the rights of creditors to a much greater degree than other countries (La Porta et al. 1998). La Porta et al. (1998) also show that countries with a French legal tradition tend to have comparatively inefficient contract enforcement and higher levels of corruption with negative repercussions for financial-sector performance.

We first examine the relationship between legal origin and the structure of the financial system. To do this, we create the dummy variable English that takes on the value of 1 if the country has a Common Law legal tradition. We also create the dummy variable French, which equals 1 if the country has French civil law origins. We do not focus on German Civil Law and Scandinavian civil law countries because there are relatively few and because the main distinctions are between the Common Law and French Civil Law countries (La Porta et al. 1998). Table 3.13 divides countries into those with underdeveloped, bank-based, and market-based financial systems. It then presents the average values of the legal, regulatory, tax, and macroeconomic determinants and tests whether there are significant differences in the means of these determinants across the different financial structures.[7] Table 3.14 presents simple correlations. Underdeveloped, Bank, and Market in table 3.14 are simple dummy variables taking the value 1 if a country is classified as an underdeveloped, bank-based, or market-based economy, respectively. Structure is the structure index reported in table 3.11. Finally, table 3.14 also presents evidence on the partial correlation between the financial structure variables and the determinants after controlling for the level of GDP per capita.

Countries with market-based financial systems are much more likely to have Common Law origins than underdeveloped or bank-based systems. Similarly, Common Law countries tend to have

Table 3.13
Determinants of Financial Structure: Means Tests

	English	French	SRIGHTS	CRIGHTS	Enforce	Corrupt	Account	RESTRICT	Deposit insurance	Dividend disadvantage	Capital gain disadvantage	Inflation
Underdeveloped	0.38	0.56	2.86	2.29	5.49	4.60	49.53	2.50	0.61	0.23	0.19	25.23
Bank-based	0.19	0.50	2.54	2.08	8.68	7.37	63.17	1.90	0.83	0.18	0.14	3.91
Market-based	0.69	0.08	3.69	2.54	8.54	8.44	71.69	1.96	0.54	0.16	0.09	4.31
Means-test (t-statistics)												
Underdeveloped versus bank	0.19 (0.175)	0.06 (0.704)	0.33 (0.464)	0.20 (0.702)	-3.18 (0.001)	-2.77 (0.001)	-13.63 (0.005)	0.61 (0.013)	-0.22 (0.174)	0.05 (0.451)	0.05 (0.565)	21.32 (0.037)
Underdeveloped versus market	-0.31 (0.059)	0.48 (0.002)	-0.83 (0.061)	-0.25 (0.635)	-3.04 (0.001)	-3.84 (0.001)	-22.16 (0.001)	0.54 (0.017)	0.07 (0.656)	0.07 (0.249)	0.10 (0.252)	20.92 (0.064)
Bank versus market	-0.50 (0.005)	0.42 (0.013)	-1.15 (0.040)	-0.46 (0.346)	0.14 (0.809)	-1.07 (0.195)	-8.53 (0.021)	-0.07 (0.769)	0.29 (0.124)	0.02 (0.768)	0.05 (0.619)	-0.40 (0.690)

Note: p-values are given in parentheses.

Table 3.14
Determinants of Financial Structure: Correlations

Variable		English	French	SRIGHTS	CRIGHTS	Enforce	Corrupt	Account	RESTRICT	Deposit insurance	Dividend disadvantage	Capital gain disadvantage	Inflation
Under-developed	correlation coefficient	-0.032 (0.803) 63	0.249 (0.049) 63	-0.096 (0.516) 48	-0.013 (0.934) 46	-0.728 (0.001) 48	-0.626 (0.001) 59	-0.654 (0.001) 40	0.442 (0.002) 45	-0.070 (0.610) 56	0.178 (0.235) 46	0.162 (0.283) 46	0.346 (0.005) 63
	regression coefficient	-0.165 (0.107) 63	0.142 (0.158) 63	-0.032 (0.433) 48	-0.095 (0.014) 46	-0.135 (0.032) 48	-0.055 (0.133) 59	-0.014 (0.003) 40	0.171 (0.051) 45	0.197 (0.077) 56	0.028 (0.928) 46	0.147 (0.498) 46	0.004 (0.027) 63
Bank	correlation coefficient	-0.250 (0.048) 63	0.065 (0.611) 63	-0.215 (0.142) 48	-0.096 (0.525) 46	0.429 (0.002) 48	0.275 (0.035) 59	0.115 (0.482) 40	-0.270 (0.072) 45	0.208 (0.125) 56	-0.062 (0.682) 46	-0.028 (0.854) 46	-0.222 (0.080) 63
	regression coefficient	-0.161 (0.133) 63	0.120 (0.256) 63	-0.076 (0.095) 48	0.018 (0.694) 46	0.044 (0.541) 48	-0.029 (0.463) 59	-0.006 (0.294) 40	-0.084 (0.402) 45	0.057 (0.619) 56	0.129 (0.706) 46	0.057 (0.813) 46	-0.002 (0.226) 63
Market	correlation coefficient	0.308 (0.014) 63	-0.377 (0.002) 63	0.323 (0.025) 48	0.108 (0.476) 46	0.388 (0.006) 48	0.460 (0.001) 59	0.564 (0.001) 40	-0.221 (0.145) 45	-0.120 (0.379) 56	-0.137 (0.364) 46	-0.152 (0.315) 46	-0.187 (0.141) 63
	regression coefficient	0.326 (0.001) 63	-0.263 (0.007) 63	0.108 (0.020) 48	0.077 (0.118) 46	0.091 (0.224) 48	0.084 (0.021) 59	0.021 (0.001) 40	-0.088 (0.424) 45	-0.253 (0.031) 56	-0.156 (0.677) 46	-0.204 (0.443) 46	-0.002 (0.349) 63
Structure index	correlation coefficient	0.184 (0.170) 57	-0.260 (0.051) 57	0.310 (0.036) 46	-0.004 (0.979) 44	0.182 (0.227) 46	0.375 (0.005) 54	0.460 (0.004) 38	-0.158 (0.312) 43	-0.054 (0.712) 50	-0.157 (0.308) 44	-0.230 (0.133) 44	0.091 (0.501) 57
	regression coefficient	0.418 (0.060) 57	-0.354 (0.111) 57	0.195 (0.035) 46	0.037 (0.709) 44	-0.053 (0.722) 46	0.144 (0.080) 54	0.044 (0.001) 38	-0.148 (0.507) 43	-0.338 (0.204) 50	-0.581 (0.434) 44	-0.707 (0.177) 44	0.004 (0.230) 57

Note: Regressions include the log of per capita income p-values in parentheses, number of observations.

market-based financial systems even after controlling for the level of GDP per capita. Underdeveloped and bank-based financial systems are more likely to have French legal origins than market-based systems and there is a positive correlation between French Civil Law countries and underdeveloped financial systems.

Legal Codes

Countries with legal codes that rigorously protect the rights of minority shareholders tend to have market-based financial systems. Countries with legal codes that stress the rights of creditors and shareholders are much less likely to have underdeveloped financial systems.

We now examine the relationship between particular legal codes and financial structure. Here we use two variables. SRIGHTS is La Porta et al.'s (1998) index of the degree to which the legal codes of the country protect monetary shareholder rights.[8] La Porta et al. (1998) note that to the extent that a country's laws help potential shareholders feel confident about their property and voting rights, this should be reflected in larger, more active, and hence more efficient equity markets. La Porta et al. (1997) and Levine (forthcoming) confirm this hypothesis. The second variable, CRIGHTS is an index of the degree to which the legal codes of the country protect purchasers of debt contracts, which is also based on the La Porta et al. (1998) database.[9] If the legal environment makes banks confident about their claims, this should encourage the development of an active banking sector.

Market-based economies tend to have much stronger shareholder rights than either bank-based or underdeveloped financial systems (table 3.13). Table 3.14 also shows that there is a significant positive correlation between market-based systems and the strength of shareholder rights protection even after controlling for the level of GDP per capita. In terms of creditor rights, however, there is little difference between bank-based and market-based financial systems. Note, however, that countries with legal systems that stress the rights of creditors tend not to have underdeveloped financial system after controlling for differences in GDP per capita.

Enforcement

Poor contract enforcement goes hand-in-hand with underdeveloped financial systems, contract enforcement is not strongly linked with whether a country's financial system is bank-based or market-based.

Laws are important, but the enforcement of those laws is frequently more important for financial development (La Porta et al. 1998). We use an index of contract enforcement that measures whether the country's laws are efficiently and impartially enforced and whether governments tend to change the nature of contracts ex post.[10] Higher values of ENFORCE indicate greater efficiency in enforcing contracts. Improved contract enforcement lowers transactions costs and should facilitate equity and debt contracting (La Porta et al. 1997, 1998; Levine 1999, forthcoming). There are not good a priori reasons to believe that efficient contract enforcement will favor debt or equity contracting relative to the other.

Countries with underdeveloped financial systems are more likely to have low levels of contract enforcement (table 3.13). There is little difference between bank-based and market-based financial systems in terms of contract enforcement. The strong negative connection between the efficiency of contract enforcement and the degree of overall financial sector development holds even after controlling for differences in income per capita (table 3.14).

Corruption

A strong positive link exists between corruption and financial underdevelopment. Countries with lower levels of corruption tend to have more market-based financial systems.

Corruption, if it exists, can severely undermine enforcement of legal codes. We use an index of corruption, CORRUPT, which measures corruption in government (La Porta et al. 1997). Lower scores indicate that government officials are likely to demand special payments in the form of bribes throughout all levels of government.

Countries with underdeveloped financial systems are much more likely to have high levels of corruption in government (table 3.13). To the extent that corruption reflects poor enforcement of legal codes, countries with poorly operating legal systems tend to have less well-developed financial systems.

Corruption tends to hurt development of markets disproportionately since well-enforced shareholder rights are essential for market-based financial systems. Indeed, lower levels of corruption are correlated with more market-based financial structures (table 3.14).

3.4.2 Regulatory Environment

Government regulations and guidelines materially affect the functioning of the financial sector. Through listing requirements, regulations, policies, and tax laws, governments influence accounting practices, permissible practices of banks, and deposit insurance. Each of these strategies may affect the operation of banks and markets. We now empirically examine accounting standards and bank regulations.

Accounting
Countries with strong accounting standards tend to have market-based financial systems and are unlikely to have underdeveloped financial systems.

Information about corporations is critical for exerting corporate governance and making investment decisions. Accounting standards that simplify the interpretability and comparability of information across corporations will facilitate financial contracting. Furthermore, financial contracting that use accounting measures to trigger particular actions can more usefully be used with effective accounting standards. Governments impose an assortment of regulations regarding information disclosure and accounting standards. This chapter examines a measure of the quality of information disclosed through corporate accounts from La Porta et al. (1998).

ACCOUNT is an index of the comprehensiveness of company reports. The maximum possible value is 90 and the minimum is 0. The Center for International Financial Analysis and Research assessed general accounting information, income statements, balance sheets, funds flow statement, accounting standards, and stock data in company reports in 1990.

Underdeveloped financial systems are much less likely to have high accounting standards (table 3.13). Furthermore, the positive relationship between financial development and accounting standards holds even after controlling for the level of real per capita GDP. Finally, comprehensive, high-quality information about firms is very strongly correlated with market-based systems. Thus, the easy availability of good, comparable corporate financial statements is particularly important for the operation of equity markets.

Bank Regulations

Countries with regulations that restrict the rights of banks to engage in securities market activities, real estate, and insurance are more likely to have underdeveloped financial systems.

This section uses data on allowable nontraditional activities of banks from Barth, Caprio, and Levine (2001). We consider the degree to which a country's regulatory system allows banks to engage in the following four nontraditional activities:

• Securities: the ability of banks to engage in the businesses of securities underwriting, brokering, dealing, and all aspects of the mutual fund business

• Insurance: the ability of banks to engage in insurance underwriting and selling

• Real Estate: the ability of banks to engage in real estate investment, development and management

• Nonfinancial Firm Ownership: the ability of banks to own and control nonfinancial firms

After assessing each country's regulations, a number between one and four was assigned to each activity: Securities, Insurance, Real Estate, and Nonfinancial Firm Ownership. The assigned numbers are interpreted as follows: 1 indicates unrestricted: banks can engage in the full range of the activity directly in the bank; 2 indicates permitted: the full range of those activities can be conducted, but all or some of the activity must be conducted in subsidiaries; 3 indicates restricted: banks can engage in less than full range of to activity, either in the bank or subsidiaries; 4 indicates prohibited: the activity may not be conducted by the bank or subsidiaries.

RESTRICT is a summary index of overall regulatory restrictiveness. RESTRICT equals the average value of Securities, Insurance, Real Estate, and Nonfinancial Firm Ownership, so that RESTRICT takes on values between 1 (least restrictive) and 4 (most restrictive). The average value of RESTRICT is 2.2, with a standard deviation of 0.6. The United States has a value of 3.

As shown in table 3.13, countries with underdeveloped financial systems tend to have much greater restrictions on the activities of their banks. The negative relationship between regulatory restrictiveness and financial sector development holds after controlling for the level of GDP per capita at the 0.05 significance level (table 3.14).

Thus, while Barth, Caprio, and Levine (2001) show that greater restrictiveness tends to increase the fragility of the banking system, this chapter shows that greater restrictiveness is also associated with a generally underdeveloped financial system.

Deposit Insurance
Countries with explicit deposit insurance systems are less likely to have market-based financial systems.

Explicit deposit insurance systems may increase confidence that the general public has in the formal banking system. This may allow easier entry of new banks and operation of smaller banks that have reputation disadvantages.

To assess if there is any link between deposit insurance and financial structure we use *Deposit insurance*, a dummy variable that takes on the value one for countries with explicit deposit insurance and zero for those that do not. As shown in table 3.13, countries with explicit deposit insurance are most likely to have bank-based financial systems and least likely to have market-based systems. Although the correlation between bank-based financial systems and explicit deposit insurance is not significant, the negative correlation between market-based systems and deposit insurance holds when we control for differences in income per capita.

Taxes
There is not a strong link between financial structure and tax distortions favoring either dividends or capital gains relative to interest income.

We consider two tax variables. *Dividend disadvantage* equals the degree to which the tax laws discriminate against dividend income relative to interest income.[11] Higher values signify greater tax disadvantage for dividend income. *Capital gains disadvantage* equals the degree to which the tax system discriminates against capital gains income relative to interest income.[12] As shown in table 3.13, we could not find a strong link between the tax distortions and financial structure.

3.4.3 Macroeconomy

High-inflation economies are much more likely to have underdeveloped financial systems, but inflation is not strongly linked with whether a country's financial system is bank-based or market-based.

Macroeconomic instability may importantly distort and complicate financial contracting. Huybens and Smith (1999) show theoretically and Boyd, Levine, and Smith (2001) confirm econometrically that higher levels of inflation produce smaller, less active, and less efficient banks and markets.[13] This subsection examines the relationship between financial structure and inflation. As shown in table 3.13, economies with underdeveloped financial systems tend to have higher inflation rates than either bank-based or market-based systems. Inflation, however, is not significantly different in bank- versus market-based systems. The correlation table confirms this. Inflation is positively correlated with financial *underdevelopment* even after controlling for the level of GDP per capita, but no significant inflation rate differences exist between bank-based and market-based systems.[14]

3.5   Conclusions

In this chapter we used newly collected data on a cross-section of up to 150 countries to illustrate how financial systems differ around the world. In providing the first systematic examination of financial structure and economic development since Goldsmith's 1969 seminal book, we had three goals. First, we analyzed how the size, activity, and efficiency of financial systems—banks, other financial institutions, and stock markets—differ across different income per capita groups. Second, we defined different indicators of financial structure—financial intermediaries relative to markets—and look for patterns as countries become richer. Third, we investigated legal, regulatory, and policy determinants of financial structure after controlling for the level of GDP per capita.

Looking at financial systems across different income groups, we saw a clear pattern emerge. Banks, other financial intermediaries, and stock markets all get larger, more active, and more efficient as countries become richer. Thus, financial-sector development tends to be greater at higher income levels.

Next, we analyzed differences in financial structure across different income groups. We saw that size measures of financial structure do not follow a clear pattern, as countries become richer. However, patterns did emerge when we looked at activity and efficiency indicators. In higher-income countries, stock markets become more active and more efficient relative to banks. Using an aggregate index of financial structure, we saw that in higher-income countries financial systems tend to be more market-based.

We then classified countries as market-based or bank-based using this aggregate index of financial structure. To avoid classifying a country as bank-based (market-based) when it has poorly developed banks (markets) by international standards, we also distinguished those countries with underdeveloped financial systems from those with developed financial systems. We identified a country as having an underdeveloped financial system if it had both poorly developed banks and markets.

Finally, we analyzed legal, regulatory, tax, and macroeconomic determinants of financial structure by looking at correlations and simple regressions that control for the level of real GDP per capita. We saw that countries with a Common Law tradition, strong protection for shareholder rights, good accounting standards, low levels of corruption, and no explicit deposit insurance tend to be more market-based, even after controlling for income. On the other hand, countries with a French Civil Law tradition, poor protection of shareholder and creditor rights, poor contract enforcement, high levels of corruption, poor accounting standards, heavily restricted banking systems, and high inflation tend to have underdeveloped financial systems in general, even after controlling for income.

In this chapter our goal has not been to test specific hypotheses rigorously. Rather, our objectives have been to compile and compare different indicators of financial structure, make an initial attempt at identifying certain interesting patterns and highlight suggestive correlations. We hope the most important contribution of this chapter will be to stimulate additional research in the area of financial structures and economic development.

Appendix 3.1:   Financial Systems Evolve over Time

3A.1   Intermediaries over Time

This section examines the evolution of financial systems over time. In the case of banks, data exist from the 1960s onward. Thus, we examine how financial intermediary size as a share of GDP changes over the last four decades. The intertemporal patterns are very similar to the cross-country patterns.

Banks and other financial intermediaries have grown as a share of GDP over the decades.

To illustrate this, we first construct the income quartiles discussed in the text for the 1960s, 1970s, 1980s, and 1990s. Figure 3A.1 presents these quar-

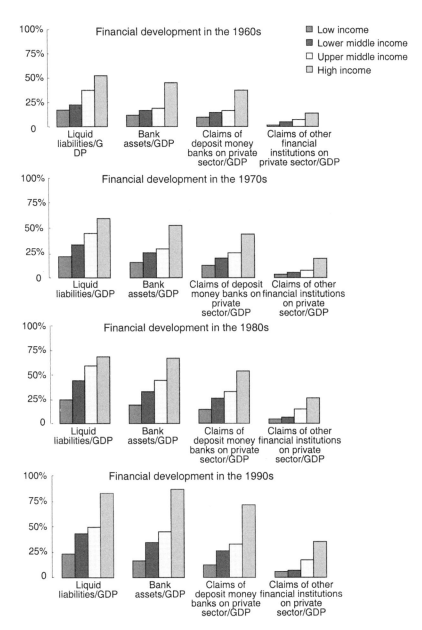

Figure 3A.1
Financial intermediary development over time.

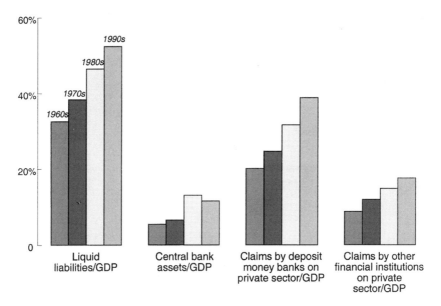

Figure 3A.2
Financial intermediary development over time.

tile graphs and makes two points. First, the cross-country patterns illustrated with data from the 1990s holds for each of the four decades. Second, financial intermediary size as a share of GDP grows in all income quartiles over time. *Liquid liabilities/GDP, Claims of Deposit money banks on private sector/GDP*, and *Claims of other financial institutions on private sector/GDP* all rise as we move from the 1960s to the 1970s, 1980s, and 1990s. This can, perhaps, be seen more clearly in figure 3A.2. Figure 3A.2 averages financial data across all countries with data for the entire sample period for each of the decades. As depicted, banks and other financial institutions become larger as a share of GDP over time. While central banks tend to play smaller role in credit allocation in richer countries, there is a small increase in this role over time.

3A.2   Equity Markets over Time

Stock markets have tended to become larger, more active, and more efficient over time. As shown in figures 3A.3 and 3A.4, *Market capitalization as a share of GDP, Total value traded as a share of GDP*, and *Turnover ratio* have risen in all income quartiles when comparing the 1970, 1980s, and the 1990s. Also note that the cross-country patterns observed in the 1990s are consistent with those observed in the 1980s: As we move from the poorest quartile of countries across to the highest quartile of countries, stock markets are more developed.

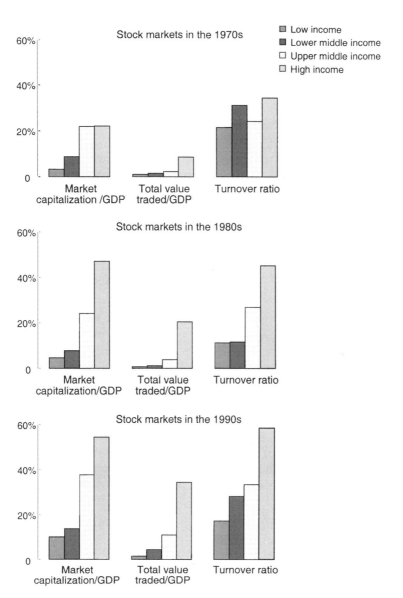

Figure 3A.3
Equity market development over time.

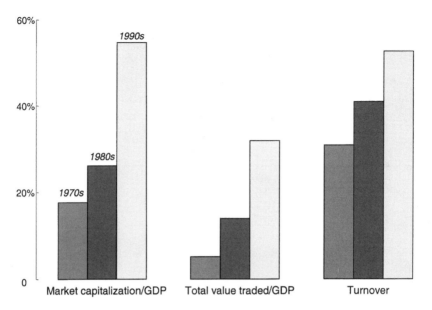

Figure 3A.4
Equity market development over time.

3A.3 Nonbank Financial Intermediaries across Countries

Insurance companies, pension funds, mutual funds, and other nonbank
financial intermediaries tend to become larger as a share of GDP as countries
become richer. Here we face considerable data problems because information on nonbanks becomes scarce for earlier years. Figure 3A.5 shows that
insurance companies, pension funds, mutual funds, and other nonbank
financial intermediaries tend to be larger in the 1990s than they were in
the 1980s. Furthermore, the cross-country patterns noted above hold over
decades.

Notes

1. See citations and discussion in Allen and Gale 2000 and Levine 1999.

2. While other differences (e.g., fiscal, monetary, and regulatory policies) could have
perfectly balanced the growth effects of differences in financial structure, this seems
unlikely. Furthermore, past studies of financial structure do not control for differences
in nonfinancial-sector policies.

3. The figures are based on the full sample whereas the tables and correlations only
include 63 countries for which we have complete data.

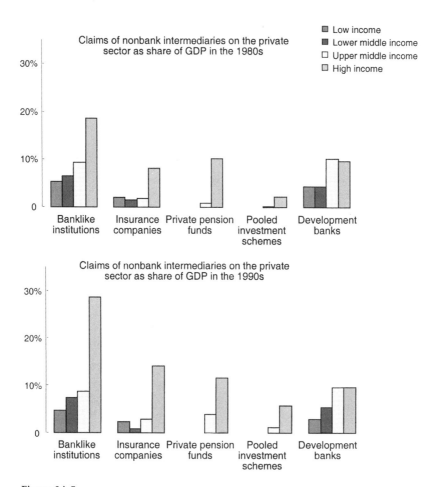

Figure 3A.5
Nonbank intermediary development over time.

4. Countries are classified according to their 1995 GNP per capita. Low is $765 or less; lower middle is $766–$3,035; upper middle is $3,036–$9,385; and high is $9,386 or more.

5. Specifically, Cyprus, Egypt, Honduras, Zimbabwe, Panama, Barbados, Costa Rica, Nepal, Iceland, Tunisia, Bangladesh, Kenya, Mauritius, Iran, and Trinidad and Tobago, Ecuador, and Colombia have high values of *Bank credit vs. trading* because the value of domestic stock transactions sums to less than two percent of GDP.

6. As a robustness check, we combined *Private Credit by deposit money banks* with *Private credit by other financial intermediaries* to create an overall measure of financial intermediary development. We want to evaluate whether the inclusion of nonbanks materially influences the classification of countries. After re-doing the above analysis

with this financial intermediary variable, we find few changes. Panama, Portugal, Belgium, and Italy were classified as bank-based but underdeveloped systems. Canada, Sweden, Thailand, and South Africa were classified as intermediary-based rather than market-based systems. Finally, Ireland was classified as intermediary-based but developed rather than underdeveloped.

7. The four-way split in table 3.12, or a two-way bank-based vs. market-based split without taking into account financial development, does not produce significant results. Differences in means become significant only if we analyze underdeveloped countries as a single group. Thus we look at differences among underdeveloped and (developed) bank-based and (developed) market-based financial structures. However, this classification is less important when we look at correlations, since correlations with the continuous structure index also produce consistent results.

8. Shareholder rights, *SRIGHTS*, is an index that is formed by adding 1 when (1) the country allows shareholders to mail their proxy vote to the firm, (2) shareholders are not required to deposit their shares prior to the General Shareholders' Meeting, (3) cumulative voting or proportional representation of minorities in the board of directors is allowed, (4) an oppressed minorities mechanism is in place, (5) the minimum percentage of share capital that entitles a shareholder to call for an Extraordinary Shareholders' Meeting is less than or equal to 10 percent (the sample mean), or (6) shareholders have preemptive rights that can only be waved by a shareholders' vote. The index ranges from 0 to 6.

9. *CRIGHTS* is an index aggregating different creditor rights. The index is formed by adding 1 when (1) the country imposes restrictions, such as creditors' consent or minimum dividends to file for reorganization, (2) secured creditors are able to gain possession of their security once the reorganization petition has been approved (no automatic stay), (3) secured creditors are ranked first in the distribution of the proceeds that result from the disposition of the assets of a bankrupt firm, and (4) the debtor does not retain the administration of its property pending the resolution of the reorganization. The index ranges from 0 to 4.

10. This enforcement variable, *ENFORCE*, averages the contract risk and law and order variables collected by La Porta et al. (1998), as discussed in Levine 1998.

11. Assuming that marginal investor is a private individual who is sufficiently wealthy to be paying personal income taxes at the highest rate, dividend disadvantage equals the extent to which net income per $1 of dividends is less than net income from $1 of interest income.

12. Assuming that marginal investor is a private individual who is sufficiently wealthy to be paying personal income taxes at the highest rate, capital gains disadvantage equals the extent to which net income per $1 of capital gains is less than net income from $1 of interest income.

13. Boyd, Levine, and Smith (2001) highlight the nonlinear relationship between inflation and financial sector performance.

14. We also investigated the linkages between financial structure and growth in GDP per capita, existence of black market premium, and equality of income distribution. There is no correlation between black market premium and financial structure. While there is some indication that countries with more equal income distribution and higher growth are more likely to have market-based financial structures, the statistical significance of these results is low.

References

Allen, Franklin, and Douglas Gale. 2000. Comparing financial systems. Cambridge, MA: MIT Press.

Barth, James, Gerard Caprio, and Ross Levine. 2001. Banking systems around the globe: Do regulation and ownership affect performance and stability? In *Financial Supervision and Regulation: What Works and What Doesn't?*, ed. Fredrick Mishkin. Washington, DC: National Bureau of Economic Research.

Beck, Thorsten, Ross Levine, and Norman Loayza. 2000. Finance and the sources of growth. *Journal of Financial Economics* 58(1):261–300.

Boyd, John H., Ross Levine, and Bruce D. Smith. 2001. The impact of inflation on financial sector performance. *Journal of Monetary Economics* 47(2):221–248.

Demirgüç-Kunt, Aslı, and Ross Levine. 1996. Stock market development and financial intermediary growth: Stylized facts. *World Bank Economic Review* (May).

Demirgüç-Kunt, Aslı, and Vojislav Maksimovic. 1998. Law, finance, and firm growth. *Journal of Finance* 53(6):2107–2137 (December).

Demirgüç-Kunt, Aslı, and Vojislav Maksimovic. 1999. Institutions, financial markets, and firm debt maturity. *Journal of Financial Economics* 54:295–336.

Goldsmith, Raymond W. 1969. *Financial Structure and Development*. New Haven, CT: Yale University Press.

Huybens, Elizabeth, and Bruce Smith. 1999. Inflation, financial markets, and long-run real activity. *Journal of Monetary Economics* 43(2):283–315.

King, Robert G., and Ross Levine. 1993a. Finance and growth: Schumpeter might be right. *Quarterly Journal of Economics* 108(3):717–738 (August).

King, Robert G., and Ross Levine. 1993b. Finance, entrepreneurship, and growth: Theory and evidence. *Journal of Monetary Economics* 32(3):513–542 (December).

La Porta, Rafael, Florencio Lopez-de-Silanes, Andrei Shleifer, and Robert W. Vishny. 1997. Legal determinants of external finance. *Journal of Finance* 52(3):1131–1150 (July).

La Porta, Rafael, Florencio Lopez-de-Silanes, Andrei Shleifer, and Robert W. Vishny. 1998. Law and finance. *Journal of Political Economy* 106(6):1113–1155 (December).

Levine, Ross. 1998. The legal environment, banks, and long-run economic growth. *Journal of Money, Credit, and Banking* 30(3, Pt. 2):596–613 (August).

Levine, Ross. 1999. Law, finance, and economic growth. *Journal of Financial Intermediation* 8(1/2):36–67 (January).

Levine, Ross. Forthcoming. Napolean, Bourses, and economic growth: With a focus on Latin America. In *Market augmenting government*, ed. Omar Azfar and Charles Cadwell. Ann Arbor: University of Michigan Press.

Levine, Ross, and Sara Zervos. 1998. Stock markets, banks, and economic growth. *American Economic Review* 88(3):537–558 (June).

Levine, Ross, Norman Loayza, and Thorsten Beck. 2000. Financial intermediation and growth: Causality and causes. *Journal of Monetary Economics* 46(1):31–77 (August).

Park, Yung Chul. 1993. The role of finance in economic development in South Korean and Taiwan. In *Finance and development: Issues and experience*, ed. Alberto Giovanni. Cambridge: Cambridge University Press.

Rajan, Raghuram G., and Luigi Zingales. 1998. Financial dependence and growth. *American Economic Review* 88(June):559–586.

III

Financial Structure and
Economic Growth across
Countries

4   Does Financial Structure Matter for Economic Growth? A Corporate Finance Perspective

René Stulz

4.1   Introduction

This chapter examines how the organization of financial activities within a country affects economic growth through its impact on how corporations raise and manage funds. In principle, how a financial system performs any of its functions can affect economic growth.[1] For instance, the organization of a country's payment system affects growth by making it easier for economic agents to trade. Often, policymakers and academics take it as given that savings will be invested efficiently, so that firms do not matter. This view rests on traditional neoclassical principles. In a simple world of perfect capital markets and risk-neutral agents, the interest rate determines which investment opportunities are valuable and all investment opportunities that are valuable are exploited.[2] This is not the world we live in. Even though a country has savings, its growth can be stunted because its financial system fails to direct these savings where they can be invested most efficiently. This chapter, therefore, examines how the organization of financial activities affects the efficiency with which corporations invest savings and take advantage of valuable investment opportunities.

The fact that savings can be invested inefficiently because of how financial activities are organized has been at the core of the intense debate on the comparative benefits and costs of the Anglo-Saxon model and the bank-centered model. When the U.S. economy's performance seemed poor in contrast to the performance of the Japanese economy in the 1980s, the bank-centered model was viewed as a key determinant of why the performances of the two economies differed. A typical view of that period is represented by Thurow's argument that the United States has organized a system that is the exact

opposite of that of Germany and Japan. Those countries have organized a system (business groups) to minimize the influence of impatient shareholders, while the United States has organized a system
(fund dominance) to maximize the influence of impatient shareholders.[3] According to this view, Japanese firms could invest in long-
term projects because of their long-term shareholders, while American
firms could not afford to do so. The poor performance of the Japanese
economy in the 1990s has led many to reassess the evidence on the
benefits of the Japanese system. In particular, there is now evidence
that bank-dependence can make funds more costly for firms because
banks extract rents from their corporate customers.[4] Further, bank
finance is not as important for Japanese firms now as it was in the 1960s
or 1970s. As a result, Japan is now much less the prototypical bank-
centered economy than it used to be.

The argument that Thurow (1992) makes that U.S. managers evaluate projects differently from Japanese managers because of different
corporate governance arrangements emphasizes the impact of how
the organization of financial activities affects firm investment
policies. This argument would be irrelevant in a neoclassical world
because in such a world, a manager takes all projects that have a
positive net present value (where the net present value of a project is
its expected cash flows discounted at the expected rate of return
investors require for such a project). In a world with agency problems and information asymmetries, managers may not want to undertake or may be unable to undertake some projects that would
have a positive net present value in a neoclassical world. In fact,
managers might even choose to invest in projects that have a negative net present value. If two firms located in different countries
make different decisions on the same project, it has to be because
the cost of capital differs or because the incentives and monitoring of
management differ. The differences in incentives and monitoring
of management might lead management in one country to take on
bad projects or not to take on good projects either because it is not
sufficiently rewarded for making the right decisions or not sufficiently punished for making the wrong ones. Though Thurow correctly emphasizes the importance of how financial activities are
organized, we will see throughout this chapter that the differences he
focuses on between Japan and the United States are only a small part
of the issues one should consider when trying to understand how
the organization of financial activities affects economic growth.

If economies are not integrated internationally, the cost of capital can differ across countries simply because each economy is an island and the cost of capital has to balance investment and savings within that economy. However, if economies are integrated internationally, capital flows equalize the expected rate of return on securities with identical risk across countries. In perfectly integrated financial markets therefore, this value of the same cash flows to capital providers will be the same across countries. Nevertheless, identical projects can produce different cash flows to capital providers because of differences in how financial activities are organized.

To make the point that project evaluated by firms located in countries that organize their financial activities differently will differ in their profitability, consider a project consisting of building a plant in the United States. Let's assume that the project would be profitable in a neoclassical world. If the project is considered by a U.S. company, shareholders will be concerned about whether the project is undertaken to benefit management rather than the shareholders. As a result, shareholders will be skeptical about the claims management makes about the profitability of the project. If the project is evaluated by a Japanese firm, shareholders might worry that banks would insist on using the cash flows to build the firm's liquidity to reduce the firm's credit risk but banks might be willing to finance the project when the equity markets would not because the firm can provide more information to banks than to the equity markets. Finally, if the project is evaluated by a firm located in a country with poor protection of minority shareholder rights, the project might contribute little to firm value because its cash flows might be siphoned off by majority shareholders. Because the value of the project differs depending on the firm that undertakes the project, it is perfectly possible that the project might be undertaken by one firm but not by another one.

This chapter examines how the organization of financial activities affects growth through its effect on the funds firms can raise and on how firms are managed. I call the first issue the financing problem and the second one the governance problem. As the earlier example shows, the two problems are closely related. If management maximizes the value of the firm for capital providers, it can raise more funds for a project than management that pursues its own goals. The way the firm finances its activities affects how the governance problem is resolved. For instance, debtholders can intervene in the firm only if the firm is in default while shareholders can affect the actions of management when the firm is not in default.

It is important to emphasize that this paper focuses completely on the impact of financial structure on how firms raise and manage capital. It therefore ignores how financial structure affects growth and welfare through other channels. In particular, Allen and Gale (1995) have emphasized the risk-sharing aspects of financial structures. These risk-sharing aspects are important in welfare comparisons of financial structures and affect growth in a number of ways, but we have nothing to say on these issues. In contrast to Allen and Gale 1995, this chapter therefore does not focus on system comparisons.

The chapter is organized as follows. Section 4.2 first defines what is meant by organization of financial activities and contrasts this concept to the development of the financial sector. I then define a perfect markets benchmark and discuss how the cost of capital differs from its perfect markets benchmark and why this wedge offers a useful measure of how the organization of financial activities affects economic growth. Section 4.3 examines how financial structure affects the cost of capital for an entrepreneur who wants to start a new firm. Section 4.4 examines examine how the organization of financial activities affects the cost of capital for an established firm. In section 4.5, I discuss briefly how existing empirical work is supportive of our analysis. Concluding remarks are provided in section 4.6.

4.2   Perfect Markets and Financial Structure

4.2.1   Defining Financial Structure

Merton (1995) argues that a financial system provides (1) a payment system, (2) a mechanism for pooling funds, (3) a way to transfer resources across space and time, (4) a way to manage uncertainty and control risk, (5) price information to allow the economy to implement a decentralized allocation of investment, and (6) a way to deal with the asymmetric information problems that arise when one party to a financial transaction has information that the other party does not have. These functions can be performed in different ways in different economies.

A country's financial structure is defined as the institutions, financial technology, and rules of the game that specify how financial activity is organized at a point in time. A useful analogy is that financial structure is to the financial system what a foundation is to a house. Many different houses can be built on the same foundation. However, at the same time, a foundation makes it impossible to build some types of houses. If the foundation is designed for a one floor house, it cannot be used to build a skyscraper. Though there has been much focus on the distinction between bank-based economies and market-based economies, our definition of financial structure is much broader. Undoubtedly, bank-based economies and market-based economies have different financial structures. However, as we will see in this chapter, other financial structure characteristics matter a great deal for how the financial system performs its functions. As a result, the distinction between bank-based and market-based economies may have obscured rather than enriched our understanding of how financial structure affects economic growth. For instance, following La Porta, Lopez-Silanes, Shleifer, and Vishny 1998, much recent research has emphasized the importance of the protection of minority shareholders for financial development. With our definition of financial structure, a country's degree of protection of minority shareholders is an attribute of that country's financial structure.

The same function of a financial system can be performed by different institutions or according to different rules. There is no direct relation between a country's economic development and its financial structure. For instance, Japan and the United States or Germany and England had quite different financial structures at the same level of economic development. Hence, no case can be made that the financial structure is completely endogenously determined.

It is important to distinguish financial structure from financial development. Research has focused on the relation between financial development and economic growth.[5] Indicators of financial development that have been used in the literature consist of measures like the turnover of the stock market, stock market trading relative to GDP, stock market capitalization relative to GDP, the proportion of funds raised externally by firms, and so on. All these measures of financial development can be dramatically different for the same financial structure. Hence, there is no one-to-one relationship between financial development and financial structure. For instance, reliance on external funding might be the same in an economy where the stock market plays an important role and in an economy where banks play an important role. Financial structure can hinder or promote financial development, however. Policies can have a direct impact on financial structure, but they can only have an indirect impact on financial development. Policymakers cannot legislate changes in the degree of financial development but they can legislate changes in the financial structure. This makes it especially important to understand how financial structure affects economic growth.

4.2.2   A Perfect Markets Benchmark

Many results in financial economics require the assumption that markets are perfect. If markets are perfect, contracting is costless, and the Coase theorem applies.[6] This means that whenever there is a reallocation of resources that creates value, it can be implemented at no cost. In a world of perfect markets, contracting can be complete. In other words, the actions of an economic agent or the payoffs of individual securities can be specified for each state of the world at no cost. The actions of the agent are observable and contracts specifying actions in each state of the world can be enforced costlessly. With perfect markets, a firm specifies in each state of the world what the providers of capital will receive. The value of a firm for the providers of capital is the present value of the cash flows the firm will pay out to them.

If capital markets are perfect and there are no restrictions to capital flows, it does not matter where investors in a project are located. All investors value a project in the same way. There are no differences in the cost of capital across countries. A project is funded if it is expected to earn at least its cost of capital. This means that the present value of the cash flows of the project is positive. All projects that are valuable get funded irrespective of where they are located.

4.2.3   Deviations from the Perfect Markets Benchmark

In perfect financial markets, the firm can finance any project that management finds valuable. Two key market imperfections destroy this property of perfect financial markets. First, investors do not see all actions management takes. Second, management has information that investors do not have. Arrow (1979) named the first problem the hidden action problem and the second the hidden information problem. These hidden action and hidden information problems create an agency problem between management and investors. If management knows that a project will most likely be a bad project, it may want to raise funds for it anyway because generally it benefits from managing a larger firm by having more perks and a higher salary. If the project fails, management does not get all the blame because it could be bad luck. If the project succeeds, management gets the benefit of firm growth. Hidden information and hidden actions give management discretion that it can use to pursue its own objectives.

With hidden information and hidden actions, investors no longer automatically believe what management says about the cash flows they will receive from a project. This is for several reasons. First, investors know that management has incentives to overstate the cash flows and they generally cannot verify management's statements. Second, through hidden actions, management can affect cash flows later on. In particular, management can work less hard, which reduces cash flows, or alter cash flows in other ways to pursue its own goals. Third, investors generally cannot specify the use of the cash flows from a project. Because of this, management may choose to invest too much in the firm because it gets more benefits from investing than paying out the surplus cash flow to shareholders. In the extreme case, these problems imply that no funds can be raised. For instance, if management can take the funds raised and use them for consumption without penalty, the firm cannot raise funds even though it might have good projects.

In the presence of the hidden information and hidden action problems, management cannot go to the markets and announce that it has projects with a given cash flow distribution and expect investors to finance it. Consider a firm that requires funds to finance existing activities and grow. The extent to which it can raise these funds depends on the cash flows that the providers of these funds believe will accrue to them. Consequently, the firm could have a project that would be financed in perfect capital markets but would not be in imperfect capital markets because the providers of funds do not believe that they will receive sufficient cash flows from the project. In such a situation, the neoclassical capital budgeting approach is no longer useful. This is because the project would be worthwhile at the neoclassical cost of capital, but the firm cannot raise funds at that cost of capital. To secure external funding, the existing owners may have to agree to costly restrictions on the actions they can take so that the capital providers are more secure in their beliefs that they will not be taken advantage of by the owners. The cost of external funding for the firm must take into account the deadweight costs associated with these restrictions. As a result, the cost of external funding for the firm exceeds the cost of capital for investors because of the hidden information and the hidden action problems.

The best way to consider the difference between the cost of capital for investors and the cost of external funding for the firm is to focus on an entrepreneur who is seeking funding for a project. The value of the project for investors is the present value of the cash flows they would expect to receive if they owned the right to all the cash flows from the project using the appropriate discount rate given the risk of these cash flows. For the entrepreneur, the cost of external funding is the discount rate that equates the present value of the cash flows given up to secure external funding to the funds raised. These two costs of capital are identical in perfect capital markets. Market imperfections create a wedge between these two costs of capital. As the wedge increases for the entrepreneur, there is a point where the project is no longer worthwhile and investment does not take place.[7]

Consider a project that would be worthwhile in perfect financial markets. In my framework, the entrepreneur cannot undertake this project if his cost of external finance is such that the funds that could be raised are not sufficient for the investment required. In such a situation, investors will not provide the funds, so that the entrepreneur is rationed.[8] Such a situation will arise if the cash flows generated by the project in perfect markets cannot be contracted to be paid to the investors. In the extreme case, legal enforcement could be so poor that the entrepreneur could steal all the cash flows with impunity, so that the investors would get nothing and the cost of capital to the entrepreneur would be infinite. However, it could simply be that because of hidden information and hidden action problems, the cash flows are lower than in perfect capital markets because the entrepreneur cannot credibly commit to work as hard when his effort is not observable as when it is.

Let's now consider the situation of an established firm trying to raise funds. In this case also, there is a distinction between the discount rate of investors and the firm's cost of external finance. The discount rate of investors is chosen in the same way as in the case of the entrepreneur. The funds raised by the firm are equal to the present value of the cash flows the investors expect to receive. However, the firm's total value does not necessarily increase by the funds raised. The value of the firm is given by the discounted value of the cash flows the providers of capital expect to receive. This value is less than the value of the firm in the absence of the hidden information and hidden action problems if these problems lead management to make investment decisions that would not be optimal if financial markets were perfect. For instance, management could use the funds to invest in projects that have a negative net present value using the neoclassical cost of capital but have private benefits for management.

The possibility of overinvestment as well as the possibility of underinvestment create the wedge between the cost of external finance of the firm and the discount rate of the capital providers. If the firm overinvests, it means that it takes on projects it should not. These projects reduce the firm's cash flows relative to what they would be with perfect capital markets because these projects do not earn the discount rate required by investors. If the firm underinvests, it means that it does not exploit opportunities that it should take advantage of. Again, this reduces firm value relative to what it would be in perfect markets where the firm would take these projects. To examine how financial structure affects the possibility of overinvestment and the possibility of underinvestment, I organize my discussion around the life cycle of a firm. The next section starts by examining the problem of the entrepreneur seeking funding of a new project. I then investigate how financial structure affects the activities of established firms in section 4.4.

4.3 Financing the Entrepreneur

4.3.1 The Importance of Staged Financing

Consider an entrepreneur who has an idea for a project. This project has a positive net present value in the absence of the hidden information and the hidden action problems. The entrepreneur cannot finance the project on his own. He therefore has to find investors who will provide the necessary funds. To do so, he has to be able to convince investors that they can expect a return on their investment equal to their required discount rate. Investors will only finance the project if they expect to earn the opportunity cost of their funds.

Suppose first that there is no information asymmetry between the entrepreneur and the investors concerning the cash flows of the project. In this case, the project could be funded if investors believe that they will receive those cash flows from the project promised to them. This means that investors have to be confident that there are no other claims on these cash flows which requires that property rights be well defined and enforceable.

Countries differ in the extent to which investors can be assured to receive the cash flows promised to them. In countries with the worst legal enforcement, domestic investors have little chance of receiving what is promised to them if the entrepreneur does not want to pay. In other countries, domestic investors have greater expectations of receiving the promised cash flows than foreign investors. The degree of legal enforcement affects directly the entrepreneur's ability to finance his project with outside finance.[9] As legal enforcement increases, the entrepreneur becomes less likely to be able to divert funds from the firm and outside investors expect to receive more dividends. With weak legal enforcement, one expects therefore that many projects never get started unless private contracting can be used to avoid the problems created by weak legal enforcement. By building a reputation for not diverting funds from the firm's capital providers, the entrepreneur can eventually raise funds even with weak legal enforcement. Diamond (1991) shows that this reputation leads firms to avoid opportunistic actions reducing the value of the securities they have issued that they would not avoid otherwise. Gomez (forthcoming) provides a model where reputation makes equity valuable even in the absence of a legal system that protects minority shareholders. Unfortunately, reputation is most likely to work as a substitute for legal enforcement only for projects that are highly divisible, so that the entrepreneur can get started with little funding. For projects that initially require large amounts of funding, the entrepreneur will have to raise these amounts without having a reputation. His only choice will be to rent somebody else's reputation if profitable to undertake the project or give up the project otherwise.

Weak legal enforcement does not necessarily prevent entrepreneurship. Legal enforcement was weak in the United States during the second half of the last century. Minority shareholder rights were typically trampled on. Coffee (2000) argues that investment banks enabled entrepreneurs to raise funds from foreign investors in the United States because of their role in making sure that foreign investors would not be taken advantage of. He also points out that institutions such as the New York Stock Exchange that could serve as substitutes for governmental legal enforcement were also important.

However, for private institutions to emerge that facilitate contracting when legal enforcement is deficient, it must be that government institutions do not stand in the way. Excessive regulation or political interference in economic activity could easily prevent the emergence of such institutions.

For a given level of legal enforcement, the entrepreneur's problem is that he has more information about the project than investors. There is no reason for investors to believe that the entrepreneur is telling the truth when he describes the project. This is because the entrepreneur can benefit from undertaking the project even if the project has little chance to succeed. If he does not raise funds to undertake the project, the entrepreneur's equity is worthless. As long as the entrepreneur has an equity claim in the project, he benefits if the project does well, but if the project does poorly, the investors lose more than the entrepreneur. The information asymmetry between investors and the entrepreneur makes it often impossible for the entrepreneur to fund the project by issuing shares to new investors in public markets. Since the entrepreneur would want to sell shares even if there was no project, investors cannot take at face value the statements of the entrepreneur. Therefore, the entrepreneur cannot raise the funds for the project by simply describing the project and asking the investors to believe that the project is profitable. Even if the project has a high value and would be funded in perfect financial markets, it will not be funded when the hidden information problem is sufficiently important.

To initiate the project, the entrepreneur may start on a scale where investors can learn about the project and stop funding it if they discover that it will not be profitable. Generally, therefore, the method of financing involves financing in stages, where future financing depends on how the project is evolving.[10] Capital markets are generally ill suited to stage financing for at least two reasons. First, stage financing requires an investor to provide new funds under some conditions. This means that a security that provides stage financing does not have the property of limited liability. However, securities without limited liability have essentially disappeared from the capital markets.[11] If a security requires its owner to make payments in the future, its value depends on whether the payments will be made if the conditions of the security are met. To insure this requires limitations on trading. Otherwise, the securities have most value for those individuals with the least amount of wealth who cannot make the subsequent payments. Second, even if it were possible to have traded securities without limited liability, it is generally not possible to specify all the conditions under which the additional financing would be provided. Success in a project has many dimensions. However, with publicly traded securities, it will generally not be possible to set up a mechanism where the owners of the securities act collectively to figure out whether funds should be provided.[12]

4.3.2   The Role of Financial Intermediaries in Financing the Entrepreneur

The solution to finance the entrepreneur's project generally involves staged financing obtained from financial intermediaries such as banks, bank substitutes, and possibly venture capitalists. Banks effectively provide staged financing. They do so in the form of loans that they renew and expand as the entrepreneur makes his case for financing more compelling. The use of debt financing economizes on monitoring costs. If the entrepreneur repays the debt, there is no reason for the bank to expend resources on figuring out the true value of the entrepreneur's assets.[13] With such a financing mechanism, the bank provides funds in the form of debt and the entrepreneur, his friends, and possibly venture capitalists own the equity.

Competition among potential providers of funds has the effect of reducing the interest rate charged to the entrepreneur. This would seem to be good for economic growth, but things are not this simple. If financing has to be staged, as one learns about the project, new financing decisions are taken. At each stage of the project, the financial intermediary has to assess whether the project should be pursued and under which conditions. At that point, the financial intermediary can contribute value to the project by having specialized skills that it can apply to evaluate the project and increase its probability of success.

The extent to which a financial intermediary expends resources on a project depends on the extent to which the intermediary can benefit from expending these resources. The financial intermediary cannot make profits when the project fails and must therefore make profits when projects succeed. This means that if a project succeeds the financial intermediary has to be able to extract rents.[14] Lack of competition among financial intermediaries increases the ability of a financial intermediary to extract rents from successful projects, thereby justifying the expenditure of resources on projects to increase their probability of success. Some ability to extract rents is therefore necessary for relationship lending.[15]

Competition among financial intermediaries limits the incentive for financial intermediaries to invest resources in projects when they can only be compensated for doing so through a relationship with the firm. When competition is strong, established firms can walk away from a relationship with a financial intermediary. Therefore, the financial intermediary cannot benefit as much from having helped the firm succeed. When competition becomes too strong, the financial intermediaries do not develop expertise, so that they cannot assess projects and hence do not finance them. Further, projects that get started but do not benefit from relationship financing are less likely to succeed. Without relationship financing, therefore, fewer projects get started. The projects that get started are those where the financial intermediary can finance investments that are not project-specific and can be used as collateral. In other words, if relationship financing is not available, the entrepreneur can borrow to buy a building but not to finance improvements in machinery that are project-specific. At the same time, however, with too little competition, financial intermediaries can expropriate the entrepreneur if the project is successful by increasing the cost of finance when the project turns out to be successful. As the ability to extract rents increases, however, the payoff to the entrepreneur from his idea falls.

The relationship between the entrepreneur and the financial intermediary is complicated by the fact that the financial intermediary has private information about the project's entrepreneur. The existence of this private information means that if the financial intermediary withholds funds from the entrepreneur, other financial intermediaries will infer from this decision that there is adverse information about the project. Consequently, it may be difficult for the entrepreneur to seek other sources of funds if the financial intermediary increases the cost of its financing regardless of the degree of competition among financial intermediaries.

Another area where the financial intermediary may impose costs on the entrepreneur has to do with the continuation and expansion decision. With debt claims, financial intermediaries have incentives to push the entrepreneur to avoid risks since the value of debt claims falls as risk increases. Consequently, the financial intermediary evaluates the continuation decision differently from the entrepreneur. If continuation involves an increase in risk, the financial intermediary may choose to discontinue the project if the proceeds from liquidation are high enough. The possibility that the financial intermediary may prevent continuation of the project when it would be optimal for the entrepreneur to continue means that the entrepreneur's payoff is decreased and his incentives to work hard fall.

The extent to which the financial intermediary makes suboptimal continuation decisions is affected by whether the financial intermediary holds equity. If the financial intermediary holds debt and equity in the same proportions as in the firm's capital structure, its incentives are to maximize firm value. The problem of suboptimal continuation can be resolved also by having different financial intermediaries for debt and equity. By providing the entrepreneur with more equity, it becomes less likely that he will not be able to pay interest to the bank and the influence of the bank becomes less important.

The provision of private equity plays a crucial role in financing entrepreneurs for another reason. The use of debt requires the availability of collateral. Debt that does not have a specific collateral, such as a building, is collateralized by the whole firm. Some activities of a firm do not yield collateral that can be used to raise debt. For instance, with R&D investments, the bank that seizes the firm faces the problem that it has no assets that it can sell or even evaluate. Equity enables firms to raise funds by pledging a share of random future cash flows.

The problem of suboptimal continuation is exacerbated by funding risks. Staged financing requires that the commitment to continue financing will be honored. This commitment cannot be honored if the financial intermediary is bankrupt or is unable to lend money when the entrepreneur expects to receive additional funds. Instability and/or political intervention in the banking sector therefore reduce the expected payoff from entrepreneurship. As the entrepreneur invests his sweat equity, he has to believe that funds will be available when he reaches a point where he can demonstrate the value of the project better. However, if capital constraints on banks or lending directives prevent them from lending to the entrepreneur, the project will have to be discontinued even though it is a valuable project. If this possibility is high enough, the entrepreneur will not undertake the project in the first place. Viewed from this perspective, governments that encourage growth in some sectors of the economy by pushing banks to lend more to those sectors and less to others take the risk of decreasing entrepreneurial activity by making the availability of funds for successful entrepreneurs less predictable.

Access to public markets for the entrepreneur is expensive unless the value of the project can be established by public investors with sufficient precision so that the project can be funded. Public investors do not have access to the same information as financial intermediaries because the firm cannot communicate some types of information publicly without reducing its value. This might suggest that public capital markets are therefore not important. Yet, they serve four purposes. First, public capital markets allow the entrepreneur to escape the bank.[16] They make it possible for the entrepreneur to have an alternative source of financing if the bank tries to expropriate too much of the profits from the project. Consequently, even though entrepreneurs are financed initially through bank finance, the availability of public markets can play a crucial role in promoting entrepreneurship by limiting the ability of financial intermediaries to extract rents. Second, public markets make it possible for the entrepreneur to realize profits from a successful project. Without public markets, the entrepreneur's stake is illiquid. If the entrepreneur sells his stake, he will face a limited market and hence get a low price. With public markets, the payoff from the project for the entrepreneur increases. Third, public markets aggregate information and therefore provide valuable information about the value of firms and projects that can be used for making investment decisions.[17] Fourth, the existence of public equity markets makes possible the emergence of financial intermediaries who provide funds in exchange for equity and can therefore share the entrepreneur's risks. A country can have public markets, yet these markets might not be easily available to new firms. From this discussion, having public markets available to new firms plays a key role in encouraging entrepreneurial activity. Public equity markets may be difficult to access for firms because of, among other reasons, high costs of going public, restrictions on listings, and poor liquidity.

Intermediated finance is critical for entrepreneurship, but absent an exit opportunity for entrepreneurs through equity markets, the rent-seeking of financial intermediaries lowers the gains to entrepreneurship and may hinder it significantly. Intermediated finance is informationally intensive. Generally, it cannot take place at too much of a distance.[18] There are obvious exceptions, however. The monitoring component of intermediated finance requires the financial intermediary to have skills that enable it to evaluate the progress of the entrepreneur. In some cases, it may well be that these skills are simply not available locally. In these cases, therefore, financial openness enables local entrepreneurs to obtain financing that otherwise they could not get. With equity markets, however, location is much less important. Foreign firms, particularly Israeli firms, will at times list first on NASDAQ even though they are in countries with local equity markets. Consequently, as long as the firms in a country have free access to foreign markets, some foreign financial institutions can substitute for local ones.

4.3.3   Financial Structure and Entrepreneurial Finance

The following characteristics of a country's financial structure are important for the creation and growth of new firms:

1. Well-defined property rights so that entrepreneurs can sell rights to future cash flows

2. Availability of staged financing

3. Stability of the financial sector so that implicit commitments of stage financing can be honored by financial intermediaries

4. Availability of private equity financing

5. Availability of uncollaterized debt

6. Availability of an exit option of public equity markets for young firms

Without these characteristics, a financial structure hinders the emergence of firms where the hidden information and hidden action problems are important. If a country's financial structure is such that such firms cannot be financed, that country's growth suffers. Importantly, however, financial structure choice does not reduce to a choice between markets and banks. In our analysis, it is clear that both markets and banks are required.

In section 4.2 contrasted financial structure with financial development. The requirements for entrepreneurial finance discussed here make it possible to emphasize the importance of this difference. If one were to summarize the key requirement of a financial structure from the perspective of entrepreneurial finance, it is that it supports sophisticated private explicit and implicit contracting. For such contracting to take place, a country needs stability and an effective legal system. These requirements facilitate financial development, but financial development is not a condition for these requirements to be met. Some of these requirements may be met because of events that took place a long time ago. For instance, the type of law that a country has might be the result of colonization and other past events. At the same time, however, all these requirements are susceptible to policy interventions. Further, laws themselves are not enough. It matters how they are enforced. For instance, a legal system that protects the rights of the creditors is useless if it takes ten years to enforce a claim.

4.4   Monitoring Established Firms

Section 4.3 showed that as firms grow and become better established, they rely more on public markets. Their equity becomes publicly traded and they can issue public debt. In the United States, the established firm has dispersed shareholders. Berle and Means (1932) emphasized the governance problem resulting from having dispersed shareholders. In a firm with a large body of atomistic shareholders, costs of collective action among shareholders are too high for the shareholders to cooperate effectively. As a result, management can pursue its own objectives with more freedom than if the firm is controlled by large shareholders. As shown by La Porta et al. (2000), in most countries besides the United States, established firms have large shareholders that can affect directly the firm's policies. In many ways, these shareholders are more similar to management in a firm with dispersed ownership than to small shareholders. Like management in a firm with dispersed ownership, they may choose to make decisions that do not increase the value of a firm's equity because they receive other benefits from these decisions. Though I talk explicitly about the problems associated with large shareholders in section 4.4.1, many of the issues I discuss when analyzing management apply equally well to large shareholders who derive private benefits from their control of the firm.

Managerial discretion means both that an incompetent manager can keep his job and that a competent manager can use the firm's resources to pursue his own goals. If the firm has valuable investment opportunities, there is little reason in general for management to work against the interests of shareholders. In this case, if management fails to take properly advantage of these investment opportunities, it is because it is misinformed or incompetent. If a firm does not have valuable investment opportunities, well-informed and competent management could prefer to invest the firm's cash flow in poor projects rather than return it to the shareholders.[19] This implies that large firms held by atomistic shareholders are likely to overinvest and consume excessive perquisites rather than repurchase shares or increase dividends when faced by poor investment opportunities. The other side of the coin is, however, that precisely because management is reluctant to return cash flow to shareholders, the firm is limited in its ability to raise funds.[20] This is because capital providers, knowing that management pursues its own goals, cannot be assured that the funds it provides will be put to good use. Management that always wants to invest cannot raise funds by claiming that it has good projects. As a result, management might not be able to invest when it has good projects because of an inability to raise funds.

The extent to which management in large firms has incentives to maximize firm value is crucial for economic growth. As management becomes more likely to pursue its own objectives, it becomes less able to raise funds and the funds it raises have a higher cost. The mechanisms used to monitor management and provide it with incentives to maximize shareholders wealth differ across economies. The main devices used to discipline management and provide it with incentives are the composition of equity ownership, the market for corporate control, the role of the board of directors of the firm, its capital structure, and the compensation of managers. The usefulness of these devices depends crucially on the role the capital markets play in an economy. Without capital markets, there is no market for corporate control in that unsolicited bids for a firm are not possible and managers cannot be compensated directly as a function of their impact on shareholder wealth. Hence, having an unrestricted market for corporate control has no value in an economy where most firms have no traded equity. The rest of section 4.4 focuses successively on the role of ownership, of the market for corporate control, and of debt in monitoring management before considering the impact of financial openness, reputation, and product market competition on how financial structure affects established firms.

4.4.1 Ownership, Managerial Discretion, and Managerial Incentives

Though diffuse ownership is common for large companies in the United States, it is not so in the rest of the world. Based on the difficulty of collective action for dispersed shareholders, one might be tempted to believe that concentrated ownership is necessarily better and that having firms with large shareholders leads to greater economic growth. The difficulty is that concentrated ownership does not necessarily lead to better investment decisions. It may simply lead to a situation where decisions are made to the benefit of the large shareholder and of management. For instance, the large shareholder can insure that the firm buys from other companies the shareholder owns at favorable prices. Control of a corporation can be achieved with substantially less than majority ownership of the rights to the firm's cash flows. Consequently, large shareholders can extract benefits from the corporation that reduce the value of the firm at the expense of the other shareholders. Barclay and Holderness (1989) show that these benefits can be considerable even in the United States. Zingales (1994) discusses evidence showing that these benefits are large in other countries. As smaller shareholders become disenfranchised, the cost of capital for the corporation increases because shareholders who buy shares expect to receive a smaller fraction of the firm's cash flows.

To the extent that small shareholders cannot be expropriated, however, there is a benefit to the firm from having large shareholders. These shareholders have stronger incentives to monitor the firm because they capture more of the benefit from gathering information that can be used profitably by the firm. A small shareholder cannot gain substantially from finding out that the firm could invest more efficiently and does not have the influence over the firm that would allow him to change the firm's investment policy. Large shareholders can further play a useful role also in making a takeover possible. Grossman and Hart (1980) document the problem that shareholders have little incentive to tender their shares if a bid is made for them because they can capture the benefits from a takeover by holding onto their shares. Since no atomistic shareholder views himself as pivotal to the outcome of the takeover attempt, each atomistic shareholder refrains from tendering. A large shareholder knows that a takeover is much less likely to succeed if he does not tender. Consequently, as demonstrated by Shleifer and Vishny (1986), takeovers that might not be possible in the absence of large shareholders might be possible in their presence. In the presence of private benefits of control for large shareholders, however, the large shareholder may prevent a takeover from taking place to preserve the benefits from control.

It follows from this analysis that no case can be made that either diffuse ownership or control by large shareholders is necessarily better for economic growth. Whether having a large shareholder control a firm increases firm value depends critically on the extent to which the large shareholder can expropriate other capital providers, including minority shareholders, to increase his private benefits from control. If the large shareholder is unable to increase his private benefits from control by expropriating other capital providers, he can increase his wealth only by increasing the value of the firm. However, otherwise, he may choose to focus on generating private benefits even when he could increase substantially the value of the firm through his actions. This is because he gets all the private benefits but only a share of the value-increasing actions he takes. To the extent that noncontrolling shareholders are well protected, having a large shareholder is advantageous. As the large shareholder's stake in the firm increases, he cares more about the value of his stake than he does about the value of private benefits of control. Unfortunately, as La Porta, Lopez-Silanes, and Shleifer (1999) show, large shareholders are less important in countries where the rights of noncontrolling shareholders are well protected. One interpretation of this result is that it makes sense to acquire large stakes only to the extent that they provide large private benefits.

The liquidity of the stock market plays a key role in allowing investors to build large stakes and enabling them to sell large stakes. In an illiquid stock market, investors cannot build large stakes without paying a substantial premium to induce investors to sell their shares. As a result, they might have to give up to selling shareholders much of the benefits that they expect to get from their stake. Similarly, investors with a large stake may find themselves in a situation where they cannot sell it without discounting the shares substantially to attract buyers. An illiquid stock market can therefore both prevent large blocks from being created and large blocks from being dissolved.[21] Bhide (1993) and others have therefore argued that making the stock market less liquid could make large shareholders more active because they might just sell their shares in a more liquid market if they were to conclude that the firm is poorly run. Making the stock market less liquid seems to require ownership to be concentrated already since otherwise it may be too expensive for investors to build large blocks. Further, if existing large block holders cannot sell, they might promote more conservative investment policies.

In the United States, it is extremely rare to observe a hostile takeover of a firm where management owns more than 10 percent of the value of the firm. It is generally the case throughout the world that to exert effective control of a firm a shareholder does not require a majority stake. Depending on the country, however, it is easier to exert control with a small stake using pyramids and/or shares with differential voting rights. For instance, in some countries, exchanges allow firms to list many types of shares but in others they do not. Shares with differential voting rights enable a large shareholder to exert control when he owns only a small claim to cash flows. In this case, the shareholder has less of an incentive to use his votes to maximize firm value. For instance, the shareholder can be better off by diverting cash flow from the firm toward private benefits since he receives all of the private benefits but only a fraction of the cash flow. Pyramids have the same impact.[22] If it were costless to establish firms, a 5-cent investment would make it possible to have working control of General Motors (GM). One could use this five cent investment to float a firm with capital of nine cents, which could then borrow some. This firm would then have assets of say 15 cents that it could use to buy 51 percent of the shares of a company with equity worth 30 cents. This company itself could borrow and then buy a 51 percent stake in a company which then could be worth 80 cents. This could go on until the final company owns half the shares of GM.

The problem with establishing a pyramid or creating shares with differential voting rights is that such devices to capture private benefits of control generally require control to start with. Otherwise, the cost of these devices may be too high irrespective of the magnitude of the private benefits from control. To see this, consider the situation of an individual who has no shares in a corporation and wants to acquire control through a pyramid. Those who sell the shares to the individual know that eventually he can obtain large private benefits from control. They will therefore attempt to set a price for the shares they sell that enables them to capture some of the benefits that the pyramid builder will eventually get from control. There is no reason, however, for only one individual to try to start a pyramid if building pyramids is profitable. Consequently, all the rents from having a pyramid will be expropriated and no pyramid will exist. In contrast, if a shareholder has control, he can decrease his capital invested in the firm by creating a pyramid. Since he has control of the firm, his private benefits will stay constant. However, by selling shares, he increases his resources. The same arguments work for the case where a shareholder wants the firm to have differential voting rights.

Having votes proportional to ownership of cash flows is a powerful device to insure that the controlling shareholder maximizes firm value. This solution does not prevent pyramids, however. With a pyramid, a large shareholder could exert control over a majority of the shares even though his own financial stake might be small. It is interesting to note, however, that differential voting rights and pyramids could lead to greater firm value if the private benefits from control for the large shareholder are fixed and cannot be increased. In this case, the benefit from controlling more voting rights comes only from the ability of the shareholder to increase firm value. It would then be better for management to be monitored by a shareholder that has control than not being monitored. For instance, incompetent management could stay in place if shareholders are atomistic but not if there is a large shareholder in charge. The problem is that it may not be possible to insure that a large shareholder cannot extract private benefits from control that decrease firm value relative to what it would be in the absence of the large shareholder.

Not much attention has been paid in the corporate finance literature to the issue of why managers and large shareholders acquire stakes in firms. This issue is reasonably well understood for an entrepreneur who seeks to raise public funds.[23] For such an entrepreneur, selling all the equity he owns to the public would lead potential investors to be skeptical both about the value of the shares and about the incentives of the entrepreneur to maximize the value of the firm. Consequently, the entrepreneur keeps a fraction of the shares to insure that he can sell the rest at an acceptable price. This motivation for the entrepreneur to hold a large block of shares leads to the existence of large shareholders. For instance, the heirs of the entrepreneurs may have large blocks. As shown by La Porta, Lopez-Silanes, and Shleifer (1999), families are often large block holders.

Because of the private benefits from control, a block is worth more held together than dispersed, so that owners of blocks will attempt to sell them whole.

What is not well understood is why, in a large public firm, management or other investors would acquire large blocks. One can think of a number of reasons for an investor or management to build a large stake, but no evidence exists for the empirical importance of these reasons. First, management or a large shareholder may acquire shares to get private benefits from control. Second, management or a large shareholder may have private information that indicates that the shares are undervalued. One would not expect undervaluation to lead investors to hold a large block of shares for a long period of time. Third, management can acquire shares to commit to a policy of maximizing firm value and hence increase the value of the firm. Doing so can prevent a takeover by increasing firm value. Fourth, management may build a stake to preserve private benefits from control. Fifth, a large shareholder may acquire a stake because of its ability to alter the actions of management in a way that increases value. In all these cases, the acquisition of shares has benefits that would lead existing shareholders to sell their shares only if the price reflects some or all of the benefits that accrue to the new owners. In many cases, however, large blocks are built through direct acquisition of shares from the firm. For instance, the firm may issue stock that it gives to managers or sells to investors. Interestingly, the empirical evidence both for Japan and the United States is that firms that sell a large block of equity to an investor (or organized group of investors) increase in value.[24]

Some of the motivations to build a large stake increase firm value and decrease the cost of capital. Other motivations may have the opposite effect. If management has a small stake or no stake at all, it may have little incentive to worry about the wealth of shareholders. Hence, an increase in management's stake would be a positive development in aligning management's incentives more with those of the shareholders. It might also prevent takeovers with too low a premium from succeeding.[25] However, as management's stake increases, management can effectively prevent the firm from being taken over and can pursue its own objectives without having to worry about discipline from the market for corporate control. Based on these considerations, one would expect firm value to be a concave function of managerial ownership. Morck, Shleifer, and Vishny (1988) provide evidence supportive of this prediction for the United States.

It is often argued that the concentration of ownership in the Japanese or German systems is valuable. Based on our discussion, it is not clear that this is correct. In Japan, companies often have corporate shareholders (banks and nonbanks) which hold together a controlling stake. These holdings are generally reciprocal, so that company A holds shares of company B, and reciprocally. Such a structure can lead to monitoring of management (see Berglof and Perotti 1994). It can force management to pay attention to the other firms in the group. Such a structure also makes it impossible for a firm to be taken over. Morck and Nakamura (1999) argue that the motivation for corporate cross-holding was to prevent firms from being taken over. In other words, the same structure can lead to firm value maximization because managers across firms monitor each other or it can lead to a loss of value because managers collude to protect their firms from the pressures of the market for corporate control.

In a closed economy, a firm is constrained by the financial structure of the economy it is in. As a result, if the economy does not have a reputable stock exchange or investment banks, there is nothing that the firm can do. In open economies, firms can in some circumstances use the financial structure of foreign countries when the financial structure of their country is deficient. We already saw that entrepreneurs can issue equity on foreign markets. However, the problems in using foreign markets or institutions are much more substantial for young firms than they are for more established firms.

Consider a firm that is in a country where minority shareholder rights are not protected. That firm can develop a reputation for protecting minority shareholder rights, but the reputation mechanism has limits. The majority owners of a firm that does not need external financing has no reason to keep a reputation of not taking advantage of minority shareholders. As a result, reputation may be hard to establish when a firm is seeking external financing. However, a listing on a foreign exchange can help a firm located in a country that protects minority shareholder rights poorly. By listing abroad, the firm may subject itself to different laws and to different levels of scrutiny. The firm can list on an exchange as a way to commit to more frequent and detailed disclosure. Cantale (1998) and Fuerst (1998) develop theoretical models where firms reveal their good prospects by listing abroad.

4.4.2   The Market for Corporate Control and Managerial Incentives

If the market for corporate control forces management to take actions that reduce firm value in the long run, then having large shareholders who prevent the firm from being taken over against the wishes of management can increase firm value in the long run. This raises the question of how an active market for corporate control affects economic growth. On the one hand, such a market leads to the removal of inefficient management. On the other hand, though, it can lead management to reject investments that would be profitable. This is because outside investors and potential bidders may not have information that allows them to assess the profitability of such investments. As a result, the value of the firm may fall when such investments are undertaken even though they are profitable when evaluated with the information that management has. A concern has been, therefore, that investments for which information asymmetries are more important may be postponed or avoided altogether by management when it believes that potential bidders are monitoring its actions actively. Viewed from this perspective, Stein (1989) argues that insulating management from takeover pressure can be valuable.

Much attention has been paid to R&D investments from this perspective. R&D investments are hard to evaluate because the firm cannot communicate much about such investments. One would therefore think that takeover pressure would lead firms to decrease R&D investment. Though this argument seems intuitively convincing, it lacks empirical support. For instance, Meulbroek et al. (1990) examine R&D expenditures by firms that adopt antitakeover amendments and find no evidence that the adoption of such amendments leads to an increase in R&D expenditures. Recent research also shows Japanese firms are as quick to cut R&D investment in downturns as American firms.[26] This suggests that the Japanese economy may not be that different from the U.S. economy with respect to R&D investment.

There is some evidence indicating that management's possible preoccupation with short-term investors may affect the cost of capital within the American economy. If management puts a lot of weight on short-term investors, it is less likely to issue equity when the firm is underpriced. The reason for this is that issuing equity under such circumstances is costly for shareholders who plan to sell equity in the short-run. These investors lose because of the dilution of their stake as equity is issued. Since they will be gone when the market learns the true value of the firm, having the firm issue equity does not help them by allowing the firm to take on valuable projects.

The deadweight loss of projects not financed is therefore the cost of short-termism. The evidence that the stock price falls in the United States when a firm announces an equity issue is consistent with the existence of such a cost. If management always issues equity to finance new positive net present value projects and maximizes firm value based on its information, an equity issue does not convey information that the firm is undervalued. Interestingly, the stock price does not fall in Japan when an equity issue is announced. In Japan during the 1980s, the stock price actually increased when a firm announced that it would issue equity.[27] One could therefore argue that a bank-centered economy leads to more efficient investment because firms issue equity when they would not in the U.S. economy, so that firms do not give up valuable projects when firms in the U.S. would give up such projects. Based on the existing evidence, this is a plausible explanation.[28]

If the evidence on security issues in Japan can be interpreted as evidence of a focus of managers in the long term, the question that arises is whether this is due to a lack of hostile takeovers. Another way to put the question is whether Japanese firms would behave the same way if they could be taken over. This seems unlikely. In an economy where hostile takeovers cannot take place but alternate governance mechanisms are nonexistent, short-termism would seem to be the price to pay for having management monitored. In this case, there would be no alternative to having management removed through a takeover if it is inefficient, and firm value would be too low relative to what it could be with better decisions from management. Unfortunately, besides having the effect of forcing management to put more weight on the short-term, the corporate control market has the defect of being a very costly device that leaves much inefficiency unchecked. To gain control of a corporation is expensive, so that bidders attempt to do so to change management only when the gains are extremely large. In the United States, irrespective of how one measures hostile takeovers, they were extremely rare and are rarer now. This raises the issue of alternative monitoring devices for management that help improve managerial performance when management does not perform poorly enough to justify a takeover.

An important consideration that affects the efficiency of the take-over market in insuring better performance from management is that management can influence the probability that the firm will be taken over. Management can put in place antitakeover measures. How-ever, management can also hoard resources so that if a takeover bid is made, it can use these resources to defeat it. Hence, a bidder could identify an inefficiently managed firm and yet be unable to take that firm over because management has the resources to fight off the bid. In this case, the bid may force management to sell poor investments, disgorge excess cash, and even issue debt to commit to maximizing firm value in the future. Hence, the bid will make the firm more efficient. Unfortunately, the fact that management might repel the bid may decrease the probability that the bid will take place. This may lead to a situation where there are too few takeover bids.

Takeovers are rare and expensive, but this does not mean that they have little impact on firms in general. Suppose that bidders cannot fully tell whether firm value is low because of poor decisions or bad luck. There is therefore a risk of a takeover if value falls. In such a situation, it becomes valuable for management to find ways to make commitments to maximize firm value. Management can make such commitments in a number of different ways. It can recruit a board that is more independent and more active. It can change its com-pensation so that it is tied more closely to changes in the value of the firm. It can repurchase shares to signal that firm value is higher than reflected in the share price.

Management can be removed because shareholders decide that doing so will increase firm value. This can take place when the firm is healthy because management misses opportunities to create wealth for shareholders. Such a situation is rare, since it is difficult for outsiders to know about investments management could have made but did not because of lack of ability or foresight. In contrast, it is much more likely that management will be removed because the firm is doing poorly. In that case, the governance role of share-holders is often secondary. As the firm does poorly, the creditors play a large role because they can put the firm into bankruptcy. This means that when shareholders do not perform their role, possibly because they face excessive costs of collective action, creditors may end up monitoring management.

4.4.3 Debt and Managerial Incentives

Debt exerts discipline on management by preventing management from overinvesting and monitoring management. As a result, managers would generally prefer low leverage. Berger, Ofek, and Yermack (1997) provide evidence to this effect. There is evidence, however, that management departs from policies of low leverage when doing so allows it to prevent the firm from being taken over. By issuing debt, management can commit to a policy of asset sales to get the firm more focused or can finance a share repurchase. In either case, firm value may increase sufficiently to make a hostile bid no longer possible.[29] Conservative capital structures give more discretion to management, since it can choose riskier projects without having to worry about losing its position or its power through default. Managerial discretion can be valuable, however, when the firm has good investment opportunities. A firm that is too highly levered may not be able to invest in new projects because shareholders do not want to raise new funds.[30] Raising new funds for such a firm can decrease shareholder wealth because the new funds increase the value of the debt.

Leverage differs across countries, but some of the differences seem overstated. Though the bank-centered systems are often viewed as having greater leverage than the Anglo-Saxon economies, most measures of leverage indicate that Japanese firms do not have systematically higher leverage than comparable American firms.[31] What is true, however, is that the Japanese firms before the mid-1980s had mostly bank debt and only a trivial amount of public debt. The composition of a firm's debt is as important as the amount of a firm's debt, but much more effort has been focused in the finance literature on explaining the amount of debt a firm has than the composition of its debt.

The extreme view on leverage is that bankruptcy has a very low cost. In this case, high leverage works as an incentive and monitoring device. Management that makes mistakes ends up not being able to repay the debt. Consequently, the firm defaults and the creditors get to decide what steps should be taken.[32] It could be that management is removed, but alternatively, management could be kept and the firm could be provided with more resources. As bankruptcy and default become costly, these benefits of debt still exist, but the optimal debt ratio falls. The key in these arguments for the benefit of leverage is, however, that creditors can intervene efficiently and make choices that maximize firm value. This requires the layers of a firm's debt that trigger default if things go poorly to be provided with funds where the costs of collective action for creditors are low.

The costs of collective action for creditors are high when debt is public. In this case, any changes in the debt covenants require an agreement of the debtholders. In contrast, with nonpublic debt, ownership is generally concentrated. This means that nonpublic debtholders can negotiate directly with management. Debtholders can influence management only if the firm faces difficulties in making debt payments. Otherwise, debtholders have no legal rights and management can safely ignore them. As a result of this feature of debt, the type of debt the firm issues plays a crucial role in the extent to which creditors can monitor management. At one extreme, the firm could have long-term zero coupon debt. Such debt would lead to no monitoring of management through debt until maturity of the debt. This is because there are no debt payments until the debt matures. Suppose alternatively that the firm has substantial short-term debt that can be rolled over. In this case, each possible rollover becomes an opportunity for the debtholders to monitor management.

The extent to which a rollover creates an opportunity for the debtholders to monitor management depends crucially on financial structure. To see this, consider one extreme case where nonpublic debtholders face intense competition from the capital markets. In this case, as long as the firm is not in default, if the nonpublic debtholders do not roll the debt over, the managers can issue public debt provided that its value is not too low. This means that nonpublic debtholders have little ability to monitor management at loan renewals. At the other extreme, if there are no alternative sources of funds, debtholders exert considerable control over the firm. The costs of bankruptcy and default also play an extremely important role in the ability of debtholders to monitor the firm. If the costs of default and bankruptcy are very large, debtholders have no bargaining power and cannot monitor. This is because they cannot withhold funds.

It follows from this discussion that short-term debt can be an extremely powerful tool to monitor management when the costs of collective action on the part of the short-term debtholders are low. For that to be the case, the debt cannot be public debt. This assumes, however, that the creditors are able to renew loans if doing so creates value. If there is some chance that banks, which are the main providers of non-public debt, may not have the resources to renew loans, then the benefits from short-term debt fall and short-term financing can force firms to abandon valuable projects because of lack of financing. For instance, Kang and Stulz (2000) provide evidence for Japan that a firm's bank dependence is costly when banks are doing poorly. They find that Japanese firms that were more bank-dependent at the end of the 1980s experienced a sharper stock-price downfall in the early 1990s and invested less than firms that were less bank-dependent. When bank finance is not fully reliable, long-term debt becomes more valuable, but firm value is less than it would be if reliable short-term debt were available. In this perspective, a strong banking sector is important not because of the funding that it makes available but because of the monitoring of management that it makes possible. U.S. evidence of this monitoring role is that the announcement of the renewal of bank loans has a significant positive effect on firm value, while the announcement of the first public debt offering of a firm has a significant negative impact on its stock price.[33] Kang (1993) provides evidence on the monitoring role of banks for Japanese firms by showing that firms make better acquisitions in the United States when they have a main bank, in that the market reacts more favorably to their acquisition announcement.

Banks are important, but they care about being repaid more than they care about firm value unless they hold equity. In other words, intermediated finance can insure that management cannot reduce firm value too much, but cannot insure that management increases firm value as much as is possible.[34] If the banks hold equity, then they care more about increasing firm value. However, the cost of having banks hold equity is that they become more vulnerable.

There is a paradox about asking banks to monitor management that needs to be explained. If management of a nonfinancial company has to be monitored, why is it that the management of a bank will do so and who monitors the bank's management? The answer here is straightforward for two reasons. First, banks diversify across loans. Diamond (1984) showed that it therefore possible for bank investors to assess management's performance more easily than to assess the performance of management in an undiversified firm. Second, banks have considerable short-term financing. Consequently, if the management of banks makes poor decisions, in principle punishment is swift since the providers of short-term funds— the depositors—withdraw their funds.[35] Viewed from this perspective, bank bailouts have a pervasive cost: They make bank management less efficient and consequently decrease the efficiency of the economy as a whole. At the same time, however, if banks are short of capital, projects have to be interrupted.

There is evidence that distress and default have different implications in the Japanese system than in the U.S. system. Japanese banks seem to intervene more quickly than U.S. banks and firms within a Keiretsu group seem to obtain more funds to remedy the distress.[36] There is evidence that U.S. banks are reluctant to renegotiate the terms of loans, so that the flexibility of bank loans relative to public debt is not taken advantage of.[37] In principle, bank debt should be easier to renegotiate, so that financial distress for firms with substantial bank debt could be remedied more effectively through renegotiation. However, banks that are constrained by capital requirements may have little room to negotiate. It could even be the case that banks allow firms to continue activities that have negative value by funding these activities to prevent default. All this means that relying on banks to monitor management requires critically that banks be able to perform that role and have the incentives to do so.

4.4.4   Financial Structure and Established Firms

For established firms, then, the financial structure has to insure that management is monitored and that large shareholders cannot expropriate the other capital providers. The following characteristics of the financial structure help to achieve this:

1. Laws and enforcement of laws that prevent the expropriation of claimholders, especially minority shareholders, by management and large shareholders.

2. A market for corporate control puts a limit to management's use of its discretion to pursue its own goals.

3. Because of the existence of information asymmetries, firms have to have some ability to protect themselves from hostile takeovers

when the bid price is too low in light of management's information about the true value of the firm. Otherwise, management will shy away from investments for which information asymmetries are important.

4. Large shareholders can play an important role in monitoring management. Laws should therefore not attempt to prevent the existence of such shareholders or to prevent coordination among large shareholders.

5. Leverage is an important monitoring tool. Though management generally prefers low leverage, the discipline of debt is advantageous. One would therefore expect financial structures that do not penalize debt to be more favorable to growth.

6. In principle, bank debt is especially valuable because it has low costs of collective action and is flexible.

7. For leverage to play its role, bankruptcy has to be cheap and the rights of creditors have to be well defined.

8. Financial stability is critical if bank financing plays its appropriate role in an economy. In the absence of such stability, activities where flexible financing is important cannot take place.

9. Firms have to be able to place equity with private investors.

It should be clear from this section that the relation between economic growth and the public capital markets is ambiguous. A firm financed only through atomistic investors is likely to be a firm with higher distress and bankruptcy costs, and its management is likely to be less monitored than if the firm has other sources of financing and possibly has some large shareholders. If takeovers are difficult or impossible, the management of a firm financed through atomistic investors becomes largely unmonitored as long as the firm is not in default. Further, public funding is likely to be too expensive when information asymmetries are important. As a result, an economy that relies too much on funding from the capital markets would be one specialized in industries where information asymmetries are not important. Though protection of minority shareholders is important, one also has to worry about who will monitor management. If management is insufficiently monitored, large firms may end up investing too much. It should be clear, however, that both banks and markets are important. Intermediated finance has a role to play with established firms, but so do capital markets.

4.5 The Impact of Financial Structure on Growth

This section discusses some empirical evidence that is supportive of the arguments advanced in this chapter. A growing recent literature shows that aspects of financial structure as defined here matter for the development of finance and for economic growth. As countries grow, one expects their financial structure to change. This can make it difficult to make the case that financial structure has an independent influence on financial development and economic growth. The work of La Porta et al. (1997, 1998) has been highly successful in making such a case. They have demonstrated the importance of the origin of a country's legal system in its financial and economic development. In their work, they show that common law countries differ strikingly in their financial development from civil law countries. Since a country's legal system was determined in some cases centuries ago, often through colonization, it would seem that no case can be made that financial and economic development affect the origin of the legal system of a country. La Porta et al. (1998) show that ownership is more concentrated when the legal system does not protect small shareholders well and find that common law countries protect small shareholders better. La Porta et al. (1997) add to these findings by showing that the equity markets and external finance are more important in common law countries. Among other results, they point out that countries with civil law have fewer initial public offerings (IPOs). Modigliani and Perotti (1998) argue that poorer legal protection increases the importance of debt financing relative to equity financing and find some supportive data.

Though the research focusing on legal protection has been extremely successful, it has three limitations whose implications ought to be investigated thoroughly. First, a country's legal origin was determined a long time ago.[38] This makes it difficult to distinguish between a situation where legal origin explains the importance of financial markets with a situation where legal origin happens to be correlated with variables that explain the importance of financial markets. If legal origin and the other variables that might affect the importance of financial markets changed over time, the issue of the importance of omitted variables might be resolved. Unfortunately, legal origin is constant. Second, the legal origin variables have shown themselves to have considerable explanatory power for post–World War II studies. Yet, the United States had poor protection of minority shareholder rights during the last century. In many countries, as emphasized by Rajan and Zingales (1999), attitudes toward markets changed dramatically during the first half of this century, so that countries that were favorably disposed toward markets stopped being so disposed. Legal origins cannot explain these changes.

Third, the policy relevance of legal origin or other legal variables is not clear. Nothing can be done about legal origin. A country might be encouraged to change its laws about the protection of shareholder minority rights and to enforce these laws. It is not clear that changing laws or the enforcement of laws by itself will have much impact, however. It does not follow from the fact that financial markets are weak absent protection of minority shareholders that they become strong simply by having such protection. None of the existing empirical studies conduct a study of countries that changed these laws or the degree of enforcement of these laws. A study of such countries would provide a good natural experiment to evaluate the significance of legal variables.

Demirgüç-Kunt and Maksimovic (1998) provide evidence that relates the use of external financing to characteristics of a country's financial markets. They find that greater respect for the law leads to greater use of external finance for firms. They also show that existence of a well-functioning stock market leads to greater external financing of firms. Rajan and Zingales (1998) provide a complementary perspective by showing that industries that rely more on external finance in the United States grow more in countries with better financial development. King and Levine (1993) and Levine and Zervos (1993) argue that greater financial development increases economic growth. Levine and Zervos show that growth is related to stock market activity, among other variables. Levine (1999) shows that there is a relation between measures of the development of the financial intermediation sector and measures of creditors' rights and contract enforcement. He then proceeds to test for an impact of these determinants of financial intermediation development on economic growth and finds a significant effect.

We considered a number of elements of financial structure in this chapter. It would therefore be useful to know which ones are most important for economic growth. Levine (1999) organizes a horse race where he compares, on the one hand, the relation between growth and law variables, and on the other hand, the relation between growth and the importance of banks. He finds evidence that law variables help predict growth while the importance of banks does not. Keeping everything else unchanged, the evidence tells us that increasing the relative importance of banks has no impact on economic growth. However, the importance of banks is determined endogenously. Banks can be important because of impediments to the development of markets or because of political intervention. Hence, a large banking sector might be evidence of distortions in the workings of market forces, which one would not expect to be associated with greater growth. Nevertheless, this evidence shows that the relative importance of banks is not a useful variable to explain economic growth.

In addition to the recent cross-country evidence, there is a lot of evidence at the country level showing that the sources of finance and the governance mechanisms are important for firms. In particular, there is much evidence at this point permitting a comparison of Japanese firms and U.S. firms. There is less evidence on German firms. The traditional view of this comparison, mentioned in the introduction, is that Japanese firms have a sizable fraction of their shares held by stable corporate shareholders, high leverage, bank finance, and no hostile takeovers. In contrast, U.S. firms have atomistic shareholders, lower leverage, less bank finance, and hostile takeovers. This sharp contrast was correct at one point. However, it is less so now. Japanese firms still have substantial holdings by corporate shareholders. Despite all the difficulties the Japanese economy has had since 1990, these holdings have decreased only slowly in the aggregate. With few exceptions, Japan still does not have hostile takeovers. However, the role of banks and bank finance has decreased steadily for the last fifteen years. There are three reasons for this decrease. First, banks are most influential when firms are credit-constrained. As Japanese firms generated large cash flows, they became independent of banks because their financing was less important. Second, deregulation made it possible for Japanese firms to obtain funds from other sources than Japanese banks. Third, since the early 1990s, Japanese banks have suffered from a lack of capital which has decreased their ability to lend new funds.

The decrease in the importance of banks in Japan shows that the bank-centered system of Japan at its peak may simply not have been stable for two reasons. First, managers want to be independent of banks if they can, so that they try to escape their influence. Banks can prevent managers from acquiring independence from them when firms have trouble paying off their bank loans, but not otherwise.[39] Second, as a country's transactions with foreigners become liberalized, firms can turn to foreign sources of funds.[40] This limits bank influence. The evolution of the Japanese bank-centered system therefore suggests that contrasting the Japanese system to the U.S. system should not be interpreted as indicating that one could actually choose to recreate the Japanese system if one wanted to. Japanese banks played a key role in the financing and governance of firms for a long time not because some financial planner decided that this was best for economic growth but because these banks had enough political power to keep markets in check.[41]

There is considerable evidence that the Japanese system had benefits for firms that led to a lowering of the cost of capital. First, Hoshi, Kashyap, and Scharfstein (1991) show that the investment of Japanese firms belonging to keiretsus was less sensitive to liquidity. The sensitivity of investment to liquidity has often been described as a direct implication of the cost of capital wedge we discussed earlier. For instance, Fazzari, Hubbard, and Petersen (1988) argue that the dependence of investment on liquidity increases as firms face greater difficulties and cost in obtaining external funds and provide supportive evidence for the United States. The evidence of Hoshi, Kashyap, and Scharfstein seems to imply that the determinants of investment differ between the United States and Japan. From our analysis, one would expect this to be the case if funds are more easily provided in periods of distress and if the use of funds is more efficiently monitored. Some authors—for instance, Kaplan and Minton (1994) and Kang and Shivdasani (1997)—demonstrate that banks are active when a firm faces difficulties. They provide funds, change management, and provide expertise. This interpretation of the evidence is not without controversy, however. Morck and Nakamura (1999) argue that what is going is simply that keiretsus prop up their sick members.

A second area in which evidence has been developed shows that information asymmetries are less important in Japan. We explained earlier that information asymmetries increase the cost of capital. The evidence on information asymmetries is somewhat indirect, however. From the U.S. evidence, we know that information asymmetries lead to negative stock-price reactions to issues of information-sensitive securities. These negative stock-price reactions are not observed in Japan. Further, Dewenter and Warther (1998) show recently that Japanese firms do not set their dividend policies in the same way as U.S. firms do. It seems that U.S. firms are much more concerned about the information conveyed by changes in dividends than Japanese firms.

The evidence we have just surveyed tells us nothing about whether firms invest too much. The largest investments firms typically make are acquisitions of other firms. There is considerable evidence for the United States that since the early 1980s the market reacts unfavorably when a firm announces that it is making a bid for another firm. A possible interpretation of this evidence is that these bids are not in the interest of shareholders. Another possible interpretation, however, is that bids reveal that the firm does not have valuable investment opportunities. It is interesting to note that the evidence for Japan is different. On average, Japanese bidders experience positive abnormal returns when they announce acquisitions. Further, these positive abnormal returns seem to be closely associated to the influence of main banks, suggesting therefore that bank relationships lead firms to make better investment decisions. Much recent research has focused on investment within diversified firms. Evidence that diversified firms sell at a discount in the United States relative to matched portfolios of specialized firms is viewed as evidence that diversified firms invest inefficiently. Interestingly, Lins and Servaes (1997) indicate that there is no diversification discount in Germany and that the diversification discount in Japan is about half what it is in the United States. One might conclude from this that investment is less inefficient in Japan and Germany. However, a well-known argument for diversification at the firm level is that it creates an internal capital market that enables firms to invest efficiently when information asymmetries would make it difficult to raise funds externally. It could therefore be the case that diversification has more value in Japan and Germany because external capital markets are not as well developed. In a recent paper, Fauver, Houston, and Naranjo (1998) show that the diversification discount is closely related to financial structure across a large number of countries. More specifically, the value of diversification seems to be negatively related to the level of capital market development and to the degree of shareholder protection.

The country-level evidence shows that firms act differently in countries that differ in financial structure. One should be careful not to overstate these differences, however. For instance, Kaplan (1994) shows that the differences in how managers are compensated and fired between Japan and the United States do not seem economically important and Rajan and Zingales (1995) show that leverage decisions in Japan and the United States can be explained by similar variables. One should also be careful to remember that the country-level studies focus on specific aspects of financial structure. As a result, it is perfectly possible for a financial structure to have positive effects as well as negative effects.

The country studies must therefore be viewed more as evidence that financial structure matters than as evidence that one type of financial structure dominates other types of financial structure.

4.6   Conclusion

Financial structure determines the extent to which firms can limit the adverse impact of the hidden information and the hidden action problems on their cost of capital. With a poor financial structure, the cost of capital is too high so that it is difficult for entrepreneurs to create firms and for these firms to invest efficiently. It should be clear from the analysis presented in this chapter that both financial intermediaries and capital markets have a key role to play for economic growth to take place efficiently. Financial structure has to be designed so that both financial intermediaries and capital markets can play their role effectively.

The analysis in this chapter has been mostly static, in that we have discussed attributes of financial structures that are valuable. A key part of this analysis has been that financial structures have to make it possible for financial intermediaries and investors to develop specialized knowledge that enhances their usefulness to firms and their ability to monitor firms. As a result, financial structures thrive on stability and property rights. Uncertain regulatory environments, political interferences, and crisis-prone economies decrease the benefits from developing specific knowledge. This is especially the case for banking crises which ruin existing relationships if mishandled and hence not only hurt growth when they happen but also hurt future growth.

There is a complex relationship between macroeconomic stability and financial structure that has to be studied further. To wit, with a poor financial structure, there is no room for long-term relationships. Poor bankruptcy laws put a premium on short-term debt because such debt gives the creditors a chance to withdraw their funds ahead of a default. However, short-term debt itself can be a source of instability since exogenous shocks to banks can force them to withdraw funding to firms and hence force firms to cut back on investment, thereby magnifying the shock to banks. Similarly, a poor financial structure can force firms to seek financing offshore without having the ability to hedge the resulting foreign currency exposure. This again can lead to increased instability because of the sensitivity of such funding to macreconomic and exchange rate shocks as well as to political risk. This does not imply that such funding should be taxed or limited. If one were to do so, investment that otherwise would take place will be curtailed. Rather, it suggests that the impediments to local currency borrowing that lead firms to borrow abroad should be eliminated. As a result, progress made in making a country's financial structure mode efficient can also lead to decreasing macreconomic instability in that country by allowing firms to obtain more stable financing.

The globalization of financial markets and capital account liberalization raise important questions for the role of financial structure that need further study. In this chapter, I have emphasized that globalization makes it possible for established firms to often bypass much of the local financial structure. Doing so is much harder and often impossible for new firms. These firms rely on intermediated finance that generally cannot be provided from abroad. Such firms could be affected adversely by globalization if its means greater instability of financial intermediaries. However, globalization can improve the stability of financial intermediaries. In particular, with financial liberalization, local financial intermediaries can fund themselves abroad and can diversify their risks abroad, so that they become more insulated from local shocks. Globalization can also improve local intermediated finance by increasing competition and opening financing alternatives for local firms.

Notes

1. See Levine 1997 for a review of how finance affects growth.

2. I define here perfect capital markets to be markets with no transaction costs, no contracting costs, no taxes, no information asymmetries, and no restrictions to trades in financial assets.

3. Thurow 1992.

4. See Weinstein and Yafeh 1998.

5. See Levine 1997 for a review.

6. See Fama 1978.

7. See Fazzari, Hubbard, and Petersen 1988 for a discussion of this wedge and its implications for investment equations.

8. See Stiglitz and Weiss 1981.

9. Shleifer and Wolfenson (2000) provide a model that relates legal enforcement to firm value and to ownership of cash flow rights by the entrepreneur. In their model, the entrepreneur has to contribute more of his own funds per dollar invested as legal enforcement falls. As a result, the scale of the projects falls as legal enforcement falls since the resources of the entrepreneur are finite. With a model where the project requires a minimum investment scale, fewer projects would get started.

10. See Admati and Pfleiderer 1994. Gompers 1995 provides empirical evidence on stage financing.

11. Historically, there have been securities without limited liability. In particular, bank equity in the United States often did not have limited liability before the 1930s. Consequently, if a bank's capital fell, the shareholders could be called upon to invest more funds. See Winton 1993 for a theory of limited liability and a discussion of how it evolved over time.

12. See Roe 1987.

13. See Townsend 1979.

14. See Sharpe 1990 and Rajan 1992.

15. Boot and Thakor (1998) discuss how the supply of relationship lending by banks depends on competition within the banking sector as well as from the capital markets.

16. Myers (2000) discusses the role of the public markets as a way for the entrepreneur to prevent his efforts from being destroyed through rent-seeking. Black and Gilson (1998) argue that a dynamic venture capital sector exists only in stock-market-based economies as opposed to economies dominated by banks and argue that this is because venture capital requires the exit option that arises through access to capital markets.

17. Subrahmanyam and Titman (1999) develop a model where a firm seeks funding from the capital markets when investors who spend resources to acquire information about the firm get different information and complementary information. In this case, public funding is valuable because the public markets aggregate this diverse information efficiently. In contrast, firms seek private funding when investors would get the same information since in that case it is inefficient for more investors to spend resources to acquire the same information.

18. See Lerner 1995 for evidence of the proximity of venture capitalists to the firm they help finance within the United States.

19. Jensen (1986) argues that free cash flow, namely, cash flow that is not required to finance valuable projects, creates agency costs.

20. See Stulz 1990 for an analysis of this problem.

21. See Maug 1998.

22. See Wolfenzon 1999 for an analysis of pyramids.

23. See, for instance, Leland and Pyle 1977.

24. See, for instance, Wruck 1989 for the United States and Kato and Schalheim 1993 and Kang and Stulz 1996 for Japan.

25. See Stulz 1988 for a model of this effect.

26. See Hall and Weinstein 1996.

27. See Kang and Stulz 1996.

28. Kim, Kang, and Stulz (forthcoming) show that firms issuing equity in Japan have negative long-run equity abnormal returns. If one adds these long-run abnormal returns to the event abnormal return, the stock-price reaction to equity issues in Japan is not different from the stock-price reaction to equity issues in the United States. However, if one believes that financial markets are efficient, then they impound all the information received from the corporate event into the stock price immediately, in which case the Japanese evidence is the opposite of the U.S. evidence.

29. See Safieddine and Titman 1999 for evidence that firms that increase their leverage to fight off a takeover perform well subsequently.

30. See Myers 1977.

31. See Rajan and Zingales 1995 for a study of leverage across countries.

32. Harris and Raviv 1990 provide an analysis where default makes it possible to gather information and select optimal investment policies.

33. See James 1987 and Lummer and McConnell 1989 for stock-price reactions to bank loans and Datta, Iskandar-Datta, and Patel 2000 for the evidence on initial public offerings of debt.

34. See Macey and Miller 1997 for an analysis of this point in the context of Japan.

35. See Diamond and Rajan 2000.

36. See Kaplan and Minton 1994 and Kang and Shivdasani 1997.

37. See Asquith, Gertner, and Scharfstein 1994.

38. See Glaeser and Shleifer 2000 for a theory of legal origins.

39. See Hoshi, Kashyap, and Scharfstein 1991.

40. See Kang et al. 1995.

41. See Rosenbluth 1989.

References

Admati, Anat R., and Paul Pfleiderer. 1994. Robust financial contracting and the role of venture capitalists. *Journal of Finance* 49:371–402.

Allen, Franklin, and David Gale. 1995. A welfare comparison of intermediaries and financial markets in Germany and the U.S. *European Economic Review* 19:179–209.

Arrow, Kenneth J. 1979. Pareto efficiency with costly transfers. *Economic Forum* 10:1–13.

Asquith, Paul, Robert Gertner, and David Scharfstein. 1994. Anatomy of financial distress: An examination of junk-bond issuers. *Quarterly Journal of Economics* 109:625–658.

Barclay, Michael, and Clifford Holderness. 1989. Private benefits from control of public corporations. *Journal of Financial Economics* 25:371–395.

Berger, Philip G., Eli Ofek, and David L. Yermack. 1997. Managerial entrenchment and capital structure decisions. *Journal of Finance* 52:1411–1438.

Berglof, Erik, and Enrico Perotti. 1994. The governance structure of the Japanese financial keiretsu. *Journal of Financial Economics* 36:259–284.

Berle, Adolf, and Gardiner Means. 1932. *The modern corporation and private property.* New York: Macmillan.

Bhide, Amar. 1993. The hidden cost of stock market liquidity. *Journal of Financial Economics* 34:31–51.

Black, Bernard S., and Ronald J. Gilson. 1998. Venture capital and the structure of capital markets: Banks versus stock markets. *Journal of Financial Economics* 47:243–277.

Boot, Arnoud W. A., and Anjan V. Thakor. 1998. Can relationship banking survive competition? Unpublished working paper, University of Michigan, Ann Arbor, Michigan.

Cantale, Salvatore. 1998. The choice of a foreign market as a signal. Unpublished working paper, A. B. Freeman School of Business, Tulane University, New Orleans, LA.

Coffee, John C. Jr. 2000. Convergence and its critics: What are the preconditions to the separation of ownership and control. Working Paper No. 179, The Center for Law and Economic Studies, Columbia Law School, New York, NY.

Datta, S., M. Iskandar-Datta, and A. Patel. 2000. Some evidence on the uniqueness of initial public debt offerings. *Journal of Finance* 55(2):715–743.

Demirgüç-Kunt, Aslı, and Vojislav Maksimovic. 1998. Law, finance, and firm growth, *Journal of Finance* 53(6):2107–2137.

Dewenter, Kathryn L., and Vincent A. Warther. 1998. Dividends, asymmetric information, and agency conflicts: Evidence from comparison of the dividend policies of Japanese and U.S. firms. *Journal of Finance* 53:879–904.

Diamond, Douglas W. 1984. Financial intermediation and delegated monitoring. *Review of Financial Studies* 51:393–414.

Diamond, Douglas W. 1991. Monitoring and reputation: The choice between bank loans and directly placed debt. *Journal of Political Economy* 99:689–721.

Diamond, Douglas, and Raghuram Rajan. 2000. A theory of bank capital. *Journal of Finance* 55(6):2431–2465.

Fama, Eugene F. 1978. The effects of a firm's investment and financial decisions. *American Economic Review* 68:272–284.

Fauver, Larry, Joel Houston, and Andy Naranjo. 1998. Capital market development, legal systems, and the value of corporate diversification: A cross-country analysis. Unpublished working paper, University of Florida, Gainesville, FL.

Fazzari, Steven M., Robert Glenn Hubbard, and Bruce C. Petersen. 1988. Financing constraints and corporate investment. *Brookings Papers on Economic Activity*, no. 1:141–195.

Fuerst, O. 1998. A theoretical analysis of the investor protection regulations: Argument for global listing of stocks. Working paper, Yale School of Management, New Haven, CT.

Glaeser, Edward. S., and Andrei Shleifer. 2000. Legal origins. Unpublished working paper, Harvard University, Cambridge, MA.

Gomez, Armando. Forthcoming. Going public without governance: Managerial reputation effects. *Journal of Finance*.

Gompers, Paul A. 1995. Optimal investment, monitoring, and staging of venture capital. *Journal of Finance* 50:1461–1489.

Grossman, Sanford, and Oliver Hart. 1980. Takeover bids, the free-rider problem, and the theory of the corporation. *Bell Journal of Economics* 11:42–64.

Hall, B. J., and D. E. Weinstein. 1996. The myth of the patient Japanese: Corporate myopia and financial distress in Japan and the United States. Unpublished working paper, Harvard University, Cambridge, MA.

Harris, Milton, and Artur Raviv. 1990. Capital structure and the informational role of debt. *Journal of Finance* 45:321–350.

Hoshi, T., A. Kashyap, and D. Scharfstein. 1991. Corporate structure, liquidity, and investment: Evidence from Japanese industrial groups. *The Quarterly Journal of Economics* 106(1):33–60.

James, Christopher. 1987. Some evidence on the uniqueness of bank loans. *Journal of Financial Economics* 19:217–235.

Jensen, Michael C. 1986. Agency costs of free cash flow, corporate finance, and takeover. *American Economic Review* 76:323–329.

Kang, J.-K. 1993. The international market for corporate control: Mergers and acquisitions of U.S. firms by Japanese firms. *Journal of Financial Economics* 34:345–372.

Kang, J.-K., and A. Shivdasani. 1997. Corporate restructuring during performance declines in Japan. *Journal of Financial Economics* 46:29–65.

Kang, J.-K., and René M. Stulz. 1996. How Different Is Japanese Corporate Finance? An Investigation of the Information Content of New Security Issues. *Review of Financial Studies* 9:109–139.

Kang, Jun-Koo, Yong-Cheol Kim, K. Park, and René M. Stulz. 1995. An analysis of the wealth effects of Japanese offshore dollar-denominated convertible and warrant bond issues. *Journal of Financial and Quantitative Analysis* 30:257–270.

Kaplan, S. N. 1994. Top executive rewards and firm performance: A comparison of Japan and the United States. *Journal of Political Economy* 102:510–546.

Kaplan, S. N., and B. A. Minton. 1994. Appointments of outsiders to Japanese boards: Determinants and implications for managers. *Journal of Financial Economics* 36:225–258.

Kato, K., and J. S. Schallheim. 1993. Private equity financings in Japan and corporate grouping (Keiretsu). *Pacific-Basin Finance Journal* 1:287–307.

Kim, Y.-C., J.-K. Kang, and R. M. Stulz. Forthcoming. The underreaction hypothesis and the new issue puzzle: Evidence from Japan. *Review of Financial Studies*.

King, Robert G., and Ross Levine. 1993. Finance and growth: Schumpeter might be right. *Quarterly Journal of Economics* 108:717–737.

La Porta, R., F. Lopez-de-Silanes, and A. Shleifer. 1999. Corporate ownership around the world. *Journal of Finance* 54:471–517.

La Porta, R., F. Lopez-de-Silanes, A. Shleifer, and R. W. Vishny. 1997. Legal determinants of external finance. *Journal of Finance* 52:1131–1150.

La Porta, R., F. Lopez-de-Silanes, A. Shleifer, and R. W. Vishny. 1998. Law and finance. *Journal of Political Economy* 106:1113–1156.

La Porta, R., F. Lopez-de-Silanes, A. Shleifer, and R. W. Vishny. 2000. Investor protection and corporate governance. *Journal of Financial Economics* 58(1):3–27.

Leland, Hayne E., and David H. Pyle. 1977. Information asymmetry, financial structure, and financial intermediation. *Journal of Finance* 32:371–387.

Lerner, Josh. 1995. Venture capitalists and the oversight of private firms. *Journal of Finance* 50:301–318.

Levine, Ross. 1997. Financial development and economic growth: Views and agenda. *Journal of Economic Literature* 35:688–726.

Levine, Ross. 1999. Law, finance, and economic growth. *Journal of Financial Intermediation* 8(1/2):36–67.

Levine, Ross, and Sara J. Zervos. 1993. What we have learned about policy and growth from cross-country regressions? *American Economic Review* 83:426–430.

Lins, Karl, and Henri Servaes. 1997. International evidence on the value of corporate diversification. Working paper, University of North Carolina, Chapel Hill, NC.

Lummer, Scott L., and John J. McConnell. 1989. Further evidence on the bank lending process and the capital market response to bank loan agreement. *Journal of Financial Economics* 25:99–122.

Macey, Jonathan R., and Geoffrey P. Miller. 1997. Universal banks are no the answer to America's corporate governance 'problem': A look at Germany, Japan, and the U.S. *Journal of Applied Corporate Finance* 9(Winter):57–73.

Maug, Ernst. 1998. Large shareholders as monitors: Is there a tradeoff between liquidity and control? *Journal of Finance* 53:65–98.

Merton, Robert. 1995. A functional perspective of financial intermediation. *Financial Management* 24:23–41.

Meulbroek, Lisa K., Jeffry Netter, Mark Mitchell, Arnold Mulherin, and Annette Poulsen. 1990. Shark repellents and managerial myopia: An empirical test. *Journal of Political Economy* 98:1108–1117.

Modigliani, F., and E. Perotti. 1998. Security versus bank finance: The importance of proper enforcement of legal rules. Unpublished paper, University of Amsterdam.

Morck, Randall, and Masao Nakamura. 1999. Banks and corporate control in Japan. *Journal of Finance* 54:319–339.

Morck, Randall, Andrei Shleifer, and Robert Vishny. 1988. *Characteristics of Targets of Hostile and Friendly Takeovers in Corporate Takeovers: Causes and Consequences*, 101–129. National Bureau of Economic Research Project Report Series. Chicago and London: University of Chicago Press.

Myers, Stewart. 1977. Determinants of corporate borrowing. *Journal of Financial Economics* 5:147–175.

Myers, Stewart. 2000. Outside equity financing. Unpublished working paper, Massachusetts Institute of Technology, Cambridge, MA.

Rajan, Raghuram. 1992. Insiders and outsiders: The choice between relationship and arm's length debt. *Journal of Finance* 47:1367–1400.

Rajan, Raghuram, and Luigi Zingales. 1995. What do we know about capital structure? Some evidence from international data. *Journal of Finance* 50:1421–1460.

Rajan, Raghuram, and Luigi Zingales. 1998. Financial dependence and growth. *American Economic Review* 88:559–586.

Rajan, Raghuram, and Luigi Zingales. 1999. The politics of financial development. Unpublished working paper, University of Chicago, Chicago, IL.

Roe, Mark J. 1987. The voting prohibition in bond workouts. *Yale Law Journal* 97:232–279.

Rosenbluth, Frances McCall. 1989. *Financial politics in contemporary Japan*. Ithaca, NY: Cornell University Press.

Safieddine, Assem, and Sheridan Titman. 1999. Leverage and corporate performance: Evidence from unsuccessful takeovers. *Journal of Finance* 54:547–580.

Sharpe, Steven A. 1990. Asymmetric information, bank lending, and implicit contracts: A stylized model of customer relationships. *Journal of Finance* 45:1069–1087.

Shleifer, Andrei, and Robert Vishny. 1986. Large shareholders and corporate control. *Journal of Political Economy* 94:461–488.

Shleifer, Andrei, and Daniel Wolfenson. 2000. Investor protection and equity markets. Working paper 7974, National Bureau of Economic Research, Cambridge, MA.

Stein, Jeremy C. 1989. Efficient capital markets, inefficient firms: A model of myopic corporate behavior. *The Quarterly Journal of Economics* 104:655–669.

Stiglitz, J.-E., and Andrew Weiss. 1981. Credit rationing in markets with imperfect information. *American Economic Review* 71:393–410.

Stulz, René M. 1988. Managerial control of voting rights: Financing policies and the market for corporate control. *Journal of Financial Economics* 20:25–54.

Stulz, René M. 1990. Managerial discretion and optimal financing policies. *Journal of Financial Economics* 26:3–27.

Stulz, René M. 1995. Globalization and the cost of capital: The case of Nestlé. *European Financial Management* 8:30–38.

Subrahmanyam, Avanidhar, and Sheridan Titman. 1999. The going-public decision and the development of financial markets. *Journal of Finance* 54:1045–1082.

Townsend, Robert M. 1979. Optimal contracts and competitive markets with costly state verification. *Journal of Economic Theory* 21:265–293.

Thurow, L. 1992. *Head-to-head: The coming economic battle among Japan, Europe, and America.* New York: Warner Books.

Weinstein, D. E., and Y. Yafeh. 1998. On the costs of a bank centered financial system: Evidence from the changing main bank relations in Japan. *Journal of Finance* 53:635–677.

Winton, Andrew. 1993. Limitation of liability and the ownership structure of the firm. *Journal of Finance* 48:487–512.

Wolfenzon, Daniel. 1999. A theory of pyramidal ownership. Unpublished working paper, Harvard University, Cambridge, MA.

Wruck, K. H. 1989. Equity ownership concentration and firm value: Evidence from private equity financings. *Journal of Financial Economics* 23:3–28.

Zingales, Luigi. 1994. The value of the voting right: A study of the Milan stock exchange experience. *Review of Financial Studies* 7:125–148.

5

Financial Structure and Economic Development: Firm, Industry, and Country Evidence

Thorsten Beck, Aslı
Demirgüç-Kunt, Ross Levine,
and Vojislav Maksimovic

5.1 Introduction

A large body of research finds that financial development exerts a large positive impact on economic growth. The conclusion emerges from cross-country studies, industry-level studies, firm-level studies, and time-series evaluations. Furthermore, the positive link between financial development and economic growth holds after controlling for other growth determinants and possible endogeneity.[1] While still open to additional research, the positive relationship between growth and financial development prompts the following question: Which specific types of financial systems are particularly conducive to new firm formation, existing firm expansion, industrial success, and overall economic growth?

Besides examining the relationship between overall financial development and economic growth, many researchers have sought to evaluate the links between financial structure—the mixture of financial markets and institutions operating in an economy—and economic growth, the composition of industrial development, and corporate finance. In defining financial structure, historians, economists, and policymakers have focused on the relative merits of bank-based versus market-based financial systems. Besides a contentious theoretical debate about the comparative advantages of bank-based and market-based systems, empirical work over the last century has primarily involved studies of Germany and Japan as bank-based systems and the United States and the United Kingdom as market-based systems. As summarized by Allen and Gale (1999) and Stulz (chapter 4), this research has produced enormously valuable information on the operation of these country's financial systems. The small sample, however, limits the generality of the inferences that historians, economists, and policymakers can draw for other countries. The four countries have very similar long-run growth rates, so that it is difficult to correlate differences in financial structure with differences in long-run growth rates. The absence of cross-country data on financial structure has prohibited researchers from extending the analysis to a broad cross-section of countries.

This chapter expands the study of financial structure from rigorous studies of a few countries to a broad cross-section of countries by using the large international dataset constructed in chapter 2. We use (1) firm-level analyses on thirty-three countries, (2) industry-level studies on thirty-four countries, and (3) country-level investigations of forty-eight countries. Thus, we use an assortment of different datasets and econometric methodologies to assess the relationship between financial structure and economic development. In this way, we contribute to a century-long debate.

From an economic theory perspective, the chapter examines four views on financial structure: the bank-based view, the market-based view, the law and finance view, and the financial-services view. The *bank-based view* highlights the positive role of banks in mobilizing resource, identifying good projects, monitoring managers, and managing risk (Levine 1997, 2000). The bank-based view also highlights the comparative shortcomings of market-based systems. Specifically, well-developed markets quickly reveal information in public markets, which reduces the incentives for individual investors to acquire information. Thus, greater market development may impede incentives for identifying innovative projects and thereby hinder efficient resource allocation (Stiglitz 1985; Boot, Greenbaum, and Thakor 1993). Proponents of the bank-based view also stress that liquid markets create a myopic investor climate (Bhide 1993). Specifically, in liquid markets, investors can inexpensively sell their shares, so that they have fewer incentives to monitor managers rigorously. Thus, greater market development may hinder corporate control and national productivity. Moreover, Gerschenkron (1962) and others have argued that banks have advantages over markets in the early stages of economic development when the institutional environment is unable to support market activities effectively. Specifically, even in countries with weak legal and accounting systems and frail institutions, powerful banks can still force firms to reveal information and pay their debts, thereby facilitating industrial expansion (Rajan and Zingales 1999). From these vantage points, market-based systems may be less effective than bank-based systems in allocating capital to new, innovative firms.

The *market-based view* highlights the positive role of markets in promoting economic success (Beck and Levine 2000a). In particular, markets facilitate diversification and the customization of risk management devices. Furthermore, proponents of the market-based view stress deficiencies in bank-based systems. First, by acquiring expensive information about enterprises, banks can extract large rents from firms. This reduces the incentives for firms to undertake high-risk, high-return projects because firms will lose an excessively large proportion of the potential profits to banks (Rajan 1992). Second, since banks make loans, they have an inherent bias toward low-risk, and therefore, low-return projects. Thus, bank-based systems may retard innovation and growth (Morck and Nakamura 1999; Weinstein and Yafeh 1998). Furthermore, powerful banks may collude with firm managers against other investors, which stymies competition, effective corporate control, the emergence of new firms, and economic growth (Hellwig 1998). Thus, proponents of the market-based view stress that markets will reduce the inherent inefficiencies associated with banks and thereby enhance new firms formation, the ease with which firms and industry attract capital to expand, and overall economic growth.

The *law and finance view* stresses that the legal system is the primary determinant of the effectiveness of the financial system in facilitating innovation and growth (La Porta et al. 1997, 1998, 1999, 2000). Moreover, La Porta et al. (2000) reject the entire bank-based versus market-based debate. They argue instead that (1) legal systems that effectively protect outside investors, both equity and debt holders, promote overall financial development, and (2) it is overall financial development, not financial structure per se, that is critical for firm, industry, and national economic success. Thus, the law and finance view predicts that financial structure will be unrelated to new firm formation, the structure of industrial development, and economic growth after controlling for overall financial development. Instead, the law and finance view conjectures that the efficiency of the legal system will be positively related to financial development and hence innovation and growth.

Finally, the *financial-services view* stresses that financial systems provide key financial services. These financial services are crucial for firm creation, industrial expansion, and economic growth. The division between banks and markets in providing these services, however, is of secondary importance. Thus, the financial services view predicts that overall financial development is important for economic development, but financial structure per se will not add much to our understanding of the process of economic development.

This chapter examines six specific questions:

1. Do countries with bank-based financial systems grow faster than countries with market-based systems, or is financial structure unrelated to the pace of economic development?

2. Does the legal system facilitate economic growth by exerting a major impact on the overall effectiveness of the financial system?

3. Do industries that depend heavily on external finance grow faster and/or is new firm formation more likely in bank-based or market-based financial systems?[2]

4. Does the legal system importantly influence the availability of external finance and the rate of new firm creation?

5. Do firms in bank-based system have greater access to external financing and grow faster than firms in market-based financial systems?

6. Does the component of the financial system that is defined by the legal environment influence firm performance?

We use three different datasets and methodologies to examine these three questions. First, we use standard cross-country growth regressions to assess the first two questions. We average data over the period 1980–1995 and assess whether financial structure, that is, the degree to which the country is bank-based or market-based influences economic growth. We study two alternative hypotheses: (1) the level of overall financial development influences growth, but not financial structure per se, and (2) the legal system plays the critical role in facilitating financial arrangements and hence in easing new firm creation, firm access to capital, industrial development, and economic growth.

Second, to explore the impact of financial development and financial structure on industry growth and new firm creation, we use a country-industry panel. Building on work by Rajan and Zingales (1998), we test whether industries that depend more heavily on external finance, grow faster in market- or bank-based financial systems, or whether it is the overall level of financial development that is critical in accounting for cross-country differences in industrial growth patterns. We also examine whether the component of financial development that is explained by the legal system is important for explaining cross-industry growth patterns. Decomposing industry growth into the growth in new firms and the average size of firms, we also test the relevance of the bank-based, market-based financial services and law and finance views for understanding the creation of new firms.

Third, to answer the last two questions, we use firm-level data to compute the growth rates of firms as predicted by their internally available funds and short-term borrowings. We then examine whether the proportion of firms that grow faster than this predicted rate is higher in market- or bank-based financial systems, or whether the overall level of financial development and the legal rights of outside investors and their enforcement explain firms' growth across countries and over time.

Remarkably, country-level, industry-level, and firm-level investigations all tell the same story: the data provide no evidence for the bank-based or market based views. Distinguishing countries by financial structure does not help in explaining cross-country differences in long-run GDP growth, industrial performance, new firm formation, firm use of external funds, or firm growth. Most important, the data show that countries grow faster, industries that rely heavily on external finance expand more rapidly, new firms emerge more quickly, firms access to finance is easier, and firms enjoy greater growth in countries with higher levels of overall financial development and in nations with legal systems that more effectively protect the rights of outside investors.

Our results are thus consistent with the financial-services and the law and finance views. While the overall level of financial development and the efficiency of the legal system in protecting outside investors' rights are associated with higher growth rates and access to long-term finance, the distinction between market- and bank-based systems does not offer any additional information. Our findings suggest a valuable policy message. Instead of focusing on the composition of the financial system, policymakers should instead focus on strengthening the rights of outside investors and enhancing the efficiency of contract enforcement.

This chapter extends three recent papers on financial structure. Levine (2000) shows that financial structure is not a good predictor of real per capita GDP growth in a cross-country growth framework: neither bank-based nor market-based financial systems are closely associated with economic growth. He also finds that financial structure is not a good predictor of capital accumulation, productivity growth and savings rates. Levine (2000) also finds strong support for the law and finance view of financial structure. Beck and Levine (2000a) show in a country-industry panel that financially dependent industries do not grow faster in bank- or market-based financial systems. Also, the creation of new firms does not vary systematically with financial structure. Demirgüç-Kunt and Maksimovic (2000) use firm-level data and show that financial structure is not a robust predictor of the proportion of firms that grow faster than predicted by their own internal resources and short-term borrowings. While each of these papers explores only one aspect of the potential relationship between financial structure and economic development, our chapter incorporates these three different methodologies under a unified framework. Specifically, we use (1) a consistent sample of countries, (2) a consistent array of financial structure and financial development indicators for the cross-country, industry-level, and firm-level estimations, and (3) and consistent instrumental variables across the different datasets and econometric specifications. Thus, this chapter provides a comprehensive evaluation of financial structure and economic performance using firm, industry, and cross-country data in a consistent manner.[3]

The remainder of the chapter is organized as follows. Section 5.2 describes our indicators of financial development, financial structure, and the legal system. Section 5.3 explores the impact of financial structure on cross-country growth. Section 5.4 examines our four hypotheses in a country-industry panel. Section 5.5 explores whether firms' access to external resources differs across financial systems with different structures. Section 5.6 offers some conclusions.

5.2   Data

This section presents the indicators of financial development, financial structure, and the legal system that we use in the cross-country, industry-level, and firm-level analysis. We discuss other firm-level, industry-level and macro data in the respective sections. Table 5.1 presents descriptive statistics and the correlation between the different indicators. Table 5.A1 presents the different indicators for all forty-eight countries in our sample with data averaged over the period 1980–1995.

5.2.1 Indicators of Financial Development

To assess the efficiency with which financial intermediaries and markets (1) assess new projects and firms, (2) exert corporate control, (3) ease risk management and (4) mobilize savings, we need appropriate indicators. While the perfect measures certainly do not exist, the recent literature has developed indicators that proxy for financial intermediary and stock market development across countries. We use newly constructed data from chapter 2 to measure overall financial development. While previous work has focused on either financial intermediary *or* stock market development, the indicators used in this chapter combine banks and stock markets into one indicator. While this does not control for the fact that banks and stock markets might impact economic growth through different channels, as found by Levine and Zervos (1998) and Demirgüç-Kunt and Maksimovic (1998), it helps us distinguish between the effects of overall financial development and financial structure.

Our preferred measure is *Finance-activity*, a measure of the overall activity of financial intermediaries and markets. It is defined as the log of the product of Private Credit (the value of credits by financial intermediaries to the private sector divided by GDP) and Value Traded (the value of total shares traded on the stock market exchange divided by GDP). Private Credit is the most comprehensive indicator of the activity of financial intermediaries as it includes both bank and nonbank intermediaries. Recent work shows that Private Credit exerts a large, positive, robust influence on economic growth (Levine, Loayza, and Beck 2000; Beck, Levine, and Loayza 2000). Value Traded measures the activity of the stock market trading volume as a share of national output and thus indicates the degree of liquidity that stock markets provide to economic agents.[4] Levine and Zervos (1998) show that Value Traded is a robust predictor of long-run economic growth.

To test the robustness of our results, we will use several alternative measures of financial development. *Finance-size* is a measure of the overall size of the financial sector and is defined as the log of the sum of Private Credit and Market Capitalization. Market Capitalization is defined as the value of listed shares divided by GDP, and is a measure of the size of stock markets relative to the economy. While we include this in our analysis, past work suggests that market capitalization is not a very good predictor of economic performance (Levine and Zervos 1998).

Finance-efficiency measures the efficiency of financial intermediaries and markets and is defined as the log of ratio of Value Traded and Overhead Costs, which equals the overhead costs of the banking system relative to banking system assets. While subject to interpretational problems, large overhead costs may reflect inefficiencies in the banking system and therefore proxy as a negative indicator of banking-sector inefficiency.

Finance-aggregate combines the previous three measures and is thus a conglomerate indicator of the size, activity, and efficiency of the financial sector. Specifically, it is the first principal component of *Finance-activity*, *Finance-size*, and *Finance-efficiency*.

Finance-dummy isolates countries that have both underdeveloped financial intermediaries and markets. Specifically, it equals 0 if both Private Credit and Value Traded are less than the sample mean and 1 otherwise.

Our indicators of financial development exhibit a large variation across different countries, as can be seen in table 5.1. Switzerland has the highest value for Finance-activity, with Value Traded at 98 percent of GDP and Private Credit at 178 percent of GDP. Ghana, on the other hand, has the lowest value for *Finance-activity*, with Value Traded being 0.4 percent of GDP and Private Credit 3 percent of GDP. All measures of financial development are correlated with each other at the 1 percent level.

5.2.2 Indicators of Financial Structure

We also construct measures of the degree to which each country has a market- or bank-based financial system. Since there is not a single accepted definition of financial structure, we use an assortment of different measures to test the robustness of our results. We present the results on five measures of financial structure. Each of these measures is constructed so that higher values indicate more market-based financial systems. Demirgüç-Kunt and Levine (chapter 3) examine the relationship between financial structure and a variety of economic, legal, and regulatory variables. Along with many findings, they note that higher-income countries tend to have more market-oriented financial systems.

Our preferred indicator of financial structure is *Structure-activity*, which indicates the activity of stock markets relative to the activity of banks and is defined as the log of the ratio of Value Traded and Bank Credit. Bank Credit equals the claims of the banking sector on the private sector as a share of GDP. Compared to Private Credit, we exclude claims of nonbank financial intermediaries to thus focus on the commercial banking sector.

We construct several alternative measures of financial structure, along the same dimensions as the indicators of financial development, discussed in section 5.2.1. *Structure-size* indicates the size of stock markets relative to the size of the banking sector and is defined as the log of the ratio of Market Capitalization and Bank Credit. *Structure-efficiency* is defined as the log of the product of Overhead Costs and Value Traded and indicates the efficiency of the stock market relative to the banking sector. *Structure-aggregate* combines the previous three measures and is thus a conglomerate indicator of the size, activity, and efficiency of stock markets relative to banks. Specifically, it is the first principal component of *Structure-activity*, *Structure-size*, and *Structure-efficiency*. *Structure-dummy* is a simple bivariate classification of market- versus bank-based financial systems. Specifically, it equals 1 if *Structure-aggregate* is greater than the sample median and 0 otherwise. Note, however, that an economy can be classified as market-based or bank-based only relative to the other countries in the sample, since there is no absolute measure of market- or bank-based financial systems.

Our financial structure indicators vary significantly across countries. Table 5.2 presents the ranking of countries for the financial structure measures. While Taiwan (Value Traded: 150%, Bank Credit: 83%) is considered the most market-based financial system, according to *Structure-activity*, Panama is considered the most bank-based system (Value Traded: 0.3%, Bank Credit: 49%). While the classification of some countries is intuitively attractive, such as the United States, Great Britain, and Switzerland as market-based, *Structure-activity* also classifies Turkey, Mexico, and Brazil as market-based. This is, however, due to a low value of Bank Credit, rather than a high level of Value Traded. The other indicators of financial structure produce similar anomalies. Ghana is identified as the most

Table 5.1
Descriptive Statistics and Correlation

	Finance-activity	Finance-size	Finance-efficiency	Finance-aggregate	Finance-dummy	Structure-activity	Structure-size	Structure-efficiency	Structure-aggregate	Structure-dummy	Creditor	Anti-director	Rule of law
Mean	-3.84	-0.39	0.37	0.00	0.54	-2.00	-0.64	-6.48	0.00	0.50	2.12	3.10	4.03
Median	-4.05	-0.39	0.22	-0.13	1.00	-2.05	-0.58	-6.38	0.15	0.50	2.00	3.00	4.00
Standard deviation	2.07	0.72	1.80	1.00	0.50	1.16	0.76	1.42	1.00	0.51	1.35	1.28	1.61
Maximum	0.55	0.91	4.43	1.88	1.00	0.59	1.34	-3.03	1.86	1.00	4.00	5.00	6.00
Minimum	-9.07	-1.88	-2.71	-2.20	0.00	-5.17	-2.46	-9.98	-2.75	0.00	0.00	0.00	1.14
Observations	48	48	48	48	48	48	48	48	48	48	41	41	48
Correlations	Finance-activity	Finance-size	Finance-efficiency	Finance-aggregate	Finance-dummy	Structure-activity	Structure-size	Structure-efficiency	Structure-aggregate	Structure-dummy	Creditor	Anti-director	Rule of law
Finance-activity	1												
Finance-size	0.881 (0.001)	1											
Finance-efficiency	0.942 (0.001)	0.800 (0.001)	1										
Finance-aggregate	0.984 (0.001)	0.932 (0.001)	0.956 (0.001)	1									
Finance-dummy	0.690 (0.001)	0.802 (0.001)	0.654 (0.001)	0.746 (0.001)	1								
Structure-activity	0.689 (0.001)	0.347 (0.016)	0.730 (0.001)	0.618 (0.001)	0.172 (0.244)	1							
Structure-size	0.078 (0.599)	0.037 (0.803)	0.163 (0.269)	0.097 (0.512)	-0.190 (0.196)	0.544 (0.001)	1						
Structure-efficiency	0.796 (0.001)	0.513 (0.001)	0.675 (0.001)	0.693 (0.001)	0.306 (0.034)	0.862 (0.001)	0.298 (0.040)	1					
Structure-aggregate	0.655 (0.001)	0.375 (0.009)	0.651 (0.001)	0.588 (0.001)	0.142 (0.3357)	0.966 (0.001)	0.675 (0.001)	0.884 (0.001)	1				

Structure-dummy	0.518 (0.001)	0.331 (0.022)	0.568 (0.001)	0.495 (0.001)	0.167 (0.256)	0.776 (0.001)	0.607 (0.001)	0.630 (0.001)	0.791 (0.001)	1			
Creditor	−0.070 (0.663)	0.026 (0.874)	0.010 (0.949)	−0.012 (0.942)	−0.067 (0.678)	−0.161 (0.316)	0.054 (0.738)	−0.193 (0.227)	−0.136 (0.398)	−0.136 (0.398)	1		
Anti-director	0.167 (0.297)	0.246 (0.122)	0.173 (0.279)	0.203 (0.202)	0.224 (0.160)	0.154 (0.338)	0.379 (0.015)	0.091 (0.570)	0.226 (0.156)	0.072 (0.656)	0.095 (0.557)	1	
Rule of law	0.704 (0.001)	0.692 (0.001)	0.649 (0.001)	0.712 (0.001)	0.564 (0.001)	0.330 (0.022)	−0.130 (0.377)	0.454 (0.001)	0.291 (0.045)	0.208 (0.157)	−0.116 (0.470)	−0.084 (0.602)	1

Note: p-values are given in parentheses.

Table 5.2
Financial Structure across Countries

Structure-activity		Structure-size		Structure-efficiency		Structure-aggregate		Structure-dummy	
Taiwan	0.59	Ghana	1.34	Switzerland	-3.03	Taiwan	1.86	Australia	1
Malaysia	-0.32	South Africa	0.94	Taiwan	-3.62	Malaysia	1.59	Brazil	1
Switzerland	-0.39	Malaysia	0.60	United States	-4.38	Switzerland	1.58	Canada	1
United States	-0.64	Jamaica	0.08	United Kingdom	-4.79	United States	1.34	Denmark	1
Ireland	-0.64	Zimbabwe	0.03	Brazil	-4.87	United Kingdom	1.24	Germany	1
Turkey	-0.73	United Kingdom	0.02	Malaysia	-4.97	Brazil	1.01	Ghana	1
United Kingdom	-0.74	Mexico	-0.02	Israel	-5.10	Mexico	0.90	Ireland	1
Mexico	-0.85	New Zealand	-0.02	Japan	-5.24	Japan	0.86	Israel	1
Brazil	-0.92	Ireland	-0.03	Germany	-5.26	South Africa	0.85	Jamaica	1
Thailand	-0.92	Chile	-0.03	Sweden	-5.47	Canada	0.82	Japan	1
Japan	-1.00	Canada	-0.06	Thailand	-5.52	Sweden	0.80	Malaysia	1
Canada	-1.14	Peru	-0.07	Turkey	-5.54	Australia	0.80	Mexico	1
Israel	-1.15	Australia	-0.09	Australia	-5.58	Israel	0.75	Netherlands	1
Sweden	-1.18	Philippines	-0.10	Canada	-5.59	Turkey	0.71	New Zealand	1
Australia	-1.18	United States	-0.11	France	-5.60	Thailand	0.68	Peru	1
Netherlands	-1.36	Sweden	-0.15	Mexico	-5.75	Philippines	0.58	Philippines	1
Philippines	-1.47	Brazil	-0.31	South Africa	-5.91	New Zealand	0.49	South Africa	1
Germany	-1.52	Japan	-0.35	Philippines	-5.92	Peru	0.39	Sweden	1
Peru	-1.54	Belgium	-0.36	Denmark	-6.08	Jamaica	0.38	Switzerland	1
India	-1.61	Sri Lanka	-0.39	New Zealand	-6.12	Ireland	0.33	Taiwan	1
New Zealand	-1.64	Ecuador	-0.43	Jamaica	-6.12	Netherlands	0.33	Thailand	1
								Turkey	1

Denmark	−1.87	Kenya	−0.48	Spain	−6.14	Germany	0.17	United Kingdom	1
South Africa	−1.90	Taiwan	−0.53	Netherlands	−6.26	Denmark	0.17	United States	1
Jamaica	−2.04	Israel	−0.56	Argentina	−6.28	Ghana	0.16	Argentina	0
Norway	−2.06	Netherlands	−0.60	Norway	−6.49	India	0.14	Austria	0
Argentina	−2.15	India	−0.60	Peru	−6.53	Chile	0.00	Belgium	0
Ghana	−2.17	Denmark	−0.62	Italy	−6.54	Ecuador	−0.04	Chile	0
Ecuador	−2.19	Thailand	−0.66	India	−6.58	Belgium	−0.17	Colombia	0
France	−2.28	Switzerland	−0.71	Ecuador	−6.65	France	−0.17	Cyprus	0
Honduras	−2.34	Turkey	−0.74	Chile	−6.74	Argentina	−0.18	Ecuador	0
Spain	−2.36	Colombia	−0.78	Austria	−6.92	Norway	−0.23	Egypt	0
Belgium	−2.38	Pakistan	−0.98	Belgium	−6.94	Spain	−0.31	Finland	0
Chile	−2.46	Trinidad and Tobago	−1.00	Honduras	−7.06	Zimbabwe	−0.35	France	0
Pakistan	−2.51	Greece	−1.02	Finland	−7.23	Sri Lanka	−0.41	Greece	0
Italy	−2.52	Argentina	−1.09	Cyprus	−7.31	Italy	−0.55	Honduras	0
Zimbabwe	−2.58	Cyprus	−1.11	Sri Lanka	−7.37	Pakistan	−0.62	India	0
Greece	−2.65	Norway	−1.15	Greece	−7.37	Honduras	−0.63	Italy	0
Sri Lanka	−2.66	Finland	−1.29	Pakistan	−7.47	Greece	−0.66		

market-based economy, since it has an extremely low level of Bank Credit (3% of GDP). Brazil is identified as having relatively efficient markets, which is due to high overhead costs in the Brazilian banking sector. A financial system can therefore be identified as market-based either because markets are very well developed or banks are underdeveloped.

The indicators of financial structure are highly and significantly correlated with each other as indicated in table 5.1. While *Structure-activity* and *Structure-efficiency* are also positively correlated with many of the financial development indicators—indicating that financially more developed economies have more market-based financial systems—*Structure-size* is not correlated with any of the financial development measures.

Although these financial structure measures do not directly measure all of the channels via which banks and markets influence economic activity, they are the most comprehensive set of indicators that have been constructed to date for a broad cross-section of countries. Taken together, these indicators provide a measure of the comparative role of banks and markets in the economy. Furthermore, the underlying measures of bank development and stock market liquidity exert a strong influence on economic growth. Thus, the basic measures of bank development and stock market liquidity have some analytical content. Furthermore, Demirgüç-Kunt and Levine (chapter 3) show that countries with strong shareholder rights and high accounting standards tend to have more market-based financial systems. Thus, key legal and regulatory differences match up with the measures of financial structure that we use to assess the relationship between industrial performance and degree to which countries are bank-based or market-based.

5.2.3 The Legal Environment

We use three indicators of the rights of outside investors and the degree to which these rights are enforced. These data are from La Porta et al. (1998).

Creditor is an index of the degree to which the legal codes of the country protect the claims of secured creditors in the case of reorganization or liquidation of a company. It ranges from 0 to 4 and is the sum of four dummy variables that indicate whether (1) the reorganization procedure does not impose an automatic stay on assets, thereby not preventing secured creditors from taking possession of loan collateral, (2) secured creditors are ranked first in the case of liquidation, (3) management does not stay in charge of the firm during reorganization, thereby enhancing creditors' power, and (4) management needs creditors' consent when filing for reorganization. In economies with higher values of *Creditor*, outside investors have more rights relative to the management and other stakeholders, and should therefore be more willing to provide the external resources that firms need. Among the countries in our sample Ecuador, Egypt, Great Britain, India, Israel, Kenya, Malaysia, Pakistan, and Zimbabwe have very high levels of Creditor (4), whereas Colombia, France, Mexico, Peru, and the Philippines have low levels of *Creditor* (0).

Anti-director is an index of the degree to which the legal codes of the country protect minority shareholder rights. It ranges from zero to six and is the sum of six dummy variables that indicate whether (1) shareholders are allowed to mail their proxy vote to the firm, (2) shareholders are not required to deposit their shares prior to the General Shareholders' Meeting, (3) cumulative voting or proportional representation of minorities on the board of directors is allowed, (4) an oppressed minority mechanism is in place, (5) the minimum percentage of share capital that entitles a shareholder to call for an Extraordinary Shareholders' Meeting is less than or equal to 10 percent, and (6) shareholders have preemptive rights that can only be waived by a shareholders' vote. In economies with higher values of *Anti-director*, minority shareholders are better protected against expropriation by management and large shareholders and should therefore be more willing to provide external financing to firms. Canada, Chile, Great Britain, India, Pakistan, the United States, and South Africa have all very extensive minority shareholder protection (5), whereas Belgium experiences an extremely low level (0).

Rule of law is an assessment of the law and order tradition of a country that ranges from ten, strong law and order tradition, to one, weak law and order tradition. This measure was constructed by ICRG and is an average over the period 1982–1995. In countries with a higher law and order tradition, outside investors can more easily enforce their claims and rights and should therefore be more willing to provide external finance. Austria, Australia, Belgium, Canada, Denmark, Finland, the Netherlands, New Zealand, Norway, Sweden,

Switzerland, and the United States are the countries in our sample with the highest level of *Rule of law* (6), whereas there are five countries with values below two: Colombia, Pakistan, Peru, the Philippines, and Sri Lanka.

While Creditor and Anti-Director are not significantly correlated with any of the financial development and structure indicators, the correlations in table 5.1 indicate that countries with higher levels of Rule of law experience higher levels of financial development and have more market-based financial systems.

5.2.4   The Legal Origin

Legal systems with European origin can be classified into four major legal families (Reynolds and Flores 1996): the English Common Law and the French, German, and Scandinavian Civil Law countries.[5] As described by Glendon, Gordon, and Osakwe (1982), Roman law was compiled under the direction of Byzantine Emperor Justinian in the sixth century. Over subsequent centuries, the *Glossators* and *Commentators* interpreted, adapted, and amended the law. In the seventeenth and eighteenth centuries the Scandinavian countries formalized their legal code, and it has remained relatively unaffected from the far-reaching influences of the German and especially the French civil codes.

Napoleon directed the writing of the French Civil Code in 1804 and made it a priority to secure the adoption of the Code in France and all conquered territories, including Italy, Poland, the Low Countries, and the Habsburg Empire. Also, France extended her legal influence to parts of the Near East, Northern and Sub-Saharan Africa, Indochina, Oceania, French Guyana, and the French Caribbean islands during the colonial era. Furthermore, the French civil code was a major influence on the Portuguese and Spanish legal systems, which helped spread the French legal tradition to Central and South America. The German civil code *(Bürgerliches Gesetzbuch)* was completed almost a century later in 1896. The German code exerted a big influence on Austria and Switzerland, as well as China (and hence Taiwan), Czechoslovakia, Greece, Hungary, Italy, and Yugoslavia. Also, the German civil code heavily influenced the Japanese civil code, which helped spread the German legal tradition to Korea.

Unlike these Civil Law countries, the English legal system is common law, where judges trying to resolve particular cases primarily formed the laws. The Common Law tradition was spread mainly through colonialism to North America, parts of Africa, the Caribbean, and Asia.

Since most countries have acquired their legal systems through occupation and colonization, legal origin can be regarded as relatively exogenous for the period under investigation. Furthermore, La Porta et al. (1997, 1998) have shown that the legal origin of a country materially influences its legal treatment of creditors and shareholders, its accounting standards and the efficiency of contract enforcement. Levine (1998, 1999, forthcoming) and Levine, Loayza, and Beck (2000) show that the legal origin explains cross-country variations in the level of financial development.

Given its exogenous character and explanatory power, we use the legal origin of countries as instruments for financial development and financial structure, so that we can control for simultaneity bias. Specifically, we want to control for the possibilities that faster growing countries, countries with specific industrial structures, or countries with specific firm characteristics develop financial systems or structures. That is, we want to control for the possibility that financial development and structure respond to aggregate growth, industrial composition, and corporate financing. By extracting the exogenous components of financial development and structure, we isolate the impact of the financial system on economic growth, industry expansion, new firm creation, and firms' access to long-term finance.

5.3 Cross-Country Growth Regressions

This section explores the impact of financial structure on long-run economic growth in a sample of forty-eight countries, with data averaged over the period 1980–1995. We (1) describe the methodology, (2) present evidence of the impact of financial structure and financial development on economic growth, (3) discuss evidence on the law and finance approach, (4) describe different robustness tests, and (5) summarize our findings.

5.3.1 Econometric Methodology

To test the validity of the (1) market-based, (2) bank-based, (3) financial services, and (4) law and finance approach in a cross-country sample, we modify the standard growth regression as follows:

$$Growth_i = \alpha' X_i + \beta FD_i + \gamma FS_i + \varepsilon_i, \tag{5.1}$$

where *Growth* is the average annual growth rate of real per capita GDP, calculated as regression coefficient from an OLS regression, X is a set of potential growth determinants, FD is an indicator of financial development, FS is a measure of financial structure, and ε is the error term. The four competing hypotheses predict different signs for β and γ. The market-based view predicts that market-based financial systems grow faster, implying $\beta > 0$ and $\gamma > 0$. The bank-based view holds that bank-based systems are better for growth, implying $\beta > 0$ and $\gamma < 0$. The financial-services view holds that financial structure does not matter for growth and that it is overall financial development that enhances economic growth. This implies $\beta > 0$ and $\gamma = 0$. The law and finance view, finally, claims that only the part of financial development defined by the legal system is linked with economic growth. If we use the legal rights of outside investors, and the efficiency of contract enforcement as instrumental variables to extract the exogenous component of financial development, the law and finance view also predicts $\beta > 0$ and $\gamma = 0$.

We use both ordinary least square (OLS) estimations and instrumental variable (IV) estimations, using the legal origin of countries as instruments for countries, as in Levine, Loayza, and Beck (2000). IV regressions allow us to control for simultaneity bias and reverse causality from growth rates to financial development, by extracting the exogenous component of financial development and structure. To assess the law and finance view, we use Creditor, Anti-Director, and Rule of Law as instrumental variables for financial development to thus extract the component of finance that is defined by the legal system. We examine the appropriateness of the instruments with Hansen's (1982) test of the overidentifying restrictions, which is further explained by Newey and West (1987). The null hypothesis is that the instrumental variables are not correlated with the error term. The instruments are appropriate if we cannot reject the null hypothesis. We can interpret this result as indicating that the instruments (legal origin or the legal system indicators) affect real per capita GDP growth only through the financial development or structure indicators *and* the variables in the conditioning information set (i.e., the other determinants of growth).

To assess the robustness of our findings, we control for other potential growth determinants in equation (5.1). Specifically, we use two different sets of conditioning information. The *policy conditioning information set* contains the log of real per capita GDP in 1980 to control for convergence and the average years of schooling to control for the effect of human capital accumulation. Furthermore, we include (1) the logarithm of one plus the average rate of inflation, (2) the logarithm of one plus the average black market premium, (3) the logarithm of government size as a share of GDP, and (4) the logarithm of exports plus imports as a share of GDP. We include the inflation rate and the government size to proxy for macroeconomic stability and government intrusion, and the trade share and the black market premium to capture the degree of openness of economies. The *full conditioning information set* contains the policy information set plus a measure of ethnic fractionalization, revolutions and coups, and political assassinations.[6]

5.3.2   Financial Structure and Long-Run Growth

The results in table 5.3 indicate that financial structure is not significantly related to economic growth. For conciseness, the table only reports the results for the two variables of interest: *Finance-activity* and the financial structure indicators. Here we present only results using the policy conditioning information set. All regressions are run with OLS and using heteroskedasticity-consistent standard errors. None of the five structure indicators enters significantly in the regression. *Finance-activity*, on the other hand, enters positively and significantly in four out of five regressions. These results, therefore, do not give support to either the market- or the bank-based view. The results in table 5.4 confirm these findings, using the other indicators of financial development as control variables. The distinction between market- and bank-based financial system does not explain much of the variation in cross-country growth rates.

The results in table 5.5 confirm that financial development is positively correlated with long-run economic growth and that simultaneity bias or reverse causality does not drive these results. We present results using both OLS and IV regressions. All indicators of financial development enter significantly at the 5 percent level, except for *Finance-size*. This result is consistent with the findings of Levine and Zervos (1998). They find that market capitalization is not a robust predictor of economic growth. The liquidity of the stock market, not its pure size (market capitalization), matters for eco-

Table 5.3
Financial Structure, Financial Development and Economic Growth, OLS Regressions

Dependent variable: Real per capita GDP growth, 1980–1995

	(1)	(2)	(3)	(4)	(5)
Structure-activity	0.001				
	(0.999)				
Structure-size		−0.656			
		(0.174)			
Structure-efficiency			−0.324		
			(0.243)		
Structure-aggregate				−0.548	
				(0.220)	
Structure-dummy					−0.957
					(0.129)
Finance-activity	0.517	0.665	0.751	0.818	0.745
	(0.158)	(0.005)	(0.006)	(0.014)	(0.005)
R^2	0.388	0.428	0.399	0.407	0.420

Notes: The dependent variable is the average growth rate of real per capita GDP, calculated as regression coefficient. All regressions include the policy conditioning information set: logarithm of initial income, schooling, inflation, black market premium, government size, and trade openness. All regressions are estimated using OLS.

Structure-activity = log(total value traded divided by claims on private sector by commercials banks)

Structure-size = log(market capitalization divided by claims on private sector by commercials bank)

Structure-efficiency = log(total value traded as share of GDP × banks' overhead costs as share of total assets)

Structure-aggregate = first principal components of structure-activity, structure-size, and structure-efficiency

Structure-dummy = dummy variable that takes the value 1 if structure-aggregate is above the median, 0 otherwise

Finance-activity = log(total value traded as share of GDP × claims on private sector by financial institutions as share of GDP)

nomic growth. The tests of overidentifying restrictions for the IV regressions indicate that we cannot reject the null hypothesis that the instruments are not correlated with the error terms.

The results in table 5.5 are not only statistically significant, but also economically important. Consider Argentina that had a value of *Finance-activity* of −5.99 over the period 1980–1995. If Argentina had enjoyed a level of financial development as Thailand (*Finance − activity* = −1.98), a country with lower real per capita GDP in 1980, the regression results suggests, that Argentina would have grown two percentage points faster over this period.

Table 5.4
Financial Structure and Economic Growth, Sensitivity Analysis

Dependent variable: Real per capita GDP growth, 1980–1995

Explanatory variable	Coefficient	Standard error	t-statistic	p-value	R-squared
1. Controlling for Finance-size					
Structure-activity	0.539	0.305	1.770	0.085	0.353
Structure-size	−0.327	0.469	−0.697	0.490	0.290
Structure-efficiency	0.377	0.281	1.343	0.187	0.319
Structure-aggregate	0.436	0.332	1.312	0.197	0.310
Structure-dummy	0.191	0.517	0.369	0.714	0.282
2. Controlling for Finance-efficiency					
Structure-activity	−0.346	0.355	−0.973	0.337	0.433
Structure-size	−0.739	0.416	−1.775	0.084	0.474
Structure-efficiency	−0.032	0.202	−0.159	0.875	0.424
Structure-aggregate	−0.455	0.372	−1.222	0.229	0.442
Structure-dummy	−1.390	0.612	−2.270	0.029	0.486
3. Controlling for Finance-aggregate					
Structure-activity	0.134	0.383	0.350	0.729	0.384
Structure-size	−0.734	0.480	−1.529	0.134	0.429
Structure-efficiency	−0.033	0.244	−0.135	0.894	0.382
Structure-aggregate	−0.275	0.351	−0.783	0.439	0.388
Structure-dummy	−0.937	0.585	−1.600	0.118	0.412
4. Controlling for Finance-dummy					
Structure-activity	0.329	0.248	1.325	0.193	0.428
Structure-size	−0.174	0.459	−0.379	0.707	0.405
Structure-efficiency	0.188	0.229	0.822	0.416	0.413
Structure-aggregate	0.213	0.269	0.792	0.433	0.410
Structure-dummy	−0.054	0.465	−0.116	0.908	0.402

Notes: The dependent variable is the average growth rate of real per capita GDP, calculated as regression coefficient. All regressions include the policy conditioning information set: logarithm of initial income, schooling, inflation, black market premium, government size, and trade openness. All regressions are estimated using OLS.

Structure-activity = log(total value traded divided by claims on private sector by commercials banks)

Structure-size = log(market capitalization divided by claims on private sector by commercial banks)

Structure-efficiency = log(total value traded as share of GDP × banks' overhead costs as share of total assets)

Structure-aggregate = first principal components of structure-activity, structure-size, and structure-efficiency

Structure-dummy = dummy variable that takes the value 1 if structure-aggregate is above the median, 0 otherwise

Table 5.5
Financial Development and Economic Growth

Dependent variable: Real per capita GDP growth, 1980–1995

1. OLS regressions

Explanatory variable	Coefficient	Standard error	t-statistic	p-value	R-squared
Finance-activity	0.517	0.193	2.684	0.011	0.388
Finance-size	0.885	0.796	1.113	0.273	0.280
Finance-efficiency	0.582	0.186	3.127	0.003	0.424
Finance-aggregate	1.070	0.427	2.507	0.016	0.382
Finance-dummy	1.882	0.736	2.559	0.014	0.401

2. IV regressions

Explanatory variable	Coefficient	Standard error	t-statistic	p-value	$N \times J$ statistic
Finance-activity	0.630	0.282	2.232	0.031	2.141
Finance-size	1.725	1.206	1.430	0.160	3.286
Finance-efficiency	0.752	0.291	2.586	0.014	1.652
Finance-aggregate	1.336	0.616	2.169	0.036	2.272

Notes: The dependent variable is the average growth rate of real per capita GDP, calculated as regression coefficient. All regressions include the policy conditioning information set: logarithm of initial income, schooling, inflation, black market premium, government size, and trade openness.

Finance-activity = log(total value traded as share of GDP × claims on private sector by financial institutions as share of GDP)

Finance-size = log(market capitalization and claims on private sector by financial institutions as share of GDP)

Finance-efficiency = log(total value traded as share of GDP divided by banks' overhead costs as share of total assets)

Finance-aggregate = first principal component of finance-activity, finance-size, and finance-efficiency

Finance-dummy = takes value 0 if claims on private sector by banks as share of GDP and value traded as share of GDP are less than sample mean, 1 otherwise

The results in tables 5.3, 5.4, and 5.5 give support for the financial-services view by underlining the importance that overall financial development has for economic growth. The results are not consistent with either the market- or the bank-based view.

5.3.3   The Law and Finance View and Long-Run Growth

The results in table 5.6 are consistent with the law and finance view. Here we use as instruments specific elements of the legal system that

Table 5.6
Financial Development and Economic Growth: The Legal-Based View

Dependent variable: Real per capita GDP growth, 1980–1995

Explanatory variable	Coefficient	Standard error	*t*-statistic	p-value	N × J statistic
1. Policy conditioning information set					
Finance-activity	0.747	0.348	2.144	0.040	0.814
Finance-size	1.653	0.717	2.307	0.028	1.468
Finance-efficiency	0.692	0.340	2.034	0.050	0.913
Finance-aggregate	1.255	0.559	2.246	0.032	1.102
2. Full conditioning information set					
Finance-activity	0.970	0.277	3.498	0.002	0.329
Finance-size	2.282	0.699	3.266	0.003	2.122
Finance-efficiency	0.878	0.311	2.827	0.008	0.729
Finance-aggregate	1.757	0.521	3.373	0.002	0.931

Notes: N × J statistic is distributed chi-squared with two degrees of freedom.
At the 10 percent level, the critical value is 4.61. At the 5 percent level, the critical value is 5.99. The dependent variable is the average growth rate of real per capita GDP, calculated as regression coefficient. Policy conditioning information set: simple set, plus inflation, black market premium, government size, and trade openness. Full conditioning information set: policy set, plus a measure of ethnic fractionalization, revolutions and coups, and political assassinations. We use creditor, anti-director, and rule of law as instruments for financial development.

Finance-activity = log(total value traded as share of GDP × claims on private sector by financial institutions as share of GDP)

Finance-size = log(market capitalization and claims on private sector by financial institutions as share of GDP)

Finance-efficiency = log(total value traded as share of GDP divided by banks' overhead costs as share of total assets)

Finance-aggregate = first principal component of finance-activity, finance-size, and finance-efficiency

are important for financial development. Specifically, we use *Creditor, Anti-director,* and *Rule of law* as instruments for the indicator of financial development. All indicators of financial development enter significantly in the regression at the 5 percent level. Furthermore, the regressions pass the test of the overidentifying restrictions. That is, the data do not reject the hypothesis that Creditor, *Anti-director,* and *Rule of law* influence growth only through their effects on financial development or the other explanatory variables. The coefficients show similar sizes as when using the legal origin as instruments and are larger than in the OLS regressions. Thus, the data are consistent with the view that the component of overall financial development explained by legal codes and their enforcement is positively and significantly related to economic growth.

5.3.4 Sensitivity Analysis

Our results are robust to several robustness checks. First, we rerun the regressions in tables 5.3, 5.4, and 5.5 using the full conditioning information set. The structure indicators never enter significantly. Second, we include a dummy for very undeveloped financial systems in the regressions with financial structure. This does not alter our results. None of the structure indicators enters significantly. Third, we use *Creditor, Anti-director,* and *Rule of law* as instruments for financial structure. Again, the indicators of financial structure do not enter significantly. Finally, we examine unbalanced financial systems. While financial structure might not matter, financial systems with a distorted structure might impede the efficient provision of financial services. We therefore create a dummy variable that takes the value 1 if Value Traded is above the sample mean and Bank Credit below the mean or vice versa. Using this indicator of unbalanced financial systems does not change our results—classifying countries, as having unbalanced financial systems does not explain long-term economic growth.

5.3.5 Summary

Our findings are consistent with the financial services and the law and finance views. Financial development and the component defined by the legal protection of outside investors explain long-term cross-country growth rates. Financial structure, namely, the distinction between market- and bank-based financial systems, does not offer any additional information. These results are robust to the use of different indicators of financial development and structure and different conditioning information sets. These results are also robust a battery of sensitivity tests (Levine 2000), including tests of whether bank-based systems are more effective at promoting growth at low-levels of economic development (Boyd and Smith 1996, 1998).

5.4 Industry-Level Results

This section explores our four competing hypotheses in a panel data set of thirty-four countries and thirty-six industries. Specifically, we explore (1) whether industries that depend heavily on external finance grow faster in market- or bank-based financial systems, and (2) new firms are more likely to form in bank-based or a market-based financial systems. Thus, unlike in the section 5.3, we focus on a specific channel through which financial development and potentially financial structure affects economic activity and industrial structure. We first discuss the econometric methodology and the additional data we use. We then explore whether externally dependent industries grow faster in market- or bank-based financial systems or whether it is the overall level of financial development that determines industrial growth patterns across countries. In a second step, we decompose industry growth into its two components—growth in the number of firms and growth in the average size of firms—and analyze whether financial structure and development determines the creation of new firms. Finally, we test the importance of the legal system for industry growth and new firm creation.

5.4.1 Econometric Methodology and the Data

We use a panel of thirty-four countries and thirty-six industries to test our four hypotheses. We build on work by Rajan and Zingales (1998) and explore the interaction of industry and country characteristics, that is, the dependence of industries on external finance and the level and structure of financial development across countries. This subsection describes the methodology and data.

Methodology

Financial intermediaries and markets help overcome market frictions that drive a wedge between the price of external and internal finance. Lower costs of external finance facilitate firm growth and new firm formation. Therefore, industries that are naturally heavy users of external finance should benefit disproportionately more from greater financial development than industries that are not naturally heavy users of external finance. That should be especially true for new firms in these industries.

Rajan and Zingales (1998) find evidence consistent with the hypothesis that industries that rely more heavily on external finance grow faster in countries with a better-developed financial system. Furthermore, Rajan and Zingales show that the effect of financial development on the industrial growth runs mostly through growth in the number of establishments rather than through growth in the average size of establishments. Financial development improves disproportionately the prospects of young firms in industries that rely heavily on external finance.

We extend the work by Rajan and Zingales and explore whether industries with a high need of external finance grow faster in economies with bank- or market-based financial systems. We use the following regression to assess the impact of financial development and financial structure on industry growth and the creation of new firms:

$$Growth_{i,k} = \sum_j \alpha_j Country_j + \sum_l \beta_l Industry_l + \gamma\, Share_{i,k}$$

$$+ \delta_1(External_k * FD_i) + \delta_2(External_k * FS_i) + \varepsilon_{i,k}, \qquad (5.2)$$

where $Growth_{i,k}$ is the average annual growth rate of value added or the growth in number of firms in industry k and country i. $Country$ and $Industry$ are country and industry dummies, respectively, and $Share_{i,k}$ is the share of industry k in manufacturing in country i in 1980. $External_k$ is the measure of dependence on external finance for industry k as measured for a sample of U.S. companies over the period 1980–1989. FD_i and FS_i are indicators of financial development and financial structure for country i, respectively. We interact the external dependence of an industry ($External$) with both (1) a measure of overall financial development (FD) and (2) an index of the degree of market-based versus bank-based, namely, an index of financial structure (FS).[9] The dummy variables for industries and countries correct for country and industry specific characteristics that might determine industry growth patterns. We thus isolate the effect that the interaction of external dependence and financial development/structure has on industry growth rates relative to country and industry means. By including the initial share of an industry we control for a convergence effect; we expect industries with a large share to grow more slowly, and therefore a negative sign on γ.[10]

The different hypotheses imply different predictions about the sign and significance of δ_1 and δ_2. The market-based view predicts that industries that are dependent on external finance grow faster in economies with market-oriented financial systems and higher levels of financial development, thus implying $\delta_1 > 0$ and $\delta_2 > 0$. The bank-based view predicts that industries that are dependent on external finance grow faster in economies with bank-oriented financial systems and higher levels of financial development, thus implying $\delta_1 > 0$ and $\delta_2 < 0$. The financial-services view predicts that industries dependent on external finance grow faster in economies with a higher level of overall financial development, whereas the financial structure should not matter, thus implying $\delta_1 > 0$ and $\delta_2 = 0$. The law and finance view predicts that industries dependent on external finance grow faster in economies that protect the rights of outside investors more efficiently, whereas financial structure should not matter. If we replace FD_i with indicators of these legal rights and contract enforcement, this implies $\delta_1 > 0$ and $\delta_2 = 0$.

We run both OLS and IV regressions. IV regressions allow us to address the issue of endogeneity of independent variables. Specifically, we control for the endogeneity of the level overall financial development and the structure of the financial system. As above, we use the legal origin of countries to extract the exogenous component of financial development and structure. We also use the religious composition of countries as additional instruments.[11] La Porta et al. (1999) show that the dominant religion of a country influences institutional development.

External Dependence

We use industry-level data on external dependence from Rajan and Zingales (1998). Their underlying assumption—and ours—is that for technological reasons some industries depend more heavily on external finance than others. Unfortunately, we can only observe the actual use of external finance, but not the demand for it. For countries with well-developed financial systems, Rajan and Zingales note that external funds will be supplied very elastically, so that the actual use of external finance would primarily reflect the demand for external finance. Assuming that the variance of the need for external finance across industries persists across countries, we can thus use the actual external dependence of industries as observed in a country with a well-developed financial system as a proxy for the "natural" dependence of industries on external finance. As discussed in Rajan and Zingales (1998), we use the United States to compute the natural external dependence of industries.

The data are from Standard and Poor's *Compustat* for U.S. firms in thirty-six industries. This database contains only publicly listed firms. A firm's dependence on external finance is defined as the share of investment that cannot be financed through internal cash flows; or as capital expenditures minus cash flow from operations divided by capital expenditures. Both numerator and denominator are averaged over the 1980s to smooth temporal fluctuations. The industry values are calculated as medians rather than means to thus prevent outliers from dominating the results. Table 5.A2 lists the external dependence for all thirty-six industries. The drug industry is the industry most dependent on external finance, whereas the tobacco industry has no demand for external finance, namely, our dependence measure is less than zero.

Industry Growth Rates
Our dependent variable is the average annual growth rate of value added. We use the data obtained by Rajan and Zingales (1998) from the *Industrial Statistics Yearbook* database put together by the United Nations Statistical Division (1993). We also use a decomposition of the industry growth rate. Specifically, we consider the growth in the number of establishments, as opposed to the growth in the average size of establishments.[12] The decomposition of industry growth therefore provides both a robustness test of the previous results and a more detailed exploration of the mechanisms through which financial development and financial structure influence industrial growth patterns across countries.

5.4.2   Financial Structure and Industry Growth

The results in table 5.7 indicate that financial structure does not have an independent impact on industrial growth patterns across countries.[13] Although the interaction terms of external dependence with *Structure-activity* and *Structure-aggregate* show coefficients that are significant at the 5 percent level in the OLS regressions, these results are not confirmed by the instrumental variable regressions. None of the interaction terms with financial structure enters significantly at the 5 percent level. These results are not consistent with the market- or the bank-based view.

The results in table 5.8 support the financial-services view and thereby strengthen the previous findings. The interaction terms with financial development always enter significantly at the 5 percent level level. None of the interaction terms with financial structure enters significantly. These results indicate that externally dependent industries grow relatively faster in countries with better-developed

Table 5.7
Financial Structure and Industry Growth

Dependent variable: Industry growth, 1980–1989				
	Structure-activity	Structure-size	Structure-aggregate	Structure-dummy
1. OLS regressions				
Interaction (external dependence × structure-activity)	0.887 (0.033)			
Interaction (external dependence × structure-size)		0.698 (0.144)		
Interaction (external dependence × structure-aggregate)			0.914 (0.046)	
Interaction (external dependence × structure-dummy)				1.101 (0.233)
R^2	0.311	0.309	0.310	0.309
Number of observations	1016	1016	1016	1016
2. IV regressions				
Interaction (external dependence × structure-activity)	1.407 (0.064)			
Interaction (external dependence × structure-size)		1.119 (0.246)		
Interaction (external dependence × structure-aggregate)			1.415 (0.121)	
Number of observations	1016	1016	1016	

Notes: The dependent variable is the annual compounded growth rate in real value added for 1980–1990 for each industry in each country.

The p-values for heteroskedasticity robust standard errors are reported in parentheses. All regressions also include the industry's share of total value added in manufacturing in 1980. We use the British, French, and German legal origin dummies as instruments for financial structure in the IV regressions.

Structure-activity = log(total value traded divided by claims on private sector by commercials banks)

Structure-size = log(market capitalization divided by claims on private sector by commercial banks)

Structure-aggregate = first principal components of structure-activity and structure-size

Structure-dummy = dummy variable that takes the value 1 if structure-aggregate is above the median, 0 otherwise

Table 5.8
Financial Development, Financial Structure, and Industry Growth

Dependent variable: Industry growth, 1980–1989

	Structure-activity	Structure-size	Structure-aggregate
Interaction (external dependence × structure-activity)	−1.314 (0.308)		
Interaction (external dependence × structure-size)		−0.103 (0.892)	
Interaction (external dependence × structure-aggregate)			−0.416 (0.640)
Interaction (external dependence × finance-activity)	1.350 (0.033)	0.719 (0.018)	0.842 (0.022)
Number of observations	1016	1016	1016
Interaction (external dependence × structure-activity)	−0.868 (0.435)		
Interaction (external dependence × structure-size)		−0.175 (0.825)	
Interaction (external dependence × structure-aggregate)			−0.441 (0.628)
Interaction (external dependence × finance-size)	3.659 (0.029)	2.494 (0.010)	2.843 (0.014)
Number of observations	1016	1016	1016
Interaction (external dependence × structure-activity)	−1.137 (0.346)		
Interaction (external dependence × structure-size)		−0.151 (0.845)	
Interaction (external dependence × structure-aggregate)			−0.461 (0.609)
Interaction (external dependence × Finance-Aggregate)	2.742 (0.029)	1.629 (0.013)	1.899 (0.016)
Number of observations	1016	1016	1016

Notes: The dependent variable is the annual compounded growth rate in real value added for 1980–1990 for each industry in each country. The p-values for heteroskedasticity robust standard errors are reported in parentheses. All regressions also include the industry's share of total value added in manufacturing in 1980. All regressions are IV. We use the British, French, and German legal origin dummies and the share of Catholic, Muslim, and Protestant population in total population as instruments for financial development and financial structure development and financial structure.

Finance-activity = log(total value traded as share of GDP × claims on private sector by financial institutions as share of GDP)

Finance-size = log(market capitalization and claims on private sector by financial institutions as share of GDP)

Finance-aggregate = first principal component of finance-activity and finance-size

Table 5.8
(continued)

Structure-activity = log(total value traded divided by claims on private sector by commercial banks)

Structure-size = log(market capitalization divided by claims on private sector by commercial banks)

Structure-aggregate = first principal components of structure-activity and structure-size

financial systems, while the specific structure of the financial system does not have any impact on industrial growth patterns.

5.4.3 *Financial Structure and the Creation of New Firms*

The results in table 5.9 indicate that new firms are more easily created in countries with higher levels of financial development, but financial structure does not explain industry patterns in the growth of new firms across countries.[14] None of the interaction terms with financial structure enters significantly in the regressions. The interaction terms with the financial development indicators, however, enter significantly at the 10 percent level in the regressions with *Structure-size* and *Structure-aggregate*. They do not enter significantly in the regressions with *Structure-activity*. We can explain this inconsistency with the fact that *Structure-activity* is the structure measure that shows the highest correlation with the indicators of financial development. Overall, these results are again consistent with the financial-services view and are inconsistent with the market- or bank-based view.

5.4.4 *Industry Growth, New Firm Creation, and the Law and Finance View*

The results in table 5.10 show that externally dependent industries grow faster and new firms are created more easily in countries with higher levels of creditor and shareholder rights and more effective enforcement of those rights. While none of the interaction terms with financial structure enters significantly, the interaction terms with the three legal variables enter jointly significantly at the 10 percent level in all six regressions. The p-values on the individual coefficients indicate that it is especially the enforcement of laws that is important for the growth of externally dependent industries and the creation of new firms in these industries.

Table 5.9
Financial Development, Financial Structure, and the Growth in Number of Firms

Dependent variable: Growth in the number of firms, 1980–1989

	Structure-activity	Structure-size	Structure-aggregate
Interaction (external dependence × structure-activity)	0.127 (0.905)		
Interaction (external dependence × structure-size)		0.729 (0.310)	
Interaction (external dependence × structure-aggregate)			0.571 (0.474)
Interaction (external dependence × finance-activity)	0.659 (0.227)	0.572 (0.015)	0.521 (0.092)
Number of observations	903	903	903
Interaction (external dependence × structure-activity)	0.275 (0.748)		
Interaction (external dependence × structure-size)		0.786 (0.282)	
Interaction (external dependence × structure-aggregate)			0.609 (0.427)
Interaction (external dependence × finance-size)	1.969 (0.169)	1.914 (0.014)	1.746 (0.074)
Number of observations	903	903	903
Interaction (external dependence × structure-activity)	0.179 (0.852)		
Interaction (external dependence × structure-size)		0.747 (0.302)	
Interaction (external dependence × structure-aggregate)			0.574 (0.465)
Interaction (external dependence × finance-aggregate)	1.400 (0.193)	1.268 (0.014)	1.163 (0.081)
Number of observations	903	903	903

Notes: The dependent variable is the log difference between the number of establishments in 1990 and 1980 for each industry in each country. The p-values for heteroskedasticity robust standard errors are reported in parentheses. All regressions also include the industry's share of total value added in manufacturing in 1980. All regressions are IV. We use the British, French, and German legal origin dummies and the share of Catholic, Muslim, and Protestant population in total population as instruments for financial development and financial structure.

Finance-activity = log(total value traded as share of GDP × claims on private sector by financial institutions as share of GDP)

Finance-size = log(market capitalization and claims on private sector by financial institutions as share of GDP)

Finance-aggregate = first principal component of finance-activity and finance-size

Table 5.9
(continued)

Structure-activity = log(total value traded divided by claims on private sector by commercial banks)

Structure-size = log(market capitalization divided by claims on private sector by commercial banks)

Structure-aggregate = first principal components of structure-activity and structure-size

5.4.5 Sensitivity Analysis

Our findings are robust to a number of sensitivity checks (Beck and Levine 2000a). First, when we use a larger sample of forty-two countries (some of which are not in this chapter's 48-country sample), our conclusions do not change. While industries with higher need of external finance grow faster in economies with better-developed financial sectors and better protection of outside investors, financial structure cannot explain industry growth patterns across countries. Second, we use alternative measures of external dependence. Specifically, we use external dependence measured for a sample of Canadian firms to thus test whether our results are due to peculiarities of the U.S. financial system. The results do not change. We also use a measure of external finance computed from a sample of firms that have gone public over the previous ten years, since young firms are especially dependent on external finance. Again, our main findings hold. Finally, we use an indicator for unbalanced financial systems to explore whether the growth of industries that depend heavily on external finance is impacted by distorted financial systems. As in the cross-country analysis, we do not find any significant impact of the unbalanced indicator.

5.4.6 Summary

Our findings from the country-industry panel confirm the results from the cross-country regressions and provide support for the financial services and law and finance view. Industries that depend relatively more on external finance grow faster in economies with higher levels of financial development and legal systems that better protect the rights of outside investors. Industries that are heavy users of external finance do not grow faster and new firms are not created more rapidly in either a market- or bank-based financial system. It is

Table 5.10
Financial Structure, the Legal Environment, and Industry Growth

	Structure-activity	Structure-size	Structure-aggregate
Dependent variable: Industry growth, 1980–1989			
Interaction (external dependence × structure-activity)	−1.494 (0.124)		
Interaction (external dependence × structure-size)		−0.543 (0.695)	
Interaction (external dependence × structure-aggregate)			−1.651 (0.243)
Interaction (external dependence × creditor)	0.229 (0.687)	0.300 (0.614)	0.181 (0.756)
Interaction (external dependence × anti-director)	1.327 (0.078)	0.598 (0.594)	1.455 (0.178)
Interaction (external dependence × rule of law)	1.179 (0.001)	0.818 (0.001)	1.059 (0.001)
F-test creditor, anti-director, and rule of law	4.77 (0.003)	4.95 (0.002)	4.92 (0.002)
Number of observations	1016	1016	1016
Dependent variable: Growth in the number of firms, 1980–1989			
Interaction (external dependence × structure-activity)	−0.858 (0.329)		
Interaction (external dependence × structure-size)		0.104 (0.926)	
Interaction (external dependence × structure-aggregate)			−0.564 (0.650)
Interaction (external dependence × creditor)	0.749 (0.138)	0.788 (0.118)	0.749 (0.137)
Interaction (external dependence × anti-director)	1.175 (0.126)	0.440 (0.069)	0.928 (0.343)
Interaction (external dependence × rule of law)	0.719 (0.012)	0.472 (0.010)	0.588 (0.024)
F-test creditor, anti-director, and rule of law	2.49 (0.059)	3.05 (0.028)	2.39 (0.067)
Number of observations	903	903	903

Notes: The dependent variable in the top panel is the annual compounded growth rate in real value added for 1980–1990 for each industry in each country. The dependent variable in the bottom panel is the log difference between the number of establishments in 1990 and 1980 for each industry in each country. The p-values for heteroskedasticity robust standard errors are reported in parentheses. All regressions also include the industry's share of total value added in manufacturing in 1980. All regressions are IV. We use the British, French, and German legal origin and the legal determinants.

Table 5.10
(continued)

Structure-activity = log(total value traded divided by claims on private sector by commercials banks)

Structure-size = log(market capitalization divided by claims on private sector by commercial banks)

Structure-aggregate = first principal components of structure-activity and structure-size

Creditor = index of secured creditor rights

Anti-director = index of minority shareholder rights

Rule of law = measure of the law and order tradition of a country

thus the overall level of financial development, but not a specific structure of the financial system that enables especially new firms to overcome barriers in obtaining external funding.

5.5 Firm-Level Results

In this section we use firm-level data from a panel of thirty-three countries and six years between 1990 and 1995 to explore whether firms' access to external finance varies across financial systems with different structures, or whether the overall level of financial development and the legal system determine firms' access to external finance. We next describe the methodology and data that we use; assess the market-based, bank-based, and financial-services view; and explore the importance of legal institutions for firms' access to external finance.

5.5.1 Econometric Methodology and Data

We follow an approach developed by Demirgüç-Kunt and Maksimovic (1998, 2000) to measure whether firms' growth in an economy is financially constrained. Simple correlation between firms' growth and financial development and structure does not control for differences in the amount of external financing needed by firms in the same industry but in different countries. These differences may arise because firms in different countries may employ different technologies, because profit rates may differ across countries, or because investment opportunities and demand may differ. In our empirical tests we take into account the possibility that these factors may affect the demand for external capital. To control for these differences at the firm level, we calculate for each firm in an economy the rate at which it can grow, using (1) only its internal funds or (2) using its internal funds and short-term borrowing. We then compute the percentage of firms that grow at rates that exceed each of these two estimated rates. These statistics yield estimates of the proportion of firms in an economy relying on external financing to grow.

The firm-level data consist of accounting data for the largest publicly traded manufacturing firms in thirty-three countries, using data from the Worldscope database. We estimate a firm's potential growth rate using the standard "percentage of sales" financial planning model (Higgins 1977). This approach relates a firm's growth rate of sales to its need for investment funds, based on three simplifying assumptions. First, the ratio of assets used in production to sales is constant. Second, the firm's profits per unit of sales are constant. Finally, the economic depreciation rate equals the accounting depreciation rate. Under these assumptions, the firm's financing need in period t of a firm growing at g_t percent per year is given by

$$EFN_t = g_t * Assets_t - (1 + g_t) * Earnings_t * b_t, \tag{5.3}$$

where EFN_t is the external financing need and b_t is the fraction of the firm's earnings that are retained for reinvestment at time t. Earnings are calculated after interest and taxes. While the first term on the righthand side of equation (5.1) denotes the required investment for a firm growing at g_t percent, the second term is the internally available funds for investment, assuming a constant retention rate b_t.

We use two different estimates of a firm's attainable growth rate. The internally financed growth rate IG_t is the maximum growth rate that can be financed with internal resources only. Assuming that the firm retains all its earnings, that is, $b_t = 1$, equating EFN_t to 0 and solving equation (5.1) for g_t, we obtain

$$IG_t = ROA_t/(1 - ROA_t), \tag{5.4}$$

where ROA_t is the firm's return on assets (*Earnings/Assets*). The definition of IG thus assumes that firm does not rely on any external source to finance its growth.

The short-term financed growth rate SG_t is the maximum growth rate that can be obtained if the firm reinvests all its earnings and obtains enough short-term external resources to maintain the ratio of its short-term liabilities to assets. To compute SG_t, we first replace total assets in equation (5.1) by assets that are financed by new long-term capital, calculated as total assets times one minus the ratio of short-term liabilities to total assets. SG_t is then given by

$$SG_t = ROLTC_t/(1 - ROLTC_t), \tag{5.5}$$

where $ROLTC_t$ is the ratio of earnings, after tax and interest, to long-term capital. The definition of SG thus assumes that the firm does not access any long-term borrowings or sales of equity to finance its growth.

The estimates of IG and SG are conservative for several reasons. First, we assume that a firm utilizes the unconstrained sources of finance—trade credit in the case IG, and trade credit and short-term borrowing in the case of SG—no more intensively than it is currently doing. Second, firms with spare capacities do not need to invest and may grow at a faster rate than predicted without accessing external resources. Third, the financial planning model abstracts from technical advances that reduce the requirements for investment capital. Thus, it may overstate the costs of growth and underestimate the maximum growth rate attainable using unconstrained sources of financing.

For each country we then calculate the percentage of firms whose realized annual real growth rate of sales exceeds the predicted rates IG_t and SG_t, respectively. $STCOUNT_t$ is calculated as $\sum_f d_{fit}/n_{it}$, where n_{it} is the number of firms in country i in period t and d_{fit} takes the value 1 if the firm f's real growth rate of sales exceeds IG_{fit}, and 0 otherwise. $LTCOUNT_{it}$ is calculated in a similar way, using IG_{fit}. $STCOUNT_t$ is thus an estimate of the proportion of firms in country i that obtain external funding at time t, and $LTCOUNT_{it}$ is an estimate of the proportion of firms in country i that obtain long-term external financing at time t.

Table 5.11 presents the average values for $STCOUNT$ and $LTCOUNT$ for all thirty-three countries in our sample. There is a large variation in the proportion of firms that obtain external resources. Only 26 percent of firms in New Zealand grow at rates requiring external financing, while 100 percent of firms in Austria do. Only 17 percent of firms in Chile grow beyond the rate predicted by the use of internal and short-term external funds, but 100 percent in Austria. These differences are likely to be affected by the availability of external finance both directly and indirectly, as the composition of firms in each economy evolves through mergers and diversification to take advantage of the available sources of financing.

Table 5.11
Firm Growth across Countries

Country	STCOUNT	LTCOUNT
Argentina	0.51	0.46
Australia	0.46	0.39
Austria	1.00	1.00
Belgium	0.45	0.38
Brazil	0.49	0.48
Canada	0.65	0.61
Chile	0.29	0.17
Colombia	0.33	0.33
Denmark	0.43	0.35
Finland	0.47	0.42
France	0.38	0.29
Germany	0.93	0.92
Great Britain	0.39	0.28
Greece	0.36	0.28
India	0.53	0.38
Ireland	0.64	0.55
Israel	0.58	0.46
Italy	0.41	0.35
Japan	0.43	0.36
Malaysia	0.54	0.49
Mexico	0.52	0.47
Netherlands	0.36	0.26
New Zealand	0.26	0.23
Norway	0.46	0.41
Pakistan	0.46	0.32
Philippines	0.35	0.30
Portugal	0.40	0.36
South Africa	0.27	0.19
Spain	0.38	0.32
Sweden	0.46	0.38
Switzerland	0.33	0.28
Thailand	0.49	0.35
United States	0.44	0.39

Notes: STCOUNT is the share of firms that grow faster than predicted by the use of internal resources. *LTCOUNT* is the share of firms that grow faster than predicted by the use of internal resources and short-term borrowings. Data are averaged over the period 1990–1995.

To analyze our different hypotheses in our sample of thirty-three countries and six years, we run the following regressions:

$$y_{it} = \beta_1 FD_{it} + \beta_2 FS_{it} + \beta_3 CV_{it} + \varepsilon_{it}, \tag{5.6}$$

where y is either STCOUNT or LTCOUNT, FD is one of the five indicators of financial development, defined above, FS is one of the five indicators of financial structure, CV is a set of control variables, and ε is the error term.

We estimate equation (5.6) using IV techniques to control for simultaneity bias and reverse causality. Specifically, as in sections 5.3 and 5.4, we will be using the legal origin of countries to extract the exogenous component of the level of financial development and structure.

To assess the robustness of the link between the proportion of firms that receive external resources and the level of financial development and structure, we include several control variables. Specifically, we include the average size of firms, since firms that are larger relative to the economy might enjoy better access to external financing than smaller firms. We include the inflation rate to control for measurement errors in firms' financial statements in highly inflationary economies. We include the level and the growth rate of real per capita GDP. We include the level of real per capita GDP to control for determinants of firms' access to external financing that are related to the level of economic development, but are independent of the financial system. We include the growth rate of real per capita GDP to control for the possibility that firms' desire to grow depends on the rate of growth of the economy. Finally, we include Rule of law to control for effects of the legal system that are independent of the effect of the financial system.

5.5.2 Excess Growth of Firms and Financial Structure

The results in table 5.12 indicate that the share of firms growing at rates requiring external financing does not vary across countries with different financial structures. For conciseness, the table only reports the results for the variable of interest—financial structure. The top panel reports the results for STCOUNT, the bottom panel for LTCOUNT. Except for Structure-Size, none of the indicators of financial structure enters significantly at the 5 percent level in the regressions of either STCOUNT or LTCOUNT. These findings are not consistent with either the market- or the bank-based view.

Table 5.12
Financial Structure and Firm Growth

Explanatory variable	Coefficient	Standard error	t-statistic	p-value	Number of observations	Countries
1. Dependent variable: *STCOUNT*						
Structure-activity	−0.010	0.020	−0.479	0.632	172	33
Structure-size	−0.091	0.024	−3.846	0.000	172	33
Structure-efficiency	−0.014	0.017	−0.829	0.408	172	33
Structure-aggregate	−0.031	0.018	−1.757	0.081	172	33
2. Dependent variable: *LTCOUNT*						
Structure-activity	−0.010	0.021	−0.494	0.622	172	33
Structure-size	−0.100	0.024	−4.098	0.000	172	33
Structure-efficiency	−0.010	0.017	−0.566	0.572	172	33
Structure-aggregate	−0.032	0.019	−1.738	0.084	172	33

Notes: STCOUNT is the share of firms that grow faster than predicted by the use of internal resources. *LTCOUNT* is the share of firms that grow faster than predicted by the use of internal resources. Conditioning information set: level and growth rate of real per capita GDP, inflation rate, total assets of firms in a country divided by GDP, and rule of law. We use the British, German, and French legal origin as instruments for financial structure.

Structure-activity = log(total value traded divided by claims on private sector by commercial banks)
Structure-size = log(market capitalization divided by claims on private sector by commercial banks)
Structure-efficiency = log(total value traded as share of GDP × banks' overhead costs as share of total assets)
Structure-aggregate = first principal components of structure-activity, structure-size, and structure-efficiency

The table 5.13 results provide evidence for the financial services view. We again report only the variable of interest—financial development. All four indicators of financial development enter significantly positive at the 5 percent level in the regressions of *STCOUNT*. This indicates that firms are more likely to grow at rates that require external financing in economies with higher level of financial sector development. All four indicators of financial development enter significantly positive at the 10 percent level in the regressions of *LTCOUNT*. We interpret this as evidence that the share of firms that grow at rates requiring long-term external financing is higher in countries with better-developed financial sector.

5.5.3   *Excess Growth of Firms and the Law and Finance View*

To explore the law and finance view, we first regress our indicators of financial development on our three legal indicators, *Creditor*, *Antidirector*, and *Rule of law*. The fitted values of these regressions indicate the level of financial development predicted by the legal environment of a country. We also use the residual from each regression—*Excess-finance*—to indicate the component of financial development that is not predicted by the legal environment. In the second stage, we then run equation (5.7) including both the predicted value of financial development from the first stage and *Excess-finance*. The law and finance view predicts a positive coefficient on the fitted value of *Finance* and an insignificant coefficient on *Excess-finance*. A significantly positive coefficient on *Excess-finance* would indicate an importance of other components of the financial sector not predicted by the legal systems for firms' growth. A significantly negative coefficient on *Excess-finance* would indicate that a financial sector growing beyond the legal infrastructure is damaging for firms' growth.

The results in table 5.14 provide support for the law and finance view. We report only the coefficient on the fitted values of our indicators of financial development and on the respective *Excess-finance*. The results in the top panel indicate that firms are more likely to grow at rates requiring external finance in economies in which the legal system is conducive to the development of large, active, efficient banks and stock markets. With the exception of Finance-Size all predicted indicators of financial development enter significantly positive. None of the Excess-Finance variables enters significantly in the regressions. The results in the bottom panel are even stronger. All indicators of predicted financial development enter significantly

Table 5.13
Financial Development and Firm Growth

Explanatory variable	Coefficient	Standard error	t-statistic	p-value	Number of observations	Countries
1. Dependent variable: *STCOUNT*						
Finance-activity	0.056	0.025	2.219	0.028	172	33
Finance-size	0.154	0.069	2.248	0.026	172	33
Finance-efficiency	0.059	0.028	2.134	0.034	172	33
Finance-aggregate	0.092	0.041	2.230	0.027	172	33
2. Dependent variable: *LTCOUNT*						
Finance-activity	0.049	0.026	1.897	0.060	172	33
Finance-size	0.143	0.070	2.029	0.044	172	33
Finance-efficiency	0.048	0.029	1.661	0.099	172	33
Finance-aggregate	0.080	0.043	1.887	0.061	172	33

Notes: *STCOUNT* is the share of firms that grow faster than predicted by the use of internal resources. *LTCOUNT* is the share of firms that grow faster than predicted by the use of internal resources. Conditioning information set: level and growth rate of real per capita GDP, inflation rate, total assets of firms in a country divided by GDP, and rule of law. We use the British, German, and French legal origin as instruments for financial development.

Finance-activity = log(total value traded as share of GDP × claims on private sector by financial institutions as share of GDP)

Finance-size = log(market capitalization and claims on private sector by financial institutions as share of GDP)

Finance-efficiency = log(Total value traded as share of GDP divided by banks' overhead costs as share of total assets)

Finance-aggregate = first principal component of finance-activity, finance-size, and finance-efficiency

Table 5.14
Firmg Growth and the Legal-Based View

Explanatory variable	Coefficient	Standard error	t-statistic	p-value	Number of observations	Countries
1. Dependent variable: *STCOUNT*						
Finance-activity	0.057	0.029	1.998	0.046	172	33
Excess-finance-activity	0.013	0.017	0.760	0.447		
Finance-size	0.100	0.066	1.511	0.131	172	33
Excess-finance-size	−0.013	0.047	−0.283	0.778		
Finance-efficiency	0.074	0.033	2.236	0.025	172	33
Excess-finance-efficiency	0.021	0.018	1.145	0.252		
Finance-aggregate	0.090	0.046	1.972	0.049	172	33
Excess-finance-aggregate	0.019	0.030	0.651	0.515		
2. Dependent variable: *LTCOUNT*						
Finance-activity	0.080	0.029	2.761	0.006	172	33
Excess-finance-activity	0.022	0.017	1.262	0.207		
Finance-size	0.150	0.067	2.227	0.026	172	33
Excess-finance-size	0.010	0.048	0.199	0.842		
Finance-efficiency	0.093	0.034	2.757	0.006	172	33
Excess-finance-efficiency	0.025	0.018	1.371	0.170		
Finance-aggregate	0.123	0.046	2.665	0.008	172	33
Excess-finance-aggregate	0.033	0.030	1.094	0.274		

Notes: *STCOUNT* is the share of firms that grow faster than predicted by the use of internal resources. *LTCOUNT* is the share of firms that grow faster than predicted by the use of internal resources. All regressions are estimated using panel data with random effects. Conditioning information set: level and growth rate of real per capita GDP, inflation rate, total assets of firms in a country divided by GDP, and rule of law.

Finance-activity, size, efficiency and aggregate are the predicted values from a regression of finance-activity, size, efficiency, and aggregate on creditor, anti-director, and rule of law. Excess-finance refers to the residuals from the respective regression.

Finance-activity = log(total value traded as share of GDP × claims on private sector by financial institutions as share of GDP)
Finance-size = log(market capitalization and claims on private sector by financial institutions as share of GDP)
Finance-efficiency = log(total value traded as share of GDP divided by banks' overhead costs as share of total assets)
Finance-aggregate = First principal component of finance-activity, finance-size, and finance-efficiency

positive in the regressions, while none of the Excess-Finance indicators does. This indicates that the share of firms that grow at rates requiring external long-term financing is higher in economies with a contracting environment that favors financial development.

5.5.4 Sensitivity Analysis

We confirm our main findings using a larger sample of thirty-eight countries, some of which are not included in the forty-eight-country sample of this chapter.[15] While firms grow at rates requiring external financing in economies with higher level of financial development and economies with better protection of outside investors, financial structure and financial development beyond the component predicted by the legal system does not have any explanatory power for firms' growth.

Demirgüç-Kunt and Maksimovic (2000) take a different approach to test the law and finance view. Specifically they allow banking-sector and stock market development to take different coefficients. In the first stage they regress an indicator of banking-sector development on *Rule of law*, the common legal origin dummy, *Creditor* and the inflation rate, and an indicator of stock market development on *Rule of law*, the Common legal origin dummy, *Anti-director*, and the inflation rate. They show that while the predicted level of banking-sector and stock market development can explain the share of firms that grow at rates requiring external financing, the residuals from the first-stage regressions do not have any explanatory power. In the regressions of *LTCOUNT* only the predicted level of stock market development enters significantly, while the predicted level of banking-sector development does not enter significantly. Again, the residuals from the first-stage regressions do not have any explanatory power. This indicates that any financial development beyond the level predicted by the macroeconomic environment and the legal system does not explain firms' growth.

5.5.5 Summary

Using firm-level data we confirm our previous findings. Financial structure does not explain the growth of firms beyond the rates predicted by the internal resources and short-term borrowings. This is inconsistent with both the market- and the bank-based view. The share of firms that grow at rates requiring external financing is higher in countries in countries with higher levels of financial-sector development, which is consistent with the financial-services view. Furthermore, we find that firms are more likely to grow at rates that require external finance in countries in which the contracting environment favors financial sector development. Financial sector development beyond the level that is predicted by the legal system does not have any explanatory power for firms' growth. This is consistent with the law and finance view.

5.6   Conclusions

This chapter explored the relationship between financial structure —the degree to which a financial system is market- or bank-based— and economic development. We use three methodologies. The cross-country approach uses cross-country data to assess whether economies grow faster with market- or bank-based financial systems. The industry approach uses a country-industry panel to assess whether industries that depend heavily on external financing grow faster in market- or bank-based financial systems, and whether financial structure influences the rate of new firm creation. Finally, the firm-level approach uses firm-level data across a broad selection of countries to test whether firms are more likely to grow beyond the rate predicted by internal resources and short-term borrowings in market- or bank-based financial systems.

The cross-country regressions, the industry panel estimations, and the firm-level analyses provide remarkably consistent conclusions. Financial structure is not an analytically useful way to distinguish among financial systems. More precisely, countries do not grow faster, financially dependent industries do not expand at higher rates, new firms are not created more easily, firms' access to external finance is not easier, and firms do not grow faster in either market- or bank-based financial systems.

We do find strong evidence in favor of the both the financial services and law and finance views of financial structure. We find that economies grow faster, industries depending heavily on external finance expand at faster rates, new firms form more easily, firms' access to external financing is easier, and firms grow more rapidly in economies with a higher levels of overall financial-sector development and in countries with legal systems that more effectively protect the rights of outside investors. These results are consistent with both the financial services and the law and finance theories.

Appendix 5.1

Table 5A.1
Indicators of Financial Development, Financial Structure and the Legal System across Countries

Country	Finance-activity	Finance-size	Finance-efficiency	Finance-aggregate	Finance-dummy	Structure-activity	Structure-size	Structure-efficiency	Structure-aggregate	Structure-dummy	Anti-director	Credi-tor	Rule of law	Legal origin
Argentina	-5.99	-1.62	-1.91	-1.39	0	-2.15	-1.09	-6.28	-0.18	0	4	1	3.21	F
Australia	-2.14	0.22	1.71	0.84	1	-1.18	-0.09	-5.58	0.80	1	4	1	6.00	E
Austria	-3.36	-0.06	0.48	0.26	1	-3.04	-2.46	-6.92	-1.27	0	2	3	6.00	G
Belgium	-4.37	-0.47	0.19	-0.16	0	-2.38	-0.36	-6.94	-0.17	0	0	2	6.00	F
Brazil	-4.14	-1.01	-0.62	-0.53	0	-0.92	-0.31	-4.87	1.01	1	3	1	3.79	F
Canada	-2.14	0.20	1.84	0.86	1	-1.14	-0.06	-5.59	0.82	1	5	1	6.00	E
Chile	-3.96	-0.07	0.20	0.10	1	-2.46	-0.03	-6.74	0.00	0	5	2	4.21	F
Colombia	-6.31	-1.09	-2.51	-1.31	0	-3.04	-0.78	-7.50	-0.75	0	3	0	1.25	F
Cyprus	-4.44	-0.04	-1.06	-0.21	1	-3.62	-1.11	-7.31	-1.05	0			3.59	E
Denmark	-3.63	-0.45	0.58	0.05	0	-1.87	-0.62	-6.08	0.17	1	2	3	6.00	S
Ecuador	-5.75	-1.25	-1.52	-1.10	0	-2.19	-0.43	-6.65	-0.04	0	2	4	4.00	F
Egypt	-6.85	-1.11	-1.55	-1.23	0	-4.14	-1.54	-9.60	-2.09	0	2	4	2.50	F
Finland	-3.52	-0.16	0.98	0.28	1	-2.72	-1.29	-7.23	-0.76	0	3	1	6.00	S
France	-2.57	0.10	0.64	0.50	1	-2.28	-1.42	-5.60	-0.17	0	3	0	5.39	F
Germany	-1.76	0.10	1.91	0.89	1	-1.52	-1.53	-5.26	0.17	1	1	3	5.54	G
Ghana	-9.07	-1.88	-2.71	-2.20	0	-2.17	1.34	-8.52	0.16	1			2.00	E
Greece	-5.05	-0.73	-0.92	-0.62	0	-2.65	-1.02	-7.37	-0.66	0	2	1	3.71	F
Honduras	-5.15	-1.08	-0.76	-0.77	0	-2.34	-1.46	-7.06	-0.63	0			2.07	F
India	-4.35	-0.92	0.52	-0.30	0	-1.61	-0.60	-6.58	0.14	0	5	4	2.50	E
Ireland	-2.41	-0.11	4.14	1.11	1	-0.64	-0.03	-8.02	0.33	1	4	1	4.68	E
Israel	-2.52	-0.23	1.43	0.51	1	-1.15	-0.56	-5.10	0.75	1	3	4	2.89	E

											1	2		
Italy	-3.89	-0.47	0.13	-0.09	1	-2.52	-1.45	-6.54	-0.55	0	1	2	5.00	F
Jamaica	-4.82	-0.66	-0.96	-0.55	0	-2.04	0.08	-6.12	0.38	1			2.11	E
Japan	-0.43	0.88	3.32	1.76	1	-1.00	-0.35	-5.24	0.86	1	4	2	5.39	G
Kenya	-6.83	-0.90	-2.30	-1.27	0	-3.93	-0.48	-8.88	-1.37	0	3	4	3.25	E
Malaysia	-1.08	0.63	3.27	1.52	1	-0.32	0.60	-4.97	1.59	1	4	4	4.07	E
Mexico	-4.50	-1.13	0.23	-0.49	0	-0.85	-0.02	-5.75	0.90	1	1	0	3.21	F
Netherlands	-1.41	0.52	2.95	1.35	1	-1.36	-0.60	-6.26	0.33	1	2	2	6.00	F
New Zealand	-3.14	-0.06	1.07	0.42	0	-1.64	-0.02	-6.12	0.49	1	4	3	6.00	E
Norway	-2.91	0.04	0.91	0.47	1	-2.06	-1.15	-6.49	-0.23	0	4	2	6.00	S
Pakistan	-5.41	-1.13	-0.45	-0.78	0	-2.51	-0.98	-7.47	-0.62	0	5	4	1.82	E
Panama	-6.55	-0.55	-1.76	-0.95	1	-5.17	-1.94	-9.98	-2.75	0			2.11	F
Peru	-6.60	-1.84	-2.02	-1.62	0	-1.54	-0.07	-6.53	0.39	1	3	0	1.50	F
Philippines	-4.17	-0.69	0.03	-0.26	0	-1.47	-0.10	-5.92	0.58	1	3	0	1.64	F
Portugal	-4.32	-0.34	-0.19	-0.17	1	-3.40	-2.10	-7.52	-1.43	0	3	1	5.21	F
South Africa	-2.81	0.74	0.75	0.79	1	-1.90	0.94	-5.91	0.85	1	5	3	2.65	E
Spain	-3.11	-0.10	0.57	0.30	1	-2.36	-1.29	-6.14	-0.31	0	4	2	4.68	F
Sri Lanka	-5.97	-1.14	-1.26	-1.03	0	-2.66	-0.39	-7.37	-0.41	0	3	3	1.14	E
Sweden	-1.91	0.39	1.49	0.92	1	-1.18	-0.15	-5.47	0.80	1	3	2	6.00	S
Switzerland	0.55	0.91	2.98	1.88	1	-0.39	-0.71	-3.03	1.58	1	2	1	6.00	G
Thailand	-1.98	-0.06	2.33	0.86	1	-0.92	-0.66	-5.52	0.68	1	2	3	3.75	E
Trinidad and Tobago	-5.32	-0.50	-1.52	-0.67	0	-3.41	-1.00	-7.72	-1.04	0			4.00	E
Tunisia	-5.52	-0.44	-1.00	-0.58	1	-4.29	-1.91	-8.90	-2.09	0			2.79	F
Turkey	-4.77	-1.61	-0.03	-0.81	0	-0.73	-0.74	-5.54	0.71	1	2	2	3.11	F
United Kingdom	-1.33	0.41	2.72	1.27	1	-0.74	0.02	-4.79	1.24	1	5	4	5.14	E
United States	-0.80	0.64	2.24	1.37	1	-0.64	-0.11	-4.38	1.34	1	5	1	6.00	E
Zimbabwe	-6.14	-1.04	-1.37	-1.04	0	-2.58	0.03	-7.88	-0.35	0	3	4	2.21	E

Table 5A.1
(continued)
Notes:

Finance-activity = log(total value traded as share of GDP × claims on private sector by financial institutions as share of GDP)

Finance-size = log(market capitalization and claims on private sector by financial institutions as share of GDP)

Finance-efficiency = log(total value traded as share of GDP divided by banks' overhead costs as share of total assets)

Finance-aggregate = first principal component of finance-activity, finance-size, and finance-efficiency

Finance-dummy = takes value 0 if claims on private sector by banks as share of GDP and value traded as share of GDP are less than sample mean, 1 otherwise

Structure-activity = log(total value traded divided by claims on private sector by commercials banks)

Structure-size = log(market capitalization divided by claims on private sector by commercials bank)

Structure-efficiency = log(total value traded as share of GDP × banks' overhead costs as share of total assets)

Structure-aggregate = first principal components of structure-activity, structure-size, and structure-efficiency

Structure-dummy = dummy variable that takes the value 1 if structure-aggregate is above the median, 0 otherwise

Creditor = index of secured creditor rights

Anti-director = index of minority shareholder rights

Rule of law = measure of the law and order tradition of a country

Legal origin: E = British, F = French, G = German, S = Scandinavian

Table 5A.2
External Dependence across Industries

ISIC code	Industrial sector	External dependence
314	Tobacco	−0.45
361	Pottery	−0.15
323	Leather	−0.14
3211	Spinning	−0.09
324	Footwear	−0.08
372	Nonferrous metal	0.01
322	Apparel	0.03
353	Petroleum refineries	0.04
369	Nonmetal mineral products	0.06
313	Beverages	0.08
371	Iron and steel	0.09
311	Food products	0.14
3411	Pulp, paper	0.15
3513	Synthetic resins	0.16
341	Paper and paper products	0.18
342	Printing and publishing	0.20
352	Other chemicals	0.22
355	Rubber products	0.23
332	Furniture	0.24
381	Metal products	0.24
3511	Basic industrial goods excl. fertilizers	0.25
331	Wood products	0.28
384	Transportation equipment	0.31
354	Petroleum and coal products	0.33
3843	Motor vehicles	0.39
321	Textile	0.40
382	Machinery	0.45
3841	Ships	0.46
390	Other industries	0.47
362	Glass	0.53
383	Electric machinery	0.77
385	Professional and scientific goods	0.96
3832	Radios	1.04
3825	Office and computing products	1.06
356	Plastic products	1.14
3522	Drugs	1.49

Source: Rajan and Zingales 1998.
External dependence is defined as capital expenditures (Compustat #128) minus cash flow from operations divided by capital expenditures. Cash flow from operations is broadly defined as the sum of Compustat funds from operations (items #110), decreases in inventories, decreases in receivables, and increases in payables

Notes

1. Specifically, firm-level studies (Demirgüç-Kunt and Maksimovic 1998, 1999), industry-level studies (Rajan and Zingales 1998; Wurgler 2000), country-case studies (Cameron et al. 1967; McKinnon 1973; Haber 1991, 1997), time-series studies (Neusser and Kugler 1998; Rousseau and Wachtel 1998), cross-country studies (King and Levine 1993a, b; Levine and Zervos 1998), cross-country instrumental variable studies (Levine 1998, 1999, 2000) and pooled cross-country, time-series studies (Beck and Levine 2000b; Beck, Levine, and Loayza 2000; Levine, Loayza, and Beck 2000; Rousseau and Wachtel forthcoming) find that the level of financial development is positively related to growth, and this relationship is not due only to simultaneity bias. Note, however, that these findings do not reject the hypothesis that economic activity influences financial development. The findings merely suggest that there is an exogenous component of financial development that positively influences economic activity, such that the strong positive relationship between the level of financial development and economic growth is not only due to economic activity's influence on financial development.

2. Everywhere in this chapter, new firm formation is proxied by new establishment formation.

3. There are, of course, some costs associated with developing this unified approach. The underlying papers perform more sensitivity analyses and robustness checks than we present in this synthesis.

4. Levine and Zervos (1998) point out a potential pitfall of Value Traded. If forward-looking stock markets anticipate large corporate profits and therefore higher economic growth, this will boost stock prices and therefore boost Value Traded. However, when we use the turnover ratio, which equals Value Traded divided by Market Capitalization, we get similar results. Turnover does not suffer from this price effect because stock prices enter into the numerator and denominator.

5. This does not include legal systems with Islamic roots or socialist systems.

6. Levine, Loayza, and Beck (2000) and Beck, Levine, and Loayza (2000) have used similar conditioning information sets in their work on the impact of financial inter-mediary development on economic growth. We also tried a full conditioning information set that comprises the policy conditioning information set and indicators of civil liberties, revolutions and coups, political assassinations, bureaucratic efficiency, and corruption. The results are similar.

7. We use the coefficient estimate for *Finance-activity* from table 5.5 (top panel).

8. Results available on request. See also Levine 2000 for further robustness tests.

9. We do not include financial development or financial structure on their own, since we focus on within-country and across-industry growth rates.

10. This does not correspond exactly to the convergence concept known from cross-country growth regressions. We include the share in manufacturing rather than the level, since we focus on within-country, across-industry growth rates. As in Rajan and Zingales (1998), γ enters significantly negative in most regressions.

11. Unlike in the cross-sectional growth regressions we include financial structure and financial development indicators at the same time, since we can exploit more variance

in these panel regressions. We therefore extend our set of instrumental variables by religious composition.

12. There are no cross-country data available on firms. An establishment is defined as a unit which engages, under a single ownership or control, in one, or predominantly one, kind of activity at a single location.

13. Since *Structure-efficiency* and *Finance-efficiency* are available only for the years 1990–1995, we do not use these measures in this section.

14. Beck and Levine (2000a) show that the growth in the average size of firms is related to neither financial development nor financial structure.

15. Results available on request.

References

Allen, Franklin, and Douglas Gale. 1999. *Comparing financial systems*. Cambridge, MA: MIT Press.

Beck, Thorsten, and Ross Levine. 2000a. Industry growth and capital allocation: Does having a market- or bank-based system matter? Mimeo, Finance Department, University of Minnesota.

Beck, Thorsten, and Ross Levine. 2000b. Stock markets, banks, and growth: Correlation or causality? Mimeo, Policy Research Department, World Bank.

Beck, Thorsten, Ross Levine, and Norman Loayza. 2000. Finance and the sources of growth. *Journal of Financial Economics* 58(1):261–300.

Bhide, Amar. 1993. The hidden costs of stock market liquidity. *Journal of Financial Economics* 34(1):1–51 (August).

Boot, Arnoud W. A., Stuart J. Greenbaum, and Anjan V. Thakor. 1993. Reputation and discretion in financial contracting. *American Economic Review* 83:1165–1183.

Boyd, John H., and Bruce D. Smith. 1996. The co-evolution of the real and financial sectors in the growth process. *World Bank Economic Review* 10(2):371–396 (May).

Boyd, John H., and Bruce D. Smith. 1998. The evolution of debt and equity markets in economic development. *Economic Theory* 12(3):519–560.

Cameron, Rondo, Olga Crisp, Hugh T. Patrick, and Richard Tilly, eds. 1967. *Banking in the early stages of industrialization: A study of comparative economic history*. New York: Oxford University Press.

Demirgüç-Kunt, Aslı, and Vojislav Maksimovic. 1998. Law, Finance, and Firm Growth. *Journal of Finance* 53(6):2107–2137 (December).

Demirgüç-Kunt, Aslı, and Vojislav Maksimovic. 1999. Institutions, financial markets, and firm debt maturity. *Journal of Financial Economics* 54:295–336.

Demirgüç-Kunt, Aslı, and Vojislav Maksimovic. 2000. Funding growth in bank-based and market-based financial systems: Evidence from firm-level data. Mimeo, Policy Research Department, World Bank.

Gerschenkron, Alexander. 1962. *Economic backwardness in historical perspective, a book of essays*. Cambridge, MA: Harvard University Press.

Glendon, M. A., M. W. Gordon, and C. Osakwe. 1982. *Comparative legal tradition in a nutshell*. St. Paul, MN: West Publishing Co.

Haber, Stephan H. 1991. Industrial concentration and capital markets: A comparative study of Brazil, Mexico and the United States, 1830–1930. *Journal of Economic History* 51(3):559–580 (September).

Haber, Stephan H. 1997. Financial markets and industrial development: A comparative study of governmental regulation, financial innovation, and industrial structure in Brazil and Mexico, 1840–1940. In *How Latin America Fell Behind*, ed. Stephan Haber. Stanford, CA: Stanford University Press.

Hansen, L. P. 1982. Large sample properties of generalized method of moments estimators. *Econometrica* 50:1029–1054.

Hellwig, Martin. 1998. On the economics and politics of corporate finance and corporate control. Mimeo, School of Business, University of Mannheim.

Higgins, Robert C. 1977. How much growth can a firm afford? *Financial Management* 6:3–16.

King, Robert G., and Ross Levine. 1993a. Finance and growth: Schumpeter might be right. *Quarterly Journal of Economics* 108:717–738.

King, Robert G., and Ross Levine. 1993b. Finance, entrepreneurship, and growth: Theory and evidence. *Journal of Monetary Economics* 32:513–542.

La Porta, Rafael, Florencio Lopez-de-Silanes, Andrei Shleifer, and Robert W. Vishny. 1997. Legal determinants of external finance. *Journal of Finance* 52(3):1131–1150.

La Porta, Rafael, Florencio Lopez-de-Silanes, Andrei Shleifer, and Robert W. Vishny. 1998. Law and finance. *Journal of Political Economy* 106(6):1113–1155.

La Porta, Rafael, Florencio Lopez-de-Silanes, Andrei Shleifer, and Robert W. Vishny. 1999. The quality of government. *Journal of Law, Economics, and Organization* 15(1):222–279.

La Porta, Rafael, Florencio Lopez-de-Silanes, Andrei Shleifer, and Robert W. Vishny. 2000. Investor protection and corporate governance. *Journal of Financial Economics* 58(1):3–27.

Levine, Ross. 1997. Financial development and economic growth: Views and agenda. *Journal of Economic Literature* 35(2):688–726 (June).

Levine, Ross. 1998. The legal environment, banks, and long-run economic growth. *Journal of Money, Credit, and Banking* 30(Pt. 2):596–620 (August).

Levine, Ross. 1999. Law, finance, and economic growth. *Journal of Financial Intermediation* 8(1/2):36–67.

Levine, Ross. 2000. Bank-based or market-based financial systems: Which is better? Mimeo, Department of Finance, University of Minnesota.

Levine, Ross. Forthcoming. Napoleon, bourses, and growth: With a Focus on Latin America. In *Market Augmenting Government*, ed. Omar Azfar and Charles Cadwell, Ann Arbor: University of Michigan Press.

Levine, Ross, Norman Loayza, and Thorsten Beck. 2000. Financial intermediation and growth: Causality and causes. *Journal of Monetary Economics* 46(1):31–77.

Levine, Ross, and Sara Zervos. 1998. Stock markets, banks, and economic growth. *American Economic Review* 88(3):537–558 (June).

McKinnon, Ronald I. 1973. *Money and capital in economic development.* Washington, DC: Brookings Institution.

Morck, Randall, and Masao Nakkamura. 1999. Banks and corporate control in Japan. *Journal of Finance* 54:319–340.

Neusser, Klaus, and Maurice Kugler. 1998. Manufacturing growth and financial development: Evidence from OECD countries. *Review of Economics and Statistics* 80:636–646 (November).

Newey, W., and K. West. 1987. Hypothesis testing with efficient method of moments estimation. *International Economic Review* 28:777–787.

Rajan, Raghuram G. 1992. Insiders and outsiders: The choice between informed and arms length debt. *Journal of Finance* 47(4):1367–1400 (September).

Rajan, Raghuram G., and Luigi Zingales. 1998. Financial dependence and growth. *American Economic Review* 88(3):559–586 (June).

Rajan, Raghuram G., and Luigi Zingales. 1999. Financial systems, industrial structure, and growth. Mimeo, School of Business, University of Chicago.

Rousseau, Peter L., and Paul Wachtel. 1998. Financial intermediation and economic performance: Historical evidence from five industrial countries. *Journal of Money, Credit, and Banking* 30(4):657–678 (November).

Rousseau, Peter L., and Paul Wachtel. Forthcoming. Equity markets and growth: Cross-country evidence on timing and outcomes, 1980–1995. *Journal of Banking and Finance.*

Stiglitz, Joseph E. 1985. Credit markets and the control of capital. *Journal of Money, Credit and Banking* 17(2):133–152 (May).

Weinstein, David E., and Yishay Yafeh. 1998. On the costs of a bank-centered financial system: Evidence from the changing main bank relations in Japan. *Journal of Finance* 53(2):635–672.

Wurgler, Jeffrey. 2000. Financial Markets and the Allocation of Capital. *Journal of Financial Economics* 58(1):187–214.

6 Financial Structure and Bank Profitability

Aslı Demirgüç-Kunt and
Harry Huizinga

6.1 Introduction

Countries differ widely in their relative reliance on bank versus market finance. Germany and Japan, for instance, are regarded as bank-based, as in these countries the volume of bank lending relative to the stock market is rather large. At the same time, the United States and the United Kingdom are considered to be more market-based. In chapter 3, Demirgüç-Kunt and Levine construct indices of the organization of the financial system, or financial structure, for a large set of developing and developed countries. They measure the relative importance of bank versus market finance by the relative size of stock aggregates, by relative trading or transaction volumes, and by indicators of relative efficiency. Developing countries are shown to have less developed banks and stock markets in general. The financial sector—banks, other financial intermediaries, and stock markets—becomes larger, more active, and more efficient, as countries become richer. Further, in developing countries financial systems tend to be more bank-based.

The variety of financial systems around the world poses economists with several interesting questions. A substantial body of literature has already shown that both banking sector development and stock market development may lead to higher growth at the firm, industry and country level.[1] However, as discussed in chapter 4, financial structure—the *relative* importance of banks versus markets—may also have important implications for firm performance and long-run economic growth. Demirgüç-Kunt and Maksimovic (2000) and Levine (2000) analyze the impact of financial structure on firm performance and economic growth, respectively.

In this chapter we focus on the performance of the banking sector itself across different financial systems. The purpose of this paper is twofold. First, we investigate the impact of financial development on bank profits and margins. Second, after controlling for the level of financial development, we examine if financial structure has an independent impact on bank performance. If banks operating in different financial structures show differences in performance (especially bank margins), this could have important implications for economic growth. After all, if financial structure differences do not translate into differences in the cost of bank financing for firms, it becomes much less clear that they are important.

To our knowledge, this is the first work to consider the impact of financial structure on bank performance. Using bank-level data for a large number of developed and developing countries over the 1990–1997 period, we investigate if there is any relationship between measures of bank performance on the one hand, and levels of bank and stock market development, and financial structure on the other.

We consider two measures of bank performance: bank profitability (measured as profits divided by assets), and bank interest margins (measured as net interest income divided by assets). As an accounting identity, the bank interest margin equals (pretax) profits plus bank operating costs, plus loan loss provisioning (and minus non-interest income). Bank profitability and bank interest margins can be seen as indicators of the (in)efficiency of the banking system, as they drive a wedge between the interest rate received by savers on their deposits and the interest paid by lenders on their loans. As such, these variables will affect the cost of bank finance for firms, the range of investment projects they find profitable and thus economic growth.

In general, we find that financial development has a very important impact on bank performance. Simple means tests show that countries with underdeveloped financial systems have significantly higher levels of bank profits and margins. Once we control for the level of financial development, however, there is no significant difference in bank profits or margins between bank-based and market-based systems.

These relationships are largely confirmed by regression analysis. Specifically, we see that higher bank development is related to lower bank profitability and interest margins. Lower profitability and lower interest margins should be reflections of increased efficiency due to greater competition among banks. Stock market development on the other hand, leads to increased profits and margins for banks especially at lower levels of financial development, indicating complementarities between bank and stock market finance. Stock market development may improve bank performance, for instance, as stock markets generate information about firms that is also useful to banks. Alternatively, the legal and regulatory environment that makes stock market development possible may also improve the functioning of banks.

The remainder of this chapter is organized as follows. Section 6.2 discusses the data. Section 6.3 presents the empirical results. Section 6.4 offers some conclusions.

6.2 The Data

This study combines bank-level data on profitability, interest margins and other bank-level variables with cross-country data on financial structure. Our bank-level data are derived from bank balance sheets and income statements, as available from the BankScope data base compiled by Fitch IBCA. The dataset covers all OECD countries as well as many developing countries. For a list of countries included in this study, see table 6.1. Bank coverage is comprehensive for most countries with covered banks roughly accounting for 90 percent of all bank assets worldwide. The sample covers the period 1990–1997.

Table 6.1 also provides mean values of the bank-level variables used in the empirical work for each country separately. Profit/ta is computed as pretax profits divided by total assets. Two countries, Argentina and Finland, experienced on average negative bank profits over this sample period. Notably low also is the average profitability of Japanese banks at 0.2 percent of assets. Next, Net Margin/ta is net interest income divided by total assets. Thus, Net Margin/ta is an ex post interest margin that differs from the ex ante interest margin (simply the loan interest rate minus the deposit interest rate) because of possible loan defaults. The Net Margin/ta variable thus adjusts for the fact that banks that charge high interest rates may experience equally high loan default rates. Lowest values of Net Margin/ta are obtained by several developed countries, notably Finland, Ireland, the Netherlands, and Switzerland. Apart from low loan default rates, low Net Margin/ta can reflect low operating costs, and low (pretax) profitability. Overhead/ta is defined as a bank's noninterest

Table 6.1
Bank Characteristics

	Profit/ ta	Net margin/ ta	Over-head/ ta	Equity/ ta	Loan/ ta	Non-interest-earning assets/ ta	Customer and short-term funding/ ta
Argentina	−0.004	0.052	0.076	0.197	0.548	0.215	0.656
Australia	0.010	0.021	0.024	0.068	0.710	0.055	0.780
Austria	0.008	0.018	0.029	0.080	0.423	0.052	0.803
Belgium	0.005	0.018	0.022	0.072	0.301	0.031	0.889
Bolivia	0.014	0.048	0.045	0.117	0.670	0.057	0.848
Canada	0.003	0.019	0.021	0.090	0.694	0.041	0.844
Chile	0.006	0.041	0.031	0.155	0.545	0.153	0.746
Colombia	0.020	0.066	0.083	0.164	0.597	0.153	0.732
Denmark	0.013	0.047	0.035	0.105	0.526	0.036	0.825
Ecuador	0.018	0.069	0.078	0.133	0.530	0.117	0.679
Finland	−0.030	0.015	0.023	0.070	0.446	0.092	0.633
France	0.003	0.029	0.036	0.100	0.488	0.056	0.768
Greece	0.009	0.029	0.037	0.076	0.389	0.084	0.868
Guatemala	0.009	0.062	0.059	0.096	0.487	0.165	0.695
Honduras	0.031	0.076	0.044	0.109	0.552	0.124	0.779
India	0.002	0.030	0.028	0.053	0.445	0.071	0.868
Indonesia	0.016	0.040	0.028	0.115	0.686	0.038	0.759
Ireland	0.010	0.017	0.011	0.144	0.496	0.033	0.849
Italy	0.010	0.033	0.038	0.092	0.455	0.066	0.742
Japan	0.002	0.019	0.014	0.038	0.708	0.032	0.882
Jordan	0.010	0.024	0.025	0.093	0.436	0.099	0.854
Kenya	0.018	0.049	0.040	0.102	0.560	0.127	0.826
Korea	0.003	0.021	0.026	0.084	0.554	0.102	0.751
Malaysia	0.017	0.027	0.015	0.082	0.590	0.093	0.815
Mexico	0.012	0.043	0.046	0.177	0.568	0.126	0.773
Nepal	0.034	0.044	0.024	0.072	0.519	0.060	0.865
Netherlands	0.007	0.014	0.014	0.090	0.451	0.029	0.776
N. Zealand	0.013	0.025	0.025	0.041	0.753	0.045	0.886
Nigeria	0.025	0.059	0.084	0.092	0.260	0.139	0.675
Norway	0.009	0.027	0.023	0.057	0.771	0.041	0.800
Panama	0.015	0.027	0.020	0.101	0.629	0.046	0.849
Paraguay	0.023	0.067	0.067	0.137	0.548	0.227	0.822
Peru	0.018	0.072	0.082	0.121	0.571	0.125	0.803
Philippines	0.023	0.043	0.041	0.159	0.589	0.072	0.693
Singapore	0.014	0.021	0.012	0.153	0.579	0.163	0.828
S. Africa	0.019	0.046	0.038	0.155	0.768	0.027	0.788

Table 6.1
(continued)

	Profit/ ta	Net margin/ ta	Over-head/ ta	Equity/ ta	Loan/ ta	Non-interest-earning assets/ ta	Customer and short-term funding/ ta
Sri Lanka	0.023	0.041	0.038	0.135	0.529	0.091	0.662
Swaziland	0.020	0.058	0.062	0.065	0.647	0.066	0.876
Sweden	0.004	0.022	0.022	0.056	0.390	0.065	0.762
Switzerland	0.015	0.017	0.045	0.183	0.521	0.048	0.629
Thailand	0.008	0.028	0.019	0.073	0.841	0.039	0.857
UK	0.014	0.028	0.028	0.135	0.385	0.076	0.744
US	0.017	0.039	0.036	0.081	0.603	0.088	0.741
Zambia	0.045	0.119	0.123	0.131	0.240	0.237	0.768
Average	0.013	0.039	0.039	0.106	0.545	0.089	0.784

Note: Ratios are calculated for each bank in each country and then averaged over 1990–1997. All variables are divided by total assets. Data are from Bankscope data base of IBCA. Detailed variable definitions are given in appendix 6.1.

expenses (mostly wages) divided by total assets. Countries with low Net Margin/ta indeed tend to also have low Overhead/ta. In the sample average values for profit and margin are 1.3 percent and 3.9 percent, respectively.

Next, the table provides information about several balance-sheet items. These balance-sheet items are direct indicators of the earning power and the cost side of banks. Hence, in empirical work relating bank profitability and interest margins to financial structure variables, we use bank-level variables derived from balance sheet as controls. Equity/ta is defined as book equity divided by total assets. International variation in Equity/ta reflects differences in capital adequacy as well as different definitions of book equity. Loan/ta is defined as total loans divided by total assets, while Non-Interest-Earning Assets/ta is defined as cash, real estate and other non-interest-earning assets divided by total assets. Finally, Customer & Short-Term Funding/ta is deposits and other short-term funding divided by total assets.

Country averages of the financial development and structure variables are presented in table 6.2. First, there are three size variables. Bank/gdp is the ratio of the total domestic assets of deposit money banks divided by GDP, providing a measure of the overall

Table 6.2
Financial Development and Structure

	Bank/ GDP	Central bank/ GDP	Mcap/ GDP	Bank credit/ GDP	Tvt/ GDP	Structure	Market
Argentina	0.216	0.034	0.130	0.164	0.043	−0.104	0
Australia	0.767	0.030	0.713	0.696	0.331	0.111	1
Austria	1.261	0.004	0.123	0.932	0.078	−0.284	0
Belgium	1.175	0.013	0.355	0.563	0.052	−0.191	0
Bolivia	0.367	0.224	0.017	0.357	0.000	−0.389	0
Canada	0.656	0.039	0.588	0.565	0.292	0.091	1
Chile	0.465	0.197	0.838	0.451	0.085	0.321	1
Colombia	0.177	0.020	0.132	0.158	0.014	−0.033	0
Denmark	0.475	0.016	0.340	0.375	0.157	0.036	1
Ecuador	0.175	0.094	0.104	0.170	0.013	−0.217	0
Finland	0.799	0.010	0.295	0.771	0.118	−0.144	0
France	1.021	0.011	0.329	0.887	0.170	−0.171	0
Greece	0.413	0.193	0.149	0.183	0.058	−0.171	0
Guatemala	0.145	0.011	0.009	0.123	0.000	−0.399	0
Honduras	0.253	0.073	0.049	0.208	0.020	−0.249	0
India	0.344	0.129	0.277	0.242	0.076	0.022	1
Indonesia	0.492	0.020	0.184	0.460	0.077	−0.168	0
Ireland	0.361	0.010	0.265	0.293	0.141	−0.024	0
Italy	0.740	0.103	0.166	0.521	0.076	−0.228	0
Japan	1.311	0.047	0.792	1.169	0.284	−0.063	0
Jordan	0.713	0.211	0.649	0.620	0.124	0.028	1
Kenya	0.288	0.114	0.160	0.212	0.005	−0.146	0
Korea	0.551	0.011	0.372	0.532	0.439	0.142	1
Malaysia	0.816	0.012	2.015	0.748	1.140	1.301	1
Mexico	0.240	0.015	0.318	0.215	0.126	0.297	1
Nepal	0.216	0.111	0.050	0.162	0.002	−0.331	0
Netherlands	1.116	0.009	0.686	0.904	0.428	−0.012	0
N. Zealand	0.852	0.034	0.493	0.779	0.143	−0.103	0
Nigeria	0.110	0.201	0.058	0.083	0.001	−0.163	0
Norway	0.689	0.018	0.256	0.574	0.143	−0.142	0
Panama	0.576	0.206	0.086	0.558	0.003	−0.339	0
Paraguay	0.164	0.069	0.020	0.163	0.002	−0.361	0
Peru	0.134	0.003	0.145	0.116	0.050	0.097	1
Philippines	0.367	0.092	0.516	0.281	0.150	0.290	1
Singapore	0.952	.	1.365	0.829	0.702	0.399	1
S. Africa	0.662	0.028	1.658	0.613	0.148	0.629	1
Sri Lanka	0.271	0.097	0.161	0.211	0.021	−0.149	0
Swaziland	0.207	0.003	0.181	0.202	0.056	0.049	1

Table 6.2
(continued)

	Bank/ GDP	Central bank/ GDP	Mcap/ GDP	Bank credit/ GDP	Tvt/ GDP	Structure	Market
Sweden	0.537	0.060	0.623	0.460	0.332	0.347	1
Switzerland	1.769	0.015	0.981	1.647	0.755	0.008	1
Thailand	0.824	0.015	0.570	0.784	0.400	0.066	1
UK	1.160	0.030	1.126	1.137	0.551	0.149	1
US	0.731	0.050	0.799	0.644	0.616	0.319	1
Zambia	0.118	0.483	0.074	0.062	0.002	−0.303	0
Average	0.600	0.068	0.483	0.512	0.221	−0.006	0.477

Note: Data are averages for the period 1990–1997. Detailed definitions and sources are given in appendix 6.1.

size of the banking sector. From the table, we see that richer countries generally have larger banking sectors. Next, Central bank/gdp is defined as the total assets of the central bank divided by GDP. Several developing countries (Bolivia, Jordan, Nigeria, and Panama) stand out with central bank assets exceeding 20 percent of GDP, while the size of central bank assets tends to be far more modest for developed countries. Thus in developing countries, the central bank plays a relatively large role in credit provision. As a final index of financial size, Mcap/gdp is the stock market capitalization divided by GDP. Again, there is a general tendency for richer countries to have larger stock markets. Some developing countries, notably Malaysia, Chile, and Jordan, also have well-developed stock markets.

Next, the table contains two variables reflecting the volume or activity of the banking sector and the stock market, respectively. Bank credit/gdp is the credit to the private sector by deposit money banks divided by GDP. Hence, this variable proxies for the credit activity of the banking system. As seen, credit in Japan is relatively important at 117 percent of GDP. It is similarly very important in Switzerland (at 165%) and the United Kingdom (at 113%), which are countries with major international banking sectors. Poorer countries are shown to have comparatively little credit activity. Next, Tvt/gdp is the total value of stocks traded divided by GDP, as an indicator of stock market activity. Some developing countries, such as Bolivia, Guatemala, Nepal, Nigeria, Paraguay, and Zambia, have hardly any stock market activity at all at 0.2 percent of GDP or less. Among the developed countries, Austria, Greece, and Italy also have relatively dormant stock markets with trading volume at less than 10 percent of GDP.

In the empirical work, we also examine how the performance of the banking sector (in terms of profits and the net interest margin) is related to the *relative* development of the banks and stock markets. To capture whether a financial system is bank-based or market-based, we use an index of financial structure constructed in chapter 3. Specifically, this Structure index is the means-removed average of relative size, relative activity and relative efficiency measures. Relative size here is calculated as the ratio of the stock market capitalization to total assets of deposit money banks; relative activity is defined as the total value of stocks traded divided by bank credit to the private sector; relative efficiency, finally, is given by the product of total value traded and average overhead costs of banks in the country. Higher values of Structure indicate a more market-based financial system. We classify countries with values of the Structure variable above (below) the mean as market-based (bank-based) financial systems. Further, Market is a dummy variable that takes the value 1 for market-based systems and 0 for bank-based systems. The table shows that there is wide variation in financial structure within income groups as well as across income groups.

6.3 Empirical Evidence

This section presents empirical evidence on the relationship between bank performance and financial structure. As an initial look at this relationship, panel A of table 6.3 provides the mean values of the Profit/ta and Net Margin/ta variables for bank-based and market-based systems separately. The numbers show that both profits and margins of banks are lower in market-based financial systems, although only the difference in margins is statistically significant at the 5 percent level. These mean figures can be misleading, however, since they do not control for the development of the financial sector or other determinants of profits and margins.

In panel B of table 6.3, we look at differences in means for three groups of countries: underdeveloped, bank-based, and market-based financial systems. A country's financial system is classified as underdeveloped if its bank and stock markets are *both* underdeveloped. A country's banking system or stock market, in turn, is considered underdeveloped if Bank credit/gdp or Tvt/gdp are below the sam-

Table 6.3
Bank Performance and Financial Structure

	N	Mean	Standard deviation	Minimum	Maximum
Panel A:					
Bank-based					
Profit/ta	23	.014	.015	−.030	.045
Net margin/ta	23	.045[a]	.025	.015	.119
Market-based					
Profit/ta	21	.012	.006	.002	.023
Net margin/ta	21	.032[a]	.015	.014	.072
Panel B:					
Underdeveloped					
Profit/ta	19	.018[d,e]	.011	−.005	.045
Net margin/ta	19	.055[b,c]	.022	.017	.119
Developed and bank-based					
Profit/ta	10	.005[d]	.013	−.030	.016
Net margin/ta	10	.025[b]	.008	.015	.040
Developed and market-based					
Profit/ta	15	.010[e]	.005	.003	.019
Net margin/ta	15	.027[c]	.011	.014	.047

Note: Countries with underdeveloped financial systems have below mean values for both bank and market development. Countries are defined to have market-based financial systems if the value of their structure index is above the sample mean. Structure index is the means-removed average of relative size, relative activity and relative efficiency indicators as defined in Demirgüç-Kunt and Levine 1999.

[a], [b], [c], [d], and [e] denote pairs that are significantly different at 5 percent or lower significance level.

ple mean, respectively. Accordingly, we now only classify financial systems as bank-based or market-based if the financial system is not deemed underdeveloped. This three-way classification points at a real difference between developed and underdeveloped financial systems. Indeed, bank margins and profits decline significantly, as financial systems become developed. Further, bank profits and margins are higher in market-based systems than in bank-based systems, although these differences are not statistically significant.

Next, we study these relationships more formally within a regression setting. Our empirical framework extends the work in Demirgüç-Kunt and Huizinga (1999) on the determinants of bank profitability and interest margins to include indices of financial structure. The basic regression equation is as follows:

$$I_{i,j} = \alpha + \beta B_i + \gamma X_j + \delta S_j + \varepsilon_{i,j}, \tag{6.1}$$

where $I_{i,j}$ is the dependent variable (either Profit/ta or Net Margin/ta) for bank i in country j; $B_{i,t}$ are bank variables for bank i; X_j are country variables for country j; S_j are financial development and structure variables for country j; and $\varepsilon_{i,j}$ is an error term. Versions of equation (6.1) are estimated with either bank-level data or country-level data. The bank-level specifications use bank mean values over the sample period for each bank. Country-level specifications instead use country mean values for bank and other variables. We report White's heteroskedasticity-consistent standard errors. Detailed variable definitions and sources are provided in appendix 6.1.

Table 6.4 reports the results of Profit/ta regressions along the lines of equation (6.1). In the first three specifications we include bank and stock market size measures among the independent variables to control for the level of financial development, while in the last three specifications we include activity measures instead. Specifications 1 and 4 use bank-level data, and the rest of the specifications use country-level data. We also try two different measures of financial structure. Specifications (1) and (2) use the Structure index. In specification (3) we replace Structure by Market, which, as indicated, is a dummy variable based on Structure.

In table 6.4, the bank-level and macroeconomic independent variables are the same across all specifications. Consistent with the evidence in Demirgüç-Kunt and Huizinga (1999), Profit/ta is positively related to the lagged equity variable, Equity/ta$_{t-1}$. This may indicate that well-capitalized banks face lower expected bankruptcy costs for themselves and their customers, thereby reducing their cost of funding. Profits appear to decline with a greater proportion of Non-Interest-Earning Assets/ta. Customer and short term funding develops mixed results in the bank-level versus country-level specifications. On average, this type of customer funding may carry a low interest cost, but it is costly in terms of the required branching network. The Overhead/ta variable fails to be significant, suggesting that banks can fully pass on their noninterest expenses to their customers.

The macro variables are mostly insignificant except for inflation which is significant and positive throughout. This suggests that banks tend to profit in inflationary environments. We also see that Profit/ta is significantly and positively related to Tax Rate in the bank-level specifications. Tax rate is the effective tax rate on bank income constructed as the ratio of a bank's tax liability to its pretax profits. The positive coefficient on the Tax Rate variable suggests that banks in high-tax environments have to earn higher pretax profits to

Table 6.4
Bank Profitability and Financial Structure

	(1)	(2)	(3)	(4)	(5)	(6)
Bank level and macro controls						
Equity/ta$_{t-1}$	.024***	.059	.065	.026***	.096**	.092**
	(.008)	(.041)	(.052)	(.008)	(.043)	(.044)
Loan/ta	−.002	.000	.002	.000	.004	−.001
	(.003)	(.008)	(.008)	(.003)	(.008)	(.008)
Non-interest-earning assets/ta	−.026*	−.078**	−.078*	−.026*	−.068**	−.073**
	(.015)	(.039)	(.044)	(.015)	(.031)	(.035)
Customer and short term funding/ta	−.009**	.042	.043	−.007*	.062**	.068**
	(.004)	(.035)	(.036)	(.004)	(.031)	(.034)
Overhead/ta	.025	.136	.155	.009	.079	.135
	(.053)	(.130)	(.144)	(.054)	(.121)	(.137)
GNP/capita	.0003***	.000	.000	.000	.000	−.000
	(.0001)	(.000)	(.000)	(.000)	(.000)	(.000)
Growth	.001**	.000	.000	.001	−.001	−.000
	(.000)	(.001)	(.001)	(.000)	(.001)	(.001)
Inflation	.001***	.001**	.001**	.001***	.001**	.001**
	(.000)	(.000)	(.000)	(.000)	(.000)	(.000)
Tax rate	.004**	.001	.005	.005**	.001	−.001
	(.002)	(.013)	(.018)	(.002)	(.011)	(.012)
Financial development and structure						
Bank/GDP	−.011***	−.010*	−.003			
	(.003)	(.006)	(.005)			
Central bank/GDP	.055***	.019	.027*			
	(.011)	(.014)	(.014)			
Bank credit/GDP				−.011***	−.010*	−.006
				(.003)	(.006)	(.006)
Mcap/GDP	.011***	.015**	.005**			
	(.003)	(.006)	(.002)			
Tvt/GDP				.019**	.029***	.020**
				(.004)	(.009)	(.008)
Structure	−.002	−.018*		−.002	−.015**	
	(.004)	(.010)		(.004)	(.006)	
Market			−.003			−.005
			(.003)			(.003)
Adj R2	.10	.35	.32	.10	.43	.39
Number of countries	43	43	43	44	44	44
Number of observations	2237	43	43	2249	44	44

Note: Columns (1) and (4) are estimated using mean values for each bank for the 1990–1997 time period. Columns (2) and (5) are estimated using country means over the sample period. Columns (3) and (6) replace structure in specifications (2) and (5) by market. Dependent variable is profit/ta which is before tax profits divided by total assets. Detailed variable definitions and data sources are given in appendix 6.1. White's heteroskedasticity consistent standard errors are given in parentheses.

*, **, and *** indicate significance levels of 10, 5, and 1 percent, respectively.

pay these taxes. This also suggests that banks are able to pass on at least part of their taxes to their customers.[2]

Next, we turn to the financial system variables. We want to explore the role of financial structure on bank performance, while controlling for the level of bank and stock market development. In the first three specifications, we control for financial development by including Bank/gdp, Central bank/gdp, and Mcap/gdp, as indicators of (central) bank and stock market size. In the last three specifications, we instead include Bank credit/gdp and Tvt/gdp as indicators of bank and stock market activity.

In all specifications, we see that private bank development measures, whether relating to size or activity, have negative signs, with statistically significant coefficients in four of the six regressions. This may suggest that banks in a well-developed banking market face tougher competition, and therefore lower profitability. We also see that Central bank/gdp enters with a positive coefficient. Since a high level of central bank activity is an indicator of lower (private) financial system development this is consistent with the previous result (see also chapter 3).

Next, we see that Mcap/gdp and Tvt/gdp both obtain positive and significant signs in all specifications. This suggests that controlling for the level of bank development in countries with well-developed stock markets banks have greater profit opportunities. Why would stock market development ever increase bank profitability? A possible explanation is that stock market development allows firms to be better capitalized, thereby reducing risks of loan default. Also, at a higher level of stock market development, much information on publicly traded firms is made available that also enables banks to better evaluate credit risk. However, the impact of stock market development on bank performance is not linear. Specifically, when we add a squared term of stock market development into our specifications, this squared term enters with a negative and significant coefficient. This suggests that at some point the potential gains of stock market development for bank performance have been realized. After this point, it may become immaterial whether further financial development takes the form of bank market or stock market development (as is consistent with the Demirgüç-Kunt and Maksimovic 1996).

In specifications 1,2 and 4,5 we include the Structure index to capture whether a country is market-based or bank-based. Structure enters all four specifications with a negative sign, but it is only significant in the country-level regressions in specifications 2 and 5. This suggests that after controlling for the level of financial development, there is some evidence that a more market-based financial structure would lead to lower levels of bank profits. However, the correlations between the Structure index and measures of stock market development tend to be very high at over 80 percent. Therefore, in specifications 3 and 6 we replace the Structure variable with the Market dummy variable, with lower levels of correlation with our stock market indicators at about 60 percent. Using this indicator of financial structure, we no longer see a significant effect of financial structure on bank profits.

Table 6.5 presents the results of the Net Margin/ta regressions. Apart from the different dependent variables, the regressions in tables 6.4 and 6.5 are completely analogous. Clearly, Profits/ta and Net Margin/ta are interrelated, as a bank's net interest income is a major determinant of its profitability.[3] The Net Margin/ta variable perhaps more accurately reflects how financial structure affects the bank's financial customers (depositors and lenders) rather than the bank itself. However, most of the results in tables 6.4 and 6.5 are similar. In our discussion of table 6.5, we will therefore focus on how the results in table 6.5 differ from those in table 6.4.

Starting with the bank-level variables, we see that the coefficient of Loan/ta is positive and significant in three specifications. This sensibly reflects that loans are interest-paying (as opposed to say the cash on the balance sheet), thereby increasing net interest income. Overhead/ta enters all specifications with positive coefficients which are significant in four cases. This suggests that banks pass on their noninterest expenses, such as wages, to their financial customers (in terms of lower deposit rates and/or higher lending rates).

Turning to the financial structure variables, we see that the results in table 6.5 are largely similar to those in table 6.4. Looking at the separate bank and stock market variables, we see that they are significant with the same signs as before. The Structure index is again negative throughout but now only significant in one specification. When replaced with the Market variable, the impact of financial structure on bank margins is no longer significant.

Our raw data indicate that bank profits and margins tend to be relatively high in underdeveloped financial systems regardless of financial structure. This suggests that financial structure is particu-

Table 6.5
Bank Interest Margins and Financial Structure

	(1)	(2)	(3)	(4)	(5)	(6)
Bank level and macro controls						
Equity/ta$_{t-1}$	.024***	.021	.026	.026***	.028	.023
	(.008)	(.035)	(.037)	(.008)	(.036)	(.036)
Loan/ta	−.002	.013	.015*	.000	.022**	.020**
	(.003)	(.009)	(.009)	(.003)	(.008)	(.008)
Non-interest earning assets/ta	−.026*	.023	.025	−.026*	.038	.039
	(.015)	(.032)	(.036)	(.015)	(.028)	(.029)
Customer and short term funding/ta	−.009**	.031*	.031*	−.007*	.030*	.031*
	(.004)	(.017)	(.018)	(.004)	(.017)	(.018)
Overhead/ta	.025	.452***	.474***	.009	.437***	.459***
	(.053)	(.129)	(.151)	(.054)	(.136)	(.143)
GNP per capita	.0003***	.000	−.000	.000	.000	−.000
	(.0001)	(.000)	(.000)	(.000)	(.000)	(.000)
Growth	.001**	−.000	−.001	.001	−.001	−.001
	(.000)	(.001)	(.001)	(.000)	(.001)	(.001)
Inflation	.001***	.001**	.001**	.001***	.001**	.001**
	(.000)	(.000)	(.000)	(.000)	(.000)	(.000)
Tax rate	.004**	.013	.018	.005**	.016	.016
	(.002)	(.012)	(.016)	(.002)	(.011)	(.016)
Financial development and structure						
Bank/GDP	−.011***	−.023***	−.015**			
	(.003)	(.007)	(.006)			
Central bank/GDP	.055***	.006	.016			
	(.011)	(.017)	(.018)			
Bank credit/GDP				−.011***	−.015**	−.013**
				(.003)	(.007)	(.006)
Mcap/GDP	.011***	.016***	.004**			
	(.003)	(.005)	(.002)			
Tvt/GDP				.019***	.011*	.006*
				(.004)	(.006)	(.004)
Structure	−.002	−.021**		−.002	−.007	
	(.004)	(.008)		(.004)	(.005)	
Market			−.003			−.002
			(.003)			(.003)
Adj R2	.10	.87	.85	.10	.86	.85
Number of countries	43	43	43	44	44	44
Number of observations	2237	43	43	2249	44	44

Note: Columns (1) and (4) are estimated using mean values for each bank for the 1990–1997 time period. Columns (2) and (5) are estimated using country means over the sample period. Columns (3) and (6) replace structure in specifications (2) and (5) by market. Dependent variable is the net margin/ta defined as interest income minus interest expense over total assets. Detailed variable definitions and data sources are given in appendix 6.1. White's heteroskedasticity consistent standard errors are given in parentheses.

*, **, and *** indicate significance levels of 10, 5, and 1 percent, respectively.

larly important at lower levels of economic development. To test whether this is the case, we estimate regressions as in tables 6.4 and 6.5 including an interaction term of the Structure variable and gdp per capita. The interaction term is not statistically significant and leaves the other results unchanged in the unreported regressions.

As an additional test, we include several institutional variables reflecting the legal and regulatory environment to the various specifications. We include these institutional variables as controls since they can be expected to have a direct impact on bank profitability. To a large extent, the institutional environment is expected to shape the financial structure, and therefore the impact of financial structure may be weaker after we control for the underlying institutional environment. Indeed, there is no clear role left for financial structure, after we include measures of legal code and effectiveness and restrictions on bank activities.[4] These results are also not reported.

6.4   Conclusion

The empirical evidence of this chapter suggests that banks have higher profits and margins in underdeveloped financial systems. Once we control for the level of financial development, financial structure (i.e., the relative development of banks versus markets) does not have an independent effect on bank profitability or margins. In developed financial systems, bank profits and margins are indeed not statistically different across bank-based systems and market-based systems.

Regression results indicate that greater bank development lowers bank profits and margins. Underdeveloped banking markets tend to be rife with inefficiencies and less-than-competitive pricing behavior, as also suggested by their relatively high profitability and net interest margins. Thus greater bank development brings about tougher competition, higher efficiency and lower profits.

We also see that in underdeveloped financial systems stock market development improves bank profits and margins. This reflects the complementarities between bank and stock market development. Specifically, stock market development and the improved availability of equity financing to firms may increase their borrowing capacity. Furthermore, the better and more easily available information which stock markets demand also enables banks to better evaluate credit risk. This can lead to an increase in bank profits.

However, at higher levels of stock market development we no longer observe these complementarities.

Overall, our results provide evidence that differences in bank and stock market development do translate into differences in the cost of bank financing for firms. Indeed, for countries with underdeveloped financial systems, greater financial development would improve the efficiency of the banking sector, potentially leading to increases in growth, both at the micro or firm level and at the macro level. However, we find that financial structure per se does not have a significant, independent influence on bank profits and margins.

Appendix 6.1:   Variable Definitions and Sources

6A.1   Bank Characteristics

Net margin/ta. Interest income minus interest expense over total assets.

Profit/ta. Before tax profits over total assets.

Equity/ta. Book value of equity (assets minus liabilities) over total assets.

Loan/ta. Total loans over total assets.

Non-interest-earning assets/ta. Cash, non-interest-earning deposits at other banks, and other non-interest-earning assets over total assets.

Customer and short-term funding/ta. All short-term and long-term deposits plus other nondeposit short-term funding over total assets.

Overhead/ta. Personnel expenses and some other non-interest expenses over total assets.

Source: All bank-level variables are obtained from BankScope database of IBCA.

6A.2   Macro Indicators

Gnp/cap: Real GNP per capita.

Growth: Annual growth rate of real GDP.

Inflation: The annual inflation from the GDP deflator.

Source: The above data are from World Bank National Accounts.

Tax rate: Total taxes paid divided by before tax profits for each bank, obtained from Bankscope.

6A.3   Financial Structure

Bank/gdp: Total assets of the deposit money banks divided by GDP.

Central bank/gdp: Total assets of the central bank divided by GDP.

Bank credit/gdp: Credit to the private sector by deposit money banks divided by GDP.

Mcap/gdp: Stock market capitalization divided by GDP.

Tvt/gdp: Total value of stocks traded divided by GDP.

Mcap/bank: Stock market capitalization divided by total assets of the deposit money banks.

Tvt/bank credit: Total value of stocks traded divided by bank credit to private sector.

*Tvt*overhead costs:* Total value of stocks traded multiplied by average overhead/ta of banks in the country.

Structure: Means-removed average of Mcap/bank, Tvt/bank credit, and Tvt * overhead costs, as described in Demirgüç-Kunt and Levine 1999. Higher levels indicate market-based systems.

Source: These variables are constructed as described in chapter 2. Stock market information is from the Emerging Markets database of the International Finance Corporation. The rest is from the International Financial Statistics of the International Monetary Fund.

6A.4 Legal and Institutional Indicators

Stockholder rights: An index of shareholder rights from La Porta et al. (1998). The index is formed by adding 1 if (1) the country allows the shareholders to mail their proxy to the firm; (2) shareholders are not required to deposit their shares prior to the General Shareholders' Meeting; (3) cumulative voting or proportional representation of minorities in the board of directors is allowed; (4) an oppressed minorities mechanism is in place; (5) the minimum percentage of share capital that entitles a shareholder to call for an Extraordinary Shareholders' Meeting is less than or equal to 10 percent (the sample median); or (6) shareholders have preemptive rights that can only be waived by a shareholders' vote. The index ranges from 1 to 6.

Creditor rights: An index of creditor rights from La Porta et al. (1998). The index is formed by adding 1 if (1) the country imposes restrictions, such as creditors' consent or minimum dividends to file for reorganization; (2) secured creditors are able to gain possession of their security once the reorganization petition has been approved (no automatic stay); (3) secured creditors are ranked first in the distribution of the proceeds that result from the disposition of assets of a bankrupt firm; and (4) the debtor does not retain the administration of its property pending the resolution of the reorganization. The index ranges from 0 to 4.

Contract enforcement index: Produced by Business Environmental Risk Intelligence (BERI), this index measures the relative degree to which contractual agreements are honored and complications presented by language and mentality differences. It is scored from 1 to 4, with higher scores for greater enforceability.

Common Law: A dummy variable that takes the value one for Common Law countries and the value zero otherwise. *Source:* La Porta et al. 1998.

Restrictions on banking: An aggregate index of restrictions on banking business, including securities underwriting, insurance underwriting, real estate, and owning and controlling nonfinancial firms. Ranges from 1 to 4, with higher scores indicating tighter restrictions. *Source:* Barth, Caprio, and Levine 2001.

Notes

1. See King and Levine 1993a, b and Levine and Zervos 1998 for evidence regarding financial development and economic growth. Rajan and Zingales (1998) show that industries that rely more heavily on external finance grow faster in countries with better-developed financial systems. Demirgüç-Kunt and Maksimovic (1998) show that firms in countries with an active stock market and large banking sector grow faster than predicted by individual firm characteristics.

2. Demirgüç-Kunt and Huizinga (forthcoming) examine how the pass-through of taxes by banks to their customers depends on whether the bank is domestic or foreign.

3. To be precise, pretax profits are equal to net interest income, plus noninterest income, minus overhead, minus loan loss provisioning by the income statement identity.

4. As institutional measures, we have used indicators of stockholder rights, creditor rights, contract enforcement, common law, and restrictions on banking. See appendix 6.1 for definitions.

References

Barth, James, Gerard Caprio, and Ross Levine. 2001. Financial regulation and performance: Cross-country evidence. In *Financial Supervision and Regulation: What Works and What Doesn't?*, ed. Fredrick Mishkin. Washington, DC: National Bureau of Economic Research.

Demirgüç-Kunt, Aslı, and Harry Huizinga. 1999. Determinants of commercial bank interest margins and profitability: Some international evidence. *World Bank Economic Review* 13:379–408.

Demirgüç-Kunt, Aslı, and Harry Huizinga. Forthcoming. The taxation of domestic and foreign banks. *Journal of Public Economics* 79:429–453.

Demirgüç-Kunt, Aslı, and Vojislav Maksimovic. 1996. Stock market development and firms' financing choices. *World Bank Economic Review* 10:341–369.

Demirgüç-Kunt, Aslı, and Vojislav Maksimovic. 1998. Law, finance and firm growth. *Journal of Finance* 53(6):2107–2137.

Demirgüç-Kunt, Aslı, and Vojislav Maksimovic. 2000. Funding growth in bank-based and market-based financial systems: Evidence from firm level data. Mimeo, Policy Research Department, World Bank.

King, Robert G., and Ross Levine. 1993a. Finance, enterpreneurship, and growth: Theory and evidence. *Journal of Monetary Economics* 35:513–542.

King, Robert G., and Ross Levine. 1993b. Finance and growth: Schumperer might be right. *Quarterly Journal of Economics* 108:717–738.

La Porta, Rafael, Florencio Lopez-de-Silanes, Andrei Shleifer, and Robert Vishny. 1998. Law and finance. *Journal of Political Economy* 106(6):1113–1155.

Levine, Ross. 2000. Bank-based or market-based financial systems: Which is better? Mimeo, Department of Finance, University of Minnesota.

Levine, Ross, and Sara Zervos. 1998. Stock markets, banks, and economic growth. *American Economic Review* 88:537–558.

Rajan, Raghuram G., and Luigi Zingales. 1998. Financial dependence and growth. *American Economic Review* 88:559–586.

7   International Evidence on Aggregate Corporate Financing Decisions

Ian Domowitz, Jack Glen,
and Ananth Madhavan

7.1   Introduction

Primary capital markets involve the exchange of cash for claims against the issuers, either in the form of equity or debt, or some other derivative instrument. These markets are of considerable interest to financial economists because they represent the link between corporate issuers and investors with capital to spare.[1] The literature on primary market activity has concentrated on the pricing of initial public offerings and the performance of newly listed companies, typically within one country. However, in the absence of data on primary markets, even the most basic questions about international financing decisions remain unanswered.[2] For example, what factors cause corporations to seek foreign capital as opposed to relying on domestic markets? Do these factors differ between emerging and developed markets? How do corporate decisions regarding the mix between debt and equity financing affect future financing choices? How do the institutional framework and macroeconomic environment influence financing choices? This chapter attempts to further our understanding of how and why primary markets develop using unique panel data on thirty countries from 1980 to 1997.

We provide two contributions to the literature. First, we use new data on primary market activity for both developed and emerging markets to provide a macro overview of the role played by these markets. Although this portion of the chapter is largely descriptive, it is worth emphasizing that until now there has been no attempt to systematically document the magnitude of primary market financing, both across countries and over time. Second, we examine the determinants of primary market activity, focusing on the role of various institutional, financial structure, and macroeconomic factors.

Collectively, the analysis yields considerable insight into the operation of primary markets and the role of public policy in furthering their development.

The results shed light on current debates regarding the choice of debt and equity financing, and competition between foreign and domestic financing. We find complex and significant intertemporal correlations among the various financing choices. In particular, privatization activity is initially followed by foreign equity issuance, but eventually leads to a higher level of domestic bond issuance. We also show that macroeconomic stability is highly correlated with the development of bond markets. Finally, the data suggests that the institutional framework also plays an equally crucial role in financing decisions, which is consistent with the evidence reported by Levine (1997, 1998) and Demirgüç-Kunt and Levine (chapter 3). Key institutional factors include liquidity in the stock market, concentration in the banking system, and the relative sizes of the banking sector and stock market. Overall, our results suggest that the more stable the macroeconomy and the more mature a country becomes in the state of its financial institutions, the more significant the role of bond markets.

Although we do not provide direct statistical tests of the links between the nature of the financial system and its level of development on financing decisions, some evidence is obvious. Using primary market issues as the measure of development, we find little evidence that more wealthy economies have more equity market issuance (either domestic or international, relative to GDP). This appears to be at odds with the positive correlation noted by Demirgüç-Kunt and Levine (chapter 3) between stock market secondary trading and income. One explanation is that, perhaps, in less developed economies primary issues are purchased largely by institutional investors who have little interest in secondary market trading, whereas in more wealthy economies trading by retail investors and mutual funds drive secondary market activity.

Alternatively, Domowitz, Glen, and Madhavan (2000) show that stock market transaction costs are much higher in most emerging markets, a factor that has direct implications for trading volume, but which may have little impact on issuance activity. Regardless of the reason, the evidence in their paper must be qualified by the fact that issuance in emerging markets developed very rapidly over the period 1980–1997; at the beginning of that period the stock markets in emerging markets were much less developed than at the end of the sample period. For that reason, although there is no obvious link between income and stock issuance, stock issuance did increase at the same time that growth in emerging market GDP took place, although it is likely that the catalyst for stock market development was related to changes in the institutional framework rather than growth alone.

Unlike the equity market, the evidence here suggests that the level of issuance activity in corporate bond markets is closely related to economic development. Emerging markets had much smaller bond markets (both domestic and international) than more wealthy economies. Once again, however, tremendous growth occurred over the sample period, suggesting that changes in the environment might have played an important role, perhaps even a dominant role, in promoting market development.

The role of the institutional framework for development of both equity and bond markets is complicated and involves many issues that are not readily apparent. Peru provides a good example of this, where the high levels of inflation that characterized the 1980s induced companies to use only modest amounts of debt. When stability arrived in the 1990s, companies naturally chose to issue debt, but denominated in dollars, reflecting the ongoing mistrust that investors have in the local currency. But institutional features played a role as well because, coincident with macroeconomic stability, the government also introduced a private pension system which had a large demand for privately issued securities. The constraints on their portfolios, however, induce the pension funds to buy more debt than equity, which influences relative prices of debt and equity and overall issuance activity.[3]

Recognition of these factors is crucial to understanding and correctly interpreting the operation and development of primary markets. And while this paper cannot reveal all such influences, it begins the process of understanding and characterizing markets by their macroeconomic and institutional environments.

The chapter proceeds as follows: Section 7.2 describes our evidence on the trends in primary market issuance across countries and over time; section 7.3 examines the relative importance of each of the various sources of external finance. Section 7.4 analyzes the relation between financing choices and various institutional and macroeconomic factors. Section 7.5 offers concluding remarks.

7.2   Evidence on International Primary Market Issues Data

7.2.1   Sources and Procedures

As noted above, research on primary markets has been limited by the lack of data. We compiled aggregate annual data on a select group of countries from a variety of sources. This section describes the data collection effort and also reports summary statistics on primary market activity.

Data on international issues of both equity and corporate bonds are obtained from Bondware, a commercial database that captures *all* international issues of securities on a security-by-security basis. Data on international loans were obtained from Loanware, another commercial source. For data on domestic lending, we employ data on the stock of bank lending to the private sector which comes from the International Financial Statistics (IFS) maintained by the IMF.

To obtain a complete picture of primary market activity, we need to augment these data with information on domestic issues of equity and debt. We obtained annual data on gross issues of equity and debt for the years 1980–1997 from a variety of national sources, including stock exchanges, central banks, and capital markets regulatory authorities. These data span nineteen emerging markets and three Asian Tigers. Issues data for eight industrial economies were also compiled from published secondary sources. All data sources and contributing organizations are listed in appendix 7.1. Countries were included in the final sample provided sufficient data were available for both equity and debt. Most of these data are appearing internationally for the first time through this work. We also use financial structure variables compiled by Demirgüç-Kunt and Levine (chapter 3).

Auxiliary macroeconomic data related to GDP, exchange rates, and inflation were obtained from Global Development Indicators (GDI), published by the World Bank. Country market characteristic indicators, such as accounting standards and foreign investor entry restrictions come from the annual Factbooks published by IFC.

There are data collection issues that merit discussion. The data reported to us are the data recorded by the local authorities. We are not certain of the extent to which these recordings are comprehensive. Two examples will illustrate possible sources of under-reporting. First, only public issues are recorded in most countries, which means that private placement issues and (equity) rights issues made to existing shareholders (which are not necessarily considered as public issues in some countries) may not be reported. We have no estimate of the extent to which these problems bias the reported issuance figures downward.

Second, the finite term of debt securities is problematic when comparisons with the volume of equity issues are made. This is a 'roll-over problem' that is most acute for short-term debt securities, but is present to some degree for long-term debt securities as well. For example, when focusing on gross issuance volumes over a ten-year period, the volume of ten-year debt issues can be compared to the volume of equity issues since the ten-year debt does not roll over in this time frame. However, a two-year note that is rolled over five times in ten years will record five times the gross issuance volume as a ten-year note issued once, but will represent the same amount of financing for the issuer. The extent of this problem depends on the maturity structure of debt, the length of sample period and the extent to which issuers actually choose to roll over issues. We have no measure of the extent to which this biases our measures of debt upward, however, given that our data frequency is annual and that we use only long-term debt issues (which are defined as having maturities of at least one year), the bias should be very limited.

7.2.2 Descriptive Statistics

Global Behavior
The dollar value of issues over the period 1980–1997 is summarized in table 7.1. Aggregate gross issuance of private securities in all countries over 1980–1997 amounted to $18.9 trillion.[4] Of that total, domestic debt represented 76 percent, domestic equity represented 13 percent, international bonds were 10 percent, and international equity was 1 percent. Relative to country GDP, the value of capital raised through primary markets grew sharply over the period, increasing from 1.8 percent of GDP over 1980–1985 to 4.3 percent over 1991–1997.

Domestic Equity Markets
The global total for domestic issues of equity amounted to $2.4 trillion over 1980–1997. The G4 countries accounted for 77 percent of this total, other OECD countries accounted for 9 percent, the Asian

Table 7.1
Summary Statistics

	U.S.\$ billions				Percent of GDP			
	1980–1985	1986–1991	1992–1997	1980–1997	1980–1985	1986–1991	1992–1997	1980–1997
Domestic equity								
Emerging markets	10.37	44.42	171.65	226.43	0.33	0.64	1.33	0.76
Asian Tigers	5.40	51.74	68.82	125.96	0.74	1.67	1.35	1.25
G4	278.69	708.58	857.66	1,844.93	0.70	1.30	1.00	1.00
Other OECD	44.75	70.87	90.92	206.54	1.00	1.59	1.19	1.26
Total	339.21	875.61	1,189.05	2,403.86	0.51	0.96	1.27	0.91
International equity								
Emerging markets	0.00	5.32	43.43	48.75	0.00	0.03	0.22	0.08
Asian Tigers	0.14	1.44	9.70	11.28	0.03	0.17	0.22	0.14
G4	3.59	50.45	111.28	165.32	0.03	0.17	0.21	0.13
Other OECD	0.84	4.62	16.87	22.33	0.02	0.13	0.37	0.17
Total	4.57	61.83	181.27	247.67	0.01	0.07	0.24	0.11
Domestic bonds								
Emerging markets	9.12	40.87	148.75	198.73	0.14	0.54	0.86	0.51
Asian Tigers	19.81	93.39	279.00	392.20	1.41	2.57	3.45	2.44
G4	1,308.26	4,489.18	7,722.90	13,520.33	4.84	6.85	7.88	6.52
Other OECD	36.97	101.42	103.10	241.49	2.42	4.14	1.58	2.73
Total	1,374.15	4,724.85	8,253.75	14,352.76	1.20	2.07	2.20	1.81

International bonds

Emerging markets	1.36	2.60	88.63	92.59	0.01	0.01	0.31	0.11
Asian Tigers	0.68	4.94	31.64	37.26	0.12	0.61	0.46	0.39
G4	108.72	550.32	947.22	1,606.27	0.30	1.15	1.49	0.98
Other OECD	14.76	43.33	52.84	110.93	0.33	0.76	0.67	0.59
Total	125.52	601.19	1,120.33	1,847.05	0.10	0.32	0.54	0.32
Grand total	1,843.46	6,263.48	10,744.33	18,851.27	1.82	3.43	4.25	3.14

Note: This table reports summary statistics, in billions of U.S. dollars and as a percentage of GDP, of external equity and debt issuances in the period 1980–1997, for a cross-section of thirty countries grouped by region and level of development. Data sources are documented in appendix 7.1.

Tigers accounted for 5 percent, and the emerging market countries the remaining 9 percent.[5] In relative terms, the volume of issues in the equity markets was small, representing only 13 percent of the global total for all securities, of which 10 percent was issued in the G4 countries. The global volume of equity issuance increased by 158 percent between the first and second half of the 1980s, but from these levels growth over 1991–1997 was only 36 percent.

Domestic equity market activity increased over the 1980s when financial liberalization in the major industrial countries in the early 1980s and strengthening economic activity over most of the decade supported business expansion. In the G4 countries overall, aggregate issues of equity more than doubled from $279 billion in the early 1980s to $708 billion in the second half of the 1980s. Aggregate equity issuance fell sharply in 1990 with the onset of global recession and remained depressed until 1993 when renewed demand for capital goods supported a buoyant market in new issues. For the G4 as a group, there was much slower growth over 1991–1997, however there were striking differences between countries. After reaching high levels in 1988 and 1989, primary equity issuance in Japan fell dramatically in the early 1990s and remained low during the prolonged Japanese recession. In the United States, by contrast, equity issuance did not grow appreciably over the 1980s but roughly doubled in volume in the early 1990s.

In the Asian Tigers, the growth in equity issuance has followed a similar pattern to that of the G4, except that growth over the 1980s was even more dramatic, with a ninefold increase in primary market issuance between 1980–1985 and 1986–1991. From a level of around $300 million per country in the early 1980s, issuance activity rose to a rate of $2.9 billion per country in the late 1980s, then to $3.8 billion per country in the early 1990s. All of the Tigers saw similar growth occur, however the exceptional $10.6 billion and $21.8 billion new equity issued in Korea in 1988 and 1989 was particularly notable, mirroring the extraordinarily high level of Japanese issuance in those years.

In the emerging market countries, equity issuance activity increased 327 percent from a relatively low base between 1980–1985 and 1986–1991. From a level of around $90 million per country on average in the early 1980s, issuance activity rose to a rate of about $390 million per country in the late 1980s then to nearly $1.5 billion per country per year in the early 1990s, though most of this activity was concentrated in only a few countries.

Despite the large growth in nominal dollar amounts raised in the equity markets, the size of those markets globally has increased only slightly over the sample period, remaining at around 1 percent of GDP over the entire period under investigation. That global average, however, hides the fact that growth relative to GDP was strong in both the emerging markets and the Asian Tigers, albeit from very low bases. This rapid growth has made the equity markets of both the Asian Tigers and the emerging markets slightly larger (relative to GDP) than the G4 countries.

Relative to the size of their domestic stock markets, equity issues remained relatively stable over time at about 6 percent of total market capitalization. Within the three groups of countries, the emerging markets excelled, with equity issues representing 8.6 percent of total stock market capitalization over the period 1980–1997, compared to just 1.9 percent in the G4 countries and 3.7 percent in the Asian Tigers. Moreover, emerging primary equity markets equaled 3.0 percent of total bank loans outstanding to the private sector in their countries—the same as in the Asian Tigers—whereas the comparable number was only 1.5 percent in the G4 countries. By either measure, primary emerging equity markets account for a larger share of total financing activity than is the case in more developed countries.

Domestic Bond Markets

Globally, private bond markets grew rapidly over the sample period, increasing from just $1.4 trillion over 1980–1985 to $8.3 trillion over 1992–1997, an increase of more than 490 percent. Issuance of private debt in the G4 amounted to $13.5 trillion, or 94 percent of the global total, which is only slightly above the percentage of total government borrowing undertaken by that group of countries. Total domestic bonds issued by the Asian Tigers amounted to $0.4 trillion over 1980–1997, which is equal to 3 percent of the total, nearly double the total for the nineteen emerging market countries combined. While total issuance in the emerging markets was only half that of the Asian Tiger countries, the corporate debt market in emerging markets still recorded a tripling in size between the late 1980s and the early 1990s and, in the later period, averaged $33 billion per annum. Relative to their respective GDPs, the debt markets have shown remarkable growth in all three groups of countries, but growth was by far the highest in the emerging markets.

The private debt markets also grew relative to the size of each region's banking sector, nearly doubling on a global basis from 3.7 percent of bank loans outstanding in 1980–1985 to 6.3 percent in 1991–1995. In the Asian Tigers, private debt issues grew to equal 15 percent of bank loans outstanding for 1991–1995, up from only 9.2 percent over 1980–1985. Private debt markets grew in the G4 countries as well, but ended the period at only 9.7 percent of the banking sector. In contrast, even with very strong growth over the period, the emerging market debt markets totaled only 4 percent of their domestic banking sectors in 1991–1995, up from a minimal 1.3 percent over 1980–1985.

7.2.3   International Issues of Equity and Long-Term Private Debt

In conjunction with the development of domestic markets for debt and equity, international issues of both equity and debt have taken off in recent years.

International Equity

International equity issues grew dramatically over the sample period, increasing from only $4.6 billion globally over 1980–1985 to $181 billion over 1992–1997. By far, the bulk of those issues came from the G4 countries, which issued 61 percent of the total. But equity issues were also strong in the emerging markets and Asian Tigers, which saw issues increase from near zero over 1980–1985 to $43 and $10 billion respectively over 1992–1997. Growth was fastest in the period 1992–1997, which saw issues in emerging markets increase nearly eight times its level over 1986–1991, well above the rates of growth for either the G4 or Asian Tiger countries. International issues accounted for 9 percent of total issues of equity over 1992–1997, up from only 1 percent over 1980–1985. This dramatic evidence of globalization is likely to have a substantial impact on the expected rate of return of equity.[6] Relative to GDP, growth in international equity issuance has also been impressive. Globally, issuance was only marginal over 1980–1985, but increased consistently over the next decade to reach 0.2 percent of GDP over 1992–1997.

Of particular interest, there is little statistical relation between the levels of domestic and international issues of equity. In a pooled sample of all countries, a regression of domestic issues on international issues (not reported) produces an insignificant slope coefficient. Thus, it does not appear that increased international financing is associated with a direct reduction in domestic market activity. This point is especially important for emerging markets where domestic capital markets are often in their infancy.

7.2.4 *International Bonds*

As in the domestic markets, international bond issues also greatly exceeded international issues of equity. Starting from a low of $125 billion over 1980–1985, global issues increased to $1.1 trillion over 1992–1997, six times the level of international equity issues. As with equity, debt issues were dominated by the G4, which accounted for 87 percent of the total, but growth in the emerging market and Asian Tiger countries was impressive.

Globally, international issues accounted for 12 percent of all debt issues over 1992–1997, up only slightly from the 8 percent that they represented over 1980–1985. In emerging markets, international debt issues accounted for nearly 32 percent of total debt issues, well above the global average and even above the level of international equity issuance. Relative to GDP, international bond issues have nearly doubled over each of the subperiods, well above the rate of growth of the domestic debt markets. Growth was actually negative relative to GDP in the Asian Tigers over 1992–1997, but issuance activity in those countries remained well above the level of the emerging markets.

In contrast to the equity markets, there is a strong statistical link between domestic and international issues of debt. In a pooled sample of countries, a regression of domestic issues of debt on international issues produces a slope coefficient that is statistically indistinguishable from one.

7.2.5 *External Financing Choices*

While the investment needs of any company can be met through both internal and external sources, we limit our analysis to the external sources of finance from capital markets. Under that constraint, total finance is defined as the sum of domestic and foreign sources. Each of these components can be further expanded to include bank, bond and equity financing. In all, then, there are six sources of finance considered: domestic and foreign bank lending; domestic and foreign equity; and domestic and foreign bonds. Our objective is to examine the relative importance of each of those six sources for the countries in our sample over the period 1980–1997. Relative importance is defined as the size of each variable, relative to total external finance.

Table 7.2 provides summary statistics for the four securities market sources of external finance (excluding domestic and foreign bank lending) for each of the countries, averaged over the period 1980–1997. The table illustrates the relative importance of the different types of securities in each country. For example, in Germany domestic bond markets provided over 91 percent of all external finance over the period, whereas in the U.S. domestic bond markets provided only 77 percent. In many other countries, domestic bond markets are much less important; for example, in Turkey domestic equity accounted for 83 percent of all external finance and in Sri Lanka it accounted for 98 percent. In general, domestic bond markets are much less developed in emerging markets than in the other countries. On the other hand, foreign financing is sometimes much more important in emerging markets, as illustrated by foreign bonds for Mexico and foreign equity for China.

Table 7.3 provides summary statistics for total financing ratios, where domestic and foreign bank lending is included. In all countries domestic banks provide the largest amount of external finance, usually in excess of 80 percent, and often more than 90 percent. In contrast, foreign bank finance is a relatively small part of the total, usually less than 4 percent, in no country does it exceed 6 percent when averaged over the sample period. The inclusion of bank finance with sources from securities markets is problematic for two reasons. First, the measures of bank finance that are available are stock measures of outstanding credit, as opposed to the flow measures for securities markets that we employ. For that reason the two measures are not compatible. Second, perhaps because of the first reason, the size of bank finance is so large as to overwhelm the other sources, making even large percentage changes in, for example, foreign bonds, have very little impact on the total. For these reasons, we concentrate on financing ratios which exclude bank finance in what follows.

Domestic bond markets are an important source of finance in some countries—13.7 percent in New Zealand—but are much less impor-

Table 7.2
Mean Financial Ratios by Country (percent)

	Bonds		Equity	
	Domestic	Foreign	Domestic	Foreign
Emerging markets				
Argentina	42.0	29.1	17.8	11.1
Brazil	28.9	31.4	37.6	2.1
Chile	65.7	6.9	19.2	8.2
China	45.9	12.3	8.2	33.6
Colombia	35.7	10.6	49.4	4.4
Greece	2.6	4.3	90.4	2.8
India	45.9	11.5	34.2	8.4
Indonesia	8.4	11.1	72.1	8.4
Jordan	0.4	0.0	99.6	0.0
Malaysia	42.3	3.4	53.2	1.1
Mauritius	16.3	12.0	71.1	0.7
Mexico	0.2	53.6	23.7	22.5
Pakistan	0.0	0.6	70.4	4.0
Peru	82.4	1.7	1.0	15.0
Philippines	16.5	22.4	40.5	20.6
Portugal	41.4	2.0	51.8	4.8
Sri Lanka	0.4	0.0	97.8	1.8
Turkey	7.0	1.4	83.1	8.5
Venezuela	15.7	1.0	58.1	25.1
G4				
Germany	91.3	2.2	5.5	1.0
Japan	90.3	5.9	3.7	0.1
United Kingdom	4.7	60.0	26.3	9.0
United States	76.6	9.5	12.7	1.1
Asian Tigers				
Korea (South)	81.9	5.7	11.2	1.2
Singapore	33.8	13.9	36.5	15.8
Taiwan, China	17.6	8.5	67.6	6.3
Other OECD				
Belgium	30.2	16.8	40.2	12.8
Canada	32.2	23.8	41.0	3.0
Finland	58.1	14.6	15.7	11.7
New Zealand	35.4	15.6	41.2	7.8

Note: This table reports the percentage of external finance in equity and debt, and in international and domestic markets, in the period 1980–1997, for a cross-section of thirty countries grouped by region and level of development. Data sources are documented in appendix 7.1.

Table 7.3
Mean Total External Finance Ratios by Country (percent)

	Bank		Bond		Equity	
	Domestic	Foreign	Domestic	Foreign	Domestic	Foreign
Emerging market countries						
Argentina	93.3	1.8	2.2	1.6	0.6	0.6
Brazil	96.1	0.8	1.1	0.6	1.4	0.1
Chile	90.2	2.3	4.7	0.5	1.9	0.4
China	99.6	0.1	0.3	0.0	0.0	0.0
Colombia	82.2	3.8	8.2	0.4	5.2	0.1
Greece	96.3	1.5	0.0	0.1	2.0	0.1
India	96.4	0.5	1.2	0.2	1.3	0.3
Indonesia	93.5	4.1	0.2	0.1	1.8	0.2
Jordan	94.2	0.5	0.3	0.0	5.0	0.0
Malaysia	93.5	0.0	2.5	0.2	3.8	0.1
Mauritius	95.2	0.0	0.3	3.2	1.3	0.0
Mexico	92.5	4.1	0.0	1.8	0.8	0.8
Pakistan	97.8	1.3	0.0	0.0	0.7	0.1
Peru	96.0	1.5	1.7	0.0	0.2	0.6
Philippines	93.2	2.1	1.0	0.8	2.1	0.8
Portugal	93.9	0.0	2.8	0.1	3.0	0.2
Sri Lanka	98.5	0.0	0.0	0.0	1.4	0.1
Turkey	93.5	3.2	0.6	0.1	2.4	0.2
Venezuela	90.3	1.9	3.0	0.1	3.9	0.9
G4						
Germany	88.8	0.2	10.2	0.1	0.6	0.1
Japan	90.1	0.0	8.4	0.7	0.8	0.0
United Kingdom	91.6	4.1	0.4	2.0	1.6	0.3
United States	86.5	5.2	6.1	0.8	1.4	0.1
Asian Tigers						
Korea (South)	83.7	2.2	10.7	0.5	2.7	0.1
Singapore	94.0	3.0	0.6	0.8	1.2	0.3
Taiwan, China	98.1	0.3	0.3	0.1	1.1	0.1
Other OECD						
Belgium	97.3	0.0	0.7	0.3	1.5	0.2
Canada	87.3	4.7	2.6	1.7	3.4	0.2
Finland	92.2	1.3	3.9	1.1	1.2	0.4
New Zealand	78.4	3.9	13.7	0.6	3.2	0.2

Note: This table reports the percentage of external finance in bank lending, equity and debt, and in international and domestic markets, in the period 1980–1997, for a cross-section of thirty countries grouped by region and level of development. Data sources are documented in appendix 7.1.

tant in others—0.0 percent in Greece. The G4 countries—except for the United Kingdom—have relatively well developed domestic bond markets, but a few other countries, such as Korea, also use domestic bond markets as an important source of external finance. While domestic equity markets are usually less significant sources of external finance than are domestic bond markets, that is not always the case. Many of the emerging markets, and some Asian Tiger and OECD countries, have raised more capital through domestic equity markets than domestic bond markets over this sample period.

Generally, foreign bond and equity markets have played a limited role in providing finance. With the exception of Brazil, Greece, Indonesia, Mexico, Philippines, and the United Kingdom, all countries issued more bonds domestically than internationally. Only Peru issued more international equity than domestic equity.

Table 7.4 summarizes the financing ratios across countries for each year, illustrating how much change there has been in the relative importance of each of these external sources over time. The table shows that there is much volatility in the ratios, suggesting that macroeconomic factors or the relative cost of each of the instruments may influence the choice of finance. It also suggests that there have been trends over time; foreign sources of finance became more important in the period 1990–1997 then previously. Also note the significant decline in domestic bank lending from 96 percent of all external finance in 1980 to 85 percent in 1997. Over the same period, however, foreign bank lending increased from only 1 percent to more than 5 percent.

Not obvious from the summary tables are the differences between different countries. For example, for emerging market countries domestic equity issuance increased from less than one percent of total finance in the 1980s to around 3 percent in the 1990s. In contrast, no obvious change occurred in the level of domestic equity finance in the G4 countries, but there was a notable increase in domestic bond finance (from about 5 percent to about 7 percent) over the same period of time.

7.3   The Determinants of Financing Choices

In this section we examine the relationship between various institutional factors, the macroeconomic environment and the financing ratios introduced in the previous section. The analysis employs con-

Table 7.4
Mean Financial Ratios across Countries by Years (percent)

	Banks		Bonds		Equity	
	Domestic	Foreign	Domestic	Foreign	Domestic	Foreign
1980	96.2	1.0	1.6	0.1	1.1	0.0
1981	95.5	1.4	1.7	0.2	1.2	0.0
1982	95.5	1.1	2.3	0.1	1.0	0.0
1983	95.5	0.8	2.4	0.0	1.3	0.0
1984	95.6	1.0	2.2	0.2	1.0	0.0
1985	94.5	1.2	2.8	0.5	1.0	0.1
1986	90.1	1.2	5.4	0.6	2.7	0.0
1987	93.2	1.3	3.1	0.4	2.0	0.1
1988	93.5	1.6	3.0	0.4	1.6	0.1
1989	90.0	1.7	4.9	0.4	2.8	0.1
1990	93.3	1.6	2.6	0.2	2.1	0.1
1991	93.4	1.1	2.8	0.4	2.1	0.4
1992	93.0	1.3	2.7	0.5	2.2	0.4
1993	91.1	1.8	3.0	1.0	2.6	0.5
1994	89.5	2.3	2.8	1.0	3.6	0.8
1995	90.2	3.6	2.8	0.8	2.3	0.3
1996	88.9	3.4	3.4	1.1	2.1	1.1
1997	85.0	5.5	3.3	3.5	2.0	0.6

Note: This table reports the percentage of external finance in bank lending, equity and debt, and in international and domestic markets, in the period 1980–1997, for a cross-section of thirty countries grouped by region and level of development. Data sources are documented in appendix 7.1.

ditional means as the primary methodology for examining the link between various values of a conditioning variable—for example, the level of accounting standards—and the relative amounts of debt and equity financing. This univariate approach—while admittedly very simple—sheds considerable light on the role of these factors and the extent to which they help to explain the aggregate data. We leave a multivariate analysis to future work.

7.3.1 Institutional Factors

As an initial step toward understanding the factors that influence the choice of external financing source, we examine the relationship between financial ratios and four institutional features: accounting standards, level of investor protection, market entry restrictions, and the level of concentration in the banking system. In each case, factor indices make it possible to divide the sample of countries annually into two or three groups and then to calculate the mean level of the six financing ratios (where we include two ratios for total domestic and total foreign financing) for each group. These factors were chosen because they are important indicators of the level of development of the markets, they are policy choices made by local regulators, and indices are publicly available from an independent source. While not based on a specific model of market development, one would expect investor interest in markets to be enhanced by better accounting standards, better investor protection, and more open access to foreign investors. To the extent that this reduces the cost of capital, one would expect to see more issuance activity.

Unlike the other three factors that are closely associated with equity and bond markets, the impact of the bank concentration factor, which is identified by Demirgüç-Kunt and Levine (chapter 3) as an important indicator of financial system development more generally, is less obvious. To the extent that bank concentration is associated with less competition within the banking system, one might see higher levels of primary market development. Conversely, to the extent that bank concentration is associated with political power that restricts market-friendly regulation, then one may see lower levels of market development associated with it.

Table 7.5 presents the conditional means for the four different market factors. Consider first accounting standards. In this case the index sorts countries annually into three groups: those with poor, average, and good accounting standards. These statistics suggest that the relationship between accounting standards and the financing mix is complicated. For all countries, as standards improve the level of domestic securities issues declines, although average standard countries have the highest level of domestic issues. Foreign issues are highest in countries with high standards, but that result is clearly driven by the nonemerging market countries, where the importance of domestic markets decreases (not reported) as standards improve. The t-test does not reject the hypothesis, however, that the ratios for either domestic or foreign securities are equal for the poor and good accounting standard countries.

The mix between bonds and equity also changes as a function of accounting standards. Over all countries, the relative amount of do-

Table 7.5
Mean Financial Ratios Conditional on Institutional Factors (percent)

	All securities		Bonds		Equities	
	Domestic	Foreign	Domestic	Foreign	Domestic	Foreign
Accounting standards						
Poor	80.2	19.8	18.3	7.5	61.9	12.3
Average	88.0	12.0	41.0	5.8	47.0	6.2
Good	75.2	24.8	38.4	18.6	36.8	6.3
t-test	0.54	0.54	2.11	2.28	3.27	2.78
Investor protection						
Poor	79.9	20.1	30.4	6.4	49.6	13.7
Average	86.0	14.0	29.9	6.5	56.1	7.5
Good	76.1	23.9	46.8	18.9	29.3	5.0
t-test	0.54	0.54	2.11	2.28	3.27	2.78
Entry restrictions						
Restricted	84.7	15.3	34.3	7.8	50.5	7.4
Open	78.8	21.2	41.1	15.5	37.6	5.8
t-test	1.91	1.91	1.70	3.23	3.20	0.99
Bank concentration ratio						
Below median	89.3	10.7	49.2	7.7	40.1	3.0
Above median	82.3	17.7	29.1	13.0	53.3	4.7
t-test	3.36	3.36	6.65	2.97	4.13	1.88

Note: This table presents mean financing ratios for all countries grouped conditional on the level of accounting standards, investor protection, entry restrictions and bank concentration ratios. The sample period varies by country and data availability. The t-test is for the difference between the values of the financial ratio conditional on the lowest and highest value of that conditioning variable.

mestic equity issues declines as accounting standards improve, with that decline being largely offset with domestic bond issues. There is also a decline in the issuance of foreign equity as standards improve, which is offset with an increase in foreign bonds. For all ratios, the t-test rejects the hypothesis that the poor and good standard countries are equal. Note that the impact on debt-equity ratios is dramatic. The ratio for countries with poor accounting standards is 0.3, compared to 1.3 for countries with good standards. Clearly, bond markets are much more important sources of finance in countries with good accounting standards.

Regarding investor protection, the index sorts countries into three groups again, those with poor, average and high levels of investor protection. The story that emerges is very similar to that for accounting standards. Once again, as investor protection reaches its maximum, the amount of capital raised through domestic equity markets declines and the amount raised through domestic and foreign bond markets increases. This result, however, largely reflects the experience in nonemerging markets (not reported) as the trend in emerging markets was for no difference between the poor and good investor protection regimes. Foreign bond issuance was significantly higher in the good investor protection countries, for all three groups of countries. Foreign equity issuance generally declined with improved investor protection, although there was a slight increase in nonemerging markets countries. The one enigma here is for those countries that are rated as average in investor protection, where the amount of domestic equity actually increases, at the expense of foreign equity. In all cases for specific security types, the t-test rejects equality of the ratios for the poor and good investor protection regimes. Once again, the impact on debt-equity ratios is dramatic: 0.6 for countries with poor investor protection versus 1.9 for countries with strong protection. As with accounting standards, countries with better investor protection have more developed bond markets.

Next we consider the role of entry restriction to foreign investors, where the sorting is into countries that have open entry and those that restrict entry. Here we see that countries with open markets have lower levels of domestic and foreign equity issuance and higher levels of both domestic and foreign bond issuance. This is especially true for the nonemerging markets countries (not reported), which behave quite differently from the emerging market countries in this regard. Overall, open markets lead to more foreign securities issues and less dependence on domestic issues, results that are statistically significant. Here again, the impact on debt-equity ratios is strong: 0.7 for countries with foreign entry restrictions versus 1.3 for open countries.

Finally, we consider the relationship between the level of concentration in the banking system and corporate financing decisions. Here the conditioning variable is the level of bank concentration, defined as the percent of total bank system assets controlled by the largest three banks. This index of competition in the banking sector was introduced into the debate on financial market development by Demirgüç-Kunt and Levine (1999), where they document that richer countries have lower levels of bank concentration. The results for the financial ratios are presented in table 7.5, where we see that countries with more concentrated banking systems have significantly lower levels of domestic issuance and higher levels of foreign issuance (both bond and equity). This effect is most notable for developed countries, with very little impact in emerging markets (not reported). It is consistently true, however, that bond market issuance activity is significantly lower for countries where bank concentration is high. Mean financial ratios for domestic bonds are 35 percent lower in emerging markets where bank concentration is above the median, and 31 percent lower for developed countries. Conversely, domestic equity market issuance increases significantly (by 33% for all countries) where bank concentration is high.

Overall this conditional means analysis suggests that institutional factors are highly correlated with the relative amounts of domestic and foreign securities, as well as the relative amounts of debt and equity. Markets with better accounting standards, higher levels of investor protection and more foreign entry tend to depend more on domestic bond markets and foreign markets generally, and less on domestic equity markets. Countries with concentrated banking systems tend to have less domestic bond issuance and more domestic equity issuance. Collectively, these results suggest very strongly that better institutional features are highly correlated with the development of bond markets, both domestic and foreign.

7.3.2 Macroeconomic Factors

Our analysis of macroeconomic factors and financing ratios is limited to three conditioning variables: percentage change in GDP, inflation and the total size of the financial system relative to GDP. For the first two variables we employ two methodologies for sorting country-years into two groups: high and low. One methodology—which we label the Business Cycle approach—calculates the median percentage change in the relevant conditioning variable, say percentage change in GDP, for each country over the sample period, and then assigns each country-year to either the high or low group of countries depending on whether any given year is above or below the median for that country. Once each country-year has been designated as either a high or low country-year, the mean across all country-years for each group is computed. Those mean values are reported in the tables. The idea behind this methodology is to characterize each country as in a high or low growth cycle, relative to its own historical performance under the belief that relative macroeconomic performance is important in determining corporate performance. For example, companies in a high-growth country may feel distress even if growth is positive when growth is below historical performance. Conversely, companies in countries with relatively low historical rates of growth may look at even modest bursts of growth as important.

The second methodology for calculated conditional means, which we label the Long-Term Growth approach, calculates a grand median across all countries for all country-years. Each individual country-year is then compared with this overall median and designated as either high or low for the relevant conditioning variable. Once grouped, the means of these two groups are computed and those means are reported in the tables. The logic behind this methodology is that performance relative to the global sample is also important. Companies operating in countries with high growth or low inflation relative to the global sample may behave in a different manner from companies in low-growth or high-inflation countries.

Conditional means for the six financing ratios using both conditioning methodologies for GDP and inflation are reported in table 7.6. The Business Cycle estimates suggest that countries with below median performance experience significantly higher levels of equity issuance and significantly lower levels of bond issuance in their domestic markets. Both foreign equity and bond issuance is higher during growth cycles, but that impact is statistically insignificant. While this result is statistically interesting, it is also perplexing because the switch into domestic equity during periods of low growth is at odds with the conventional wisdom that interest rates and stock market valuations are higher during periods of growth.

The second panel of table 7.6 presents the conditional means based on Long-Term Growth rates. Here the results are sharply different. Countries with growth rates below the global median use significantly less domestic equity, more domestic bonds and higher levels of foreign finance. Nearly all differences are statistically different. This result reflects in part the split in the sample between developed and emerging markets. Emerging markets had generally higher GDP growth rates during the sample period, and they also tend to have less developed bond markets.

We also examined mean values conditional on the Long-Term Growth rates for each of three six-year subperiods (not reported).

Table 7.6
Mean Financial Ratios Conditional on GDP Growth Rate and Inflation (percent)

	All securities		Bonds		Equity	
	Domestic	Foreign	Domestic	Foreign	Domestic	Foreign
GDP						
Business cycle						
Low	86.3	13.7	34.7	9.7	51.6	4.0
High	83.1	16.9	41.3	11.7	41.8	5.2
t-test	1.53	1.53	2.20	1.17	3.19	1.21
Long-term growth rate						
Low	82.4	17.6	45.2	11.9	37.2	5.7
High	86.9	13.1	31.5	9.6	55.4	3.5
t-test	2.14	2.14	4.63	1.32	6.06	2.26
Inflation						
Business cycle						
Low	84.5	15.5	35.2	10.9	49.2	4.7
High	85.4	14.6	40.7	10.3	44.7	4.3
t-test	0.42	0.42	1.81	0.32	1.48	0.33
Long-term growth rate						
Low	81.7	18.3	45.0	13.3	36.6	5.1
High	87.6	12.4	31.6	8.4	55.9	4.0
t-test	2.84	2.84	4.52	2.86	6.47	1.06

Note: This table presents mean financing ratios for six securities types conditional on the rates of GDP growth and inflation using a methodology for calculating the median value of the conditioning variable described in chapter 7.

Those statistics suggest that much of the difference reported in the second panel was driven entirely by events that transpired during the period 1986–1991, when low growth countries used significantly higher levels of domestic bonds, and lower levels of equity and foreign bonds.

Table 7.6 also presents mean financing ratios conditional on low and high values of domestic inflation. The Business Cycle estimate of median inflation in the first panel shows little difference statistically between countries with low and high inflation, although there is evidence that periods of high inflation were associated with higher levels of domestic bonds largely offset by lower issues of domestic equity. This is a rather counterintuitive result as one normally associates inflation with uncertainty for fixed-income instruments and, hence, one would expect to see lower levels of issuance during periods of inflation. The expected result does appear in the Long-Term Growth rates, which describe a very different picture. Here, we see that countries with above global levels of inflation used significantly more equity and significantly less debt, both domestic and foreign. As with the GDP growth rate, most of the high inflation countries were also emerging markets, however not all emerging markets have experienced high rates of inflation. The results for the three subperiods (not reported) suggest that most of the differences for the Long-Term Growth rates come from the two subperiods 1986–1991 and 1992–1997. Overall, these differences are reflected in debt-equity ratios that are twice the level for low inflation countries (1.4) relative to the high inflation countries (0.7).

Our third macroeconomic variable—total size of the financial sector—is taken directly from Demirgüç-Kunt and Levine (1999),[7] and is measured as the sum of domestic assets of deposit money banks and stock market capitalization divided by GDP. It provides a simple measure of the overall level of development of the financial system, although it looks only at the amount of trading activity in the stock market, ignoring both equity issuance activity and bond markets. Demirgüç-Kunt and Levine (chapter 3) find that this measure is significantly related to level of GDP. In our case, we use the measure of total size to sort countries into two groups, those that have financial systems that are greater than the median and those that are below.

Table 7.7 presents the mean financial ratios conditional on total size of the financial system. Overall, when one uses the grand median as the conditioning variable, the impact of larger financial systems is for higher levels of domestic bond issuance (roughly double the level in above median countries) and much lower levels of domestic equity issuance, reflecting the fact that most developed countries have much more developed domestic bond markets. The nearly complete offset between domestic bond and equity markets is reflected in nearly no change between domestic and foreign sources of financing.

The most striking effects in table 7.7 appear among developed countries, where larger financial systems are associated with higher levels of foreign financing, primarily foreign bonds, and higher levels of domestic equity issuance. Note in particular that the level of domestic bond issuance in developed countries declines by 24 percent in the countries with above-median financial systems, while the amount of foreign bond issuance increases 74 percent. In emerging

Table 7.7
Mean Financial Ratios Conditional on Size of the Financial System (percent)

	All securities		Bonds		Equities	
	Domestic	Foreign	Domestic	Foreign	Domestic	Foreign
All countries						
Below median	85.6	14.4	25.3	9.9	60.3	4.5
Above median	85.9	14.1	50.7	10.8	35.3	3.3
t-test	0.16	0.16	8.56	0.46	8.20	1.30
Emerging markets						
Below median	89.5	10.5	30.4	6.1	59.2	4.4
Above median	84.9	15.1	26.9	11.1	58.0	4.0
t-test	1.61	1.61	0.94	2.11	0.28	0.35
Developed countries						
Below median	87.5	12.5	65.3	9.9	22.2	2.6
Above median	78.7	21.3	49.8	17.2	28.9	4.1
t-test	3.04	3.04	3.33	2.89	2.06	1.47

Note: This table presents mean financial ratios for six securities types conditional on the median value of the total size of the financial system (domestic assets of deposit money banks + stock market capitalization/GDP). For the set of all countries the median value is the grand median, whereas for the two subsets of countries the median is the median for each subset.

markets, we also see a significant increase in foreign bond issuance, and a decrease in domestic security issuance, but the impact is much more muted than for the developed countries.

Collectively, these results suggest that there are strong links between macreconomic behavior and primary market behavior. High growth countries depend much more on domestic equity. Once economies have matured, domestic bond markets become more important as sources of finance. Unlike growth, inflation has less impact on issuance activity in the short run. For countries with persistently high inflation, however, equity, both domestic and foreign, dominates bond finance. As countries develop domestic banking systems, the data suggests that domestic bond markets also become more important relative to domestic equity markets.

7.3.3 Financial Structure

The results in table 7.7 suggest that the overall size of the financial system, at least as measured in that table, has some explanatory power for the choice of bonds and equity but does little to explain the choice of foreign and domestic sources of finance. One reason for this may be that the structure of the financial system, rather than just size, has an important influence on the choice of finance. For that reason, in this section we explore different measures of financial structure in order to learn more about the implications not only of size, but also the nature of the financial system on corporate financing decisions. To do that, we employ three additional indicator variables used by Demirgüç-Kunt and Levine (chapter 3): total value traded in the stock market relative to GDP; the ratio of claims by deposit money banks on the private sector to total value traded on the stock market; and a financial structure index, which Demirgüç-Kunt and Levine (chapter 3) construct based on several variables in order to classify countries as either bank-based or market-based.

We start with the ratio of total value traded in the stock market (relative to GDP) as an indicator of stock market development. Intuitively, more developed stock markets should be correlated with lower costs of equity capital and higher levels of equity issuance. Alternatively, to the extent that stock market development is an indicator of financial market development more generally, more developed stock markets might be uncorrelated with the choice between bonds and equity. In that case, however, one might still see a higher level of domestic market issuance relative to foreign issuance.

In that regard, it is interesting that the evidence in table 7.8 suggests that stock market development is associated with statistically higher levels of foreign issuance, although the economic difference between the above-median and below-median countries is only marginal. Note also that the higher level of foreign activity applies to both emerging and developed countries, with the level of drop of domestic issuance in both sets of countries being about the same order of magnitude. What is striking, however, is that more developed stock markets are closely linked to higher levels of domestic bond issuance, with above-median countries issuing roughly 50 percent more domestic bonds than below-median countries. This result, however, is clearly driven by developed countries, which represent a large part of the above-median sample (relative to the grand median) and which have generally more developed bond markets. When we look at the subgroups of countries, in fact, we see that for the developed countries, above-median countries have ratios of domestic bond finance that are 28 percent lower than below-median countries.

Table 7.8
Mean Financial Ratios Conditional on Financial Structure Variables (percent)

	All securities		Bonds		Equities	
	Domestic	Foreign	Domestic	Foreign	Domestic	Foreign
Total value traded						
All countries						
Below median	87.9	12.2	30.7	7.7	57.1	4.5
Above median	84.1	15.9	46.0	12.6	38.1	3.3
t-test	1.79	1.79	4.91	2.75	6.06	1.27
Emerging markets						
Below median	90.8	9.2	28.4	5.1	62.4	4.0
Above median	83.6	16.4	28.5	12.2	55.1	4.3
t-test	2.60	2.60	0.00	2.98	1.78	0.19
Developed countries						
Below median	87.6	12.4	66.7	8.6	20.9	3.8
Above median	78.6	21.4	48.1	18.8	30.6	2.7
t-test	3.10	3.10	4.08	4.09	3.03	1.11
Bank/stock trading index						
All countries						
Below median	83.2	16.8	40.6	13.0	42.6	3.8
Above median	88.4	11.6	37.6	7.7	50.8	3.9
t-test	2.49	2.49	0.93	2.98	2.53	0.11
Emerging markets						
Below median	84.2	15.9	31.2	10.4	53.0	5.5
Above median	90.2	9.8	25.4	7.2	64.8	2.7
t-test	2.14	2.14	1.61	1.34	2.92	2.18
Developed countries						
Below median	82.4	17.6	56.9	15.2	25.6	2.3
Above median	85.1	14.9	60.4	10.5	24.7	4.5
t-test	0.89	0.89	0.73	1.85	0.26	2.12
Financial structure index						
All countries						
Bank-based	89.4	10.6	37.8	7.1	51.7	3.5
Market-based	80.7	19.3	40.9	15.0	39.9	4.3
t-test	4.15	4.15	0.97	4.43	3.64	0.86
Emerging markets						
Bank-based	90.4	9.6	22.9	6.2	67.5	3.4
Market-based	82.0	18.0	36.6	12.7	45.4	5.3
t-test	2.95	2.95	3.81	2.69	5.55	1.45
Developed countries						
Bank-based	87.6	12.4	66.7	8.6	20.9	3.8
Market-based	78.6	21.4	48.1	18.8	30.6	2.7
t-test	3.10	3.10	4.08	4.08	3.03	1.11

Note: This table presents mean financial ratios for six securities types conditional on the median of the total value traded in the stock market relative to GDP, the ratio of claims on deposit money banks on the private sector relative to total value traded on the stock market, and the financial structure index developed by Demirgüç-Kunt and Levine (chapter 3) in each country. For the set of all countries, the conditioning variable is the grand median across all countries, whereas for the two subsets of countries the median of each subset is used.

The difference across emerging markets for domestic bond finance is economically almost null.

On the equity side, overall above median countries show an average decline in the ratio of equity finance of 33 percent relative to below-median countries, and that decline is statistically significant at the 1 percent level. That result, as in the case of domestic bond markets to which it represents the complement, appears driven by the wide difference between developed and emerging markets. Looking at the level of domestic equity finance, it is obvious that domestic equity plays a much more important role in emerging markets than in developed markets and the overall result largely reflects this difference. Within the two subgroups of countries, one sees very different reactions to stock market development. In developed countries, above-median countries have significantly higher levels of domestic equity finance and marginally lower levels of foreign equity finance. Conversely, in emerging markets, more stock market trading is associated with lower levels of reliance on equity and slightly higher levels of foreign equity.

Our next measure of financial system structure is the ratio of claims on money deposit banks to the private sector relative to value traded on the stock market. Demirgüç-Kunt and Levine (chapter 3) find that this measure is correlated with GDP and is an indicator of the relative importance of banks versus markets in the financial system. Intuitively, the higher this ratio, the more bank-based the system. For our financial ratios, less market-based systems might be inclined toward foreign sources of finance.

The results in the second panel of table 7.8 suggest that countries with above-median levels of bank/trading ratios in fact have higher levels of domestic securities issuance, a result that is statistically more significant than it is economically. Note, however, that the result holds for both subgroups of countries, although insignificantly so for developed countries. Overall, and for emerging markets in particular, there is a strong tendency for countries with more bank-based systems to go for domestic equity, which increase by nearly 20 percent, at the expense of both domestic and foreign bonds. In the case of the developed countries, there was not much difference in the level of domestic bonds and equity associated with the bank/trading volume measure, but there was a significant drop in foreign bonds that was almost exactly offset with an increase in foreign equity.

Our last financial structure variable is an overall index developed by Demirgüç-Kunt and Levine (chapter 3) that classifies countries on the basis of a set of indicators that include market capitalization versus bank assets, trading volume versus bank credit, and trading volume versus bank overhead costs. The resulting index sorts countries into two subgroups: market-based and bank-based.[8] Demirgüç-Kunt and Levine (chapter 3) document that higher income countries tend to be more market based. For our data, one would expect more market-based systems to rely on domestic securities, however the split between bonds and equity is ambiguous.

The third panel of table 7.8 presents the results for the financial structure index. Overall they suggest that market-based countries actually are more dependent on foreign securities, issuing 82 percent more foreign securities relative to domestic securities. Looking at the subgroups, one is inclined to attribute much of the difference to the disparity between emerging and developing countries. But actually the level of the foreign financing ratio is very similar in the two countries and the level of increase associated with being a market-based system is also about the same on average, both increasing by more than 70 percent. Also, in both cases, the increase in foreign issuance is a result of foreign bonds rather foreign equity, with foreign equity actually declining slightly for developed countries.

Overall, the market-based countries depend much less on equity than bank-based systems, with the domestic equity ratio falling by 23 percent on average between the two groups of countries. That fall, however is largely driven by the emerging markets both because they rely more on domestic equity than do developed countries and also because those emerging markets that are classified as market-based have significantly less reliance on domestic equity than bank-based emerging markets. For developed countries, the opposite is the case; market-based developing countries rely much more on domestic equity markets than do bank-based countries, with that decline being both statistically and economically significant.

Overall the three measures of financial structure that we employ produce consistent results. The more market-based the financial system, the more reliance on foreign securities. This is driven by a reliance on foreign bonds, at the expense primarily of domestic equity. For all three measures this result is both statistically and economically significant; in the case of the financial structure index, the increase in the foreign financial ratio is 85 percent for market-based countries relative to bank-based countries.

7.3.4 Privatization

The period under investigation was one in which many countries initiated and carried out privatization of large numbers of state-owned enterprises. Depending on the manner in which these events occurred, they could have had a significant influence on issuance of either domestic or international securities. In this section we examine the impact of privatizations on financing ratios in two manners. First, we calculate the mean financial ratios conditional on whether there was privatization in a country in a given year. Then we examine the long-run impact of privatization on mean financial ratios by calculating the ratios conditional on the number of years that have transpired since a privatization program began.[9]

Table 7.9 presents the mean financial ratios conditional on privatization activity. The first panel compares countries with positive privatization sales (in any given year) to all other countries. Not surprisingly, countries with privatization exhibit significantly higher levels of domestic equity issuance. In addition, privatizations were correlated with significantly higher levels of foreign issuance, both

Table 7.9
Mean Financial Ratios Conditional on Privatization Sales (percent)

	All securities		Bonds		Equity	
	Domestic	Foreign	Domestic	Foreign	Domestic	Foreign
No sales	87.5	12.5	38.6	9.3	48.9	3.2
Sales	69.6	30.4	32.5	18.3	37.1	12.1
t-test	6.29	6.29	1.46	3.81	2.71	6.62
Conditional on years after start of privatization						
0–3 years	74.2	25.8	34.5	14.4	39.7	11.3
4–7 years	68.4	31.6	35.3	21.4	33.1	10.2
8–11 years	68.4	31.6	50.2	23.2	18.2	8.4
t-test	0.71	0.71	1.63	1.51	2.37	0.53
F-test	25.1	25.1	1.0	11.7	9.7	23.3

Note: This table presents mean financing ratios conditional on the existence of a privatization program in each country and on the number of years since the initiation of that program.

equity and debt. Note that the level of foreign issuance is 143 percent higher for countries with privatization than other countries. Note also that the mean debt/equity ratio for countries with privatizations was 1.03, above the level of 0.9 for countries with no privatizations.

The second panel of table 7.9 presents mean financing ratios conditional on the numbers of years since privatization sales began. These numbers present a very striking pattern of domestic bond market development over time following privatization. Domestic bond markets in the early years following privatization contribute about 35 percent of all external finance, but that ratio increases uniformly over time until reaching 50 percent eight to eleven years later, an increase of 45 percent. Foreign bond issuance also increases, and although the absolute numbers are smaller, the percentage increase is a full 61 percent. Both of these increases are offset by declines in equity issuance, with domestic equity issuance declining by 55 percent, and foreign issuance decreasing by 26 percent. Note also that the overall debt/equity pattern of issuance changes as a result, with the ratio increasing from 1.0 in the early years following privatization to more than 2.7 in the later years.

7.4 Conclusions

Primary markets are a potentially vital source of capital for firms. To date, however, these markets have not been extensively studied. This chapter examines the pattern of primary market financing for a broad cross-section of countries for 1980–1997. The analysis provides several insights into the problems facing corporations in raising capital.

At the aggregate level, in both industrialized and emerging countries, there has been rapid growth in the issuance of both corporate debt and equity in the 1990s. As a percentage of GDP, many emerging equity markets now exceed the level of the major developed markets. Although this is less true for debt markets, issuance of private debt continues to be an important vehicle for the raising of capital in some countries. For emerging countries, access to international primary markets resumed quickly in the 1990s after defaults in the 1980s, but with a much larger equity component. These aggregate figures conceal considerable variation across nations.

These findings have direct applications to public policy. In particular, our work suggests that primary market development is related to both macroeconomic factors and market-specific aspects including the accounting framework, the level of investor protection and the extent of access for foreign investors. While financial market development may aid in achieving macroeconomic goals, such as boosting the growth rate and taming inflation, the statistics also suggest that more stable economic environments are associated with higher levels of domestic financial markets. Finally, we find that there is a strong correlation between privatization and the development of domestic bond markets.

Appendix 7.1:   Data Sources

A. Data on new issues of equity and debt securities were obtained from national sources, including stock exchanges, central banks and capital markets regulatory organizations.

Argentina	Bolsa de Comercio de Buenos Aires
Belgium	*OECD Financial Statistics Monthly*
Brazil	Comissão de Valores Mobiliários, Bolsa de Valores do Rio de Janeiro
Canada	Bank of Canada
Chile	Banco Central de Chile, Superintendencia de Valores Y Seguros
China, P.R.	China Securities Regulatory Commission
Colombia	Superintendencia de Valores, Banco de la República
Finland	Bank of Finland
Germany	*OECD Financial Statistics Monthly*
India	Reserve Bank of India
Indonesia	Capital Market Supervisory Agency (BAPEPAM)
Japan	*OECD Financial Statistics Monthly*
Jordan	Amman Financial Market
Korea	The Bank of Korea
Malaysia	Kuala Lumpur Stock Exchange, Bank Negara Malaysia
Mauritius	Bank of Mauritius, Stock Exchange Commission
Mexico	Bolsa Mexicana de Valores, Comisión Nacional Bancaria y de Valores
New Zealand	New Zealand Stock Exchange
Pakistan	Corporate Law Authority, Karachi Stock Exchange (Guarantee) Ltd.
Peru	Comisión Nacional Supervisora de Empresas Y Valores
Philippines	Bangko Sentral Pilipinas

Portugal	Comissão do Mercado de Valores Mobiliários (CMVM)
Singapore	Monetary Authority of Singapore
Sri Lanka	Colombo Stock Exchange, Securities and Exchange Commission of SL
Taiwan, R. C.	Central Bank of China
Thailand	Securities and Exchange Commission, The Stock Exchange of Thailand
Turkey	Capital Market Board of Turkey
United Kingdom	*OECD Financial Statistics Monthly*
United States	*OECD Financial Statistics Monthly*
Venezuela	Comisión Nacional de Valores

B. GDP in U.S. dollars at current market prices were sourced from the *World Bank National Accounts* database for the developing countries, and from the *OECD National Accounts* database for the industrial countries. GDP data for Hong Kong was taken from the Hong Kong *Monthly Digest of Statistics*. GDP data for Taiwan, China was taken from the IFC *Emerging Stock Markets Factbook* (1989, 1996). International issues of debt and equity are available for all countries from Bondware.

Notes

1. By contrast, *secondary markets are those where investors trade previously existing securities.*

2. Aggregate market development has been documented in a few country reports prepared by international agencies such as the World Bank, but there is little evidence on the way of time-series trends over a wide range of countries. An earlier analysis of primary market activity in developing countries is provided in Patrick and Wai 1973.

3. Glen and Madhavan 1999 provide details on the Peruvian market.

4. For a slightly larger sample of countries over a shorter period of time (1980–1985), Aylward and Glen (1999) report that government long-term debt was equal to about 45 percent of all long-term security issues (including equity), which means that it is nearly equal in size to the sum of all private issues.

5. Country groups are defined in table 7.1.

6. Stulz (chapter 4) argues that globalization reduces the cost of equity capital because both the expected return that investors require to invest in equity to compensate them for risk and agency costs fall.

7. Rajan and Zingales (1998) also use a similar indicator of market development.

8. See Demirgüç-Kunt and Levine chapter 3 for a more detailed explanation on the definition of the index and a list of countries with their index values.

9. Privatization data come from two sources: Candoy-Sekse 1988 and Privatization Yearbook (various issues).

References

Aylward, Anthony, and Jack Glen. 1999. Primary securities markets: Cross-country findings. Discussion Paper 39, International Finance Corporation.

Candoy-Sekse, Rebecca. 1998. Techniques of privatization of state-owned enterprises. Technical Paper 90, World Bank.

Domowitz, Ian, Jack Glen, and Ananth Madhavan. 2000. Liquidity, volatility, and equity trading costs across countries and over time. Working Paper, School of Business, University of Southern California, Los Angeles, CA.

Glen, Jack, and Ananth Madhavan. 1999. Primary securities markets in emerging nations: A case study of Peru. *Emerging Markets Quarterly* 3:30–37.

Karolyi, G. Andrew. 1996. What happens to stocks that list shares abroad? A survey of the evidence and its managerial implications. *Financial Markets, Institutions, and Instruments* 7:1–60.

Levine, Ross. 1997. Financial development and economic growth: Views and agenda. *Journal of Economic Literature* 35:688–726.

Levine, Ross. 1998. The legal environment, banks, and long-run economic growth. *Journal of Money, Credit, and Banking* 30:596–613.

Patrick, Hugh, and U. Tun Wai. 1973. Stock and bond issues and capital markets in less developed countries. *IMF Staff Papers* 20:253–317. International Monetary Fund.

Rajan, Raghu, and Luigi Zingales. 1998. Financial dependence and growth. *American Economic Review* 88(3):559–586 (June).

Stulz, René M. 1999. Globalization of equity markets and the cost of capital. Mimeo, School of Business, Ohio State University, Columbus, OH.

IV

Financial Structure and
Economic Performance:
Country Studies

8

Financial Structure in Chile: Macroeconomic Developments and Microeconomic Effects

Francisco Gallego and
Norman Loayza

8.1 Introduction

The outstanding macroeconomic performance of Chile in the late 1980s and 1990s has been portrayed as an example of successful market-oriented policies and, as such, has been the subject of numerous studies (see Bosworth, Dornbusch, and Labán 1994; Perry and Leipziger 1999). Recently, one of the areas receiving the largest attention is financial development (see Eyzaguirre and Lefort 1999). This emphasis is well justified given the remarkable growth in banking intermediation and stock market capitalization since the mid-1980s, which placed Chile as the financial leader in Latin America a decade later. By 1995, the ratio of credit allocated by deposit money banks to GDP in Chile was 49 percent, almost fifty percent larger than that of Brazil, the second country in the region in this respect. By the same year, stock market capitalization as a ratio to GDP reached 105 percent in Chile, at least three times bigger than in any other country in Latin America (see Loayza and Palacios 1997).

The objective of this chapter is to describe the developments in Chilean financial markets at the macroeconomic level and then examine their effects at the level of firms. At the macroeconomic level, we pay special attention to the evolution of financial structure, that is, the relative development of the banking sector vis-à-vis the stock, bond, and other capital markets. Analogously, at the level of firms we study not only their general access to financial markets but also how their financing (balance-sheet) decisions have evolved in the last decade.

The chapter is organized as follows. Section 8.2 reviews the macroeconomic development of financial markets in Chile in the last three decades. First, we describe the government policies toward financial markets. These have followed a rather pendulous process. They have transited from heavily interventionist (pre-1973) to radically market oriented (1974–1981) and, after a serious banking crisis, to prudentially regulated (1985–1990s). More recently, the 1990s can be considered the second wave of deregulation, as the access to and from *international* financial markets was gradually eased during this period. In section 8.2.2, we characterize the developments in the banking sector as well as in various types of capital markets (bond, stock, pension, and insurance markets). We conduct this assessment following the criteria proposed by Demirgüç-Kunt and Levine (chapter 3), that is evaluating, in turn, the size, activity, and efficiency of the most important financial markets.

In section 8.3, we analyze the changes that have occurred in a sample of Chilean firms in the last decade. The sample consists of seventy-nine firms that are quoted in the stock market and for which annual balance sheet data for the period 1985–1995 are available and complete. The purpose of this section is to estimate and test econometrically three issues. The first concerns the firms' access to financial markets. In particular, we test whether the reliance on internal funds for investment has decreased in the 1990s relative to the 1980s and, thus, whether investment has been more responsive to changes in the q-value of the firm. The second issue relates to the balance-sheet situation of the firms. Specifically, we examine whether the financial liberalization of the 1990s and the development of the banking, stock and bond markets at the aggregate level have affected the importance of debt relative to equity and long-term debt relative to short-term debt in the balance sheet of firms. The third microeconomic issue concerns the growth rate of the firm, measured by the proportional increase in the firm's operational revenue. We study the extent to which firm-specific and aggregate financial market developments have impacted the growth of our sample of firms. Section 8.4 offers some conclusions.

8.1.1   A Brief Literature Review and This Chapter's Value Added

Quite a few papers have examined the recent experience in financial markets at the macro level in Chile. The majority of them study the policy changes concerning banking regulations and supervision and their effect on the banks' assets and portfolio (see Arellano 1983; Brock 1992; Ramírez and Rosende 1992; Valdés-Prieto 1992; Larraín

1995; Budnevich 1997). Others address the financial and macro-economic effects of capital account controls and liberalization (see Johnston, Darbar, and Echeverría 1997; Soto 1997; Valdés-Prieto and Soto 1998; Gallego, Hernández, and Schmidt-Hebbel forthcoming; De Gregorio, Edwards, and Valdés 2000). Only recently, some studies have taken a broad approach on capital markets, attempting to provide a comprehensive perspective on the joint development of the banking sector, the stock and bond markets, and insurance markets in Chile (Eyzaguirre and Lefort 1999; Reinstein and Rosende 1999). Mostly based on time-series correlations, these papers agree in linking the recent improvements in financial depth and activity in Chile to its high rates of GDP growth in the late 1980s and 1990s. They provide, however, dissimilar views on the causes of financial development and the relative importance of the various components of the financial system. Sections 8.1 and 8.2, on the assessment of the financial system at the aggregate level, is similar to the latter studies. The perspective of this chapter is, however, different in that the comparisons between banking and capital markets are emphasized. This is done in an attempt to answer the question of whether the financial system in Chile has become bank-based or market-based (where the term market denotes not only the stock market but also the bond, insurance, and pension markets). Moreover, the evaluation of financial markets, following the criteria of size, activity, and efficiency, is done to guide the analysis of microeconomic evidence.

In section 8.3, we study the effect of financial development at the aggregate level on the firms' financial structure and access to credit and equity markets. Our analysis of microeconomic evidence follows three research traditions. The first studies how the investment behavior of the firm is determined by financial constraints beyond the profit-maximizing considerations imbedded in the firm's q-value (see Fazzari, Hubbard, and Petersen 1988; Hoshi, Kashyap, and Scharfstein 1991; Stein 1997; Hu and Schiantarelli 1998; Mairesse, Hall, and Mulkay 1999; Kaplan and Zingales 2000). To the extent that firms face constraints on or high costs of external financing, their investment depends not only on its profitability but is limited by both the availability of internal resources and the balance-sheet composition of the firm. Medina and Valdés (1998) provide an interesting application of this research line to the Chilean experience. In a sample of stock-market-traded firms in Chile, they find that firms' financial constraints do affect their investment behavior, particularly in the firms not regarded as investment grade. In this chapter, we assess the effect of financial development by analyzing whether firms are less dependent on their internal resources and balance-sheet composition and more responsive to their Tobin's q-value as result of financial development (for a similar application to Indonesia, see Harris, Schiantarelli, and Siregar 1994).

The second research tradition we follow studies the firm-specific and aggregate factors that determine the financial structure of the firm (see Aivazian et al. 2001; Demirgüç-Kunt and Maksimovic 1994; Lee, Lee, and Lee 1999; Schmukler and Vesperoni 2000). In this tradition, Hernández and Walker (1993) examine whether the financial crisis of 1983–1984 in Chile and the ensuing enactment of banking prudential regulations affected the debt and equity composition of domestic nonfinancial firms. They find that after the crisis the debt-equity ratio declined, particularly in firms in the tradable sector. This resulted from the liquidation of assets and corresponding debt reduction induced by the new prudential banking regulations. Focusing on the period 1985–1995, in this chapter we examine whether changes in various sectors of the Chilean financial system have had an impact on the firms' preference for and availability of equity, long-term debt, and short-term debt as alternative financing choices. Controlling for firm characteristics such as size and tangibility of assets and reported profitability, we estimate the balance-sheet effect of the size and activity of banking, stock, and bond markets.

The third empirical objective is to study the macro and micro determinants of firm growth. With this we intend to reproduce at the micro level the cross-country, time-series work that links financial development to GDP growth (see Levine 1997; Levine, Loayza, and Beck 2000). However, given that our sample of firms is not representative of all economic activities in Chile, we are careful both in accounting for firm-specific factors and in interpreting the results regarding the growth impact of macro variables (see Nickell, Wadhwani, and Wall 1992; Bernstein and Nadiri 1993; Schiantarelli and Srivastava 1996; Sena 1998). Adding this empirical exercise to those mentioned above, we intend to give a rather broad picture of how macro financial development and structure in the 1990s has affected the firms' access to financial markets, their balance-sheet structure, and their growth performance.

Finally, we must recognize two shortcomings of the chapter. We focus here on how financial development in Chile has contributed to make firm investment more responsive to its expected profitability and less restricted by the availability of internal funds. However, from the perspective of the consumer, the financial sector has a role beyond its effect on investment and growth. A well-developed financial system allows economic agents to smooth their consumption pattern over time. By shielding the consumer from the effect of temporary negative income shocks and the uncertainty associated with them, a developed financial system improves private and social welfare. Though admittedly important, the effect of financial development on consumption smoothing in Chile is beyond the scope of this chapter.[1] The second shortcoming of the chapter is related to the applicability of our firm-level results to the Chilean economy in general. Clearly our sample of firms is not representative; we work with well-established, mature firms that are quoted at the stock market and have good balance-sheet data. We can argue that banking and capital market development has a greater impact on growing and more financially constrained firms and, therefore, our results establish a lower bound for the beneficial impact of financial development. However, it is possible that this impact is characterized by nonlinearities or threshold effects that obscure the extrapolation of our results to the whole economy. We leave for future research an analysis of how firms of representative sizes, maturity levels, and sectors have been affected by the financial development in Chile.

8.2 Financial Developments at the Macro Level (1960–1997)

To examine the macroeconomic developments in the Chilean financial system in the last three decades, this section first presents a brief description of related economic policies and then describes the sector's performance over the period.

8.2.1 Financial-Sector Policies

We now review the main policies related to the Chilean financial system in the last thirty years. These policies follow a combination of historic elements (such as the country's legal tradition) and an extension of the general development model followed by the country at each point in time. The financial policy periods identified below correspond to those of general economic policies.

Financial Repression, Pre-1973

Reflecting the inward-looking development model implemented in those years in Chile and most other Latin American countries, the financial sector was extremely regulated. This meant the prevalence of controlled interest rates, quantitative restrictions on credit, mandated allocation of credit to priority sectors, and large state ownership of banks and other financial institutions, the latter specially during the 1970–1973 period.[2]

Financial Liberalization, 1974–1981

The radical shift in the country's development model started in 1974 was reflected in the removal of most regulations affecting the banking sector. Consistent with the logic of market liberalization, the determination of interest rates and domestic credit was left to market forces. Thus, interest rates were completely freed by January 1976, entry barriers in the banking industry were gradually eliminated starting in 1975, and liquidity requirement rates were diminished for the majority of deposit types between 1974 and 1980. Quantitative controls on credit were eliminated in April 1976, while a gradual opening of the capital account took place between 1975 and 1980.

An important component of the financial liberalization of the 1970s was the privatization of state-owned banks. It started in mid-1975 and was implemented through the sale of assets using a highly leveraged financing scheme. This financing mechanism allowed potential buyers to borrow from the government up to 90 percent of the sale price and to use the privatized assets themselves as the main collateral.[3] To accompany the privatization process, there was a gradual relaxation of entry restrictions to the banking sector.

Similarly, several reforms allowed the development of other capital markets such as insurance, bond, and stock markets. In 1976, a stock register was created, and the public disclosure of information was made mandatory. In 1981, a series of laws destined to protect minority shareholders and prevent the misuse of privileged information were enacted. Also in 1981, the issuance of long-term bonds was facilitated. In 1980, insurance market rates were liberalized while prudential regulations on insurance companies' portfolios were implemented. The same year, a fully funded pension system began to operate, and private institutions started to manage the pension funds by investing them in various financial instruments.

In contrast to the prudential regulation established for capital markets, the banking sector lacked a well-developed regulatory and supervisory system, including the lack of effective public disclosure mechanisms. Furthermore, two additional factors aggravated the lack of a proper regulatory system. First, there existed an implicit state guarantee on deposits, which became evident in the rescue of Banco de Osorno y la Unión and other financial institutions in 1976. Second, the financing mechanism for the purchase of state-owned banks generated the existence of highly leveraged banks, most of them belonging to economic conglomerates that were themselves highly indebted. The implicit government guarantees, the highly leveraged position of banks, the lack of appropriate banking regulation, and the preferential tax treatment of debt obligations created moral hazard problems that deteriorated the banks' asset portfolio and prepared the grounds for a banking crisis.

Banking Crisis, 1982–1984[4]

In addition to the conditions conducive to moral hazard problems, the balance sheet of banks suffered from a maturity and currency mismatch due to their investment in long-term projects in the nontradable sector that were largely financed with loans from abroad. The banks' portfolio mismatch placed them in a vulnerable position that was made manifest by the macroeconomic shocks in the first half of the 1980s. From 1981 to 1984 a negative terms-of-trade shock, a sharp increase in international interest rates, and a consequent large devaluation of the Chilean currency worsened the quality of most banks' portfolio and made some of them insolvent. Although the negative macroeconomic developments were not completely unexpected, the banks did little to adjust their portfolio probably because they expected the government to rescue them. Between 1982 and 1985, the government intervened in twenty-one financial institutions, including the Banco de Santiago and Banco de Chile, which jointly had 35 percent of the entire loan portfolio of the banking sector. Of the intervened financial institutions, fourteen were liquidated and the rest were rehabilitated and privatized. The state rehabilitated the banks by allowing them to recapitalize and issue long-term debt (which the central bank bought) to replace their existing nonperforming assets. Thus, the state assumed an important share of the costs of the 1982 banking crisis.

In the wake of this banking crisis, the liberalization process was partially reversed given that, first, the state became the manager and main creditor of rescued banks, and second, the state reinstated financial controls such as restrictions on external capital movements and suggested interest rates by the central bank.

Prudential Regulation, 1985–1990

The controls on interest rates were eliminated in 1985 and a new banking law was enacted. This established a modern prudential regulation, an enforced supervisory capacity by the state, and an explicit deposit insurance. The new banking law included (1) limits on the debt-to-capital ratio and reserve requirements related to the leverage position of the bank, (2) incentives for private monitoring of banks through both a partial public guarantee on deposits and the mandatory information disclosure to the public, and (3) separation between the core business of the bank and that of its subsidiaries.[5]

The regulatory framework for other capital markets was also improved during this period. The main changes are the following. First, a new bankruptcy law that clarified the extent of private sector responsibility in failing enterprises was implemented. Second, the purchase of equity in domestic firms by the private pension fund managers was allowed and regulated. And, third, the tax reform of 1984 eliminated the preferential treatment of debt liabilities by the firms (with respect to equity) and provided incentives for financial saving by all investors.

The privatization of large state enterprises (the telephone and power companies and some mining corporations), the recapitalization of rescued banks, and a significant external debt-to-equity conversion by private firms strongly promoted the development of the stock market and the pension fund managers (the largest institutional investors in Chile). This contributed to extend the ownership of capital throughout society.[6]

External Financial Deregulation, 1991–1999

External financial deregulation started in the late 1980s and was strengthened during the 1990s when a number of constraints related to external capital account transactions were lifted. Specifically, first, firms with good credit rating were allowed to issue bonds and shares in external markets; second, institutional investors, such as banks, pension fund managers, and insurance companies, were allowed to hold external assets; third, the permanence requirements for external investment and profits were gradually eased; and fourth, international trade payments transactions were liberalized (see Gallego, Hernández, and Schmidt-Hebbel forthcoming for more details). Until recently, however, the central bank maintained capital controls in the form of an unremunerated reserve requirement on external funds, which was advocated on the grounds that it deterred volatile short-run capital. In September 1998 this requirement was virtually eliminated.

In 1997, a new capital market law was passed by congress that regulated the participation of banks in nontraditional areas, such as factoring, nonpension insurance, and investment banking.

Finally, it is in this period when some regulations regarding the operations of private pension funds started to show some flaws. Specifically, the capital penalties imposed by law for under-performance led all private funds to mimic each other's portfolio excessively. Furthermore, the restrictions on the type of investments that private pension funds were allowed to hold produced asset portfolios not sufficiently diversified.

Indices of Financial-Sector Policies
The policy changes studied above can be summarized in financial liberalization indices. This has been done by Bandiera et al. (2000) and Morley, Machado, and Pettinato (1998). These indices are presented in figure 8.1. Both indices reflect well the five periods of Chilean financial policy, with the initial liberalization in the mid-1970s, the partial reversion after the crisis in the early 1980s, and the strengthening and expansion during the 1990s. Morley, Machado, and Pettinato's index is also available for other countries. When we compare the average for Latin America with the Chilean index, we note that for almost twenty years Chile was well above the average. Recently, however, Chile's position has become relegated to the average due to the strong financial liberalization experienced in other countries of the region.

8.2.2 Financial-Sector Performance

This section will describe the main results of the Chilean financial system, emphasizing the measures proposed by Demirgüç-Kunt and Levine in chapter 3 to determine the size, activity, and efficiency of

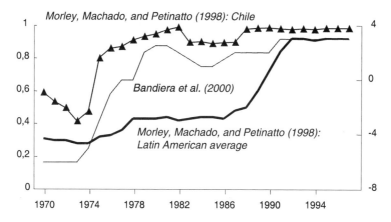

Figure 8.1
Financial liberalization index.
Sources: Authors' elaboration using Morley, Machado, and Petinatto 1998 and Bandiera et al. 2000.

banking and other financial markets. In this section, we also compare the relative development in the main financial markets. Thus, we attempt to assess whether the Chilean economy can be best characterized as bank-based or stock market–based.

Financial System: Global Results
Figure 8.2 presents the evolution of the size of the financial sector in Chile from 1960 to the present. It also presents the contribution of the main financial markets—namely, banks, the stock market, and the bond market—all relative to GDP.[7]

From the mid-1970s onward the financial system in Chile has grown relative to the size of the economy. The banking sector grew significantly in the late 1970s and moderately in the last two decades. The bond market expanded especially from 1980, while the stock market experienced a striking increase in the 1990s. Then, it appears that the overall growth of the financial sector during this period was accompanied by a significant change in its structure and composition. However, it is interesting to observe that the growth of financial markets has not been smooth but has also experienced temporary booms. For instance, the banking credit boom that took place before the 1982 crisis was mostly reversed, and so was the stock market expansion in 1983–1984. To a lesser extent, the decrease in stock

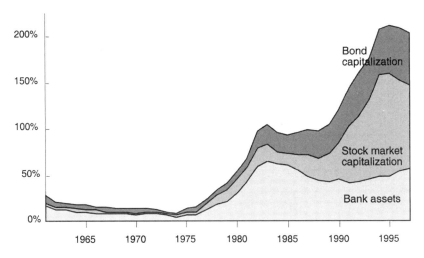

Figure 8.2
Financial market development.
Sources: Jeftanovic 1979, chapter 2 (this volume), Central Bank of Chile, and CB Capitales.

market capitalization in 1996–1997 can also be interpreted as a partial reversal of the strong expansion of the stock market in the early 1990s.

Banking Sector
Figure 8.2 shows the evolution of banks' financial assets as a fraction of GDP. It exhibits a growing trend from 1977, with a downward correction in the mid-1980s. By 1997, the financial assets of the banking sector represented 55.1 percent of GDP, a proportion higher than the world average (52.6%) and the largest in Latin America (whose average is 27.9%).

To examine the activity of the banking sector, we consider the behavior of private credit extended by commercial banks relative to GDP. As figure 8.3 shows, the evolution of banking sector activity is very similar to that of its size, with a sustained growth from 1974 to 1982, a reversal from 1982 to 1988, and a new increase from 1991. It is important to note that the reversal in the 1980s reflected, to a large degree, the correction of an unsustainable credit boom, as described in Gourinchas, Landerretche, and Valdés 1998. This alerts us to the fact that some changes, particularly short-lived ones, in these

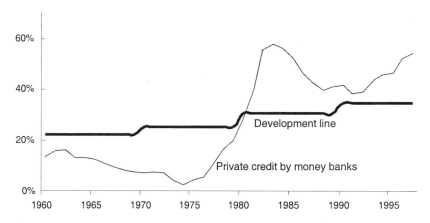

Figure 8.3
Bank activity.
Sources: Chapter 2 and Central Bank of Chile.

outcome indicators not always reflect financial development (or weakening).

In the 1990s, banking activity has experienced a moderate and steady growth, following the new regulatory framework of the late 1980s and accompanying the fast development of other financial sectors, mainly the stock and bond market.

Figure 8.3 also serves to compare banking sector activity in Chile with that of the world. The development line proposed by Demirgüç-Kunt and Levine (chapter 3) corresponds to the world average of banking activity. According to their criterion, a country's banking sector can be regarded as developed if its activity is above the development line.[8] In the case of Chile, the banking sector can be regarded as highly underdeveloped until the early 1980s; it then attains a developed status, which is maintained for the rest of the period, even at the depths of the 1980s banking crisis.

To assess the efficiency of the banking sector, we analyze the evolution of overhead costs and the sector's gross margins. We have data available for 1976–1982 (from De la Cuadra and Valdés-Prieto 1992) and for 1990–1997 (from chapter 2). Both overhead costs and gross margins of the banking sector fell notably in the late 1970s, that is, at the start of the liberalization process. In the 1990s, both indicators are relatively stable. This should not be taken to imply that the sector's efficiency has stagnated during the period. According to

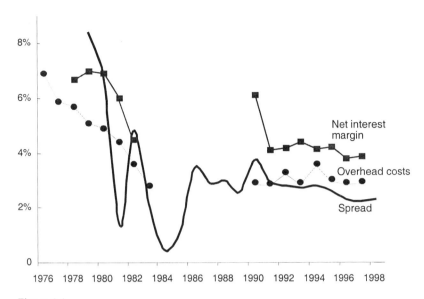

Figure 8.4
Bank efficiency
Source: Chapter 2 and De la Cuadra and Valdés-Prieto 1992.

Basch and Fuentes (1998), this stability is related to the higher degree of competition faced by banks in providing financing sources, which has led them to concentrate in alternative markets, such as personal banking or small to medium firms, which are associated with higher costs.

To complement the previous analysis (and to fill the gap for the 1980s), we also study the spreads on short-run (less than a year) banking lending and borrowing operations. As figure 8.4 shows, the behavior of banking spreads tell a similar story for the 1970s and 1990s to that of overhead costs and gross margins. The information provided by banking spreads in the early and mid-1980s should be taken with care. In particular, the sharp fall in banking spreads in 1984 reveals not a dramatic (and short-lived) improvement in efficiency but the workings of the policy of controlled and implicitly subsidized interest rates.

Stock Market
As customary, we assess the size of the stock market by its capitalization relative to GDP. Figure 8.2 shows that the size of the stock

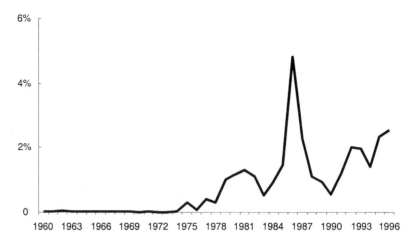

Figure 8.5
Primary equity emissions/GDP.
Sources: Valenzuela 1984 and Bolsa de Comercio de Santiago (various issues).

market grew gradually in the 1970s and 1980s and experienced a rapid expansion in the last decade, reaching 105 percent of GDP in 1995. Only in the 1990s the size of the stock market in Chile became larger than the world average (which was 18.5% in the 1970s, 28.4% in the 1980s, and 38.2% in the 1990s). Figure 8.5 presents the primary equity emissions relative to GDP over the period 1960–1997. It reveals that prior to 1974, the primary stock market was basically nonexistent. Since the mid-1970s, this measure of growth in stock market depth presents a rising trend with sporadic large expansions, mostly identified with episodes of privatization of public enterprises.

The remarkable expansion of stock market capitalization deserves further attention. The conventional measure of stock market capitalization combines stock price movements with changes in the quantity of stock shares. While both price and quantity increases indicate larger stock market depth, it can be argued that the expansion that most accurately reveals a larger availability of funds for firm investment is that related to the quantity of shares and listed companies. In figure 8.6, we report a stock market quantity index obtained by dividing the total value of the stock market by its corresponding price index. The quantity index shows a rising trend, which, however, is less pronounced than the growth rate of GDP. The conclusion that emerges from this analysis is that the strong expansion in stock market capitalization since the mid-1980s has been mostly driven by

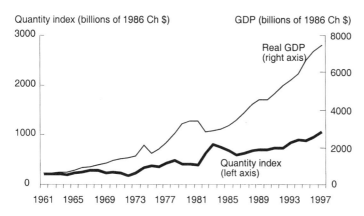

Figure 8.6
Stock market quantity index and GDP.
Source: Authors' calculations.

price effects. In fact, the behavior of the quantity of stock shares may put in question whether the growth of stock market capitalization can be identified with improved financial intermediation through stock markets. However, to the extent that stock price improvements are an incentive for firms to increase their assets through public equity offerings, the conventional measure of stock market capitalization remains relevant.

To measure the activity of the stock market, Demirgüç-Kunt and Levine (chapter 3) propose to use the stock traded value to GDP. The evolution of this variable in Chile is presented in figure 8.7. It shows a gradual increase in the 1970s and a rapid rise since 1985, which led the stock market activity to reach a peak of 17 percent of GDP in 1995. Despite this growth, using the criterion described in the section on the banking sector, the stock market in Chile would still be classified as underdeveloped. (The development line in figure 8.7, representing the world average, gives the threshold above which a country's stock market is classified as developed.)

However, as explained in the section on financial policies, starting in the 1990s it is possible for firms with good credit rating to issue shares abroad. This means that for this group of firms, the relevant stock market is not only Chile's but also that of developed countries, particularly the United States. For this reason, figure 8.7 also presents the total traded value, which is the sum of traded value in the Chilean stock market and abroad. Interestingly, the traded value of

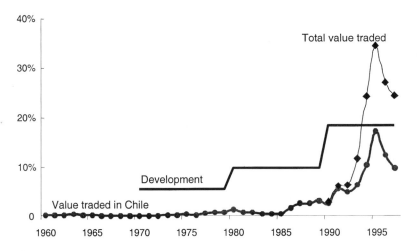

Figure 8.7
Stock market activity.
Sources: Valenzuela 1984 and chapter 2.

Chilean shares doubles when their activity in the U.S. stock markets is included (from 8.5% to 17.1% of GDP in the 1990s). However, given the large transaction costs involved in issuing share abroad, medium and small firms are in practice restricted to operate in the still relatively illiquid Chilean stock market (see Caballero 1999).

Demirgüç-Kunt and Levine (chapter 3) argue that both the stock market traded value to GDP and the turnover ratio provide information as to how efficient the stock market is. These, however, are incomplete proxies and we complement them with measures that directly address the transaction costs to participate in the stock market.[9]

Considering the turnover ratio as measure of efficiency, figure 8.8 shows the significant rise in the stock market efficiency during the 1990s, especially after 1992 when Chilean shares began to be traded offshore. Note that during the first liberalization stage (1974–1981), the turnover ratio did not rise with respect to its historical average, even though there was a significant increase in the stock market size during that period. Figure 8.8 presents the turnover ratio that includes the Chilean shares traded abroad. As in the case of the traded value to GDP, total turnover is also twice as big as that in the Santiago stock exchange. Still, total turnover remains below the world average for the 1990s.

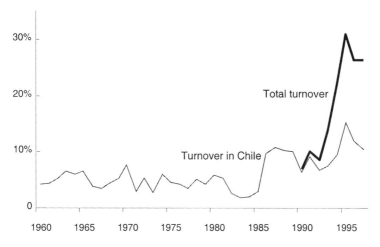

Figure 8.8
Stock market efficiency I: Turnover ratio.
Source: Valenzuela 1984 and chapter 2.

Given the incomplete information on efficiency provided by the turnover ratio, we present a complementary measure based on the costs to participate in the stock market. This is proxied by the ratio of stockbrokers' gross profit over assets. Considering that stockbrokers concentrate most of daily transactions, this measure proxies for the costs of trading in the stock market. According to this measure figure 8.9 also indicates improving market efficiency over the last decade.

Other Capital Markets

Among the other functioning financial sectors in Chile, we can cite (1) the pension fund management companies (PFMCs), (2) insurance companies, (3) mutual funds, (4) financial societies, and (5) the public and private bond market. We identify the main characteristics of the evolution of these sectors, with emphasis on its size and activity.

Pension Funds

As mentioned in section 8.2.1, in 1981 the pension system was transformed into a system of fully funded individual capitalization accounts, managed by the PFMCs. The fund administrators invest the pension savings in a series of instruments, ranging from domestic public debt to foreign bonds. These agents have mobilized a gradually increasing amount of financial resources, with a strong positive effect on the development of other financial sectors and activities.

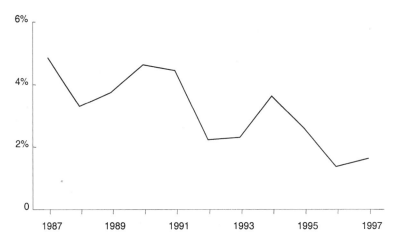

Figure 8.9
Stock market efficiency II: Stockbroker efficiency.
Source: Superintendencia de Valoresy Seguros (various issues).

Figure 8.10 shows the evolution of the PFMCs' pension assets together with their composition. The pension funds' assets have grown since their inception, reaching levels above 40 percent of GDP in the 1993–1998 period. Regarding the funds' composition by instrument, public bonds represent in average as much as 9 percent of GDP, which corresponds to about 40 percent of total public debt. Other important investment instruments used by the pension funds are mortgage bonds (4% of GDP or 60% of total mortgage bonds), corporate bonds (1.4% of GDP or 50% of total corporate bonds in Chile), and stock shares (6% of GDP in average or 10% of the total stock of shares).

It is interesting to note that the life insurance market benefited significantly from the development of the private pension funds. This occurred because of the requirement for the pension fund managers to purchase life insurance on behalf of all their contributors. Payments to insurance companies from the PFMCs averaged about 0.24 percent of GDP in 1988–1997, which represented revenues for the insurance companies of 10 percent of their assets.

Regarding the pension funds' efficiency, their average return has been very high, that is, 11 percent in average since 1981. However, the operational costs of the pension management companies have also been high in comparison with international standards, which may raise some doubts as to their efficiency.

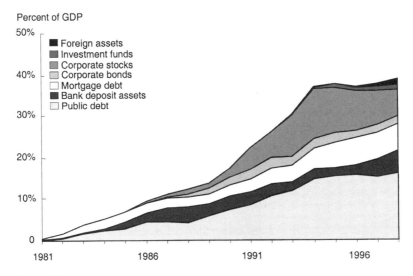

Figure 8.10
Pension funds development.
Source: Schmidt-Hebbel 1999.

Bond Market

The most active bond markets in Chile correspond to public bonds (mostly from the central bank), mortgage bonds, and corporate bonds. Figure 8.11 shows the evolution of each instrument since 1980. It can be seen that public bonds have a large jump in the early 1990s, partly due to the policy of sterilizing the large capital flows from abroad. The mortgage bonds show an important development since 1980, from an average of 1.4 percent of GDP in the previous two decades to about 6.7 percent of GDP in 1981–1997 (reaching 11% of GDP in 1997). Corporate bonds were first issued in 1975, grew slowly until the late 1980s, and increased more markedly in the 1990s. Thus, from a level of 0.2 percent of GDP in 1975–1980, corporate bond capitalization obtained an average of 2.5 percent of GDP in 1981–1997. Last, as a note of caution, we should mention that the presence of a large public bond sector is not necessarily correlated with a deeper or more active debt market for private firms.

Insurance Companies, Mutual Funds, and Financial Societies

The assets of insurance companies have grown from 0.7 percent of GDP in the late 1970s (Jeftanovic 1979) to 11 percent in 1997. This

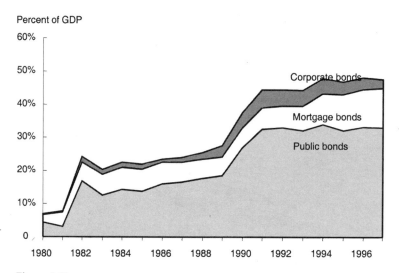

Figure 8.11
Bond market capitalization.
Sources: Superintendencia de Valoresy Seguros (various issues), Eyzaguirre and Lefort 1999, and CB Capitales.

asset growth was caused by an increase in both insurance penetration and density. Mutual funds have developed particularly since the early 1990s, reaching a level of 6 percent of GDP in 1997. Finally, financial societies flourished in the initial period of liberalization (until 1981) but suffered serious problems during the banking crisis. They have grown moderately during the 1990s but have yet to reach asset levels above 2 percent of GDP.[10]

8.2.3   Financial Structure: Bank-Based or Market-Based?

We now study whether the Chilean economy is based on banks or markets. To analyze this point, we use the approach and indicators developed by Demirgüç-Kunt and Levine (chapter 3). That is, we study the evolution of size, activity, and efficiency of the banking sector, relative to those of the stock and other capital markets. We should note that the financial indicators under consideration suffer from high volatility in annual (or higher) frequencies. This is exacerbated when we combine two or more of them. Given that we are interested in long-run trends, we work with financial structure ratios that have been smoothed by fitting a second-order polynomial.

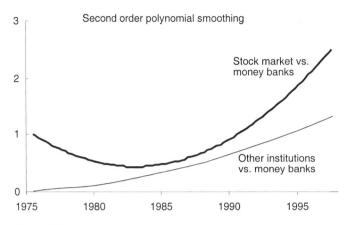

Figure 8.12
Financial structure: Size.

Relative Size

With regards to the relative size of the different sectors of the financial system, figure 8.12 shows two measures. The first compares banks and the stock market and the second, banks and other financial institutions—namely, financial societies, PFMCs, mutual funds, and insurance companies. The conclusion that emerges from this figure is that the liberalization process has been generally related to a shift in the financial structure of the economy, in a way such that the stock and other capital markets have gained importance relative to the banking sector. This trend started in the mid-1970s and has accelerated in the late 1980s and 1990s.

Relative Activity

As figure 8.13 shows, the activity of the stock and other capital markets relative to that of the banking sector has an increasing trend since the early 1970s, which mimics the trend in their relative size. These trends may be the result of an adjustment from an initial situation in which the nonbanking sector was too small for the level of development of the Chilean economy. In this sense, the change in the financial structure in Chile is analogous to a stock adjustment process: The economy accumulates the financial institutions of relative scarcity. Therefore, it is likely that the increasing trend in the relative importance of nonbanking institutions tapers off in the future.

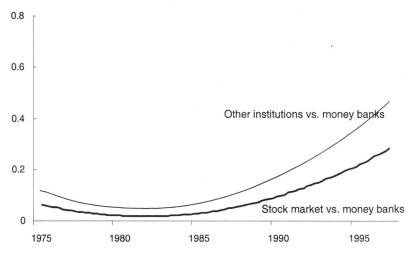

Figure 8.13
Financial structure: Activity.

Relative Efficiency

Finally, we examine two alternative indicators to study the efficiency of the stock market relative to the banking sector. The first indicator is the one proposed by Demirgüç-Kunt and Levine (chapter 3) that compares the stock market's turnover with the spreads on banking borrowing and lending operations. The second indicator is the ratio of banking spreads to stockbrokers' return on assets. A rise in both indicators represents an increase in the stock market's efficiency relative to the banks'. The evolution of these indicators is presented in figure 8.14. The results for both indicators are very similar and show that the stock market has been gaining in efficiency relative to the banking sector since the mid-1980s. This result confirms the increasing relative importance of the nonbanking sector that we see when we use size and activity as the comparison criteria.

8.3   Microeconomic Evidence

In this section, we study the access to financial markets, the balance-sheet composition, and the growth performance in a sample of Chilean firms. The emphasis of the empirical exercises presented here is on how financial developments at the macroeconomic level have affected the performance and financial structure of firms.

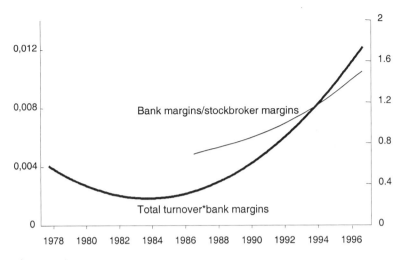

Figure 8.14
Financial structure: Efficiency.

Sample and Data

Our sample consists of seventy-nine firms that are quoted at the stock market and for which annual balance-sheet data for the period 1985–1995 are available and complete. We focus on the period from 1985–1995 because, first, it corresponds to before and after the second wave of financial liberalization in Chile; second, it is the period of significant stock market expansion; and, third, it is the period for which reliable data are accessible. Table 8.1 presents descriptive statistics for the four dependent variables examined below. This is done for the whole period as well as for the subperiods 1986–1990 and 1991–1995. As argued in the section on macro developments, the latter period is characterized by a further liberalization of domestic financial markets and an opening to international capital.

Balance-sheet data are obtained from Ficha Estadística Codificada Uniforme (FECU), which is a mandatory report submitted by corporations to the corresponding government supervisory board. The FECUs contain firms' balance sheet data on a comparable basis for the 1985–1995 period. Market value data are obtained from Reseña de la Bolsa de Comercio de Santiago (RCBS), which is the annual report of the Santiago Stock Exchange. Finally, macrofinancial data are obtained from chapter 2 and extended using the Chilean national sources cited in section 8.2. For further details on data sources and definitions, see appendix 8.1.

Table 8.1
Descriptive Statistics

Variable	Sample	Mean	Standard deviation	Minimum	Maximum
Investment/	Full-sample	0.133	0.231	−0.888	2.297
capital stock	1986–1990	0.140	0.239	−0.718	2.297
	1991–1995	0.126	0.222	−0.888	2.012
	AFP-grade	0.148	0.212	−0.616	2.297
Total debt/	Full-sample	0.576	1.170	0.000	17.851
equity					
	1986–1990	0.720	1.564	0.000	17.851
	1991–1995	0.433	0.505	0.000	3.905
Long-term/	Full-sample	1.480	4.228	0.000	65.037
short-term debt	1986–1990	1.778	5.636	0.000	65.037
	1991–1995	1.151	1.927	0.000	21.686
Sales growth	Full-sample	0.054	0.371	−2.693	4.749
	1986–1990	0.09	0.406	−2.652	4.749
	1991–1995	0.018	0.329	−2.693	1.592

Econometric Methodology

All relationships studied and estimated in this chapter are characterized by the joint endogeneity of most variables involved. That is, most explanatory variables in our models either are simultaneously determined with the dependent variable or have a two-way causality relationship with it. Thus, for example, in our investment regressions, it is likely that investment and cash flow be simultaneously determined or that investment may feed back into the firm's q-value. The joint endogeneity of the explanatory variables calls for an instrumental variable procedure to obtain consistent estimates of the coefficients of interest. Taking advantage of the panel structure of our dataset, we apply a GMM estimator based on the use of lagged observations of the explanatory variables as instruments. These are appropriate instruments under the following conditions. First, the error term must be serially uncorrelated or, at least, follow a moving average process of finite order. Second, future *innovations* of the dependent variable must not affect current values of the explanatory variables, although they can be affected by current and past realizations of the dependent variable (this being the sense in which they are jointly endogenous).

The validity of these assumptions can be examined statistically. For this purpose we use two specification tests. The first is a Sargan test of overidentifying restrictions, which examines the overall validity of the moment conditions comparing them with their sample analogs. The second is a test of serial correlation of the regression residuals. Lack of serial correlation indicates that all lagged values of the explanatory variables can be used as instruments. Serial correlation of a given order means that the residual follows a moving average process of the same order, which in turn indicates that only observations lagged more than this order are appropriate instruments.

The second issue we must address in the process of estimation is the potential presence of unobserved firm-specific effects. Ignoring them may produce inconsistent estimates given that firm-specific effects are likely to be correlated with the explanatory variables. An indication that unobserved firm-specific effects are present in a regression model is a persistent serial correlation of the residuals. When we find evidence of this type of misspecification in the regression in levels, we control for unobserved firm-specific effects following the procedure developed by Arellano and Bond (1991) and Arellano and Bover (1995). This procedure consists of combining in a system the regression expressed in levels with the regression expressed in first differences, each of them properly instrumented. The instruments for the regression in differences (which no longer contain the firm-specific effect) are the lagged levels of the explanatory variables. For the regression in levels, the instruments are the lagged differences of the explanatory variables. These are appropriate instruments under the assumption that the correlation between the explanatory variables and the firm-specific effect is constant over time. This procedure is called the *GMM system estimator*. (For a concise presentation of this methodology, see Levine, Loayza, and Beck 2000; for a survey of applications to firm investment regressions, see Mairesse, Hall, and Mulkay 1999.)

The specification tests for the *system* estimator are similar to those introduced above. The first is a Sargan test of overidentifying restrictions, and the second is a test of lack of residual serial correlation. Since in this case the residuals examined are those of the regression in differences, first-order serial correlation is expected by construction and, thus, only second- and higher-order serial correlation is a sign of misspecification.

8.3.1 Firm Investment and Financing Constraints

The first issue we study concerns the firms' access to financial markets for investment purposes. In particular, we would like to test whether, as result of the financial development experienced in the 1990s, firms are less dependent on their internal resources and balance-sheet composition and more responsive to their Tobin's q-value.

The basic regression model we estimate is as follows:

$$Inv_{i,t} = \beta_0 + \beta_1 q_{i,t} + \beta_2 Cash_{i,t-1} + \beta_3 D/K_{i,t} + \varepsilon_{i,t}, \tag{8.1}$$

where, Inv_t is the flow of annual investment as a ratio to the capital stock at the beginning of the year, q_t is the market value of the firm over its replacement value measured at the beginning of the year, $Cash_{t-1}$ is the ratio of cash flow of the previous year to the capital stock at the beginning of the year, D/K_t is the ratio of total debt to the capital stock measured at the beginning of the year, ε_t is the regression residual, and the subscript i is an index for firms. The measure of the firm's q-value is adjusted for its degree of leverage and for tax effects on the present value of adjustment costs.[11] All variables are treated as weakly endogenous, in the sense that they can be correlated with current and past realizations of the residual but are required to be uncorrelated with its future realizations. We ignore unobserved firm-specific effects because, as we discuss below, there is no persistent residual serial correlation in the levels regression.

According to the q theory of investment, in the absence of financial restrictions and corporate agency problems, firm investment depends exclusively on the value of the firm relative to its replacement value (adjusting for tax effects on capital adjustment costs).[12] However, to the extent that the firm faces constraints on external financing, its investment will be determined by its internal resources, namely, retained cash earnings. Furthermore, in the face of imperfect financial markets, the degree of leverage of the firm (here represented by its debt-to-capital ratio) may deter the availability of external financing even after controlling for Tobin's q. Therefore, we consider that a firm faces a better functioning financial system when, first, its investment is more responsive to changes in q; second, investment is less determined by the firm's *cash flow*; and, third, investment is less negatively affected by the firm's liability composition, represented by the debt-to-capital ratio.

The first empirical exercise is a comparison between all firms in the sample and two subgroups of firms that are expected to have better access to financial markets. These are, first, the group of firms in whose shares the private pension fund management companies are allowed to invest (PFMC investment grade, for short), and, second, the group of firms that are members of corporate conglomerates (see Medina and Valdés 1998). We compare the coefficients obtained for different sample groups through multiplicative dummies applied to the three variables of interest. The estimation results are presented in table 8.2. Column (1) presents estimates applied to all firms in the sample. Column (2) compares PFMC-grade firms with the rest, while column (3) compares firms belonging to conglomerate members with other firms. We focus on the GMM estimator applied to the regression in levels because it controls for the joint endogeneity of the explanatory variables and is supported by the Sargan and serial correlation specification test.[13]

The estimation results for the sample of all firms reveal that investment does not significantly depend on the firm's q-value but is driven positively by the firm's cash flow and negatively by its level of indebtedness. According to the interpretation of investment theory provided above, we can conclude that firms in the whole sample face important constraints on external finance. This conclusion, however, does not apply equally to all firms. In fact, the comparison between all firms and PFMC-grade firms indicates that investment in the latter type is significantly more responsive to changes in q and less dependent on cash flow. However, there appears to be no significant difference regarding the investment response to the debt-to-capital ratio. The results on q and cash flow are to be expected given that PFMC-grade firms are usually larger, better established, and able to enjoy the signaling derived from their investment-grade accreditation; thus, they are likely to face a more receptive financial environment than the average firm. The comparison regarding members of conglomerates indicates that they are different with respect to the rest in that their investment rate is significantly less dependent on their debt-to-capital ratio. Judging from the sign of the multiplicative dummies on q and cash flow, members of conglomerates are also more responsive to changes in the q-value of the firm and less restricted by internal resources, although these results do not have strong statistical significance.

Table 8.2
Firm Investment and Financing Constraints: Effects by Types of Firms (t-statistics are presented below their corresponding coefficients)

Estimation technique	All firms GMM-level	All vs. PFMC GMM-level	All vs. conglomerate GMM-level
Instruments	Levels (1)	Levels (2)	Levels (3)
Constant	0.071291	0.080757	0.081635
	6.777601	10.899700	11.955756
q	−0.000359	−0.013630	0.009672
	−0.034648	−2.506736	1.364845
$q \times$ PFMC grade		0.088146	
		8.089278	
$q \times$ conglomerate member			0.009672
			1.364845
Initial cash flow/capital stock	0.368475	0.423410	0.373514
	10.344349	27.603268	14.504739
Initial cash flow/capital stock × PFMC grade		−0.214116	
		−8.792866	
Initial cash flow/capital stock × conglomerate member			−0.070924
			−1.465789
Initial debt/capital stock	−0.024829	−0.038331	−0.046514
	−2.550134	−7.674725	−6.282047
Initial debt/capital stock × PFMC grade		0.008855	
		0.981647	
Initial debt/capital stock × conglomerate member			0.038950
			2.713593
Number of firms	79	79	79
Number of observations	790	790	790
Specification tests (p-values)			
(a) Sargan test	0.419	0.488	0.200
(b) Serial correlation			
First-order	0.001	0.000	0.001
Second-order	0.756	0.869	0.775
Third-order	0.842	0.815	0.794

Note: Dependent variable: investment/capital stock.

The second empirical exercise on the investment regression model consists of comparing the response coefficients in the 1990s with those of the 1980s. This exercise is central to our chapter because the 1990s is a period of significantly higher financial development than any time before (see figure 8.2). The relaxation of financial constraints for firms in the 1990s would be a strong indication of beneficial microeconomic effects from macroeconomic financial developments. Table 8.3 presents the results of comparing the 1990s with the 1980s through multiplicative dummies on the explanatory variables. We do this exercise for the samples of all, PFMC-grade, and conglomerate-member firms, respectively. In the three cases, the GMM estimator in levels is supported by the specification tests, and, thus, we base our conclusions on its results. From table 8.3, we can directly draw inferences regarding the coefficient for the 1980s and the *changes* from the 1980s to the 1990s (these are the coefficients on, respectively, a given variable and its multiplicative dummy; e.g., q and $q * D90$). Indirectly, we can also draw inferences on the total magnitude of the coefficients in the 1990s (given by the sum of the coefficients on a given variable and its multiplicative dummy; e.g., $q + q * D90$). We do statistical tests on the coefficients corresponding to the 1990s using information on the variance-covariance of all estimated coefficients.[14] The conclusions given below refer to both cases, namely, coefficient changes and total magnitudes in the 1990s.

The results on the three samples are similar in that they indicate that in the 1990s firm investment has been less financially constrained than in the 1980s. This conclusion is most strongly based on the PFMC-grade and conglomerate member sample results.[15] For those groups of firms, investment in the latter period has been less financially constrained in the three dimensions under consideration. That is, firm investment in the 1990s is positively driven by changes in Tobin's q, is not tied to internal cash flow, and is not affected by the debt-to-capital ratio. For the sample of all firms, the importance of internal resources and degree of leverage for investment decisions appear to have diminished in the 1990s; however, cash flow is still a relevant variable in their investment equation, while their q-value remains not significant.

The last empirical exercise for the investment model consists of adding some macrofinancial indicators to the regression that already considers the 1990s effect. The results are presented in table 8.4. Column (1) considers the effect of financial size variables, namely,

Table 8.3
Firm Investment and Financing Constraints: The 1990s Effect (t-statistics are presented below their corresponding coefficients)

Estimation technique	All GMM-level	PFMC grade GMM-level	Conglomerate member GMM-level
Instruments	Levels (1)	Levels (2)	Levels (3)
Constant	0.069920	0.077850	0.113306
	6.443411	5.469183	8.338725
q	−0.007274	0.049745	0.000217
	−0.530558	1.263372	0.008294
$q \times D90$	0.014713	0.051493	0.079865
	1.289299	1.312342	3.229927
Initial cash flow/capital stock	0.444121	0.447417	0.465798
	10.698994	8.754703	4.002885
Initial cash flow/capital stock $\times D90$	−0.178301	−0.463293	−0.454980
	−3.644851	−8.600985	−4.065013
Initial debt/capital stock	−0.034442	−0.067566	−0.073412
	−2.561269	−4.615293	−3.105916
Initial debt/capital stock $\times$ D90	0.021459	0.083327	0.048390
	0.963382	3.704538	1.355583
Number of firms	79	40	36
Number of observations	790	400	360
Total effects in the 1990s q90	0.007439	0.101238	0.080082
	0.510579	2.852857	2.646388
Initial cash flow/capital stock 90	0.265820	−0.015876	0.010818
	3.592555	0.088743	0.812184
Initial debt/capital stock 90	−0.012983	0.015761	−0.025022
	−0.097937	0.019153	−0.273819
Specification tests (p-values) (a) Sargan test	0.548	0.652	0.478
(b) Serial correlation First-order	0.001	0.001	0.022
Second-order	0.768	0.839	0.233
Third-order	0.763	0.256	0.495

Note: Dependent variable: investment/capital stock.

Table 8.4
Firm Investment and Financing Constraints: Macrofinancial Effects (t-statistics are presented below their corresponding coefficients)

Estimation technique	GMM-level	GMM-level
Instruments	Levels	Levels
	(1)	(2)
Constant	0.058535	0.056130
	0.900371	0.746495
q	−0.008036	−0.006055
	−0.613052	−0.464803
$q \times$ D90	0.016224	0.015266
	1.480736	1.343898
Initial cash flow/capital stock	0.455392	0.449664
	10.468945	10.440822
Initial cash flow/capital stock $\times$ D90	−0.184366	−0.181217
	−3.631141	−3.535226
Initial debt/capital stock	−0.030981	−0.033259
	−2.284139	−2.433325
Initial debt/capital stock $\times$ D90	0.007942	0.014379
	0.420875	0.693153
Bank assets/GDP	−0.004290	
	−0.031807	
Stock market capitalization/GDP	0.026322	
	1.079529	
Private credit by banks/GDP		0.022485
		0.121902
Stock market traded value/GDP		0.089983
		0.591962
Number of firms	79	79
Number of observations	790	790
Specification tests (p-values)		
(a) Sargan test	0.508	0.539
(b) Serial correlation		
First-order	0.001	0.001
Second-order	0.786	0.773
Third-order	0.768	0.762

Note: Dependent variable: investment/capital stock.

the ratio of bank assets to GDP and stock market capitalization relative to GDP. Column (2) considers measures of financial activity, that is, the ratio of private credit to GDP and the stock market traded value relative to GDP. The conclusion from this exercise is that these macro financial variables do not have an independent effect on investment once the q-value of the firm and the 1990s effect are accounted for. In other words, the effect on firm investment from macro financial development appears to work through microeconomic channels, that is, by making investment more responsive to the firm's q-value and less constrained on the use of external finance.

8.3.2 Firm Financial Structure

The second issue we study concerns the balance-sheet, financial situation of the firms. Specifically, we would like to examine whether the financial liberalization of the 1990s and the development of the banking, stock and bond markets over the last decade have affected the importance of debt relative to equity and long-term debt relative to short-term debt in the balance sheet of firms.

The basic regression model for each dependent variable is the following:

$$D/E_{i,t} = \beta_0 + \beta_1 \ln(K_{i,t}) + \beta_2 FA/TA_{i,t} + \beta_3 P/TA_{i,t}$$
$$+ \beta_4 IntEq_{i,t} + \beta_5 MFin_t + \eta_i + \varepsilon_{i,t} \tag{8.2}$$

$$LD/SD_{i,t} = \gamma_0 + \gamma_1 \ln(K_{i,t}) + \gamma_2 FA/TA_{i,t} + \gamma_3 P/TA_{i,t}$$
$$+ \gamma_4 IntEq_{i,t} + \gamma_5 MFin_t + \mu_i + \upsilon_{i,t} \tag{8.3}$$

The dependent variables, D/E and LD/SD, are the debt-to-equity ratio and the ratio of long-term to short-term debt, respectively. K represents the capital stock, which proxies for the firm's size. FA/TA represents the ratio of fixed to total assets, which is a measure of the tangibility of total assets. P/TA is the ratio of operational profits to total assets and proxies for the firm's current profitability. $IntEq$ is a dummy variable for whether the firm has been able to place its stock shares in international equity markets. $MFin$ is a vector of variables representing macro financial outcomes. All stock variables are measured at the end of the corresponding year. The regression residuals are represented by ε and υ, respectively. All explanatory variables are treated as weakly endogenous, except the macro financial variables, which are exogenous. Finally, η and μ are unobserved firm-specific effects. We consider firm-specific effects in the financial structure regression equations because the regression in levels exhibits highly persistent serial correlation, which leads us to reject the GMM levels estimator in favor of its GMM *system* counterpart. The Sargan and serial correlation tests support the model estimated with the GMM *system* procedure.

The firm-related explanatory variables are chosen in accordance with standard corporate finance theory (for recent similar applications, see Lee, Lee, and Lee 1999; Schmukler and Vesperoni 2000). In contrast to the investment regression model, for financial structure there is no clear way in which macro financial development affects the coefficients on the firm-specific variables. Therefore, our previous strategy based on analyzing slope changes is not applicable to the financial structure regressions. Instead, we directly include our measures of macro financial development in the regression model and analyze their estimated coefficients. Note that since these variables do not change across firms, they are analogous to time-specific effects.

Table 8.5 reports the results on the debt-to-equity ratio, and table 8.6, on the ratio of long-term to short-term debt. Column (1) of each table reports the results obtained with the GMM-level estimator.[16] Since the specification tests reject it, we focus on the results obtained with the GMM-*system* estimator, which are presented in the next columns of each table. Column (3) does not consider macrofinancial variables, while columns (4) and (5) consider measures of size and activity of the corresponding capital markets.

Regarding the debt-to-equity ratio (table 8.5), a rise in the firm's size and, less robustly, an increase in its assets' tangibility appear to shift the financial structure of the firm toward higher equity and lower debt. Somewhat paradoxically, the firm's access to international equity markets appears to increase the debt-to-equity ratio of the firm.[17] It is likely that the ability to issue ADRs has a positive signaling effect on the firm's creditworthiness. This effect might decrease the costs of indebtedness sufficiently to overcome the direct equity-promoting effect of issuing ADRs.

The effects of the measures of macrofinancial size and activity on the debt-to-equity ratio are similar and in agreement with our priors. Larger size and activity of the banking sector lead firms to prefer

Table 8.5
Financial Structure—Ratio of Debt to Equity: Firm and Macrofinancial Effects (t-statistics are presented below their corresponding coefficients)

Estimation technique Instruments	GMM- levels Levels (1)	GMM- system Levels and diff. (2)	GMM- system Levels and diff. (3)	GMM- system Levels and diff. (4)
Constant	1.252191	2.741988	1.403612	2.595548
	1.609277	8.891821	4.848698	9.168479
ln (capital stock)	−0.056868	−0.138326	−0.114914	−0.192560
	−1.325128	−8.366062	−7.018878	−10.381302
Fixed assets/total assets	−0.025426	0.099073	−0.217105	−0.477531
	−0.113333	0.867485	−2.013139	−3.690840
Profits/total assets	0.652228	−0.399482	−0.012718	0.171888
	2.173082	−2.693729	−0.068977	0.951840
Access to international	0.209673	0.191641	0.185700	0.218406
equity markets	1.468839	2.031269	2.146591	1.714409
Bank assets/GDP			2.455970	
			9.891957	
Stock market			−0.086684	
capitalization/GDP			−2.571706	
Private credit by				3.016378
banks/GDP				13.330112
Stock market traded				−0.527869
value/GDP				−3.983729
Number of firms	71	71	71	71
Number of observations	710	710	710	710
Specification tests (p-values)				
(a) Sargan test	0.367	0.381	0.298	0.242
(b) Serial correlation				
First-order	0.009	0.308	0.301	0.297
Second-order	0.009	0.442	0.381	0.370
Third-order	0.006	0.266	0.257	0.255

Note: Dependent variable: ratio of debt to equity.

debt over equity in their balance sheets. Conversely, larger size and activity of the stock market induce firms to expand equity relative to debt.

Regarding the ratio of long-term to short-term debt (table 8.6), asset profitability of the firm and the tangibility of its assets are positively and significantly associated with a longer maturity of the firm's debt. On the other hand, as firms get larger, their debt maturity becomes shorter. The access to international equity markets seems to lead to a larger share of long-term debt, possibly through the signaling mechanisms mentioned earlier.

As to the effect of the macro financial variables, we find that the total size of bank assets and the level of activity of private banking are not significantly related to a longer maturity of firms' debt. To study the effect of capital markets on debt maturity, we use the size and activity of the bond market (instead of the stock market, which is most relevant for questions on equity ratios, as in the previous model). The size and activity of the total (public plus private) bond market, measured by its capitalization relative to GDP, is negatively related to the long-term to short-term debt ratio. However, when we focus only on the capitalization of the *private* bond market—arguably more directly related to the firms' financing choices than the public bond market—its effect on debt maturity changes sign (column 5). That is, the size of the private bond market induces firms to have a debt structure of longer maturity.

8.3.3 Firm Growth

The third issue we would like to study concerns the growth rate of the firm, measured by the proportional increase in the firm's operational revenue. We would like to study the extent to which firm-specific and macrofinancial market developments have had an impact on the growth rate of our sample of firms.

The specification of the growth regression has been motivated by corporate finance theory and also by analogy with the macro-growth literature. As in the previous models, it considers both firm-specific and macro variables. The basic firm growth regression is the following:

$$RGr_{i,t} = \beta_0 + \beta_1 Ro_{i,t} + \beta_2 I/R_{i,t} + \beta_3 Fin_i + \beta_4 NoP_i + \beta_5 D/E_{i,t}$$

$$+ \beta_6 GDPgr_t + \beta_7 MFin_t + \varepsilon_{i,t}, \tag{8.4}$$

Table 8.6
Financial Structure—Ratio of Long-Term to Short-Term Debt: Firm and Macrofinancial Effects (t-statistics are presented below their corresponding coefficients)

Estimation technique	GMM-levels	GMM-system	GMM-system	GMM-system	GMM-system
Instruments	Levels and diff. (1)	Levels and diff. (2)	Levels and diff. (3)	Levels and diff. (4)	Levels and diff. (5)
Constant	4.026744 2.756485	1.532385 1.426523	1.652367 1.394299	1.438177 1.099103	3.192477 2.463129
ln (capital stock)	-0.1639 -2.096303	-0.108112 -1.866332	-0.056440 -0.972994	-0.077509 -0.995396	-0.201357 -2.954878
Fixed assets/total assets	-0.461493 -0.833909	2.447923 4.520499	1.335821 2.447119	1.980901 3.345182	1.865745 3.639951
Profits/total assets	-3.602144 -3.13399	3.75885 3.736814	2.012747 2.818181	2.533926 2.354454	2.747668 2.322228
Access to international equity markets	0.750394 1.284955	0.665636 2.267406	0.70412 3.209567	0.615889 2.166721	0.724933 2.400832
Bank assets/GDP			0.428348 0.731893		
Bond capitalization/GDP			-1.743874 -5.564671		
Private credit by banks/GDP				0.742750 1.218402	0.016659 0.022159
Bond market traded value/GDP				-3.400357 -2.416364	
Private bond market capitalization/GDP					1.122315 2.222603

Number of firms	71	71	71	71	71
Number of observations	710	710	710	710	710
Specification tests (p-values)					
(a) Sargan test	0.717	0.305	0.466	0.616	0.549
(b) Serial correlation					
First-order	0.054	0.152	0.154	0.153	0.154
Second-order	0.028	0.372	0.369	0.369	0.371
Third-order	0.114	0.276	0.274	0.275	0.276

Note: Dependent variable: ratio of long-term to short-term debt.

where RGr is the annual growth rate of the firm's revenues. Ro is the initial (lagged) level of revenues and is included to capture convergence effects to the firm's steady-state size. I/R is firm's investment as ratio to revenues. Fin and NoP are dummy variables for whether the firm is, respectively, a financial or a nonprofit firm; they are included to account for a potentially different growth behavior in these types of firms. D/E is the initial debt-to-equity ratio and serves to control for principal/agent effects on firm growth. $GDPgr$ is the annual growth rate of GDP and is included to account for both the business cycle and overall market expansion. $MFin$ is a vector of variables representing macrofinancial outcomes. The regression residual is represented by ε.

All explanatory variables are treated as weakly endogenous, except the macro variables, which are exogenous. We ignore unobserved firm-specific effects in the growth regression because, as we discuss below, there is no indication of persistent residual serial correlation in the regression in levels. In fact, the error term appears to be serially uncorrelated. Thus, we focus on the results obtained with the GMM estimator applied to the regression in levels. This choice is supported by the Sargan and serial-correlation specification tests.

Table 8.7 presents the results on firm's growth. The significantly negative sign of the firm's initial size reveals a convergence effect; that is, as the firm gets larger, its rate of growth slows down, ceteris paribus. Not surprisingly, the investment rate has a positive effect on the growth of firm's revenues. Financial firms do not appear to grow differently from the rest, while nonprofit firms have a poorer growth performance even accounting for the investment rate. The debt-to-equity ratio does not significantly affect firm's growth; this may suggest that if principal/agent considerations affect the growth of the firm, they would do it through the investment rate. Last, for the control variables, the GDP growth rate has a positive and significant effect on the growth rate of the firm.

Regarding the macro financial variables, the size and activity of the banking sector seem to have a positive impact on the growth rate of the firms. However, the size and activity of the stock market have a surprisingly negative effect on growth. A casual interpretation of this result would say that the development of the banking sector is more relevant than that of the stock market for the growth of the firm. However, when we use measures of stock market size that

Table 8.7
Firm Growth: Firm and Macrofinancial Effects (t-statistics are presented below their corresponding coefficients)

Estimation technique	GMM-level	GMM-level	GMM-level	GMM-level
Instruments	Levels	Levels	Levels	Levels
	(1)	(2)	(3)	(4)
Constant	0.227425	−0.172640	−0.417794	−0.447618
	2.419091	−2.091356	−5.103201	−5.258059
Initial real level of revenues	−0.012301	−0.009113	−0.011038	−0.009752
	−2.438299	−1.737221	−2.212130	−1.942987
Investment/revenues	0.004752	0.005325	0.005379	0.005357
	6.652456	6.070022	6.880249	6.420178
Financial firm	0.192124	0.223286	0.553800	0.040144
	0.245742	0.258534	0.068559	0.048545
Nonprofit firm	−0.098665	−0.080107	−0.088623	−0.083793
	−2.429645	−1.846098	−2.127454	−2.022815
Total debt/total equity	0.013719	0.014280	0.015554	0.013406
	1.144243	1.199563	1.362413	1.150187
GDP growth	0.465176	1.312682	1.592927	1.480796
	1.908803	4.913631	5.806864	5.396786
Banks assets/GDP		0.738795		0.719868
		4.960857		5.300129
Stock market capitalization/ GDP		−0.094898		
		−4.895802		
Private credit by banks/ GDP			1.410610	
			9.268829	
Stock market traded value/ GDP			−1.051936	
			−6.906845	
Real stock market capitalization/GDP				1.096829
				4.645536
Number of firms	66	66	66	66
Number of observations	660	660	660	660
Specification tests (p-values)				
(a) Sargan test	0.133	0.439	0.555	0.369
(b) Serial correlation				
First-order	0.539	0.653	0.567	0.624
Second-order	0.614	0.817	0.699	0.839
Third-order	0.239	0.245	0.240	0.248

Note: Dependent variable: revenue growth.

abstract from price effects (see column 5), the estimation results
indicate that quantity measures of stock market capitalization have a
positive and significant effect on firms' growth rate. We conduct two
additional exercises (not shown in the table) which render similar
results. First, when we use a quantity measure of traded value to
GDP as measure of market activity, we estimate a positive effect on
firms' growth rate. Second, we also obtain a positive and significant
coefficient on market activity when we use the turnover ratio as
alternative measure of stock market activity. Given that the turnover
ratio also abstracts from price effects, the conclusion from the additional exercises is that the real expansion of the stock market in terms
of shares and listed companies affects favorably the firm's growth
rate. On the other hand the price component of stock market capitalization and activity appears to be negatively correlated with the
growth rate of the firm.

8.4 Conclusion

In the last fifteen years Chile has experienced a remarkable development in its financial system. In our view, this is the happy outcome
of the union between the market-oriented policies started in the
mid-1970s and the proper regulatory framework implemented in the
1980s.

From the analysis of the size, activity, and efficiency of the different financial sectors and markets, we reach two basic conclusions:

• The banking sector experienced a significant development, quick
but with reversals in the 1970s and most of the 1980s and gradual in
the 1990s. In fact, the banking sector in Chile surpassed the world
average in the 1980s and has not fallen below it since then. The
stock and other capital markets also experienced improvement,
moderate in the 1980s and remarkable in the 1990s. Despite this improvement, the stock market in Chile has not yet reached the world
average.

• The composition (structure) of the financial system in Chile also
experienced a noteworthy change. The shift in the financial structure
of the economy has occurred in a way such that the stock and other
capital markets have gained importance relative to the banking sector. This trend started in the 1970s and has accelerated in the late

1980s and 1990s. The shift in financial structure may be the result of an adjustment from an initial situation in which the nonbanking sector was too small for the level of development of the Chilean economy. In this sense, the change in the financial structure in Chile is analogous to a stock-adjustment process; the economy accumulates the financial institutions of relative scarcity. Therefore, it is likely that the increasing relative importance of nonbanking institutions tapers off in the future.

The second objective of this chapter is to examine how these developments in the Chilean financial system have affected the performance and behavior of firms. Specifically, the paper analyzes for a sample of Chilean firms their access to financial markets for investment purposes, their financing (balance-sheet) decisions and corresponding financial structure, and their growth performance. We work with a sample of seventy-nine firms that are quoted in the stock market and for which annual balance-sheet data for the period 1985–1995 are available and complete. We now summarize the main conclusions of the analytical section of the chapter, noting the caveat presented in the introduction regarding the applicability of the results to the Chilean economy in general.

• In the second half of the 1980s—that is prior to the second wave of financial liberalization, firm investment did not significantly depend on the firm's q-value but was driven positively by the firm's cash flow and negatively by its level of indebtedness. We can conclude that firms in this period faced important constraints on external finance.

• In the 1990s, the period of largest financial development at the macro level, firm investment has been less financially constrained than in the 1980s. That is, in the 1990s firm investment has been more responsive to changes in Tobin's q, less tied to internal cash flow, and less affected by the debt-to-capital ratio. These results are larger and more significant in the cases of investment-grade firms and firm belonging to corporate conglomerates. Of the three indications of better access to financial markets, those related to the effects of q-value and cash flow are the strongest and most robust across samples.

• Regarding the effect of macro financial variables on the financial structure of the firms in the sample, we conclude that, first, a larger size and activity of the banking sector lead firms to prefer debt over equity, while not affecting the maturity of their debt obligations. Second, a larger size and activity of the stock market induce firms to expand equity relative to debt. And, third, a larger size of the *private* bond market induces firms to increase the maturity of their debt obligations. The public bond market, however, appears to have the opposite effect.

• The firm's access to international equity markets appears to increase the debt-to-equity ratio of the firm and to enlarge the maturity of its debt. The first result may seem rather puzzling. It can be explained, however, considering that the ability to issue ADRs reflects low credit risk and/or has a positive signaling effect on the firm's overall creditworthiness. This effect might decrease the costs of indebtedness sufficiently to overcome the direct equity-promoting effect of issuing ADRs.

• Regarding the effect of macrofinancial variables on the firm's revenue growth, the size and activity of the banking sector seem to have a positive impact on the growth rate of the firm. On the other hand, the size and activity of the stock market have a surprisingly negative effect on growth. However, this result changes when the measure of stock market capitalization includes only quantity effects. In fact, an expansion of the real size and activity of the stock market appears to lead to higher firm growth.

Appendix 8.1:   Data Sources and Definitions

Balance-sheet data are taken from FECUs (acronyms for Ficha Estadística Codificada Uniforme). The FECUs are available at the Superintendencia de Sociedades Anónimas and contain the full firm's balance sheet in a comparable base for the 1985–1995 period. The submission of the information collected in FECUs is legally mandated for the corporations (Sociedades Anónimas.) The variables constructed using this source are

Debt to equity ratio
Sales growth rate
Profits to total assets ratio
Long term to short term debt ratio
Fixed assets to total assets ratio

Data on the market value of the firm's equity is obtained from Bolsa de Comercio de Santiago (various issues). This publication summarizes the annual activity of the Santiago stock market.

The raw FECUs data is used to construct the following variables.[18]

Variable	Description	Variable	Description
Investment	$\dfrac{I_t}{K_{t-1}}$	Tobin's q	$(1-t) \times \left(\dfrac{D_{t-1} + \dfrac{MV_{t-1}}{(1-d+t)}}{K_{t-1}} \right)$
Cash flow	$\dfrac{CF_{t-1}}{K_{t-1}}$	Debt to capital	$\dfrac{D_{t-1}}{K_{t-1}}$
Initial level of real sales	$S_{t-1} \times \dfrac{P_{90}}{P_{t-1}}$		

Where

$K_t = A_t - STA_t$

$CF_t = OP_t + \delta_t$

$I_t = K_t + \delta_t - K_{t-1} \times \pi_t$

D = Total debt

MV = Market value of the firm equity

t = Tax on firm profits

π = Annual inflation (December to December)

d = Tax on dividends

A = Total assets

STA = Short-term assets

OP = Operational profits

δ = Depreciation

S = Sales level

P = Price level.

With respect to some firm's characteristics, we use the dummy variables defined below.

Variable	Description
PFMC grade	Firm is eligible for investment by Pension Funds Management Companies
Conglomerate	Firm is part of an economic conglomerate of firms
Nonprofit	Firm supplies a product without a clear profit motive (like schools, hospitals, and clubs, among others)
Financial	The firm's business is related to a financial activity
Access to international equity market	The firm's equity is traded in an international stock market

Finally, the macrofinancial variables are constructed using the definitions shown in section 8.2:

Variable	Description
Bank market size	Ratio of claims on government, public enterprises, and nonfinancial private sector to GDP
Stock market size	Stock market capitalization to GDP
Bond market size	Total bonds stock to GDP
Bank market activity	Private credit by banks to GDP
Stock market activity	Traded value in the stock market to GDP
Bond market activity	Traded value in the bond market to GDP
Real stock market size	Real stock market capitalization to GDP
Private bond market size	Private bond stock to GDP
Turnover ratio	Stock market activity to stock market size ratio
GDP growth	Annual GDP growth rate

Notes

1. Consumption smoothing in Chile has been the subjects of several studies, mostly following the approach in Campbell and Mankiw (1989). They focus on the estimation of the share of constrained consumption in Chile. Corbo and Schmidt-Hebbel (1991) estimate this share at 60 percent for the period 1968–1988, while Bandiera et al. (1998) find a share of 55 percent for the period 1970–1995. Most recently, Schmidt-Hebbel and Servén (2000) estimate the share of constrained consumption to be 25 percent in the period 1986–1997. The main conclusion from these studies is that liquidity constraints have become gradually less important in Chile, a fact that corresponds to the development of the financial sector in the country.

2. It is interesting to notice that this trend toward financial repression started in the 1930s. Before the Great Depression, the Chilean financial sector was relatively free and developed (Jeftanovic 1979).

3. For a detailed description of the privatization process and its consequences, see Barandiarán and Hernández 1999.

4. There is an extended literature on this period, which we only summarize in this chapter. For a complete analysis of the banking crisis, see Barandiarán and Hernández 1999.

5. For a more detailed analysis of the new law and its consequences, see Brock 1992.

6. It is important to mention that, according to the new regulatory framework, pension fund management companies (PFMC) could not directly own or manage banks, or vice versa. However, there were no restrictions on both banks and PFMCs to be part of a holding, a situation that is common today.

7. Note that the sum of the sectors included in figure 8.2 is larger than the size of the consolidated financial sector, given that these sectors have some assets in common.

8. Demirgüç-Kunt and Levine (chapter 3) argue that the development line should be based on measures of activity (liquidity) of banking and other financial markets. Thus, pure size would not be considered in this criterion for international comparisons.

9. A simple example may clarify why traded value or turnover are incomplete proxies for stock market efficiency. Suppose that domestic firms start to issue shares abroad.

This will likely lead to a decrease in the activity and liquidity of the domestic stock market. If however, domestic stockbrokers become more cost-effective to regain their market participation, then the stock market becomes more efficient even though the ratios of activity and liquidity indicate otherwise.

10. Financial societies are saving and loan institutions that, in contrast to banks, do not create money.

11. The adjustment is made following the procedure outlined in Summers 1981 and Lehmann 1991. For details see appendix 8.1.

12. The linear relationship between the investment ratio and the firm's q value in equation (8.1) follows from the assumption that adjustment is costless until some normal level of investment is reached and then marginal adjustment costs rise linearly with investment (see Summers 1981). Furthermore, in order to identify the shadow price of new capital (marginal q) with the value of the firm relative to its replacement cost (average q), we assume that the production function presents constant returns to scale and the adjustment-cost function is homogenous of degree one (see Hayashi 1982).

13. Given that there is no evidence of persistent residual serial correlation, we do not use the GMM *system* estimator but stay with the GMM estimator in levels. The correlation tests give evidence that the residual follows a moving average process of order 1; our choice of the lagged order of the instruments is consistent with this dynamic structure of the error term.

14. These tests are presented right before the specification tests.

15. This conclusion goes against our priors since it means that the most financially constrained firms have not been the largest beneficiaries of financial development.

16. The first two regressions reported in tables 8.5 and 8.6 do not include the macro financial variables. We do this to highlight the changes in the firm-specific variables that occur when the macro financial variables are included in the regression. The misspecification of the GMM-levels estimator does not improve when macrofinancial variables are included as additional regressors (this regression is not reported in the tables). Thus, we center the analysis on the results obtained with the GMM-system estimator.

17. It is interesting to note that Schmukler and Vesperoni (2000) obtain a similar result in their sample of Latin American countries but not in their East Asian sample.

18. Stocks are measured at the end of period t.

References

Aivazian, V., L. Booth, Aslı Demirgüç-Kunt, and V. Maksimovic. 2001. Capital structures in developing countries. *Journal of Finance* 56(1):87–130.

Arellano, J. P. 1983. De la Liberalización a la intervención: El Mercado de capitales en Chile, 1974–83. *Colección de Estudios de CIEPLAN* 11(December):9–37.

Arellano, M., and S. Bond. 1991. Some tests of specification for panel data: Monte Carlo evidence and an application to employment equations. *Review of Economic Studies* 58(2):277–297.

Arellano, M., and O. Bover. 1995. Another look at the instrumental-variable estimation of error-components models. *Journal of Econometrics* 68(1):29–51.

Bandiera, O., G. Caprio, P. Honohan, and F. Schiantarelli. 2000. Does financial reform raise or reduce savings? *Review of Economics and Statistics* 82(2):239–263.

Barandiarán, E., and L. Hernández. 1999. Origin and resolution of a banking crisis: Chile 1982–86. Working Paper 57, Central Bank of Chile (December).

Basch, M. and R. Fuentes. 1998. Determinantes de los Spreads bancarios: El caso de Chile. Working Paper R-329, Research Network, Inter-American Development Bank.

Beck, T., Aslı Demirgüç-Kunt, and Ross Levine. 1999. A new database on financial development and structure. Working Paper 1829, Policy Research Department, World Bank.

Bernstein, J., and M. Nadiri. 1993. Production, financial structure, and productivity growth in U.S. Manufacturing. Working Paper 4309, National Bureau of Economic Research.

Bolsa de Comercio de Santiago. 1985–1995. *Reseña Anual*. Santiago, Chile.

Bosworth, B., R. Dornbush, and R. Labán. 1994. *The Chilean economy: Policy lessons and challenges*. Washington, DC: Brookings Institution.

Brock, P. 1992. *If Texas were Chile. A primer on banking reform*. San Francisco, CA: Institute for Contemporary Studies.

Budnevich, C. 1997. Banking system regulation and supervision in Chile: Past, present, and future. Mimeo, Central Bank of Chile (July).

Caballero, R. 1999. Structural volatility in Chile: A policy report. Mimeo, Department of Economics, MIT (October).

Campbell, J., and G. Mankiw. 1989. Consumption, income, and interest rates: Reinterpreting the time series evidence. *NBER Macroeconomics Annual* 4:185–216. National Bureau of Economics Research.

Corbo, V., and K. Schmidt-Hebbel. 1991. Public policies and saving in developing countries. *Journal of Development Economics* 36(July):89–115.

De Gregorio, J., S. Edwards, and R. Valdés. 2000. Controls on capital inflows: Do they work? *Journal of Development Economics* 63(1):59–83.

De la Cuadra, S., and S. Valdés-Prieto. 1992. Myths and facts about financial liberalization in Chile: 1974–1983. In *If Texas were Chile: A primer on banking reform*, ed. P. Brock, 11–101. San Francisco, CA: Institute for Contemporary Studies.

Demirgüç-Kunt, Aslı, and V. Maksimovic. 1994. Stock market development and firm financing choices. Working Paper 1461, Policy Research Department, World Bank.

Eyzaguirre, N., and F. Lefort. 1999. Capital markets in Chile, 1985–1997: A case of successful international financial integration. In *Chile: Recent Policy Lessons and Emerging Challenges*, ed. G. Perry and D. Leipziger, 109–148. Washington, DC: World Bank.

Fazzari, S., G. Hubbard, and B. Petersen. 1988. Financing constraints and corporate investment. *Papers on Economic Activity* 1:141–195. Washington, DC: Brookings Institution.

Gallego, F., L. Hernández, and K. Schmidt-Hebbel. Forthcoming. Capital controls in Chile: Were they effective? In *Banking, financial integration, and international crises*, ed. L. Hernández and K. Schmidt-Hebbel. Santiago, Chile: Central Bank of Chile.

Gourinchas, P., O. Landerretche, and R. Valdés. 1998. Lending booms: Stylized facts. Mimeo, Central Bank of Chile (September).

Harris, J., F. Schiantarelli, and M. Siregar. 1994. The effect of financial liberalization on capital structure and investment decisions of Indonesian manufacturing establishments. *World Bank Economic Review* 8(1):17–47.

Hayashi, F. 1982. Tobin's marginal q and average q: A neoclassical interpretation. *Econometrica* 50(1):213–224.

Hernández, L., and E. Walker. 1993. Estructura de Financiamiento Corporativo en Chile (1978–1990). *Estudios Públicos* 51:87–156.

Holtz-Eakin, D., W. Newey, and H. Rosen. 1988. Estimating vector autoregressions with panel data. *Econometrica* 56(6):1371–1395.

Hoshi, T., A. Kashyap, and D. Scharsftein. 1991. Corporate structure, liquidity, and investment: Evidence from Japanese panel data. *Quarterly Journal of Economics* 106(1):33–60.

Hu, X., and F. Schiantarelli. 1998. Investment and capital market imperfections: A switching regression approach using U.S. firm panel data. *Review of Economics and Statistics* 80(3):466–479.

Jeftanovic, P. 1979. El Mercado de Capitales en Chile 1940–1978. Las Instituciones e instrumentos financieros. Working Paper No. 45, Department of Economics, University of Chile (December).

Johnston, B., S. Darbar, and C. Echeverría. 1997. Sequencing capital account liberalization: Lessons from the experiences of Chile, Indonesia, Korea, and Thailand. *IMF Working Papers* 157. Washington, DC: International Monetary Fund.

Kaplan, S., and L. Zingales. 2000. Investment-cash flow sensitivities are not valid measures of financing constraints. *Quarterly Journal of Economics* 115(2):707–712.

Larraín, C. 1995. Internacionalización y supervisión de la banca en Chile. *Estudios Públicos* 60:117–143.

Lee, J. W., Y. S. Lee, and B. S. Lee. 1999. The determination of corporate debt in Korea. Development Discussion Paper 718, Harvard Institute for International Development (July).

Lehmann, S. 1991. Determinantes de la inversión productiva privada en Chile (1981–89). *Colección de Estudios CIEPLAN* 33:19–58.

Levine, R. 1997. Financial development and economic growth: Views and Agenda. *Journal of Economic Literature* 35(2):688–726.

Levine, R., N. Loayza, and T. Beck. 2000. Financial intermediation and growth: Causality and causes. *Journal of Monetary Economics* 46(1):31–77.

Loayza, N., and L. Palacios. 1997. Economic reform and progress in Latin America and the Caribbean. Working Paper 1829, Policy Research Department, World Bank.

Mairesse, J., B. Hall, and B. Mulkay. 1999. Firm-level investment in France and the United States: An exploration of what we have learned in twenty years. *Annzles d'Economie et de Statistique*, no. 55–56:27–67.

Medina, J., and R. Valdés. 1998. Flujo de Caja y decisiones de inversión en Chile: Evidencia de sociedades anónimas abiertas. *Cuadernos de Economía* 35(106):301–323.

Morley, S., R. Machado, and S. Petinatto. 1998. Indexes of structural reform in Latin America. Mimeo, Economic Comission for Latin America and the Caribbean.

Nickell, S., S. Wadhwani, and M. Wall. 1992. Productivity growth in U.K. companies, 1975–86. *European Economic Review* 36:1055–1085.

Perry, G., and D. Leipziger, eds. 1999. *Chile: Recent policy lessons and emerging challenges*. Washington, DC: World Bank.

Ramírez, G., and F. Rosende. 1992. Responding to collapse: The Chilean banking legislation after 1983. In *If Texas were Chile: A primer on banking reform*, ed. P. Brock, 193–216. San Francisco, CA: Institute for Contemporary Studies.

Reinstein, A., and F. Rosende. 1999. Reforma financiera en Chile. Mimeo, University of Chile.

Schiantarelli, F., and V. Srivastava. 1996. Debt maturity and firm performance: A panel study of Indian public limited companies. Mimeo, Policy Research Department, World Bank.

Schmidt-Hebbel, K. 1999. Chile's pension revolution coming of age. Mimeo, Central Bank of Chile.

Schmidt-Hebbel, K., and L. Servén. 2000. Policy shifts and external shocks in Chile under rational expectations. Mimeo, Central Bank of Chile (January).

Schmukler, S., and E. Vesperoni. 2000. Does integration with global markets affect firms' financing choices? Evidence from emerging markets. Mimeo, Policy Research Department, World Bank.

Sena, V. 1998. Technical efficiency change and finance constraints: An empirical analysis for the Italian manufacturing, 1989–1994. Discussion Paper 98-08, University of York.

Soto, C. 1997. Controles a los movimientos de capital: Evaluación empírica del caso chileno. Mimeo, Central Bank of Chile.

Stein, J. 1997. Internal capital market and the competition for internal resources. *Journal of Finance* 52:111–133.

Summers, L. 1981. Taxation and corporate investment: A q theory approach. *Brookings Papers on Economic Activity* 1:67–140. Washington, DC: Brookings Institution.

Superintendencia de Valores y Seguros (SVS). 1987–1998. *Revista de Valores y Seguros*.

Valdés-Prieto, S. 1992. Ajuste estructural en el mercado de capitales: La evidencia chilena. In *El Modelo Económico Chileno*, ed. D. Wisecarver, 401–444. Santiago, Chile: CINDE-Universidad Católica.

Valdés-Prieto, S., and M. Soto. 1998. The effectiveness of capital controls: Theory and evidence from Chile. *Empirica* 25:133–164.

Valenzuela, A. 1984. El Mercado de valores chileno 1960–1983. *Serie Estudios* 1, Bolsa de Comercio de Santiago.

9 Firms' Financing Choices in Bank-Based and Market-Based Economies

Sergio Schmukler and
Esteban Vesperoni

9.1 Introduction

The late 1980s and 1990s witnessed unprecedented developments in the financial sector of emerging economies. Emerging markets became more open and integrated with the rest of the world. After lifting restrictions on capital movements, countries received record high levels of capital inflow. During the 1970s and 1980s, capital flows were directed mainly to governments or to the private sector through the banking system. Whereas, in the 1990s, capital flows took the form of foreign direct investment and portfolio flows, including bond and equity flows, companies in emerging markets are now participating in international financial markets. Equity trading is shifting from local domestic markets to international markets. As financial markets became more global, a remarkable series of financial crises occurred, with significant spillover effects across countries. Countries open to financial flows were severely affected by swings in international financial markets.

The increased integration with world capital markets and the recent crises have generated a debate on the benefits of financial integration and the role of domestic financial systems. Does the integration with world capital markets provide better financing opportunities for local firms? If so, can all firms benefit equally? Should countries promote the development of the domestic financial system or should they fully integrate with international capital markets? In light of the increasing globalization, what type of domestic financial systems is more adequate for financial development? What type of financial systems can better complement and ease the inevitable integration with world financial markets? What type of financial system can better cope with financial crises?

In a separate paper, Schmukler and Vesperoni 2000, we concentrate on the effects of globalization on firms' financing choices. In this chapter, we study the relation between the type of domestic financial sector and firms' financing opportunities. More specifically, we analyze whether the relation between firms' financing choices and firms' characteristics differs across financial systems. Additionally, we study whether the effects of integration and financial crises on firms' financing ratios are different in bank-based and market-based economies.

We focus on firms' financing choices from emerging economies. Financial choices are characterized by the following ratios: debt over equity, short-term debt over equity, long-term debt over equity, short-term debt over total debt, and retained earnings over total liabilities.[1] We construct a large panel of nonfinancial companies located in East Asia and Latin America, working with seven emerging countries that have experienced financial liberalization and crises. Our data comprise firms from Argentina, Brazil, Indonesia, Malaysia, Mexico, South Korea, and Thailand. The data cover the 1980s and 1990s. We gather information on balance sheets, firm-specific characteristics, and measures of financial integration. Our data set enables us to shed light on some aspects of the current debate about the performance of bank- and market-based financial systems.

This chapter also analyzes the previously unstudied case of Argentine firms' financing choices. This country is an interesting case study for a number of reasons. First, Argentina underwent a sharp process of financial liberalization in the early 1990s. Following the liberalization, the 1994–1995 Mexican crisis and the 1998 global crisis had strong spillover effects on the domestic economy. In the aftermath of the Mexican crisis, the government reformed and consolidated the banking sector. International banks now control most of the banking activity. Second, Argentine firms are actively raising capital in international capital markets, through bonds and equity issues. Third, the economy is highly dollarized, with a large fraction of contracts written in U.S. dollars. Unlike other countries, the Argentine data allow us to study the relation between debt maturity and debt currency denomination.

The rest of the chapter is organized as follows. Section 9.2 presents some of the arguments discussed in the literature that compares bank-based and market-based systems. Section 9.3 discusses the data and methodology used in the chapter. Section 9.4 presents the evidence for bank-based and market-based financial systems. Section 9.5 presents in detail the case of Argentina. Section 9.6 concludes.

9.2   Bank-Based and Market-Based Systems

This section presents some of the arguments raised by the literature on bank- and market-based economies. This literature studies the efficiency of different financial systems in the intermediation between saving and investment. In particular, the literature discusses the pros and cons of bank-based versus market-based models of organization.[2] In bank-based systems, banks provide most of the credit to the economy. In market-based systems, firms raise funds in capital markets (bond and equity markets).

One of the issues discussed in the literature is related to the fact that the lenders' evaluation of managers and firm performance may be an expensive activity. There is a trade-off between liquidity of financial instruments and control of debtors. Highly liquid security markets reduce incentives for traders to control the behavior of managers. Bhide (1993) argues that corporate bonds, which usually do not contain provisions for inside monitoring, can be freely traded in liquid markets. This liquidity allows bondholders to penalize bad management, which saves resources allocated to exercise some control over corporations, whereas unsecured business loans require banks to control the activities and management of borrowers, implying the costly collection of inside information. The presence of asymmetric information prevents the liquid trading of bank loans.

While market-based systems are better suited to offer liquid financial instruments to investors, bank-based systems promote long-term relationships between intermediaries and borrowers and facilitate corporate control. This implies that the two systems may be better at providing funds for different firms. Banks may be well prepared to fund start-up firms, while public markets can be better prepared to finance established firms, typically with more tangible assets. In addition, one potential advantage of inside monitoring is the development of long-term relationships between borrowers and lenders. This could extend the maturity structure of liabilities in relation to market-based economies.

Stage financing gives a different perspective to the expected maturity structure of debt contracts under bank-based and market-based systems. For example, stage financing might replace long-term loans for a series of short-term contracts in bank-based systems. This type of financing enables banks to monitor firms at different stages of investment projects. Stulz (1998) points out that banks are prepared to effectively renew and expand loans, as borrowers offer convincing information about the viability of their projects. Moreover, if a borrower pays her debts, there is no reason to spend resources trying to figure out the true value of the borrower's assets. In this way, Stulz suggests that stage financing is often an efficient solution to the intermediation problem. Thus, this sort of financing agreements implies that there is no simple relation between financial structure and maturity of financial instruments.

To shed further light on the existing literature, this chapter focuses on the effects of financial globalization and crises on firms' financing choices from bank- and market-based of systems. We study integration of firms from emerging markets to world capital markets. If the difference between firms in bank-based and marked-based economies is less important than the difference between emerging markets and developed capital markets, we would expect that integration with international markets has similar effects in firms from both systems. On the other hand, if firms from bank-based and market-based systems face different financing opportunities, access to international capital market will affect them differently.

Similarly, global financial crises may affect economies from both systems in a distinct way. Bank-based systems may encourage long-term relationships between borrowers and lenders. During a crisis, banks' inside information allows them to continue lending to sound firms. On the other hand, when foreign shocks hit the domestic economy, markets tend to become illiquid and prices for all firms decline. It might be hard for fickle investors to distinguish viable firms from nonviable firms. These reasons suggest that firms from bank-based systems might suffer less from global financial crises than firms from market-based systems do. However, if the financial crisis hits the banking sector, firms from bank-based economies will be subject to the difficulties faced by their financial intermediaries.

9.3 Data and Methodology

9.3.1 Data Description

Our sample contains data on firms from two bank-based countries (Argentina and Indonesia) and five market-based systems (Brazil,

Mexico, Malaysia, South Korea, and Thailand). The countries in the sample are of particular interest, since they have undergone periods of financial repression, followed by financial liberalization and crises. Data on firms' balance sheets come from two sources, the corporate finance database of the International Finance Corporation (IFC) and WorldScope. IFC has complete data for the 1980s; WorldScope has a large dataset for mid- and late 1990s. The data set contains a total of 1,973 firms. After removing outliers and firms that are in the sample for less than three years, we are left with around eight hundred firms.

To compare the preliberalization period (mainly the 1980s) with the postliberalization period (mainly the 1990s), we combine data from both sources. Our sample comprises annual balance sheet data of publicly traded firms, from 1980 to 1999.[3] Previous work on corporate finance, notably that of Demirgüç-Kunt and Maksimovic (1995, 1998a, b) and Aivazian et al. (2001), use similar data but only for the 1980s. We also add the case of Argentina, which was not studied before.

The data set contains detailed information on the capital structure of firms, but it does not include sources and uses-of-funds statements. We exclude from the sample financial firms and banks, given that there is lack of information on the maturity structure of time deposits and we are particularly interested about debt maturity. We also eliminate from the sample firms for which we have information for less than three periods. Given that available data only exist for publicly traded firms, we are mostly studying large companies.[4]

To measure financial integration at the firm level, we construct indicators of access to international bond and equity markets. First, we use data on international bond issues by firms from emerging economies. The data come from the database of H. Kalsi and A. Mody, World Bank Prospects Group, and JP Morgan. The data measure the access to international bond markets. Second, to capture access to international equity markets, we use the proportional value traded on American Depositary Receipts (ADRs), in the New York Stock Exchange, and on Global Depositary Receipts (GDRs), in the London Stock Exchange. This proportion is calculated relative to the total value traded for that firm's equity in all markets. Data on ADRs and GDRs come from Bloomberg.[5]

To measure financial liberalization in these economies, we employ the index of financial controls constructed by Kaminsky and

Schmukler (1999). This is a qualitative multidimensional index of financial liberalization. The index takes into account controls on interest rates, legal restrictions for firms and banks to borrow in foreign markets, level of reserve requirements, and restrictions for residents to acquire assets in foreign currency. High values of the index stand for high levels of financial liberalization.

To test whether financial choices for firms in bank-based and market-based economies are different, we use the criteria in Demirgüç-Kunt and Levine (chapter 3). They classify countries according to the characteristics of their financial sector. Following their classification, Argentina and Indonesia are bank-based financial systems, while Brazil, Mexico, Korea, Malaysia, and Thailand are market-based financial systems.

9.3.2 Variables and Methodology

This chapter studies three fundamental characteristics of firms' financial structure by estimating models with five different dependent variables. The three fundamental characteristics are (1) the choice between debt and equity financing, (2) the maturity structure of debt, and (3) the choice between internal and external financing. The five dependent variables are as follows. The variable debt-equity tracks the evolution of total debt and is defined as the ratio between total liabilities and the book value of equity. The variable short-term debt over equity captures the evolution of short-term debt. The variable long-term debt over equity is the ratio between long-term liabilities and the book value of equity. The fourth variable, short-term debt over total debt, captures the behavior of firms' maturity structure of debt. The fifth variable, retained earnings over total debt, describes the importance of internal financing.[6]

The explanatory variables can be grouped in four different categories: (1) firm-specific characteristics, (2) access to international capital markets, (3) macroeconomic factors (namely, financial liberalization, crises, and financial development), and (4) country effects. The variables in the first category focus on key characteristics of firms. They accomplish two objectives in our work. On the one hand, they allow us to analyze how different firms' characteristics affect firms' financing choices during the 1980s and 1990s. Therefore, we can compare our results with the existing literature, which only focuses on the 1980s. On the other hand, these variables work as control variables in a more general model that tests how financial liberalization and access to international markets affect firms' financing choices.

Among the firm-specific characteristics, the first variable is the logarithm of firms' net fixed assets, which is a proxy for the size of firms. The second variable, the ratio of firms' net fixed assets over total assets, is an indicator of asset tangibility. The third variable captures the capacity of firms to generate internal resources and is defined as the ratio between firms' profits after taxes over total assets. Finally, we also include a variable that reflects the production mix. This is a dummy variable that takes a value of one if the firm is a producer of tradable goods, and zero otherwise. Tradable producers have the capacity to generate revenues in foreign exchange; thus, they might be able to obtain different kinds of financing.

The variables in the second category measure the effects of expanding the financing opportunities through access to international bond and equity markets. The variable capturing access to international bond markets is a dummy variable that takes a value of 1 for periods in which a given firm issues bonds in international capital markets, and 0 otherwise.[7] The variable capturing access to international equity markets is defined as the monthly average of the proportion of equity traded in international markets relative to the total value traded for that firm in each year. This variable takes a value of 0 for firms without access to international equity markets.

The third category involves macroeconomic factors that affect firms' financing. These factors include three variables. The first one captures financial liberalization. This variable is essential, since it shows the effect of economic liberalization on financial structure. We work with the index of financial liberalization created by Kaminsky and Schmukler (1999). The index is an average of several indicators of financial liberalization in the economy. These indicators include liberalization of the domestic financial sector, as well as removals of restrictions on foreign borrowing and transactions in foreign currency. High values of the index reflect high degree of financial liberalization. The index reflects sharp liberalization processes in the following years for each country: Argentina 1991, Brazil 1990, Mexico 1993, Indonesia 1992, Malaysia 1992, South Korea 1993, and Thailand 1990.[8]

The second variable related to macroeconomic factors is the one capturing financial crises. We construct dummy variables for the years 1995, 1997, 1998, corresponding to the Mexican crisis (1995) and Asian crisis (1997 and 1998). The year 1998 also captures the Russian crisis. It has been well documented that these crises had strong spillover effects on the economies under study.[9]

Finally, we include country dummies to control for the nationality of firms. This is important in light of the previous work on corporate finance. For example, Demirgüç-Kunt and Maksimovic (1995) find that country characteristics, such as the efficiency of legal institutions and the development of capital markets in different countries, are important in explaining differences in firms' capital structure.

We run two panel regressions for each dependent variable: one for bank-based countries and one for market-based economies. In a separate set, we obtain results for Argentina. The results are displayed in tables 9.1–9.5. We report results from pooled ordinary least squares (OLS) and *within* estimators (or fixed effects), with robust standard errors. In this way, we are able to compare our results with those from the existing literature in corporate finance. Since within estimations control for firm-specific effects, these models give us intrafirm information. For example, within estimates tell how deviations from each firm's average net assets affect deviations from the average debt-equity ratio. On the other hand, OLS estimations combine both interfirm and intrafirm effects. Pooled OLS estimates do not contain firm-specific effects. Then, we are able to include country-specific effects and the variable that captures the production mix (whether firms produce tradable goods). These variables cannot be included in the within estimations because they are perfectly collinear with firm-specific effects.[10]

The OLS models estimated are

$$Y_{i,c,t} = n_c + p_{i,c} + \beta' X_{i,c,t} + \gamma' A_{i,c,t} + \theta' M_{c,t} + \omega_{i,c,t}, \tag{9.1}$$

such that $i = 1, \ldots, N$, $c = 1, \ldots, C$, and $t = 1, \ldots, T$.

$Y_{i,c,t}$ represents the five variables defined above, which measure the firms' financing choices. The subscripts i, c, and t stand for firm, country, and time, respectively. $X_{i,c,t}$ stands for the three variables capturing firm-specific characteristics. $A_{i,c,t}$ denotes access to international financial markets. $M_{c,t}$ captures the macroeconomic variables, which only vary with time but not across firms. n_c stands for the country effect. The variable takes the value one for all firms in country c. $p_{i,c}$ stands for the production mix.

The *within* models estimated are

$$Y_{i,c,t} = f_{i,c} + \beta' X_{i,c,t} + \gamma' A_{i,c,t} + \theta' M_{c,t} + \varepsilon_{i,c,t}, \qquad (9.2)$$

such that $f_{i,c}$ is the firm-specific effect. We assume that the error terms, $\omega_{i,c,t}$ and $\varepsilon_{i,c,t}$, can be characterized by independently distributed random variables with mean zero and variance $\sigma^2_{i,c,t}$.

The above estimations assume exogeneity of the explanatory variables. If some of the right-hand-side variables were endogenously determined, we would need to use valid instruments to avoid endogeneity biases. Given that the existing literature on corporate finance performs the estimations assuming exogeneity, our results are comparable to current results in the literature. However, to control for potential biases due to endogeneity and to check the robustness of the results, we estimate IV models.

The instruments are constructed as follows. In the case of the variables with continuous values, we use lagged values of the same variables as instruments. We work with two lags, to avoid cases for which there might be first-order autocorrelation of the residuals. This technique assumes that past values of the explanatory variables are uncorrelated with the contemporaneous error term. At the same time, past values of the explanatory variables are correlated with contemporaneous values of the explanatory variables.

The dummy variables (firm and country effects) are not instrumented, except the variable capturing access to international bond markets. This latter variable might be endogenous, since it could be easier for firms with a certain financial structure to issue foreign bonds. Past values of this dummy variable are not suitable instruments because of its low correlation with contemporaneous values. Therefore, we construct a new instrument that indicates the degree to which capital markets are open for the country where the firm resides. The instrument takes the value 1 if two conditions are fulfilled. First, markets are open for the country, in the sense that at least one firm from that country issues bonds in international capital markets during that period. Second, the firm is an international firm, in the sense that the firm was able to issue international bonds at least once before or at the period under consideration. Otherwise, the variable takes the value 0. This variable seems to be a valid instrument, given that the degree of market openness is expected to be uncorrelated with firm-level errors and, at the same time, it is correlated with the firm's access to international bond markets.[11]

9.4   Empirical Results

9.4.1   Stylized Facts

Before proceeding with the econometric results, we present a general overview on the behavior of different ratios that characterize firms' financing choices. We contrast firms' financial structure in bank-based and market-based economies. Figure 9.1 portrays average debt-equity ratios (for total, short-term, and long-term debt) and the proportion of short-term debt over total debt for bank-based economies (Argentina and Indonesia) and market-based economies (Brazil, Malaysia, Mexico, South Korea, and Thailand) separately. Figure 9.1 suggests two messages about the behavior of firms' financial structure.

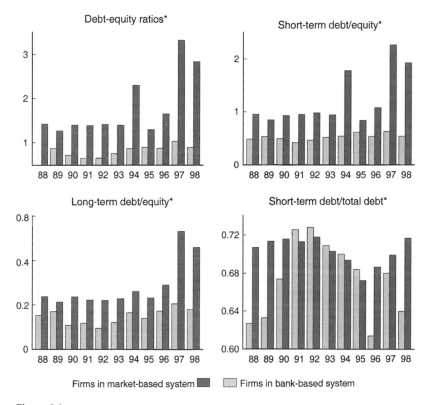

Figure 9.1
Bank-based vs. market-based financial systems.
Sources: IFC Corporate Financial Database and WorldScope.
*Ratios are averages across firms.

First, debt-equity ratios are consistently higher in market-based economies. This relation holds both for short-term and long-term debt. This is a surprising fact, given that one would expect equity values (relative to debt) to be higher in market-based economies. Perhaps, bank-based economies are liquidity constrained, with banks not issuing enough credit to firms.

Second, there are no significant differences in the maturity structure of debt in bank-based and market-based economies. As discussed in section 9.1, market-based systems are better suited to offer liquid financial instruments to investors, while bank-based systems promote long-term relationships between lenders and borrowers. Two possible explanations for this finding are as follows. One explanation is that greater liquidity does not necessarily imply short-term financial instruments. In fact, market-based systems are capable to create markets that offer liquidity to long-term financial instruments. The second explanation is related to stage financing, as explained by Stulz (chapter 4). This kind of financing does not necessarily imply that long-term lending relationships entail long-term financial instruments, because creditors might want to monitor debtors at different stages. These explanations suggest that one might not necessarily expect short-term liabilities in market-based economies and long-term liabilities in bank-based systems.

9.4.2 Econometric Results

The econometric results are displayed in tables 9.1–9.3. We estimate two sets of regressions. One set contains the countries characterized as bank-based economies. The other set includes the countries classified as market-based economies. The goal of these estimations is to compare the effect of financial liberalization and access to international capital markets on financial structure of firms from bank-based and market-based systems.

If the difference between market-based and bank-based systems is significant, one will expect differentiated effects of the integration with international financial markets. In particular, we should see differences in the variables that capture access to international financial markets. These variables measure the participation of local firms in global bond and equity markets. Consequently, these variables necessarily imply a shift towards market oriented systems. The regressions help us distinguish whether this effect is different across systems.

Table 9.1
Bank-Based versus Market-Based Systems (OLS)

Dependent variables	Total debt/equity		Short-term debt/equity		Long-term debt/equity		Short-term debt/total debt		Retained earnings/total debt	
Independent variables	Bank	Market	Bank	Market	Bank	Market	Bank	Market	Bank	Market
Firms' characteristics										
Log of net fixed assets	0.122*** (2.902)	0.032 (0.628)	0.020 (0.810)	−0.079* (−1.810)	0.102*** (4.189)	0.111*** (5.667)	−0.058*** (−6.379)	−0.039*** (−14.378)	−0.264 (−0.814)	−0.028*** (−5.941)
Net fixed assets/total assets	0.634*** (−2.720)	1.278*** (−5.588)	−0.474*** (−2.930)	−1.145*** (−5.846)	−0.159 (−1.578)	−0.133 (−1.569)	−0.045 (−1.341)	−0.185*** (−11.103)	−4.455 (−1.610)	0.062* (1.916)
Profits/total assets	1.791*** (−4.743)	9.539*** (−3.395)	−0.989*** (−3.558)	−7.625*** (−2.885)	−0.802*** (−4.820)	−1.913*** (−6.864)	0.290*** (3.672)	0.159*** (4.012)	15.583** (1.973)	2.951*** (17.672)
Tradable producers	−0.011 (−0.082)	−0.112 (−0.377)	0.052 (0.656)	0.183 (0.665)	−0.064 (−0.677)	−0.295*** (−4.220)	0.092** (2.509)	0.077*** (7.448)	0.805 (0.523)	0.019** (2.040)
Access										
Access to international bond markets	0.220** (2.070)	0.329 (1.553)	−0.011 (−0.147)	−0.048 (−0.354)	0.231*** (3.552)	0.377*** (3.494)	−0.139*** (−4.607)	−0.163*** (−7.790)	−0.540 (−0.635)	0.019* (1.846)
Access to international equity markets	0.486 (1.597)	0.000 (1.520)	0.412 (1.564)	0.000* (1.924)	0.075 (0.556)	0.000 (0.943)	−0.041 (−0.621)	0.000*** (4.041)	−3.835 (−0.966)	−0.039 (−1.027)
Financial liberalization and crises										
Financial liberalization	−0.558** (−2.522)	−0.694** (−2.058)	−0.209 (−1.320)	−0.134 (−0.480)	−0.349*** (−3.149)	−0.560*** (−3.935)	0.262*** (4.413)	0.070*** (4.473)	−1.533 (−0.454)	0.097*** (3.108)
Mexican Crisis—1995	0.114 (1.172)	−0.351 (−1.126)	0.099 (1.174)	−0.361 (−1.225)	0.015 (0.369)	0.011 (0.304)	0.014 (0.597)	−0.033*** (−2.641)	7.079 (1.064)	−0.356 (−0.252)
Asian Crisis—1997	0.295 (1.436)	1.314*** (2.728)	0.141 (1.371)	0.798* (1.816)	0.154 (0.990)	0.516*** (4.420)	−0.011 (−0.306)	−0.021 (−1.545)	−2.305 (−1.215)	0.031 (1.043)
Asian Crisis—1998	0.274** (2.093)	1.343** (2.094)	0.100 (1.203)	0.763 (1.422)	0.174** (2.428)	0.580** (2.400)	−0.050 (−1.648)	−0.032 (−1.555)	−0.548 (−0.408)	0.013 (0.340)

Country effects									
Argentina	−0.114 (−0.665)		−0.298** (−2.538)		0.184* (1.963)		−0.194*** (−4.687)		5.282 (1.414)
Brazil	−1.701*** (−2.875)		−1.437** (−2.574)		−0.264*** (−3.395)		−0.112*** (−8.166)		0.144*** (5.446)
South Korea	0.583 (1.277)		0.436 (1.076)		0.147 (1.031)		−0.018 (−1.096)		0.302*** (9.958)
Malaysia	−1.338*** (−2.928)		−1.138*** (−2.659)		−0.200*** (−2.643)		−0.069*** (−5.350)		0.029 (1.149)
Mexico	−1.386*** (−3.214)		−0.799** (−2.130)		−0.587*** (−3.860)		0.064*** (3.040)		
C	1.437** (2.313)	4.406*** (10.811)	1.271*** (2.853)	3.320*** (10.712)	0.165 (0.567)	1.086*** (5.275)	0.713*** (5.894)	0.965*** (32.474)	4.382 (0.584)
Adjusted R-squared	0.120	0.040	0.101	0.022	0.113	0.164	0.205	0.236	0.007
Fixed effects Chi-Hausman									
Number of firms	143	656	143	656	143	656	143	656	139 / 619
Number of observations	821	5316	821	5316	821	5316	821	5316	740 / 5073

Notes: Robust standard errors: White correction for heteroskedasticity. Indonesia and Thailand are the base country, for bank-based and market based systems respectively. t-statistics are in parenthesis. Bank-based countries: Argentina and Indonesia. Market-based countries: Brazil, Malaysia, Mexico, South Korea, and Thailand.

*, **, *** indicate 10, 5, and 1 percent level of significance, respectively.

Table 9.2
Bank-Based versus Market-Based Systems (within)

Dependent variables	Total debt/equity		Short-term debt/equity		Long-term debt/equity		Short-term debt/total debt		Retained earnings/total debt	
Independent variables	Bank	Market	Bank	Market	Bank	Market	Bank	Market	Bank	Market
Firms' characteristics										
Log of net fixed assets	0.064	−0.063	−0.040	−0.070	0.103	0.007	−0.026*	−0.019***	−0.478	−0.023***
	(0.461)	(−1.104)	(−0.539)	(−1.402)	(1.372)	(0.380)	(−1.954)	(−5.997)	(−1.083)	(−3.118)
Net fixed assets/total assets	0.148	−0.263	0.083	−0.134	0.065	−0.129	−0.035	−0.097***	−0.372	0.107
	(0.973)	(−0.638)	(0.997)	(−0.395)	(0.680)	(−0.863)	(−1.169)	(−3.138)	(−0.253)	(1.518)
Profits/total assets	−2.163***	−8.457**	−1.234***	−6.984**	−0.929***	−1.473***	0.108	0.195***	−6.944	3.117***
	(−4.265)	(−2.484)	(−4.079)	(−2.168)	(−3.157)	(−4.481)	(0.963)	(4.610)	(−0.483)	(17.090)
Access										
Access to international bond markets	0.049	0.079	−0.072	−0.161	0.120**	0.240***	−0.052**	−0.100***	1.081	−0.021**
	(0.649)	(0.413)	(−1.361)	(−0.991)	(1.976)	(3.889)	(−2.175)	(−6.779)	(1.200)	(−2.277)
Access to international equity markets	0.045	0.000	0.017	0.000	0.027	0.000	−0.049	0.000	−0.104	0.000
	(0.288)	(1.075)	(0.240)	(1.221)	(0.252)	(0.805)	(−1.082)	(0.492)	(−0.030)	(−1.049)
Financial liberalization and crises										
Financial liberalization	−0.410	−0.515**	−0.125	−0.400**	−0.285	−0.115	−0.015	0.025	−3.588	0.102***
	(−0.935)	(−2.040)	(−0.547)	(−2.233)	(−1.135)	(−0.820)	(−0.219)	(1.620)	(−0.744)	(2.923)
Mexican Crisis—1995	0.111	−0.104	0.082	−0.144	0.029	0.040	−0.003	−0.027***	6.477	0.001
	(1.285)	(−0.583)	(1.319)	(−0.874)	(0.656)	(1.204)	(−0.149)	(−3.141)	(1.289)	(0.068)
Asian Crisis—1997	0.327**	1.323*	0.167***	0.725	0.160	0.598***	−0.028	−0.014	0.142	0.045
	(1.969)	(1.832)	(2.650)	(1.075)	(1.130)	(5.357)	(−1.007)	(−1.507)	(0.082)	(1.570)
Asian Crisis—1998	0.256**	1.631***	0.099	1.095**	0.157**	0.536**	−0.067***	−0.006	1.535	0.017
	(2.390)	(2.809)	(1.598)	(2.292)	(2.443)	(2.359)	(−2.682)	(−0.394)	(1.048)	(0.507)
Adjusted R-squared	0.441	0.162	0.563	0.138	0.242	0.410	0.572	0.606	0.083	0.476
Fixed effects	4.273***	2.179***	7.037***	2.091***	1.969***	4.437***	5.982***	8.814***	1.433***	3.100***
Chi-Hausman	0.302	0.209	0.294	0.417	0.253	525.41***	4.564	16.124***	4.1196**	1.150
Number of firms	143	656	143	656	143	656	143	656	139	619
Number of observations	821	5316	821	5316	821	5316	821	5316	740	5073

Notes: Robust standard errors: White correction for heteroskedasticity. t-statistics are in parentheses.
*, **, *** indicate 10, 5, and 1 percent level of significance, respectively.

If the difference between market-based and bank-based systems is small, relative to the difference between emerging and developed economies, access to international financial markets should have similar effects on firms from both systems. Given that we are working with few countries, it is hard to disentangle any country specific effects from system specific effects. Therefore, these results should be subject to further research to obtain general conclusions. The evidence presented here should be considered as a first approach to the problem.

The variable financial liberalization captures, among other things, the deregulation of the domestic financial sector. During this process, economies move to financial intermediation based on market incentives. However, financial liberalization does not necessarily denote a shift toward market-based systems (as described in chapter 3). Financial liberalization can lead to the development of a competitive banking sector. As a consequence, it is less straightforward to expect a specific difference in this variable in the regressions for each system. The effect of this variable will depend on the developments in the aftermath of financial liberalizations.

The results show that firm-specific characteristics affect financial structure both in bank-based and market-based systems. The maturity structure of debt extends as firms increase their size, both in bank-based and market-based systems. In market-based systems, both short-term debt and long-term debt vary with size, although the effects on short-term debt are not strong. In bank-based systems, just long-term debt and debt-equity ratios increase with size.

Assuming that larger firms are also the more established ones, one could argue that, in market-based systems, these firms issue less risky securities. As a consequence, firms are able to shift their maturity structure to the long-term. Larger firms increase long-term debt and decrease short-term debt. Moreover, larger firms have a lower level of internal financing. In bank-based systems, one could argue that stage financing has a role. As firms grow and get established in the market, banks do not need to spend resources to control them periodically. As a consequence, long-term debt and debt-equity ratios are positively associated with firms' size.

Regarding the tangibility of assets, there is no significant difference between bank-based and market-based systems on the leverage ratios. In market-based systems, firms with more tangible assets have a longer debt maturity structure and higher level of internal

Table 9.3
Bank-Based versus Market-Based Systems (instrumental variables)

Dependent variables	Total debt/equity		Short-term debt/equity		Long-term debt/equity		Short-term debt/total debt		Retained earnings/total debt	
Independent variables	Bank	Market	Bank	Market	Bank	Market	Bank	Market	Bank	Market
Firms' characteristics										
Log of net fixed assets	0.181***	−0.039	0.032	−0.157**	0.149***	0.118***	−0.056***	−0.034***	0.432	−0.062***
	(2.932)	(−0.508)	(0.880)	(−2.354)	(4.344)	(4.617)	(−4.525)	(−7.201)	(1.103)	(−5.801)
Net fixed assets/total assets	−1.625***	−1.762***	−0.926***	−1.454***	−0.699***	−0.308**	−0.019	−0.204***	−12.371	0.148***
	(−4.211)	(−5.773)	(−4.419)	(−5.926)	(−2.808)	(−2.314)	(−0.213)	(−8.396)	(−1.528)	(3.166)
Profits/total assets	−2.523**	−20.364***	−1.415*	−16.185***	−1.098*	−4.179***	0.249	0.183	37.242	2.245***
	(−2.274)	(−4.613)	(−1.950)	(−3.880)	(−1.880)	(−6.526)	(0.989)	(1.409)	(1.262)	(6.081)
Tradable producers	−0.030	0.330	0.096	0.577	−0.125	−0.247***	0.100*	0.080***	0.097	0.048***
	(−0.101)	(0.837)	(0.722)	(1.569)	(−0.613)	(−3.094)	(1.716)	(6.421)	(0.048)	(3.142)
Access										
Access to international bond markets	1.273***	0.784	0.552*	0.261	0.722***	0.523***	−0.423***	−0.334***	−10.194	0.155***
	(2.674)	(0.917)	(1.739)	(0.326)	(3.044)	(2.669)	(−4.070)	(−6.578)	(−1.207)	(3.866)
Access to international equity markets	0.646	0.000*	0.559	0.000	0.087	0.000	0.312	0.000*	8.083	0.000
	(0.395)	(1.671)	(0.618)	(1.579)	(0.110)	(1.614)	(1.428)	(1.961)	(0.934)	(1.386)
Financial liberalization and crises										
Financial liberalization	−0.860	−0.542	−0.566	−0.051	−0.294	−0.491***	0.611	0.023	19.411	0.158***
	(−0.892)	(−1.142)	(−0.639)	(−0.124)	(−0.728)	(−2.790)	(1.143)	(1.165)	(1.345)	(4.566)
Mexican Crisis—1995	0.139	−0.798	0.119	−0.719	0.019	−0.079	0.001	−0.029*	6.137	0.004
	(1.150)	(−1.277)	(1.298)	(−1.212)	(0.350)	(−1.583)	(0.023)	(−1.844)	(1.002)	(0.222)
Asian Crisis—1997	0.326	0.873	0.145	0.435	0.181	0.438***	−0.018	−0.028*	−4.475	0.029
	(1.465)	(1.293)	(1.355)	(0.688)	(1.093)	(3.734)	(−0.472)	(−1.828)	(−1.510)	(0.883)
Asian Crisis—1998	0.353**	0.664	0.160	0.392	0.194**	0.272***	−0.051	−0.025	−3.301	0.016
	(2.110)	(0.984)	(1.460)	(0.609)	(2.436)	(2.633)	(−1.484)	(−1.205)	(−1.095)	(0.420)

Country effects										
Argentina										
Brazil	0.068	-2.445***	-0.242	-2.142***	0.310**	-0.303***	-0.249**	-0.119***	9.034	0.046
	(0.226)	(-2.896)	(-1.069)	(-2.691)	(2.038)	(-2.600)	(-2.567)	(-6.433)	(1.367)	(1.161)
South Korea		0.040		0.000		0.040		-0.062***		0.411***
		(0.052)		(0.000)		(0.228)		(-2.698)		(10.556)
Malaysia		-1.789***		-1.637***		-0.152		-0.088***		-0.054
		(-2.694)		(-2.637)		(-1.419)		(-4.856)		(-1.291)
Mexico		-1.530*		-0.877		-0.653***		0.062**		
		(-1.941)		(-1.214)		(-3.432)		(2.151)		
C	1.808	5.376***	2.020	4.336***	-0.212	1.039***	-0.041	1.030***	-45.677	0.034
	(0.884)	(7.402)	(1.105)	(7.139)	(-0.240)	(3.692)	(-0.036)	(25.755)	(-1.340)	(0.408)
Adjusted R-squared	0.074	0.030	0.047	0.017	0.096	0.160	0.196	0.21	-0.003	0.329
Fixed effects Chi-Hausman										
Number of firms	143	656	143	656	143	656	143	656	139	619
Number of observations	543	3899	543	3899	543	3899	543	3899	524	3796

Notes: Robust standard errors: White correction for heteroskedasticity. Indonesia and Thailand are the base country, for bank-based and market-based systems respectively. t-statistics are in parentheses. Bank-based countries: Argentina and Indonesia. Market-based countries: Brazil, Malaysia, Mexico, South Korea, and Thailand. Instruments are lagged explanatory variables on Firms' Characteristics (except the variable Tradable Producers), lagged values of the variable on access to international equity markets, and an indicator of countries' access to bond markets.

financing. The effects of profits over total assets on financial structure yield no differences between bank-based and market-based systems. Finally, regarding firms' characteristics, the results suggest that
tradable producers bias their maturity structure to the short-term.
There are no differences between bank-based and market-based
economies, except that tradable producers have a higher level of
internal financing in market-based systems.

Access to bond markets increases long-term debt and extends
the maturity structure of debt, both in market-based and bank-based
financial systems. Results do not only capture differences between
firms, but also within a given firm. Companies with access to bond
markets seem to react in the same way in bank-based and market-
based financial systems. In bank-based systems, the OLS and IV
estimates show that firms that access international bond markets also
increase their debt-equity ratios, suggesting that they are not just
replacing bank debt with bonds. The results suggest that bank-based
systems seem to be liquidity constrained, given that firms increase
their leverage as they access international bond markets. Also, within
regressions show that, in market economies, firms with access reduce
internal financing.

The financial liberalization variable is negatively associated with
both short-term and long-term debt in market-based economies.
However, the maturity structure moves to the short term and internal financing increases.

Regarding the crisis variables, the Mexican crisis does not have
sizable effects on capital structure, except that the maturity structure
increases in market-based systems. During the Asian crisis, market-
based economies were affected first, in 1997, with increases in most
leverage ratios. During 1998, both systems were affected. However,
bank-based economies were able to increase the maturity structure
of debt. Most likely the increase in interest rates during the crisis is
behind higher debt-equity ratios. Short-term debt is issued or rene-
gotiated at higher interest rates. Long-term debt increases under
floating rates.

9.5 The Case of Argentina

This section studies in detail the case of Argentina.[12] As mentioned
in section 9.1, this case is worth studying due to a number of reasons.
First, Argentina underwent a sharp process of financial liberalization

during the early 1990s. Second, Argentina is under a currency board system since 1991, with assets and liabilities legally held both in peso and U.S. dollars. Dollar liabilities represent a very large proportion of total liabilities, implying a high degree of dollarization. Third, some Argentine firms became rapidly integrated with world financial markets. Fourth, Argentina suffered the spillover effects of the Mexican, Asian, and Russian crises. Fifth, the Argentine financial system consolidated during the mid-1990s with a strong participation of foreign banks. Sixth, microeconomic data on Argentine corporations was not studied before in the literature. Seventh, unlike the other countries in our sample, there is information on debt currency denomination of Argentine firms.

To study Argentina, we follow the same methodology used for the rest of the chapter. The results for Argentina are presented in tables 9.4 and 9.5. The results can be summarized as follows.

9.5.1 Firm-Specific Characteristics and Financial Structure

The evidence suggests that larger firms increase their leverage. This contrasts with the East Asian experience, which suggests that larger firms increase long-term debt and reduce short-term financing. The data also show that within a given firm, changes in size are positively correlated with increases in short-term financing. Both in East Asia and Latin America, the data suggest that increases in firms' assets are negatively correlated with short-term debt. Finally, larger firms extend the maturity structure of their liabilities. The experience of Argentina is consistent with emerging economies in general and with the previous literature. Larger firms have better access to credit markets, particularly to long-term debt.

Firms with a large proportion of net fixed assets reduce leverage by decreasing both short-term and long-term debt. This effect is not significant within firms. In this regard, the behavior of firms in Argentina is more similar to the one of East Asian firms. In other Latin American countries, firms with a higher proportion of fixed assets reduce short-term debt. They do not reduce long-term financing. The effects on maturity structure are not clear, so it is hard to argue if firms in Argentina match the maturity of assets and liabilities.

Higher profits are negatively associated with leverage in Argentina. The relation holds both within firms and between firms—in the OLS and fixed effects estimations. More profitable firms increase

Table 9.4
Argentina

Dependent variables	Total debt/equity		Short-term debt/equity		Long-term debt/equity		Short-term debt/total debt		Retained earnings/total debt	
Independent variables	OLS	Within	OLS	Within	OLS	Within	OLS	Within	OLS	Within
Firms' characteristics										
Log of net fixed assets	0.263*** (4.406)	0.605*** (2.851)	0.136*** (3.114)	0.355*** (2.828)	0.127*** (4.485)	0.119 (1.288)	−0.088*** (−2.842)	−0.299*** (−2.884)	−0.356 (−0.338)	0.189 (0.157)
Net fixed assets/total assets	1.177*** (−5.188)	−0.007 (−0.008)	0.786*** (−4.644)	−0.373 (−1.153)	−0.398*** (−4.080)	0.536 (0.913)	0.070 (0.754)	−0.148 (−0.741)	−5.048 (−1.029)	6.515 (0.939)
Profits/total assets	1.681*** (−3.124)	−1.748*** (−3.197)	1.112*** (−2.949)	−1.240*** (−4.416)	−0.571** (−2.258)	−0.495 (−1.186)	−0.099 (−0.677)	−0.101 (−0.475)	16.931** (2.476)	15.944 (1.429)
Tradable producers	−0.155 (−1.034)		0.020 (0.270)		−0.176 (−1.484)		0.038 (0.721)		−0.493 (−0.253)	
Firm age	0.001 (0.746)	0.039* (1.816)	−0.003 (−0.260)	0.013 (1.088)	0.002** (2.081)	0.028* (1.921)	−0.004 (−0.812)	0.011 (1.015)	−0.031 (−1.082)	0.771 (1.292)
Domestic currency debt							0.406*** (6.742)	0.315*** (3.110)		
Access										
Access to international bond markets	0.096 (0.997)	−0.005 (−0.072)	−0.033 (−0.507)	−0.065 (−1.347)	0.127** (2.063)	0.064 (1.273)	−0.099* (−1.755)	−0.044 (−1.203)	0.009 (0.011)	0.529 (0.635)
Access to international equity markets	−0.032 (−0.209)	−0.140 (−1.059)	−0.103 (−1.223)	−0.061 (−1.005)	0.092 (1.075)	−0.101 (−0.898)	−0.071 (−0.601)	0.108* (1.849)	−0.930 (−0.585)	0.486 (0.170)

Financial liberalization and crises

Financial liberalization	0.739***	−2.065***	0.348***	−1.267***	−0.390***	−0.432*	0.511***	0.000	2.578	−2.342
	(−4.145)	(−4.003)	(−3.078)	(−3.906)	(−3.848)	(−1.806)	(4.821)	(0.000)	(0.715)	(−0.274)
Mexican Crisis—1995	0.108	−0.008	0.148	0.051	−0.037	−0.048	0.219***	0.142***	1.301	1.064
	(0.926)	(−0.125)	(1.356)	(1.096)	(−0.870)	(−1.156)	(4.956)	(2.774)	(0.593)	(0.443)
Asian Crisis—1997	0.269	0.008	0.221	0.099	0.055	−0.080			−1.303	−3.948
	(1.507)	(0.046)	(1.510)	(0.936)	(0.846)	(−0.747)			(−0.822)	(−1.447)
Asian Crisis—1998	−0.055	−0.176	−0.048	0.001	0.009	−0.162			0.445	−3.100
	(−0.372)	(−0.679)	(−0.601)	(0.017)	(0.108)	(−0.900)			(0.386)	(−0.921)
C	0.982**		0.574**		0.416		0.000		1.874	
	(2.146)		(2.314)		(1.497)		(0.000)		(0.261)	
Adjusted R-squared	0.113	0.563	0.116	0.713	0.075	0.291	0.344	0.714	0.010	0.089
Fixed effects Chi-Hausman		14.910**		14.205**	16.781***	16.781***		16.141***		8.866**
Number of firms	63	63	63	63	63	63	60	60	63	63
Number of observations	341	341	341	341	345	345	228	228	277	277

Notes: Robust standard errors: White correction for heteroskedasticity. Indonesia and Thailand are the base country. t-statistics are in parenthesis.

*, **, *** indicate 10, 5, and 1 percent level of significance, respectively.

Table 9.5
Argentina (instrumental variables)

Dependent variables Independent variables	Total debt/ equity	Short-term debt/ equity	Long-term debt/ equity	Short-term debt/ total debt	Retained earnings/ total debt
Firms' characteristics					
Log of net fixed assets	0.128	0.003	0.119***	−0.080**	0.092
	(1.367)	(0.041)	(2.598)	(−2.114)	(0.076)
Net fixed assets/total assets	−1.173***	−0.608***	−0.576**	0.176	−7.960
	(−3.131)	(−3.027)	(−2.223)	(1.491)	(−1.299)
Profits/total assets	−2.712***	−1.488**	−1.250***	−0.040	27.634**
	(−2.637)	(−2.109)	(−2.691)	(−0.125)	(2.213)
Tradable producers	−0.119	0.108	−0.224	0.056	−0.806
	(−0.465)	(0.905)	(−1.091)	(0.840)	(−0.391)
Firm age	0.000	−0.001	0.002*	0.000	−0.030
	(0.058)	(−0.820)	(1.778)	(−0.015)	(−1.078)
Domestic currency debt				0.439***	
				(5.235)	
Access					
Access to international bond markets	1.047***	0.638**	0.424**	−0.186*	−0.877
	(2.940)	(2.378)	(2.243)	(−1.961)	(−0.328)
Access to international equity markets	−0.635	−0.521	−0.052	0.000	0.541
	(−1.238)	(−1.562)	(−0.276)	(0.000)	(0.217)

Financial liberalization and crises

Financial liberalization	−0.497**	−0.178	−0.318***	0.000	2.030
	(−2.410)	(−0.945)	(−2.655)	(0.000)	(0.545)
Mexican Crisis—1995	0.217	0.225*	−0.006	0.203***	0.786
	(1.613)	(1.837)	(−0.106)	(3.828)	(0.360)
Asian Crisis—1997	0.321	0.264	0.069		−1.530
	(1.647)	(1.644)	(0.935)		(−0.916)
Asian Crisis—1998	−0.060	−0.039	0.006		0.224
	(−0.314)	(−0.378)	(0.056)		(0.160)
C	1.456*	1.074*	0.426	1.009***	0.904
	(1.752)	(1.670)	(1.057)	(3.610)	(0.103)
Adjusted R-squared	0.050	0.027	0.060	0.362	−0.011
Number of firms	63	63	63	60	63
Number of observations	278	278	282	167	274

Notes: There is not data for debt currency denomination in 1997 and 1998. Robust standard errors: White correction for heteroskedasticity. t-statistics are in parenthesis. The variable Financial Development is the interaction of domestic financial development and financial liberalization.

*, **, *** indicate 10, 5, and 1 percent level of significance, respectively.

internal financing. These results are compatible with the experience in other emerging economies.

9.5.2 Currency Denomination and Debt Maturity

The results of debt currency denomination are very interesting. The most important result is that a higher proportion of peso denominated debt is associated with a shorter debt maturity structure. This result is statistically significant in the OLS, within, and IV regressions. The findings are consistent with the fact that the Argentine economy has undergone a long and extreme inflationary process during the 1980s, which lead to a phenomenon dubbed *cortoplacismo*. This is associated with situations in which markets for long-term, domestic currency contracts tend to become thin and, in some cases, even disappear.[13] The data suggest that allowing agents to legally hold assets and liabilities in U.S. dollars has lengthened the maturity structure of debt in Argentine firms.[14]

9.5.3 Access to International Markets

There is evidence that access to international bond markets increases long-term financing, extending the maturity structure of debt. This is consistent with the evidence for other emerging economies.

The financial-sector consolidation and financial liberalization in Argentina took place through a strong participation of foreign banks. The latter replaced, in many cases, domestic financial intermediaries. These new international banks have probably not provided credit under conditions similar to the ones offered by international capital markets. Therefore, firms still benefit from accessing foreign bond markets. The evidence suggests that letting international financial agents to operate in domestic markets does not seem to be equivalent to letting firms access international capital markets directly.

9.5.4 Financial Liberalization and Crises

As in East Asia, financial liberalization seems to reduce leverage in general. In the Argentine case, there is some evidence that both short-term and long-term debt decrease. The maturity structure shifts toward the short term in Argentina. This is consistent with the experience of other emerging economies. The Mexican crisis shortens the maturity structure of debt in Argentina, in contrast with the experience of other Latin American countries.

9.6   Conclusions

Following the debate on the merits of bank-based versus market-based financial systems, this chapter analyzed cross-country microeconomic data. The chapter investigated whether the relation between financing choices and firms' characteristics differs in bank-based and market-based economies. We also studied whether financial integration and crises affect financing choices differently in bank-based and market-based systems. We used data of nonfinancial firms in emerging economies from East Asia and Latin America. We focused on leverage levels, debt maturity, and the choice between external and internal financing to study financial structure.

The results show that firm-specific characteristics affect financial structure both in bank-based and market-based systems. The maturity structure is positively related to firms' size. In market-based systems, firms are able to shift their maturity structure to the long term and have a lower level of internal financing. In bank-based systems, long-term debt and debt-equity ratios are positively associated with firms' size. The tangibility of assets and firms' profits yield no significant difference between bank-based and market-based systems on leverage ratios.

Assuming that the countries in our sample represent bank-based and market-based economies accurately, the results suggest that integration with international capital markets affect all emerging economies similarly. In other words, the difference between emerging and developed markets seems to be more important than the difference between bank-based and market-based emerging economies. Access to international bond markets increases maturity in both types of systems. The data also show that access to bond markets increases leverage in bank-based economies, suggesting that their domestic financial sector might be liquidity constrained.

Regarding the crisis variables, the Mexican crisis does not have sizable effects on capital structure, except that the maturity structure increases in market-based systems. This might be due to the non-renewal of short-term contracts and the existence of floating rates on long-term contracts. The Asian crisis seems to have affected market-based economies first.

We focused on the case of Argentina, which had not been analyzed before. The results show that, consistent with the general evidence, larger Argentine firms extend their debt maturity. In contrast to other emerging economies, larger firms also increase short-term debt. As in other countries, more profitable firms reduce leverage and increase internal financing, while more tangible assets are associated with less leverage. Access to international bond markets extends debt maturity, while access to international equity markets has the opposite effect. Consistent with the East Asian experience, financial liberalization reduces debt-equity ratios and shortens debt maturity. In contrast to other emerging economies, the Mexican crisis reduces the debt maturity structure. Finally, we found a strong relation between debt currency denomination and maturity. To extend the maturity structure, firms contract foreign currency debt.

These results suggest that the difference between bank-based and market-based emerging economies is less important than the difference between emerging and developed markets. Integration with world capital markets affects firms from bank-based and market-based systems similarly. The results from Argentina show that firms need to borrow in foreign currency to obtain long-term financing. Also, the development of a solid banking sector does not guarantee adequate financing opportunities.

One could conclude that the financial sector of emerging markets (either bank-based or market-based) needs further development and can potentially benefit from integrating with international markets. Financial integration can provide long-term financing for firms accessing international markets. The decision to develop a bank-based or a market-based system seems to be secondary. The remaining important issue is how to integrate and provide better financing opportunities to firms with no access to world markets.

Appendix 9.1:   Number of Firms and Periods Available for Each Country

Table 9A.1
Number of Firms and Periods Available for Each Country

Country	Period	Number of firms
Argentina	1988–1999	73
Brazil	1985–1998	264
Indonesia	1989–1998	185
Malaysia	1983–1998	561
Mexico	1981–1998	202
South Korea	1980–1998	410
Thailand	1980–1999	278

Notes

1. Note that the term *financing choices* in this chapter is what other works on corporate finance call *financial structure*. However, the latter term is also used to denote differences in the composition of financial systems—for example, bank-based versus market-based financial systems.

2. See Demirgüç-Kunt and Levine 1997.

3. Appendix 9.1 presents, for each country, the number of firms and time periods covered in the sample.

4. Data on publicly traded firms exist because firms have to submit their balance sheets regularly to the stock market authorities of each country. Accounting standards for other firms are different and there is no centralized agency that collects such data. If the data existed, it would be very interesting to analyze those firms.

5. Given the data availability, it is very difficult to obtain the proportional value traded of bonds in international markets, as we do for equity trading. That is why we use a dummy variable for access to international bond markets. Also, no publicly available data exists on the amount of outstanding ADRs and GDRs. That is why we use the value traded as a proxy for access to international equity markets.

6. Instead of retained earnings/total debt, the ideal variable to measure retained earnings would be retained earnings/total investment. However, the lack of firms' detailed flow statements does not allow us to properly define a ratio between the relevant flows. Then, we choose to measure the magnitude of retained earnings relative to the volume of external obligations. Note that data on retained earnings for Mexican firms are not available.

7. Notice that the variable takes a value of 1 only for the period in which a firm issues international debt.

8. To check the robustness of the results, we also used a dummy variable instead of the index of financial liberalization. The dummy variable takes the value 1 after the

dates indicated above. The results are qualitatively not different. Therefore, we report only one set of results.

9. See papers at ⟨http://www.worldbank.org/research/interest/confs/past/papersfeb3-4/agenda.htm⟩.

10. Within estimations include one dummy variable per firm. Thus, firm-specific characteristics with no time variation and country dummies would be a perfect linear combination of firm dummies.

11. Other estimations with similar instruments generated comparable results. Future research will likely come up with alternative instruments and further test the robustness of the results, but so far the existing literature has not proposed better instruments to deal with potential endogeneity biases.

12. Other papers exist that also describe country experiences. Jaramillo and Schiantarelli (1996) study the case of Ecuador, Schiantarelli and Srivastava (1996) and Samuel (1996) cover the case of India, and Gallego and Loayza (2000) analyze the case of Chile.

13. See, for example, Heymann and Leijonhufvud 1995 and Neumeyer 1999.

14. Note that since data for debt currency denomination restricts the sample significantly, we only included this variable in the regression where we expected a meaningful effect.

References

Aivazian, V., L. Booth, A. Demirgüç-Kunt, and V. Maksimovic. 2001. Capital structures in developing countries. *Journal of Finance* 56(1):87–130.

Bhide, A. 1993. The hidden costs of stock market liquidity. *Journal of Financial Economics* 34:31–51.

Demirgüç-Kunt, Aslı, and Ross Levine. 1997. Financial structure and economic development. Mimeo, Policy Research Department, World Bank.

Demirgüç-Kunt, Aslı, and V. Maksimovic. 1995. Stock market development and firm financing choices. Working Paper 1461, Policy Research Department, World Bank.

Demirgüç-Kunt, Aslı, and V. Maksimovic. 1998a. Institutions, financial markets, and firm debt maturity. Mimeo, Policy Research Department, World Bank.

Demirgüç-Kunt, Aslı, and V. Maksimovic. 1998b. Law, finance, and firm growth. *Journal of Finance* 53:2107–2137.

Gallego, F., and N. Loayza. 2000. Financial structure in Chile. Mimeo, Central Bank of Chile.

Heymann, D., and A. Leijonhufvud. 1995. *High inflation*. Oxford and New York: Oxford University Press, Clarendon.

Jaramillo, F., and F. Schiantarelli. 1996. Access to long-term debt and effects on firms' performance: Lessons from Ecuador. Mimeo, Policy Research Department, World Bank.

Kaminsky, G., and S. Schmukler. 1999. On financial booms and crashes: Regional patterns, time patterns, and financial liberalization. Mimeo, Policy Research Department, World Bank.

Neumeyer, P. 1999. Inflation-stabilization risk in economies with incomplete markets. *Journal of Economic Dynamics and Control* 23:371–391.

Samuel, C. 1996. The stock market as a source of finance: A comparison of U.S. and Indian firms. Working Paper 1592, Policy Research Department, World Bank.

Schiantarelli, F., and V. Srivastava. 1996. Debt maturity and firm performance: A panel study of indian public limited companies. Mimeo, Policy Research Department, World Bank.

Schmukler, S., and E. Vesperoni. 2000. Globalization and firms' financing choices: Evidence from emerging economies. Mimeo, Policy Research Department, World Bank.

10

Corporate Groups, Financial Liberalization, and Growth: The Case of Indonesia

Andy Chui, Sheridan Titman, and K. C. John Wei

10.1 Introduction

Developing countries can generally be characterized as having higher capital costs and lower labor costs than their more developed counterparts. Anecdotal evidence suggests that labor costs are not lower because of a lack of human capital. Indeed, engineers, computer scientists, and other skilled individuals in most developing countries receive a fraction of the salaries that their counterparts earn in developed countries in North America and Europe. A more compelling explanation for the observed difference in the returns to labor is a shortage of capital in developing countries. This is true in the public sector (e.g., public infrastructure development) as well as in the private sector (e.g., computers, telephones, etc.).

Traditional economic models suggest that in the absence of frictions, capital should flow to areas where the marginal returns to capital are highest.

This flow of capital will tend to equalize capital costs across countries, and this will, in turn, tend to equalize labor costs. However, historically, there have been a number of impediments to the free flow of capital.

To a large extent, the goal of financial liberalization is to reduce the impediments to a free flow of capital and to encourage domestic investment. Indeed, a recent paper by Henry (2000), which carefully examines twelve developing countries with policy initiatives that opened their stock markets to foreign investors, found that these countries experienced significant growth in their levels of private investment. He also found that the stock markets of these liberalizing countries experienced positive abnormal returns during the eight months leading up to the implementation of their initial efforts to open their stock markets to foreign investors. Although Henry did not include Indonesia in his sample, an earlier paper by Roll (1995) found that Indonesian stock prices approximately doubled in December 1988 when restrictions on the foreign ownership of Indonesian stocks were lifted.

There are a number of reasons why one would expect financial liberalization to promote economic growth, and there is a growing literature that suggests that there are in fact strong links between the liberalization and development of the financial sectors of countries and the growth rates of their overall economies.[1] However, at least two reasons exist why we should be somewhat cautious about the interpretation of this evidence. The first has to do with reverse causality,[2] which arises if the incentive to liberalize one's financial markets is greatest when a country's marginal return to capital is high. The second is that financial reforms generally occur along with other reforms that may also affect both the rate of investment and growth. For example, during the 1990s in Indonesia, along with financial reforms we observed a substantial amount of deregulation and privatization which probably also contributed to increased investment and economic growth.

As a first step toward addressing the possible endogeniety problems mentioned above, it is worthwhile to think about why so many of the developing countries started to liberalize their financial markets in the late 1980s and early 1990s. In particular, we must ask why, if their economies would benefit from having access to foreign equity capital, the necessary financial reforms did not take place sooner. Why, for example, did Indonesia have to wait until the late 1980s to begin liberalizing their financial markets?

Although there are a number of potential answers to this important question, the focus of this research is relatively narrow. Basically, we will compare the financial performance of two types of firms in the years following Indonesia's financial liberalization that was initiated at the end of 1988. Specifically, we compare corporate groups, which are partially owned and controlled by the most politically connected families in Indonesia, and independent firms, which are owned and controlled by individuals with less important political connections and less access to capital prior to liberalization. If financial reforms tend to hurt the politically connected firms relative to the independent firms, then we might expect to see impediments to liberalizing policies.

Financial reforms can have positive as well as negative effects on corporate groups. Suppose, for example, that successful financial reform improves the matching between entrepreneurs with good projects and capital. This, of course, is a good thing for entrepreneurs with good investment opportunities and is probably good for the overall economy. However, it may not be good for individuals and firms with less favorable investment opportunities but with relationships with policymakers and providers of capital that are likely to be less valuable in a more open and less regulated environment. These "connected" families might be hurt by financial reforms since they are placed at a disadvantage (relative to the status quo) in the competition for capital, and the increased openness of the capital markets might also lead to increased competition in the product markets as well.

If the connected families in Indonesia are hurt by financial liberalization, then they may be an impediment to reform. However, for a variety of reasons, they might also benefit from financial reforms. First, by increasing the flow of foreign capital into the country, financial liberalization might increase the value of all capital assets in the country. Moreover, the group firms, which are owned by these connected families, may actually benefit relative to the independent firms from liberalization if they enjoy some comparative advantage in accessing foreign capital. For example, they may be better able to attract analyst coverage, which may increase the liquidity of their stocks, making them more attractive to international institutional investors. Moreover, the improved information flow following liberalization may have made it more difficult for group firms to divert resources from their publicly traded companies (that the families partially own) to their private firms, which would improve the value of their public firms.

To examine these issues we examine the stock returns and capital investments of family and independent firms following financial liberalization. Specifically, we examine whether

1. stock prices of independent firms outperform the group firms after liberalization

2. valuation measures like price/earnings ratios or market to book ratios change differentially for group and nongroup firms

3. independent firms grow (invest more) relative to family firms

4. there exists a group factor that partially explains the covariation structure of returns and whether this factor became more or less important over time

5. trading volume and analyst coverage was differentially affected by financial liberalization for the two groups

For the most part, our evidence suggests that financial liberalization did not have a strong differential effect on group and independent firms. We document that the group firms have received considerably more analyst coverage than the independent firms, even after controlling for their larger size. However, we find no strong evidence that suggests that this difference in analyst coverage has had a material effect on either the stock prices or the ability of independent firms to invest.

The rest of this chapter is organized as follows: In section 10.2, we describe our data sources and in section 10.3 we give a brief description of our sample. In section 10.4 we compare the stock returns of group and independent firms and in section 10.5 and section 10.6 we examine whether differences in the analyst coverage of group and independent firms affect their valuations and return patterns. Section 10.7 examines whether there is a group factor. Section 10.8 examines the financial structures and growth rates of these firms and section 10.9 concludes the chapter.

10.2   Data Sources

Our data come from a number of sources. For financial information we use the PACAP dataset, Datastream and IBES. For the ownership structures we use data similar to those in Claessen et al. 2000. Specifically, the Worldscope database is the starting point of data collection. It provides the names and holdings of the six largest owners of the companies. The Worldscope data is supplemented with ownership information from the Asian Company Handbook 1999 and the Handbook of Indonesian Companies 1996. Other sources that identify the business groups in Indonesia are Fisman forthcoming, W. I. Carr Banque Group's 1997 publication *Indonesia Group Connections* (Jakarta, Indonesia), and Indobusiness's *Ranking of Indonesian Largest Conglomerates* (1995, 1998), available at ⟨http://indobiz.com/company/warta/conhlo/htm⟩. See Claessens et al. 2000 for a more detailed description.

The monthly stock returns, market capitalization (or firm size), and trading volume are collected from Pacific-Basin Capital Markets (PACAP; July 1985–December 1996) and Datastream (January 1997–October 1999). Since small firms are thinly traded, we use the latest monthly closing prices to compute monthly returns. Total assets, total debt, and book value of equity (BE) are also collected from PACAP (1985–1993) and Datastream (1994–1998).

The firm-specific data that we consider include firm size (SZ), book-to-market equity (B/M), turnover rate (TN), monthly return volatility (Std), debt to book assets (D/BA), and debt to market assets (D/MA). SZ is measured as the number of shares outstanding times the closing stock price at the end of June of year t. B/M is the ratio of a firm's BE at the fiscal year-end in year $t-1$ to its market value of equity (ME) at the end of year $t-1$. Debt to equity (D/E) ratio is the ratio of total debt at its fiscal year-end in year $t-1$ to its ME in December of year $t-1$. TN is calculated as twelve times the average ratio of the monthly number of shares traded to the shares outstanding. This average is computed over the period from July of year $t-1$ to June of year t. Standard deviations (Std) of returns are calculated from the period between July of year $t-1$ to June of year t. Both local currency and U.S. dollar returns are considered. To compute TN and Std, we require the stock to have at least six observations in the twelve-month period. The D/BA ratio (or D/MA ratio) is the ratio of total debt to book assets (or market assets) at the fiscal year-end in year $t-1$. Market assets are computed as the sum of total debt plus market value of equity at its fiscal year end in year $t-1$. Growth in book assets and book equity are computed as $(BA_t/BA_{t-1} - 1)$ and $(BE_t/BE_{t-1} - 1)$, respectively.

We also consider data on earnings per share (EPS), forecasted by analysts, and the number of analysts covering the stocks, which are provided from IBES. The analyst coverage of a firm is measured as the total number of analysts who provide one-year-ahead EPS forecasts of the firm in December of year t. From our earnings numbers, we calculate price to earnings (P/E) ratio, which is the ratio of the stock's closing price at the end of year t to its expected one-year ahead EPS forecasted in fiscal year t. Growth in EPS in year t is computed as $(EPS_{t+2}/EPS_{t+1} - 1) * 100$, where EPS_{t+1} and EPS_{t+2} are the expected one-year-ahead EPS and the expected two-year-ahead EPS, respectively. The coefficient of variation of EPS is the standard deviation of one-year ahead EPS forecasts divided by the mean of the one-year ahead EPS estimates. To avoid the impact of extreme values on our results, we set the values of larger than the top 1 percent or smaller than bottom 1 percent to the values equal to the top 1 percent and the bottom 1 percent break points. This trimming rule applies to return volatility, growth rates of book assets and book equity, P/E, analyst coverage, and growth rate in EPS.

10.3 Sample Description

Table 10.1 provides information about the firms in our sample for each year. This information suggests that opening the stock market to foreign investors had a profound effect on the stock market. The number of firms in our sample expanded considerably between 1989, following financial liberalization, when our sample included only 22 firms, and the start of the financial crisis in 1997, when our sample included 243 firms. The number of listed companies grew considerably in 1990 with the establishment of the PT Bursa Efek Surabaya and again in 1991 with the establishment of the PT Bursa Efek Jakarta or the Jakarta Stock Exchange.

The table indicates that a larger number of firms that were affiliated with groups listed during the first few years after liberalization. However, in the years subsequent to the financial crisis, the new listings consisted more of independent firms. The average market capitalization of Indonesian firms also increased considerably over this time period. The average market capitalization was less than U.S.$5 million prior to liberalization and grew to about U.S.$400 million in 1997. As the table indicates, group firms are on average two to three times as big as independent firms and make up the majority of the market capitalization of the Indonesian equity market. This is illustrated in figure 10.1, which plots the market capitalizations of group and independent firms over time in relation to the Indonesian GDP. As the figure illustrates, the stock market capitalization was an almost trivial fraction of GDP until 1990 and then grew steadily up to the 1997 crisis. The figure also illustrates that, with perhaps the exception of the last two years, the group firms have comprised the bulk of the economy's equity capitalization.

Table 10.1 also reveals that Indonesian companies were selling for considerably less than their book values prior to liberalization. For example, in 1987, the book to market ratio of the typical Indonesian company was around 5. Average book to market ratios fell to about 1

Table 10.1
Summary Statistics of Characteristics for Group and Independent Firms

Year		1985	1986	1987	1988	1989	1990	1991	1992	1993	1994	1995	1996	1997	1998	1999
SZ – EW	All	4.57 (15)	3.88 (16)	3.27 (18)	4.38 (19)	17.99 (22)	98.82 (83)	68.40 (112)	87.83 (134)	115.64 (133)	204.32 (155)	266.64 (189)	393.57 (154)	411.02 (243)	56.77 (266)	174.99 (259)
	Family	5.29 (8)	4.75 (8)	4.62 (8)	7.02 (8)	22.36 (10)	131.15 (49)	93.50 (63)	125.33 (75)	149.10 (81)	263.13 (95)	346.16 (105)	479.65 (113)	602.96 (122)	82.85 (120)	277.18 (119)
	Independent	3.74 (7)	3.01 (8)	2.19 (10)	2.46 (11)	14.36 (12)	52.22 (34)	36.13 (49)	40.16 (59)	63.53 (52)	111.20 (60)	167.24 (84)	156.33 (41)	217.49 (121)	35.34 (146)	88.13 (140)
SZ – VW	All	7.10 (15)	6.98 (16)	6.96 (18)	9.09 (19)	60.89 (22)	420.32 (83)	268.63 (112)	395.91 (134)	435.07 (133)	801.03 (155)	1819.78 (189)	5169.48 (154)	4293.51 (243)	1003.08 (266)	3178.80 (259)
	Family	7.68 (8)	7.79 (8)	8.71 (8)	10.93 (8)	51.26 (10)	480.52 (49)	261.03 (63)	435.82 (75)	482.49 (81)	877.40 (95)	1719.33 (105)	5546.13 (113)	5321.31 (122)	1273.73 (120)	4000.82 (119)
	Independent	6.16 (7)	5.71 (8)	4.00 (10)	5.29 (11)	73.39 (12)	202.42 (34)	293.92 (49)	237.58 (59)	261.69 (52)	514.90 (60)	2079.66 (84)	1984.50 (41)	1420.59 (121)	481.54 (146)	981.24 (140)
BM	All	3.73 (14)	3.49 (17)	5.04 (16)	1.52 (21)	1.18 (50)	1.09 (103)	1.35 (127)	1.05 (127)	0.57 (134)	0.37 (104)	0.53 (121)	0.50 (200)	0.64 (200)	0.74 (111)	N.A.
	Family	3.31 (7)	2.95 (8)	4.23 (8)	1.30 (9)	1.26 (29)	1.05 (60)	1.19 (71)	0.99 (79)	0.58 (84)	0.40 (73)	0.52 (89)	0.48 (108)	0.62 (101)	0.74 (60)	N.A.
	Independent	4.38 (7)	4.42 (9)	6.81 (8)	1.78 (12)	0.80 (21)	1.22 (43)	1.97 (56)	1.32 (48)	0.53 (50)	0.27 (31)	0.56 (32)	0.55 (92)	0.68 (99)	0.68 (51)	N.A.
BE	All	18.9 (14)	11.94 (17)	19.63 (16)	24.57 (21)	125.04 (50)	230.78 (103)	268.28 (127)	264.88 (127)	350.29 (134)	283.51 (113)	1248.31 (135)	1173.46 (201)	321.71 (200)	556.70 (111)	N.A.
	Family	17.10 (7)	10.61 (8)	15.59 (8)	28.17 (9)	144.51 (29)	264.85 (60)	300.62 (71)	293.57 (79)	393.16 (84)	126.33 (33)	524.50 (39)	400.79 (93)	411.67 (101)	764.59 (60)	N.A.
	Independent	21.69 (7)	14.25 (9)	28.48 (8)	20.40 (12)	34.87 (21)	115.44 (43)	139.35 (56)	149.92 (48)	189.52 (50)	334.90 (80)	1362.05 (96)	1445.59 (108)	142.74 (99)	128.67 (51)	N.A.

Table 10.1
(continued)

Year		1985	1986	1987	1988	1989	1990	1991	1992	1993	1994	1995	1996	1997	1998	1999
TN	All	N.A.	0.03	0.03	0.05	0.42	0.61	0.40	0.44	0.40	0.42	0.16	0.20	0.34	0.31	0.57
			(15)	(16)	(15)	(20)	(19)	(88)	(121)	(121)	(126)	(158)	(144)	(165)	(174)	(88)
	Family	N.A.	0.02	0.02	0.05	0.26	0.63	0.39	0.40	0.42	0.40	0.14	0.20	0.34	0.33	0.33
			(8)	(8)	(8)	(9)	(10)	(50)	(69)	(72)	(81)	(93)	(106)	(117)	(97)	(46)
	Independent	N.A.	0.04	0.05	0.04	0.59	0.54	0.45	0.60	0.34	0.51	0.25	0.19	0.33	0.29	1.07
			(7)	(8)	(7)	(11)	(9)	(38)	(52)	(49)	(45)	(65)	(38)	(48)	(77)	(42)
Std_LC	All	N.A.	3.58	6.16	7.41	25.82	30.64	12.13	14.80	9.35	18.14	12.68	13.11	11.60	26.77	29.40
			(13)	(13)	(14)	(18)	(18)	(70)	(102)	(108)	(113)	(136)	(127)	(144)	(218)	(228)
	Family	N.A.	3.77	6.35	7.60	31.14	31.42	12.85	14.44	8.93	17.70	12.81	13.83	11.72	26.41	27.95
			(7)	(6)	(8)	(8)	(10)	(43)	(60)	(63)	(74)	(83)	(98)	(106)	(117)	(107)
	Independent	N.A.	3.28	5.85	6.97	19.56	28.52	9.74	16.18	11.15	19.66	12.20	8.26	10.48	27.66	32.12
			(6)	(7)	(6)	(10)	(8)	(27)	(42)	(45)	(39)	(53)	(29)	(38)	(101)	(121)
Std_US	All	N.A.	3.62	9.01	7.37	25.62	30.54	12.01	14.71	9.36	18.15	12.64	13.05	11.67	28.34	39.46
			(13)	(13)	(14)	(18)	(18)	(70)	(102)	(108)	(113)	(136)	(127)	(144)	(218)	(228)
	Family	N.A.	3.82	9.03	7.55	30.91	31.34	12.73	14.36	8.93	17.70	12.77	13.76	11.78	27.46	38.39
			(7)	(6)	(8)	(8)	(10)	(43)	(60)	(63)	(74)	(83)	(98)	(106)	(117)	(107)
	Independent	N.A.	3.29	8.99	6.95	19.41	28.37	9.65	16.09	11.18	19.67	12.16	8.27	10.64	30.52	41.44
			(6)	(7)	(6)	(10)	(8)	(27)	(42)	(45)	(39)	(53)	(29)	(38)	(101)	(121)

Notes: Data on monthly returns, market equity, trading volume, and number of shares outstanding are collected from the PACAP data tapes (July 1985–December 1996) and Datastream (January 1997–October 1999). Data on book equity are also collected from PACAP (1985–1993) and Datastream, otherwise (1994–1998). This table reports the value-weighted portfolios' firm size (SZ – VW), book-to-market ratio (BM), the book value of equity (BE), turnover rate (TN), and return volatility in different years. Firm size (SZ) in June of year t is used as the weight. SZ is the market value of the firms in June of year t and is measured in million U.S. dollars. Equally weighted size (SZ–EW) is also reported. BE is observed at the firm's fiscal year end in year $t - 1$ and is measured in million U.S. dollars. BM is the ratio of BE to the market value of equity (ME) in December of year $t - 1$. TN is twelve times the average ratio of the monthly number of shares traded to the shares outstanding. This average is computed over the period from July of year $t - 1$ to June of year t. Std_LC and Std_US are the return volatility measured in local dollars and U.S. dollars, respectively. The return volatility is the standard deviation of monthly stock returns calculated from the period between July of year $t - 1$ to June of year t. To compute TN and return volatility, we require the stocks to have at least six observations in the twelve-month period. The return volatility is trimmed at the top and the bottom 1 percent. The accounting data obtained in year $t - 1$ are matched to other variables that are observed in June of year t. For example, the BM shows in the column of year 1985 are matched with the SZ in year 1986. The number of firms is in parentheses.

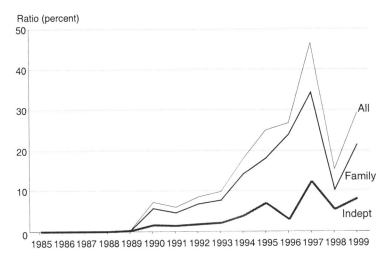

Ratio (percent)

Figure 10.1
Ratios of market capitalization to GDP (in billions of U.S. dollars) at current prices: 1985–1999.

after liberalization and went considerably below 1 in 1993. The average book to market ratio for group and independent firms are quite similar in each of the years.

Table 10.1 also reports the volatility and turnover of Indonesian stocks during our sample period. The table reveals that prior to liberalization, Indonesian stocks experienced very little turnover and very little volatility. After liberalization, turnover increased substantially, averaging a bit less than 50 percent. Volatility also increased substantially, especially in the initial years after liberalization and in the period following the financial crisis. These turnover and volatility patterns appear to be quite similar for group and independent firms.

10.4 The Stock Returns of Group and Independent Firms

This section examines Indonesian stock returns in various sample periods and compares the returns of group firms with independent firms. We will start by summarizing our stock return data for six distinct time periods:

1. The period prior to December 1988 (the prefinancial liberalization period)

2. December 1988 (the financial liberalization event month)

3. The period between 1989 and 1996

4. August 1997, when the Indonesian central government announced that they would give up the managed exchange rate system and allow its currency to freely float

5. May 1998, when Indonesia President Suharto resigned from his office

6. The period between 1997 and 1999 (the financial crisis years excluding the above mentioned months of August 1997 and May 1998)

Table 10.2 includes, for group firms and nongroup firms, the number of firms in each category and their average returns. The table documents the substantial positive equity returns in Indonesia prior to the financial crisis in 1997. For example, in December 1988, the average Indonesian stock price more than doubled. Between 1989 and 1996, Indonesian stocks continued to exhibit high average monthly returns; during this time period, the average monthly return of the value-weighted portfolio was 1.26 percent and the equally weighted index was 1.78 percent per month. However, starting with a sharp decline in August 1997, Indonesian stocks gave up all of their gains from the earlier part of the decade.

An important finding from this table is that there appears to be very little difference in the performance of group and independent firms. For the value-weighted portfolio, the group firms did slightly better than the independent firms in the period prior to liberalization and did substantially better than the independent firms in December 1988 when the stock market was opened to foreign investors. However, these return differences do not exist when one considers equally weighted portfolios. There also appears to be some evidence, looking at the value-weighted portfolios that the independent firms did somewhat better than the group firms after the financial crisis. However, again, this evidence does not seem apparent from an examination of the equally weighted portfolios.

We also examine stock returns around two major events during the financial crisis. The first event was a monetary policy shift from an exchange-rate system with a managed float to a system where the currency was freely floated. The second event was the resignation of President Suharto. In each of these two event months Indonesian

Table 10.2
Returns on Value-Weighted and Equally Weighted Portfolios in Different Sample Periods: July 1985–October 1999

Period	Return (percent, in local currency)			Return (percent, in U.S. dollars)		
	All	Family	Independent	All	Family	Independent
Panel A: Returns on value-weighted portfolios						
July 1985–	3.26	3.38	3.11	2.27	2.39	2.12
November 1988	(5.25)	(4.90)	(4.77)	(2.70)	(2.69)	(2.43)
	[14]	[7]	[7]	[14]	[7]	[7]
December 1988	90.67	102.80	63.39	89.53	101.60	64.41
	(N.A.)	(N.A.)	(N.A.)	(N.A.)	(N.A.)	(N.A.)
	[18]	[8]	[10]	[18]	[8]	[10]
January 1989–	1.60	1.51	1.73	1.26	1.18	1.39
December 1996	(1.34)	(1.18)	(1.48)	(1.06)	(0.92)	(1.19)
	[100]	[61]	[39]	[100]	[61]	[39]
August 1997	−30.38	−30.66	−29.60	−35.32	−35.58	−34.60
	(N.A.)	(N.A.)	(N.A.)	(N.A.)	(N.A.)	(N.A.)
	[226]	[115]	[111]	[226]	[115]	[111]
May 1998	−14.70	−14.96	−13.89	−8.64	−8.93	−7.79
	(N.A.)	(N.A.)	(N.A.)	(N.A.)	(N.A.)	(N.A.)
	[211]	[113]	[98]	[211]	[113]	[98]
January 1997–	2.51	2.42	2.89	0.33	0.20	0.84
October 1999	(0.96)	(0.89)	(1.13)	(0.08)	(0.05)	(0.20)
(exclude two events)	[209]	[109]	[100]	[209]	[109]	[100]
Panel B: Returns on equally weighted portfolios						
July 1985–	3.69	3.54	3.83	2.71	2.56	2.84
November 1988	(5.85)	(4.80)	(6.09)	(3.10)	(2.69)	(3.27)
	[14]	[7]	[7]	[14]	[7]	[7]
December 1988	103.63	105.90	101.82	102.42	104.67	100.62
	(N.A.)	(N.A.)	(N.A.)	(N.A.)	(N.A.)	(N.A.)
	[18]	[8]	[10]	[18]	[8]	[10]
January 1989–	2.12	1.99	2.17	1.78	1.65	1.83
December 1996	(1.76)	(1.58)	(1.81)	(1.48)	(1.31)	(1.53)
	[100]	[61]	[39]	[100]	[61]	[39]
August 1997	−26.67	−28.87	−24.39	−31.88	−33.92	−29.76
	(N.A.)	(N.A.)	(N.A.)	(N.A.)	(N.A.)	(N.A.)
	[226]	[115]	[111]	[226]	[115]	[111]
May 1998	−19.22	−20.83	−17.35	−13.48	−15.22	−11.49
	(N.A.)	(N.A.)	(N.A.)	(N.A.)	(N.A.)	(N.A.)
	[211]	[113]	[98]	[211]	[113]	[98]
January 1997–	5.96	6.33	5.84	3.92	4.29	3.83
October 1999	(1.64)	(1.62)	(1.71)	(0.76)	(0.79)	(0.77)
(exclude two events)	[209]	[109]	[100]	[209]	[109]	[100]

Notes: Monthly returns are collected from the PACAP dataset (July 1985–December 1996) and Datastream (January 1997–October 1999). Value-weighted portfolios are

Table 10.2
(continued)

formed at the end of June each year using the market value of the firms in that month as the weights. Returns on the portfolios are computed from July to June next year. Panel A (Panel B) shows the average monthly stock returns (percent) on the value-weighted (equally weighted) portfolios in different sample periods. Each cell shows three numbers. The first number is the mean, the second number is the corresponding t-statistic, and the third number is the average number of firms.

stocks dropped significantly; by about 35 percent in U.S. dollars when the currency was floated and by about 10 percent when Suharto resigned, and then continued to fall substantially in the subsequent months. Again, we do not observe significant differences between group and independent firms in any of these time periods.

Figures 10.2 and 10.3 plot the cumulated returns for the equally weighted and value-weighted portfolios from December 31, 1989, to September 30, 1999 in local currency (part A) and U.S. dollars (part B). With a volatile time series, cumulated monthly returns generally tell a much less favorable story about historical stock returns than average monthly returns and this is certainly the case here. However, again, an important observation one can take from these figures is that the performance of group and independent firms do not appear to be substantially different.

Although there does not seem to be a significant difference in the average returns of group and independent firms in this data set, a comparison of the equally weighted and value-weighted returns suggests that there is an important size effect. The equally weighted portfolios performed significantly better than the value-weighted portfolios indicating that the returns of smaller capitalization stocks outperformed the returns of the larger capitalization stocks during our sample period. Given that independent firms are on average significantly smaller than group firms, it might be the case, that after controlling for size, the group firms performed better than the independent firms.

The regressions reported in table 10.3 confirm that there is a substantial size effect; small firms generated substantially greater returns than large firms. However, after controlling for size, the evidence that group firms outperform independent firms is still quite weak. Our strongest evidence of group firms outperforming independent firms is in the month of financial liberalization followed by the period after the financial crisis.[3]

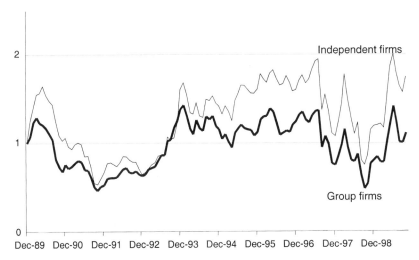

Figure 10.2A
The value of one dollar invested at the end of 1989 based on value-weighted portfolios
(local currency), January 1990–October 1999.

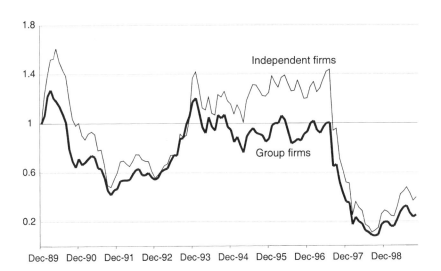

Figure 10.2B
The value of one dollar invested at the end of 1989 based on value-weighted portfolios
(U.S. dollars): January 1990–October 1999.

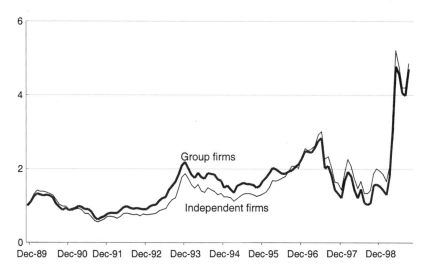

Figure 10.3A
The dollar value for one dollar invested at the end of 1989 based on equally weighted portfolios (local currency): January 1990–October 1999.

Figure 10.3B
The value of one dollar invested at the end of 1989 based on equally weighted portfolios (U.S. dollars): January 1990–October 1999.

Table 10.3
Fama-MacBeth Regressions of Returns on Firm Size and Group Dummy

Panel A: Regressions results using monthly returns
Average coefficients: July 1985–October 1999

Dependent variable	Intercept	Firm size	Group
R_{Local}	11.12 (3.76)	−0.76 (−3.21)	0.58 (1.51)
R_{US}	4.28 (2.90)	−0.76 (−3.21)	0.58 (1.49)

Time-series regressions of the coefficients estimated with R_{Local}

Dependent variable	Intercept	D2	D3	E1	E2	E3
Intercept	8.60	−2.33	11.01	314.89	−3.71	−6.69
	(1.81)	(−0.41)	(1.53)	(10.20)	(−0.12)	(−0.22)
Firm size	−0.60	0.22	−0.59	−27.44	−1.81	−0.97
	(−1.66)	(0.51)	(−1.09)	(−11.72)	(−0.77)	(−0.41)
Group	0.22	−0.02	0.98	38.80	−2.99	−2.66
	(0.34)	(−0.03)	(1.01)	(9.28)	(−0.72)	(−0.64)

Time-series regressions of the coefficients estimated with R_{US}

Dependent variable	Intercept	D2	D3	E1	E2	E3
Intercept	3.21	−0.17	3.72	110.74	−23.23	−7.17
	(1.18)	(−0.05)	(0.90)	(6.24)	(−1.31)	(−0.40)
Firm size	−0.60	0.22	−0.62	−27.27	−1.64	−1.08
	(−1.64)	(0.50)	(−1.31)	(−11.56)	(−0.70)	(−0.50)
Group	0.23	−0.03	0.95	38.56	−2.80	−2.84
	(0.35)	(−0.04)	(0.96)	(9.05)	(−0.66)	(−0.67)

Panel B: Regression results using annual returns
Average coefficients: July 1985–October 1999

Dependent variable	Intercept	Firm size	Group
R_{Local}	111.08 (2.59)	−5.71 (−1.91)	4.76 (0.66)
R_{US}	9.12 (14.28)	0.81 (4.21)	0.39 (1.80)

Time-series regressions of the coefficients estimated with R_{Local}

Dependent variable	Intercept	D2	D3
Intercept	33.99 (0.40)	84.82 (0.82)	159.26 (1.24)
Firm size	4.41 (0.81)	−12.24 (−1.96)	−17.96 (−2.31)
Group	0.37 (0.03)	−1.02 (−0.06)	24.64 (1.15)

Table 10.3
(continued)

Time-series regressions of the coefficients estimated with R_{US}

Dependent variable	Intercept	D2	D3
Intercept	9.44 (7.77)	0.10 (0.07)	−1.87 (−1.01)
Firm size	1.85 (9.52)	−1.35 (−5.66)	−1.60 (−5.37)
Group	0.43 (0.98)	−0.17 (−0.31)	0.23 (0.34)

Notes: In each month, monthly returns (in local/U.S. dollars) on individual firms are regressed on the logarithm of firm size (LnSZ) and a dummy variable, Group. Group takes a value of one if the firm belongs to the family and it takes a value of 0 otherwise. Firm size is the market value of the firm in June of year t and it is matched with the firm's returns from July of year t to June of year $t + 1$. The time-series of the estimated coefficients are regressed on D2, D3, E1, E2, and E3. D2 takes the value of one for the period from January 1989 to December 1996 and takes a value of 0 otherwise. D3 takes a value of 1 for the period from January 1997 to October 1999 (excluding the two event months) and takes a value of 1 otherwise. E1, E2, and E3 are event dummy variables. E1 takes a value of 1 in December 1988 and takes a value of 0 otherwise. E2 takes a value of one in August 1997 and takes a value of 0 otherwise. E3 takes a value of 1 in May 1998 and takes a value of 0 otherwise. The results are reported in panel A. Panel B shows the results using annual returns instead of monthly returns. Annual returns are the compounded monthly returns over the period from July of year t to June of year $t + 1$. For regressions using annual returns, D2 takes a value of 1 for the months between July 1989 and June 1997 and takes a value of 0 otherwise. Similarly, D3 takes a value of 1 for months after June 1997. The t-statistics are in parentheses.

10.5   Analyst Coverage and the Valuation of Group and Independent Firms

The number of equity analysts covering Indonesian stocks increased substantially during the 1990s. The rate of growth can be seen in table 10.4, which presents information from Institutional Brokers Estimate System (IBES) about analyst coverage for group and independent firms along with average price-earnings ratios and expected growth rates in earnings from this same data source.

The table reveals that group firms attract substantially more analyst coverage than independent firms. Throughout the postliberalization period the average number of analysts covering group firms has been more than five times as large as the number of analysts following independent firms. One reason why this might be the case is that group firms are generally bigger than independent firms and analysts tend to follow the larger firms. However, the regressions reported in table 10.5 indicate that this does not completely explain

Table 10.4
Analyst Coverage and EPS for Value-Weighted Portfolios

	Year	1990	1991	1992	1993	1994	1995	1996	1997	1998
Cover	All	1.07	3.19	5.29	5.95	9.84	10.15	8.23	10.97	9.14
		(112)	(134)	(133)	(155)	(189)	(154)	(243)	(266)	(259)
	Family	1.26	3.85	6.57	7.32	12.27	10.10	10.44	13.43	11.03
		(63)	(75)	(81)	(95)	(105)	(113)	(122)	(120)	(119)
	Independent	0.42	0.58	0.61	0.84	3.55	10.54	2.03	6.23	4.07
		(49)	(59)	(52)	(60)	(84)	(41)	(121)	(146)	(140)
P/E	All	133.53	82.03	97.35	123.64	59.37	48.50	25.86	13.96	34.97
		(31)	(75)	(77)	(83)	(97)	(99)	(103)	(95)	(73)
	Family	131.24	84.31	99.80	127.52	64.45	51.35	26.04	13.60	37.42
		(27)	(59)	(63)	(68)	(81)	(82)	(88)	(76)	(62)
	Independent	143.80	62.31	24.68	47.85	26.06	17.44	23.44	15.58	8.70
		(4)	(16)	(14)	(15)	(16)	(17)	(15)	(19)	(11)
Grw_EPS	All	25.40	19.97	20.27	23.98	27.80	26.14	19.30	19.63	82.22
		(32)	(64)	(75)	(84)	(98)	(98)	(102)	(92)	(37)
	Family	28.39	19.66	20.56	24.20	27.09	27.35	19.45	19.09	90.99
		(28)	(54)	(64)	(70)	(83)	(83)	(87)	(73)	(30)
	Independent	10.81	31.29	9.75	19.30	32.63	12.22	17.37	21.01	22.55
		(4)	(10)	(11)	(14)	(15)	(15)	(15)	(19)	(7)

Notes: This table reports the average number of analysts following the stocks in each of the value-weighted portfolios. Analyst coverage (Cover) is measured as the total number of analysts who provide one-year ahead earning forecasts of the firms in December of year t. These data are obtained from the IBES international tapes. If the stock is not covered by IBES, we set its Cover to 0. From the same data sources, we compute the P/E ratio of the firms. P/E is the firm's closing price in December of year t to the analysts' one-year-ahead forecast on earning per share (EPS). Growth rate of EPS (Grw_EPS) is computed as $100 * (FY_{2,t} - FY_{1,t})/FY_{1,t}$ where $FY_{i,t}$ is the ith year ahead forecast on EPS in December of year t. The Cover, P/E, and Grw_EPS are computed only for the firms covered by IBES and these three measures are trimmed at top and bottom 1 percent. The number of firms is in parentheses.

Table 10.5
Determinants of Analysts' Coverage Ratio in Indonesia: 1990–1998

Panel A: Results from time-series regressions

Intercept	LnSZ	Group	D3
−0.460	0.262	0.752	−0.200
(−8.52)	(22.53)	(17.47)	(−4.71)

Panel B: Results from Fama-MacBeth regressions

Intercept	LnSZ	Group	
−0.601	0.273	0.727	
(−4.71)	(8.37)	(8.07)	

Panel C: Results from Fama-MacBeth regressions with a crisis dummy

Dependent variable	Intercept	D3
Intercept	−0.550	−0.232
	(−3.69)	(−0.73)
LnSZ	0.269	0.016
	(6.83)	(0.19)
Group	0.737	−0.043
	(6.76)	(−0.19)

Notes: The logarithm of one plus analyst coverage (LnCover) is regressed on logarithm of firm size (LnSZ) and a dummy variable, Group. Analyst coverage is measured as the number of analysts who provide one-year-ahead forecasts of the earnings for the firm in December of year t. The data on coverage are obtained from IBES International tapes. If the firm is not covered by IBES, we set its coverage to 0. Firm size is the market capitalization (in million U.S. dollars) of the firm in June of year t. The dummy variable, Group, is set to 1 if the firm belongs to a family and 0 otherwise.

Panel A reports the results from the time-series regression that also includes one time-period dummy variable, D3 that takes a value of one after 1997. Panel B reports the results from the Fama-MacBeth regressions. The cross-sectional regressions are estimated every year. The means of the time-series of the estimated coefficients are reported. These time-series are also regressed on the time-period dummy variables, D3, and the results are shown in panel C. All t-statistics are in parentheses.

why analysts tend to follow group firms. These regressions indicate that even after controlling for size, group firms receive substantially greater analyst coverage than independent firms. Informal conversations with analysts suggest that there are two reasons for the greater analyst coverage of the group firms. First, the groups want analyst coverage for their smaller members, which analysts provide in order to obtain greater access to information about the larger members of the group. Second, because of the cross-holdings, the analysts need to value the smaller members of the groups in order to value the larger firms that hold their stock.

The increased coverage of group firms could potentially result in their having higher stock prices and better access to capital. The price-earnings ratios reported in table 10.4 provide some evidence that this could conceivably be the case. At least in the 1992–1995 time period, price-earnings ratios were considerably higher for group firms than for independent firms. However, this could be partly due to the group firms being larger and having somewhat greater expected earnings growth rates.

Table 10.6 examines the determinants of price-earnings ratios in more detail by regressing price-earnings ratios on the log of firm size, the debt ratio, the growth rate in earnings, the number of analysts following the stock and a dummy variable that takes on the value of 1 for firms that are in groups. The evidence suggests that size and the forecasted rate of earnings growth are the primary determinants of price-earnings ratios while membership in a group and analyst coverage do not have a detectable influence. In other words, our evidence does not indicate that the greater analyst coverage of group firms allowed them to be more favorably priced than independent firms.

10.6 Analyst Coverage, Group Affiliation, and Market Efficiency

The higher coverage of group firms suggests that these firms are more likely to be held by foreign institutional investors. Moreover, given the greater amount of analyst coverage and higher level of sophistication of their shareholders, one might conjecture that group firms are more efficiently priced than independent firms. If this is indeed the case, then the group firms may be better able to access external equity markets. There may, however, be offsetting considerations that could make the group firms less efficiently priced. The first is that while the foreign institutions may be capable of more sophisticated analysis, there may be firm specific information that locals have a comparative advantage in obtaining. Moreover, group firms may be more sensitive to shifts in the demands of international investors, which may have nothing to do with fundamentals. For example, a mutual fund specializing in Asian stocks may experience a withdrawal of funds because of a downturn in Thailand, which forces the firm to sell some of its Indonesian shares.

As a rough test of the relative efficiency of group and independent firms we first construct value-weighted portfolios of group and in-

Table 10.6
Determinants of Price-to-Earnings Ratio in Indonesia: 1990–1998

Panel A: Time-series and cross-sectional regressions

Intercept	LnSZ	D/A	Group	Grw_EPS	Lncov	D3
11.255	6.567	−1.343	13.407	0.493	−1.115	−59.915
(0.95)	(2.39)	(−0.81)	(1.48)	(5.69)	(−0.18)	(−6.46)

Panel B: Fama-MacBeth regressions: Using while period

Intercept	LnSZ	D/A	Group	Grw_EPS	Lncov
−5.174	13.920	26.773	−10.839	0.724	−14.489
(−0.20)	(2.56)	(0.67)	(−0.38)	(3.93)	(−0.86)

Panel C: Fama-MacBeth regressions: Using event dummies

Dependent variable	Intercept	D3
Intercept	7.732	−58.075
	(0.26)	(−0.90)
LnSZ	13.699	0.994
	(2.08)	(0.07)
D/A	34.306	−33.896
	(0.71)	(−0.33)
Group	−17.649	30.646
	(−0.52)	(0.42)
Lncov	−17.150	11.972
	(−0.84)	(0.28)
Grw_EPS	0.905	−0.815
	(5.34)	(−2.27)

Notes: Price-to-earnings ratio (P/E) is regressed on logarithm of firm size (LnSZ), debt-to-assets ratio (D/A), the logarithm of analyst coverage (LnCover), growth rate in earning per share (Grw_EPS) and a dummy variable, Group. P/E, D/A, analyst coverage, and Grw_EPS are observed in December of year t, while firm size is the market capitalization (in million U.S. dollars) of the firm in June of year t. The dummy variable, Group, takes a value of one if the firm belongs to a family and it takes a value of zero otherwise. Data on P/E, LnCover, and Grw_EPS are available after 1990.

Panel A reports the results from the time-series regression that also includes one time-period dummy variable, D3 that takes a value of one after 1997. Panel B reports the results from the Fama-MacBeth regressions. The cross-sectional regressions are estimated every year. The means of the time-series of the estimated coefficients are reported. These time-series are also regressed on the time-period dummy variables, D3, and the results are shown in panel C. All t-statistics are in parentheses.

dependent firms. We then regress the returns of these portfolios on their lagged values. For example, the value weighted return of the group portfolio is regressed on both its own lagged return, to measure own serial correlations, as well as the lagged return of the independent firm portfolio, to measure cross-serial correlations. The own serial correlations measure the extent to which investors over-react or underreact to information. The cross-serial correlations measure the extent that information is incorporated into one category of stocks before it is incorporated into the other category. If we believe that analyst coverage and the attention of foreign institutions make the group stocks more efficiently priced, then we might expect less serial correlation in the group stocks and the returns of the group stocks to lead the returns of the independent stocks. Alternatively, the liquidity needs of institutional investors may add noise to the group stock prices, which could induce negative serial correlation and perhaps also negative cross-serial correlations if the liquidity shocks partially spillover and affect independent stock prices.

The results in panel A of table 10.7 are inconsistent with the hypothesis that the group stocks are more efficiently priced than the independent stocks. Indeed, the evidence suggests that information is incorporated first in the independent stocks and then flow to the group stocks with a lag. Returns of group firms are positively related to the lagged returns of independent firms. However, there is a negative relation between the returns of independent firms and the lagged returns of group firms when lagged returns from group and independent firms are included in the regressions. This is somewhat surprising given the evidence in Bailey and Mao (2000) that foreign institutional investors in emerging markets generally have information that the locals do not have (or alternatively, the institutions can better interpret information).

The later result, however, is consistent with the idea that the liquidity flows of international institutions add noise to stock prices. Specifically, large buy orders from foreign institutions may temporarily push up the prices of group stocks and to a lesser extent, independent stocks. If these liquidity flows account for a greater fraction of the variance of group stocks than independent stocks, then we would expect to observe the kind of negative cross-serial correlation that we do observe.

Table 10.7
Autocorrelation and Cross-Autocorrelation of Returns for Value-Weighted Portfolios
Sorted by Dollar Trading Volume and Family Group: July 1986–October 1999

Panel A: Family versus independent firms

Dependent variable	Intercept	$R_{family, t-1}$	$R_{indept, t-1}$
$R_{family, t}$	1.37	0.13	
	(1.09)	(1.68)	
$R_{family, t}$	1.24		0.22
	(0.99)		(2.59)
$R_{family, t}$	1.23	−0.40	0.63
	(0.99)	(−1.96)	(2.78)
$R_{indept, t}$	1.33		0.15
	(1.18)		(2.01)
$R_{indept, t}$	1.45	0.08	
	(1.28)	(1.12)	
$R_{indept, t}$	1.32	−0.38	0.54
	(1.19)	(−2.04)	(2.64)

Panel B: Liquid versus illiquid stocks

Dependent variable	Intercept	$R_{liquid, t-1}$	$R_{illiquid, t-1}$
$R_{liquid, t}$	1.37	0.12	
	(1.06)	(1.50)	
$R_{liquid, t}$	1.25		0.09
	(0.96)		(1.29)
$R_{liquid, t}$	1.34	0.10	0.01
	(1.02)	(0.76)	(0.12)
$R_{illiquid, t}$	2.51		0.22
	(1.74)		(2.77)
$R_{illiquid, t}$	2.85	0.24	
	(1.99)	(2.69)	
$R_{illiquid, t}$	2.61	0.11	0.13
	(1.80)	(0.74)	(0.98)

To examine this in more detail, we examine how liquidity affects the lead-lag relationship between Indonesian stocks. Previous empirical evidence indicates that, in the U.S. market, liquid firms normally lead illiquid firms. The results in panel B of table 10.7 are consistent with the U.S. findings that liquid firms lead illiquid firms. Panel C of table 10.7 further classifies firms into four categories based on both group/independent firms and liquid/illiquid firms. The results suggest that the strongest lead-lag relation is between the independent/liquid stocks and the group/illiquid stocks. Moreover, there is some relatively weak evidence that liquid independent firms lead the liquid group firms.

Table 10.7
(continued)

Panel C: Family versus independent and liquid versus illiquid firms

Dependent variable	Intercept	R_{11t-1}	R_{12t-1}	R_{21t-1}	R_{22t-1}
Independent and thin	2.76	0.21			
	(1.77)	(2.64)			
(R_{11t})	2.53	0.14	0.19	0.18	−0.25
	(1.59)	(0.94)	(0.80)	(0.83)	(−0.95)
Independent and liquid	1.75		0.10		
	(1.50)		(1.26)		
(R_{12t})	1.43	0.17	0.24	−0.07	−0.22
	(1.21)	(1.45)	(1.39)	(−0.43)	(−1.11)
Family and thin	2.25			0.19	
	(1.55)			(2.39)	
(R_{21t})	1.82	0.08	0.48	0.08	−0.29
	(1.25)	(0.53)	(2.26)	(0.42)	(−1.18)
Family and liquid	1.42				0.11
	(1.02)				(1.35)
(R_{22t})	1.01	0.12	0.31	−0.05	−0.17
	(0.71)	(0.85)	(1.47)	(−0.27)	(−0.73)

Notes: Dollar trading volume (DTN) is measured as the past twelve-month average dollar trading volume before July of year t. Each stock should have at least six observations to compute the DTN. At the end of each June, stocks are assigned to two groups, liquid and illiquid, according to their DTN. If a stock's DTN is larger than the median of DTN, then this stock is classified as liquid and it is classified as illiquid, otherwise. The stocks are also independently assigned to two groups, Family & Independent, based on their family grouping. Stocks are further formed into four portfolios from the intersection of the two liquidity groups and the two family groups. These portfolios are value-weighted based on the stock's market capitalization in June of year t. Returns on these portfolios (% in USD) are computed from July of year t to June of year $t + 1$. $R_{family,t}$ and $R_{indept,t}$ are the returns on the portfolios of family firms and independent firms, respectively, $R_{liquid,t}$ and $R_{illiquid,t}$ are the returns on the portfolios of liquid firms and illiquid firms, respectively. R_{ijt} denotes the returns on the ij^{th} portfolio in month t, $i =$ Independent (1) or Family (2) and $j =$ Thin (1) or Liquid (2). These returns are regressed on their lagged returns and the results are reported below. The t-statistics are in parentheses.

Although we were not able to obtain data on the identity of the foreign institutions that purchase Indonesian stocks, we suspect a significant portion of the investment activity comes from U.S. and Japanese institutions. If this is the case, we can obtain more direct evidence on the influence of foreign institutions on Indonesian stocks by looking at comovements between these more developed markets and Indonesian stock returns. We hypothesize that the group stocks, which are more widely held by foreign institutions, should be more strongly influenced by the Japanese and U.S. markets.

The regression results reported in panel A of table 10.8 do not support the hypothesis that group stocks are more influenced by the foreign markets than are independent stocks. In the period prior to financial liberalization, there is no relation between Indonesian stock returns and the returns in either the United States or Japan. However, following financial liberalization, the evidence suggests that Indonesian stocks are influenced by stock returns in the United States, suggesting some degree of integration. However, the evidence fails to support our hypothesis that because foreign institutions are more likely to own shares in the group firms, that the group firm stock returns should be more highly influenced by foreign stock returns. In fact, there is no detectable difference in the sensitivity of group and independent firms to U.S. stock market returns. Moreover, these regressions fail to detect any relation between Japanese and Indonesian stocks for either group or independent stocks after the financial liberalization.

The regressions reported in panel A of table 10.8 also provide indirect evidence relating to the effect of liberalization on market efficiency and market integration. For both the group and independent stocks, the relation between returns and lagged returns declined considerably following liberalization and the relation between Indonesian stock returns and U.S. stock returns increased. To see whether this trend continued after liberalization, we divide the whole period after financial liberalization into two subperiods: 1989–1994 and 1995–1999. As indicated in table 10.8, in the most recent five-year period no discernable relation exists between the current returns and the lagged returns for either group or independent stocks, and the relation between U.S. and Indonesian stock prices has strengthened. Moreover, in the most recent period, we detect a positive and marginally significant relation between Indonesian family firms' stock returns and Japanese stock returns. This relation is weaker for independent firms.

We also examine whether the liquid stocks are more influenced by the foreign markets than are illiquid stocks. The results in panel B of table 10.8 indicate that this is indeed the case. Specifically, it is only the liquid stocks that are significantly influenced by the U.S. market after financial liberalization and this influence is increasing over time. Before financial liberalization, there is no relation between Indonesia stocks, liquid or illiquid, and the returns in either the United States or Japan. In addition, although the foreign market influence on illiquid

Table 10.8
U.S. and Japan Market Returns and Indonesia Stock Returns: July 1985–October 1999

Period	Intercept	$EMKTR_{US,t}$	$EMKTR_{JP,t}$	$R_{Family,t-1}$	$R_{Independent,t-1}$
Panel A: Family versus independent firms					
Dependent variable $R_{Family,t}$					
All months	0.62	0.60	0.22		
	(0.48)	(1.95)	(1.00)		
	0.37	0.55	0.20	−0.39	0.61
	(0.29)	(1.84)	(0.95)	(−1.91)	(2.69)
Before Dec. 1988	4.72	0.17	−0.09		
	(1.65)	(0.34)	(−0.16)		
	3.69	−0.003	0.06	−1.40	2.00
	(1.30)	(−0.01)	(0.12)	(−1.77)	(2.57)
Jan. 1989–Dec. 1994	0.70	0.80	−0.10		
	(0.41)	(1.60)	(−0.39)		
	0.15	0.77	−0.13	−0.50	0.77
	(0.09)	(1.62)	(−0.54)	(−2.40)	(2.97)
Jan. 1995–Oct. 1999	−3.30	1.22	0.83		
	(−1.25)	(1.98)	(1.79)		
	−3.09	1.18	0.84	0.21	−0.06
	(−1.16)	(1.91)	(1.80)	(0.45)	(−0.13)
After Jan. 1989	−0.88	1.01	0.19		
	(−0.58)	(2.56)	(0.79)		
	−1.08	0.96	0.17	−0.29	0.48
	(−0.73)	(2.48)	(0.72)	(−1.40)	(2.06)
Dependent variable $R_{Independent,t}$					
All months	0.62	0.62	0.14		
	(0.53)	(2.27)	(0.73)		
	0.45	0.59	0.13	−0.36	0.52
	(0.39)	(2.18)	(0.68)	(−2.00)	(2.57)
Before Dec. 1988	3.41	0.09	0.06		
	(1.76)	(0.26)	(0.16)		
	2.09	0.03	0.06	−0.59	1.32
	(1.11)	(0.10)	(0.18)	(−1.14)	(2.56)
Jan. 1989–Dec. 1994	0.93	0.77	−0.16		
	(0.60)	(1.69)	(−0.70)		
	0.52	0.78	−0.20	−0.58	0.78
	(0.35)	(1.81)	(−0.91)	(−3.01)	(3.37)
Jan. 1995–Oct. 1999	−3.02	1.34	0.66		
	(−1.16)	(2.21)	(1.43)		
	−2.85	1.33	0.67	0.28	−0.19
	(−1.08)	(2.16)	(1.45)	(0.60)	(−0.41)
After Jan. 1989	−0.62	1.06	0.08		
	(−0.43)	(2.81)	(0.37)		
	−0.77	1.03	0.07	−0.33	0.45
	(−0.54)	(2.77)	(0.29)	(−1.64)	(2.02)

Table 10.8
(continued)

Period	Intercept	$MKTR_{US,t}$	$MKTR_{JP,t}$	$R_{Liquid,t-1}$	$R_{Illiquid,t-1}$
Panel B: Liquid versus illiquid stocks					
Dependent variable $R_{liquid,t}$					
All months	0.60	0.66	0.25		
	(0.46)	(2.16)	(1.14)		
	0.44	0.65	0.24	0.11	−0.00
	(0.33)	(2.08)	(1.09)	(0.81)	(−0.03)
Before Dec. 1988	5.42	0.23	0.03		
	(1.62)	(0.41)	(0.05)		
	5.05	0.29	−0.30	1.67	−1.12
	(1.36)	(0.48)	(−0.43)	(1.53)	(−1.21)
Jan. 1989–Dec. 1994	0.65	0.81	−0.06		
	(0.41)	(1.76)	(−0.26)		
	1.07	0.67	0.02	0.37	−0.29
	(0.66)	(1.44)	(0.09)	(1.79)	(−1.70)
Jan. 1995–Oct. 1999	−3.33	1.30	0.77		
	(−1.28)	(2.13)	(1.66)		
	−3.59	1.24	0.72	−0.05	0.20
	(−1.36)	(2.03)	(1.56)	(−0.25)	(1.13)
After Jan. 1989	−0.92	1.05	0.19		
	(−0.63)	(2.78)	(0.83)		
	−1.03	1.02	0.19	0.07	0.02
	(−0.70)	(2.68)	(0.82)	(0.49)	(0.20)
Dependent variable $R_{Illiquid,t}$					
All months	2.59	0.47	0.00		
	(1.72)	(1.32)	(0.00)		
	2.05	0.43	−0.03	0.11	0.13
	(1.34)	(1.22)	(−0.12)	(0.71)	(0.97)
Before Dec. 1988	6.16	0.19	−0.06		
	(1.76)	(0.32)	(−0.09)		
	5.14	0.29	−0.52	2.06	−1.19
	(1.37)	(0.48)	(−0.73)	(1.86)	(−1.28)
Jan. 1989–Dec. 1994	2.43	0.59	−0.32		
	(1.15)	(0.96)	(−1.00)		
	2.61	0.33	−0.21	0.56	−0.33
	(1.22)	(0.55)	(−0.66)	(2.05)	(−1.45)
Jan. 1989–Dec. 1994	−0.05	0.83	0.51		
	(−0.02)	(1.21)	(0.99)		
	−0.63	0.71	0.41	−0.12	0.43
	(−0.22)	(1.09)	(0.83)	(−0.63)	(2.33)
After Jan. 1989	1.46	0.72	−0.06		
	(0.84)	(1.59)	(−0.21)		
	0.97	0.65	−0.08	0.06	0.17
	(0.56)	(1.45)	(−0.30)	(0.37)	(1.19)

Table 10.8
(continued)

Dependent variable	Intercept	$MKTR_{US,t}$	$MKTR_{JP,t}$	R_{11t-1}	R_{12t-1}	R_{21t-1}	R_{22t-1}
Panel C: Family versus independent and liquid versus illiquid stocks							
Independent and thin (R_{11t})							
Whole period	1.89	0.50	−0.04	0.13	0.18	0.20	−0.26
	(1.14)	(1.30)	(−0.15)	(0.83)	(0.78)	(0.91)	(−0.96)
Before 1988/12	5.31	0.00	−0.31	−0.46	2.41	−1.42	0.38
	(1.74)	(0.01)	(−0.54)	(−0.81)	(3.54)	(−2.57)	(0.52)
1989/01–1994/12	0.95	0.40	−0.19	0.06	0.67	0.10	−0.47
	(0.42)	(0.63)	(−0.59)	(0.21)	(2.47)	(0.36)	(−1.29)
1995/01–1999/12	2.06	1.07	0.22	0.07	−1.48	0.56	1.03
	(0.64)	(1.44)	(0.39)	(0.31)	(−2.84)	(1.36)	(1.83)
After 1989/01	0.59	0.81	−0.15	0.10	0.13	0.28	−0.29
	(0.30)	(1.62)	(−0.49)	(0.59)	(0.50)	(1.17)	(−0.97)
Independent and liquid (R_{12t})							
Whole period	0.56	0.65	0.21	0.15	0.23	−0.07	−0.20
	(0.46)	(2.33)	(1.05)	(1.34)	(1.33)	(−0.47)	(−1.03)
Before 1988/12	2.79	0.09	−0.13	−0.22	1.64	−0.93	0.23
	(1.27)	(0.25)	(−0.32)	(−0.53)	(3.35)	(−2.35)	(0.44)
1989/01–1994/12	0.74	0.83	−0.03	0.14	0.54	−0.13	−0.35
	(0.48)	(1.90)	(−0.12)	(0.70)	(2.88)	(−0.66)	(−1.40)
1995/01–1999/12	−1.31	1.19	0.70	0.17	−0.80	−0.01	0.63
	(−0.52)	(2.05)	(1.58)	(0.93)	(−1.97)	(−0.04)	(1.43)
After 1989/01	−0.52	1.04	0.14	0.14	0.18	−0.04	−0.21
	(−0.36)	(2.85)	(0.64)	(1.14)	(0.97)	(−0.22)	(−0.95)
Family and thin (R_{21t})							
Whole period	1.44	0.29	0.03	0.07	0.48	0.09	−0.29
	(0.94)	(0.83)	(0.10)	(0.47)	(2.23)	(0.44)	(−1.16)
Before 1988/12	5.34	−0.01	−0.51	−0.79	3.68	−2.08	0.21
	(1.42)	(−0.01)	(−0.72)	(−1.12)	(4.38)	(−3.04)	(0.23)
1989/01–1994/12	1.76	0.45	−0.30	−0.26	0.87	0.05	−0.21
	(0.81)	(0.73)	(−0.93)	(−0.89)	(3.31)	(0.18)	(−0.60)
1995/01–1999/12	0.44	0.31	0.75	0.13	−1.09	0.28	0.89
	(0.20)	(0.59)	(1.89)	(0.84)	(−2.98)	(0.98)	(2.25)
After 1989/01	0.45	0.46	−0.04	0.04	0.37	0.17	−0.27
	(0.26)	(1.06)	(−0.13)	(0.26)	(1.67)	(0.81)	(−1.04)
Family and liquid (R_{22t})							
Whole period	0.18	0.61	0.26	0.10	0.29	−0.06	−0.15
	(0.12)	(1.80)	(1.09)	(0.76)	(1.41)	(−0.33)	(−0.63)
Before 1988/12	6.69	0.01	−0.33	−0.85	3.36	−1.92	−0.05
	(1.84)	(0.01)	(−0.48)	(−1.25)	(4.16)	(−2.92)	(−0.06)
1989/01–1994/12	0.07	0.73	−0.04	−0.06	0.59	0.02	−0.28
	(0.04)	(1.41)	(−0.14)	(−0.25)	(2.64)	(0.09)	(−0.94)
1995/01–1999/12	−2.34	1.11	0.91	0.19	−0.98	−0.12	0.93
	(−0.87)	(1.78)	(1.91)	(1.00)	(−2.24)	(−0.35)	(1.97)
After 1989/01	−1.36	0.99	0.20	0.08	0.18	−0.00	−0.11
	(−0.84)	(2.40)	(0.26)	(0.60)	(0.85)	(−0.02)	(−0.46)

Table 10.8
(continued)

Notes: Monthly returns (percent, in USD) on the value-weighted portfolios for family (R_{Family}) versus independent ($R_{Independent}$) firms, liquid (Rliquid) versus illiquid (Rilliquid) firms, and the intersections of these four portfolios are regressed on their lagged returns and the excess returns on the U.S. and Japanese value-weighted market portfolios ($EMKTR_{US,t}$ and $EMKTR_{JP,t}$). R_{ijt} denotes the returns on the ij^{th} portfolio in month t, i = Independent (1) or Family (2) & j = Thin (1) or Liquid (2). The market returns (percent) in the United States and Japan before December of 1997 are obtained from the CRSP and PACAP, respectively. Market returns after January 1998 are obtained from Datastream. Panel A shows the results from the regressions and corresponding *t*-values are in parentheses. Panel B reports the difference in coefficients of $EMKTR_{US,t}$ (β^{US}) using R_{Family} and $R_{Independent}$ as the regressors and the difference in coefficients of $EMKTR_{JP,t}$ (β^{JP}) using R_{Family} and $R_{Independent}$ as the regressors.

stocks is insignificant, it seems to be increasing over time. Panel C of table 10.8 further suggests that it is the liquidity rather than the group affiliation that determines the relation between Indonesian stocks and foreign markets.

In summary, the Indonesian stock market appears to have become both more efficient and more integrated with global stock markets after financial liberalization. This is particularly true after the Indonesian government adopted an important deregulation package on foreign direct investment in 1994, which permits foreigners to own 100 percent of the shares of newly established Indonesian companies. Apparently, liquidity rather than group affiliation seems to have the greater influence on the extent to which Indonesian stocks are correlated with foreign markets.

10.7   Is There a Group Factor?

Our discussion up to this point suggests that group firms are fundamentally different than independent firms. Specifically, they have greater access to financial markets and have potentially valuable political connections. If group firms benefit from their political connections, then their stock prices should be sensitive to political changes that affect the value of these connections. In addition, since we believe that group firms are likely to appeal more to foreign institutions, their stock prices should be more sensitive to the changing moods of international institutional investors.

To examine the extent to which the stock prices of group firms move together we examined the return correlations between different pairs of stocks. Our unreported analysis indicates that the correlations between group firms (not in the same group) are on average higher than the average correlation between a group and independent firm. The differences between these correlations are statistically significant and support the idea that there is a group factor that reflects either the stocks' sensitivities to political changes or the influence of institutional investors. However, the magnitudes of the differences in correlations are not particularly large, and when we look at subperiods, the statistical significance arises only during the post-1997 financial crisis period.

10.8   Group Affiliation, Financial Leverage, and Growth

Up to this point we have established that Indonesia's financial liberalization had a profound effect on both the number and size of listed companies. In addition, we have established that equity analysts devoted much more attention to the group firms than to the independent firms. This has had some effect on the time series and cross-sectional correlation patterns of group and independent stocks; however, the average returns of the two categories of stocks have not been significantly different. In other words, from a valuation perspective, we cannot say that liberalization significantly favored group firms over independent firms or vice versa.

In this section, we examine the level of investment and the financing of independent and group firms during the 1990s. The evidence, reported in table 10.9 indicates that debt to equity ratios measured with book values increased substantially during our sample period. However, debt-equity ratios measured using the market value of equity increased only modestly. In any event, the evidence does not support the idea that the more efficient equity market lowered the cost of equity inducing firms to tilt away from debt financing. In addition, the evidence does not support the idea that independent firms, which may have had less access to bank debt, had debt ratios that appeared to be systematically different than the debt ratios of group firms.

Table 10.9 also presents the growth rates of both assets and equity for both group and independent firms. We use these growth rates as proxies for the firms' capital expenditures, which we observe for only a small number of companies. The numbers in these tables indicate that Indonesian firms were growing quite rapidly up until the financial crisis. However, we see no discernable difference between the growth rates of the independent firms and the group firms.

Table 10.9
Leverage and Growth Rates of Group and Independent Firms

Year		1986	1987	1988	1989	1990	1991	1992	1993	1994	1995	1996	1997	1998
D_BA	All	0.14	0.11	0.12	0.18	0.18	0.33	0.35	0.29	1.16	0.89	1.09	2.05	3.02
		(12)	(12)	(18)	(15)	(28)	(80)	(82)	(104)	(29)	(117)	(188)	(179)	(107)
	Family	0.10	0.08	0.06	0.18	0.17	0.32	0.36	0.30	1.21	0.97	1.02	2.08	3.45
		(8)	(7)	(9)	(10)	(21)	(53)	(54)	(75)	(22)	(87)	(105)	(100)	(58)
	Independent	0.32	0.20	0.24	0.18	0.22	0.38	0.30	0.27	0.61	0.44	1.28	2.00	1.98
		(4)	(5)	(9)	(5)	(7)	(27)	(28)	(29)	(7)	(30)	(83)	(79)	(49)
D_MA	All	0.32	0.36	0.19	0.10	0.14	0.36	0.36	0.20	0.21	0.24	0.26	0.39	0.39
		(12)	(12)	(18)	(15)	(28)	(80)	(82)	(104)	(97)	(117)	(188)	(179)	(107)
	Family	0.27	0.29	0.14	0.08	0.13	0.36	0.36	0.20	0.23	0.25	0.26	0.40	0.38
		(8)	(7)	(9)	(10)	(21)	(53)	(54)	(75)	(70)	(87)	(105)	(100)	(58)
	Independent	0.55	0.68	0.32	0.21	0.22	0.37	0.33	0.18	0.13	0.16	0.25	0.37	0.41
		(4)	(5)	(9)	(5)	(7)	(27)	(28)	(29)	(27)	(30)	(83)	(79)	(49)
Grw_BA	All	-0.19	0.17	0.03	0.23	0.56	0.52	0.43	0.30	-0.32	1.30	0.25	-0.25	-0.34
		(11)	(12)	(16)	(15)	(26)	(75)	(76)	(89)	(66)	(95)	(133)	(178)	(106)
	Family	-0.15	0.09	0.08	0.25	0.47	0.55	0.49	0.27	-0.31	0.47	0.25	-0.28	-0.51
		(7)	(7)	(8)	(10)	(21)	(48)	(50)	(65)	(52)	(70)	(95)	(100)	(57)
	Independent	-0.33	0.50	-0.12	0.17	1.27	0.41	0.15	0.39	-0.44	3.79	0.26	-0.16	0.07
		(4)	(5)	(8)	(5)	(5)	(27)	(26)	(24)	(14)	(25)	(38)	(78)	(49)
Grw_BE	All	-0.31	0.40	0.13	0.29	0.67	0.30	0.19	0.37	0.36	1.06	0.25	-0.76	0.54
		(11)	(14)	(16)	(17)	(37)	(94)	(101)	(108)	(74)	(95)	(133)	(178)	(105)
	Family	-0.31	0.22	0.16	0.15	0.63	0.32	0.20	0.28	0.38	0.48	0.25	-0.77	0.40
		(6)	(7)	(8)	(9)	(26)	(55)	(58)	(73)	(56)	(70)	(95)	(100)	(57)
	Independent	-0.31	0.80	0.01	0.72	1.01	0.21	0.13	0.70	0.16	2.80	0.26	-0.73	0.96
		(5)	(7)	(8)	(8)	(11)	(39)	(43)	(35)	(18)	(25)	(38)	(78)	(48)

Notes: This table shows the value-weighted portfolios' debt to book assets ratio (D/BA), debt to market assets ratio (D/MA), the annual growth rate of book assets (Grw_BA, in U.S. dollars), and the annual growth rate of book equity (Grw_BE, in U.S. dollars). Debt is the sum of long-term loans and short-term loans. All growth rates are computed as $(V_t - V_{t-1})/V_{t-1}$, where V_t is the value of the accounting variable in year t. Market assets are computed as total debt plus market value of equity (ME). Market capitalization of the firms in December of year t is used as the weight for the portfolios. All these ratios and growth rates are trimmed at top and bottom 1 percent. The number of firms is in parentheses.

10.9   Conclusion

There is now substantial evidence that suggests that a more active more open stock market promotes economic growth. If this is indeed true, then we must ask why developing countries waited until the late 1980s and early 1990s to open their stock markets to foreign investors.

There are a number of potential answers to this question. The first is that although in hindsight it looks like financial liberalization was a good thing, ex ante, opening one's financial markets to the global economy also entails risk. Indeed, the recent experience during the Asian crisis suggests that there are potential costs associated with global financial markets. A second explanation for the apparent reluctance of developing countries to open their financial markets relates to the distributional affects of a more open financial system. Specifically, politically powerful families with special access to capital may object to liberalization if it causes them to lose their comparative advantage relative to independent entrepreneurs with less access to capital.

The evidence in this chapter does not support the idea that the group firms, which are primarily controlled by powerful families in Indonesia, suffered relative to independent firms after liberalization. Indeed, in most respects, we find very little difference between group and independent firms. The most important difference between group and independent firms that we detect is that many more equity analysts follow group firms, even after controlling for size. However, our evidence is inconsistent with the hypothesis that the group firms were more efficiently priced as a result of greater analyst coverage. Moreover, we did not detect any discernable difference in their access to capital that arose from the greater analyst coverage.

The similarity between the returns of group and nongroup firms may reflect the fact that group affiliation is a poor predictor of political connections. Not all group firms are equally connected, and perhaps there are a number of independent firms with better political connections than the group firms. Future research should more carefully examine the political connections of firms (as in Fisman forthcoming) and directly examine the relation between political connections and stock returns, investment choices and financing choices around various political events.

Before concluding we should emphasize that one must be very cautious in attributing the increased investment and economic growth in Indonesia in the first half of the 1990s to the opening of its stock market. There were a number of reforms that occurred in Indonesia in the late 1980s and early 1990s, and it is impossible to disentangle the effect of any of them. For example, in addition to allowing foreign ownership of stocks, the Indonesian reforms reduced tariffs and import surcharges, deregulated banking, and ultimately led to the privatization of a number of state owned companies (e.g., Indosat). There were also efforts made to increase the information flow between corporations and investors, which could potentially improve corporate governance and efficiency. Perhaps, more important, an effort was made to reduce bureaucratic obstacles to capital formation. For example, the number of permits required to build a hotel was reduced from thirty-three to two. It is hoped that future research will help us determine which of these reforms were the most successful.

Notes

1. For an excellent review of this literature, see Levine 1997.

2. Demirgüç-Kunt and Maksimovic (1998) and Rajan and Zingales (1998) examine individual firm growth rates within developing economies and thereby avoid dealing with this causation problem.

3. We also test the group effect using time-series and cross-sectional regressions. The results show a very strong, significant group effect following the financial crisis other than the two events related to monetary and political changes.

References

Bailey, Warren, and Connie Mao. 2000. Investment restrictions and the cross border flow of information: Some empirical evidence. Working Paper, Johnson Graduate School of Management, Cornell University.

Claessens, Stijn, Simeon Djankov, Joseph P. H. Fan, and Larry Lang. 2000. Expropriation of minority shareholders in East Asia. Working Paper 2088, Financial Sector Department, World Bank.

Demirgüç-Kunt, Aslı, and Vojislav Maksimovic. 1998. Law, finance, and firm growth. *Journal of Finance* 53:2107–2137.

Fisman, Raymond. Forthcoming. Estimating the value of political connections. *American Economics Review.*

Henry, Peter Blair. 2000. Stock market liberalization, economic reform, and emerging market equity prices. *Journal of Finance* 55:529–564.

Levine, Ross. 1997. Financial development and economic growth: Views and agenda. *Journal of Economic Literature* 35:688–726.

Rajan, Raghuram, and Luigi Zingales. 1998. Financial dependence and growth. *American Economic Review* 88:559–587.

Roll, Richard. 1995. An empirical survey of Indonesia equities: 1985–1992. *Pacific-Basin Finance Journal* 3:159–192.

Index